7/6

AK

B.799.

ON AND ALONG THE THAMES

ON AND ALONG THE THAMES

THE THAMES

JAMES I. 1603-1625

BY

W. CULLING GAZE

LONDON

JARROLD & SONS, WARWICK LANE, E.C.

PREFACE.

BOOKS innumerable have been written on the scenery and certain features of the Thames, but no serious attempt has hitherto been made to treat exhaustively of the history of the famous river and its shores. The following pages attempt to tell the portion of the tale during the picturesque days of the first of the unfortunate Stuarts. Only the genius of a Gibbon could give the full dignity and pageantry to the subject, and clothe the varied and moving narrative with the proper vivid and glowing phrases.

The Nile alone of the rivers of the world can pretend to compete with the Thames on equal terms as a stream inseparable from the development of the people dwelling along its course. Alike, their spirits embody and express the genius of their children—in the former mysterious, huge and silent; in the latter energetic and bold, penetrating to the ends of the earth, and gathering to a world-centre the strands of a planet's commerce. Hundreds of other rivers scattered over the surface of the globe are more beautiful in their setting, but the framing of this river has a loveliness of tranquillity all its own. Poets and painters have dwelt with rapture on its charms; and if much of these have been destroyed by the ruthless hand of industrialism, still the associations remain, and only await the mind capable of gathering them up and combining them into an entrancing and harmonious whole. The progress and growth of English civilization are largely bound up with its story, and all but a mere sprinkling of the men and women famous in the long life of the nation have passed over its surface, or dwelt on its banks.

Apart from the rulers and high-born of the land, many pregnant glimpses will appear of the life and customs of the mass of the inhabitants along the shores of the river ; their pleasures and progress, their sorrows and struggles. The reader will gather much knowledge of the past not to be found in any history of the kingdom as a whole, and this it is hoped will aid in a wider and deeper realization that growth in all departments of life has been towards a higher state of a well-being for all.

W. Culling Gaze.

CONTENTS.

ILLUSTRATIONS.

Views of London along the Thames about 1616,
etched by W. CULLING GAZE.

On and Along the Thames.

James I.

TOWNS AND PLACES ALONG THE RIVER.

THIS section will be devoted to a fleeting glance
of the towns and villages on the banks of the Thames,
from the head to the storm-tossed mouth.

In the early days of the seventeenth century,
the river, starting from its source at the foot of the
Cotswold Hills, gathered up its roots from the grass
and sedges into a narrow meandering stream, the
haunt of the kingfisher and other shy birds and
animals, and wound its ever-widening course through
a quiet pastoral country, past villages still influenced
by the slowly dying spirit of feudalism, and past
old timbered and tiled and thatched monastic towns,
no longer haunted by the cowled figures of monks,
but shewing their empty and now despised habitations—upon which they had through generations
lavished loving care and the inspiration of religious
fervour in erecting and adorning them with the
wonders of their Gothic art—falling into ruin and
decay. When the first of the Stuarts came to the
throne much of the monastic property in buildings
and lands, broken up at the Reformation, remained
in possession of the Crown, and fragments were

granted, from time to time, to the courtiers and others, in recognition of services rendered, or in exchange for much needed money.

The tiny river flowing along through the Gloucestershire meadows passes Kemble, the first village, on a gentle eminence to the right, where the spiral steeple of the church is a landmark for some miles around. The winding current then glides past a mill and the peaceful village of Somerford Keynes on the left. The Church of All Saints has a square tower, and a gigantic stone figure of St. Christopher before the door.

A short distance on the picturesque village and Church of Holy Cross of Ashton Keynes peep out of a mass of foliage ; and then on the right appears the first town, Cricklade, of one long street, on a gentle declivity, with the quaint houses rising one above the other. This borough, sending two members to Westminster, and still redolent of monks and monasteries, has two churches—St. Mary's, the mother-church, with Norman remains and a low ivy-mantled tower, in the foreground ; and St. Samson's, with a lofty square embattled tower, on the verge of the rising ground to the right. The Priory of St. John the Baptist, near the single broad arched bridge of brick and stone, stands empty and forlorn ; and the two beautiful stone carved and traceried crosses—one in the street near the Town-house, the other in St. Mary's churchyard—no longer claim the prayers of weary wayfarers.

A mile away, on the left, rises the village of Eisey, its humble but pretty Church of St. Mary on a slight elevation overlooking the river, which wanders on to Castle Eaton, on the right, shewing a Norman and Early English Church of St. Mary with low square tower, and vestiges of the once-proud moated castle of the Zouches.

Leaving here with a widened sweep, Kempsford appears on the left, where a ford crosses the river. The village is overshadowed by the tall handsome tower of the noble Norman and Early English Church of St. Mary, on a rise near the margin of the stream. Close by the river are a few scarred remnants of the palace of the Plantagenets. During the reign, Sir Thomas Thynne built a large quadrangular mansion at Kempsford.

The old chronicles said of this district that the pasturage was so rich " that, in spring time, let it be bit bare to the roots, a 'wand' laid along therein, overnight, would be covered by new grown ' grasse ' by the next morning."

Hannington, on the right, has a Wiltshire manor-house belonging to the Freke family ; and a Norman porch is seen to its old Church of St. John the Baptist. Next comes Inglesham, and in the churchyard, close to the porch of the small isolated Norman and Early English Church of St. John the Baptist, are the pedestal and shaft of a stone cross.

Two miles south, on the left, the market town of Lechlade clusters along two long wide streets, terminating in a market place, and overlooking all is the fine Perpendicular Church of St. Lawrence, with embattled tower and well-proportioned spire. Some distance from the town, above the outfall of the Lech, is St. John's Bridge, spanning the river by five arches, with the ruined Hospital near by, and in a meadow the Priory of St. John the Baptist, deserted of its Black Canons. The town is the centre of trade for the neighbouring country, and large quantities of cheese are brought in for conveyance by barge to London.

A mile and a half on, and the small village of Buscot is seen on the right, with a square turreted tower and plain church dedicated to St. Mary. Just outside the village is the house of the Lovedens, the park skirting the river.

Opposite, bordering the stream, is Kelmscott and its towered church of St. George screened by thick trees. The little hamlet of Heighton and its humble chapel repose prettily by the river.

The village of Eaton Hastings appears now on the right remote from the water, and its Church of St. Michael is without a tower. Radcott, on the left, is a small hamlet from whence an old steep stone bridge of three Gothic arches crosses the river.

Seven miles of open country, backed by the commanding heights of Faringdon, bring us to the tiny hamlet of Duxford on the right.

The river now passes through the one-arched bridge of Tadpole, and on the right, at the foot of wooded hills, the village of Buckland nestles around an ancient towered church. Some distance on is the scanty hamlet of Chimney, in a marshy position ; and round a bend, some way from the water, we pass Shifford and its ancient chapel— once a place of considerable note.

Again a stretch of pleasant country brings us to New Bridge, a very fine stone structure of seven groined pointed arches ; the projecting piers giving shelter in their internal V-shaped angles from the great clumsy passing waggons and teams taking up all the steep narrow roadway. Leland, in the sixteenth century, wrote, " The ground all about

Newbridge lyeth in low meadows, often overflown by rage of rain."

Northmoor, on the left, with a picturesque parsonage house built in 1558, lies back from the water, verging on an extensive moor. Wooded banks enclose the stream to Ensham, once a town of some consequence, but now a very quaint Oxfordshire village near the river, which is here spanned by a stone bridge. The handsome Perpendicular Church of St. Leonard is half a mile from the water, and near it is a stone cross with an elegant tapering shaft. The ruined Benedictine convent covers an extensive area, and its crumbling architecture indicates departed magnificence.

Stanton Harcourt, at the confluence of the small river Windrush, has a Church of St. Michael in decorated Gothic mixed with Norman fragments, and a lofty square embattled tower. The house, chapel, gateway, and other buildings of the Harcourts give a fine flavour of antiquity to the village, which has been the abode of the family since Adeliza, Queen of Henry I., gave the manor of Stanton to her kinswoman Millicent, whose daughter Isabel married Robert de Harcourt.

On the elevated hills in Berkshire is Cumnor, its bounds running three miles with the river. Here on a gentle eminence towards the eastern extremity of the village, and abutting on the graveyard of the fine weather-beaten Church of St. Michael, is Hall House, once the abode of the Abbots of Abingdon, and later the scene of the love tragedy of Amy Robsart and the gay Earl of Leicester.

On the left the spire of a very ancient Church of St. Peter rises from Cassington, where are the remains of the castle of the bygone Montacutes.

Some distance from the river, on the right, is the village of Wytham, where the tradition exists of a Saxon nunnery demolished by the nuns themselves to avoid molestation from a neighbouring stronghold, probably on the site of the present moated castle. The church has a square embattled tower.

A little further on the stone two-arched Gothic bridge of Godstow crosses the river, and makes a picturesque grouping with the contiguous shell of the Benedictine nunnery, on an island formed by a branch of the main stream ; and in which tradition places the tomb of the fair Rosamond, who was kept by her royal lover (Henry II.) in strict seclusion in the neighbouring park of Woodstock (Blenheim).

In the low meadow on the right is Binsey, from whence Oxford, two miles distant, is seen across the river. The venerable Church of St. Margaret, encompassed by trees and rivulets, formerly belonged to the monastery of St. Frideswide at Osney. In the vicinity, on the margin of the water, are the remains of the buildings of Seacourt, anciently a large town full of inns for the reception of pilgrims to the Church of Binsey and St. Margaret's Well. Fragments of the bridge, which crossed at Binsey, stand out of the water.

As Oxford is approached the river separates into different channels, but the main stream arrives at Botley Bridge, one of the principal gateways of the walled city. Winding in a serpentine direction, the river skirts the south-western wall, having on the left a wide meadow, and on the right the old embattled tower of the Church of St. Thomas, and the massive grey round towers of the castle. Near the water here are the decaying, but still stately, buildings of the once magnificent abbey of Osney.

Anthony Wood, a little later, stated that the abbey in its flourishing days, with its exquisite and varied architecture rich in carving and tracery, " was not only the envy of all other monastic foundations in England, but also of those in foreign countries."

The castle, with its massive towers, though now much dilapidated, forms a splendid feature of the western portion of the city. At this period the structure was used as a prison. One of the prisoners was George Nappier, a Catholic priest, who was executed here on November 9th, 1610, and his head set upon Christ Church steeple, and his quarters fixed over the four gates of the city. Another was Sir William Cope, who, confined for debt and attempting to escape early in August, 1624, was removed by the Sheriff to the Fleet prison in London.

The city of Oxford, enclosed with thick walls, stands up a splendid and intricate network of turrets, spires and domes.

Inside the gates are noble colleges embedded in the greenery of spreading trees, and lawns, and the bright bloom of sweet-smelling gardens; and an infinite variety of quaint stone and timbered dwellings and other buildings crowd its old streets.

Churches are numerous. All Hallows, in the High Street, shews signs of age and decay. St. Mary's, in the same street, erected in 1498, has a tower and tall elegant spire. St. Martin's is the old Corporation Church, and stands near the meeting of four ways, where the Carfax conduit was built in 1610 for the convenient supply of water to the University. On March 3rd, 1606, William Davenant, then only a few days old (afterwards Sir William, poet and dramatist), son of John D'Avenant, vintner and proprietor of the Crown Tavern, was baptised

B

in St. Martin's.   John D'Avenant died in 1621, while holding the office of Mayor.

St. Peter's, the original University Church near Queen's College, is of very great antiquity.   Christchurch Cathedral was recently part of the monastery of St. Frideswide.

The colleges at this time are Merton, University, Balliol, Exeter, Hertford, Oriel, Queen's, New, Lincoln, All Souls, Magdalen with its superb tower, Brasenose, and Corpus-Christi.   Christ Church, refounded by Wolsey and completed by Henry VIII., looks fresh and new among its venerable surroundings.   Other recent foundations are Trinity, St. John's and Jesus Colleges ; and the Halls are St. Edmund's, St. Mary's, New Inn, and St. Alban's.

Dr. John Bancroft (afterwards Archbishop) was elected Master of University College, on March 2nd, 1610.   Four days later the fine dissolved Priory of the Austin Friars was purchased from the Corporation by Dorothy, widow of Nicholas Wadham, as the site of the new foundation of Wadham College.   The building was commenced in the following April, and completed July, 1613, for a warden and fifteen fellows, fifteen scholars, two chaplains, and two clerks.   In February, 1618, Dr. Anthony Blincom died at Oxford, leaving a great part of a fortune of £3,000 to Oriel College.

William Pemble, a celebrated tutor and divinity reader of Magdalen Hall, died on April 14th, 1623, at the early age of thirty-two.

Pembroke College, at first called Broadgate Hall, was founded in 1624, by means of a bequest from Thomas Tesdale of Glympton, aided by a donation from Richard Wightwick, Rector of East Ilsley, for a master, ten fellows, and ten scholars.   The placed on the right, above the junction of the narrow channel of the Ock with the river. The town is of great antiquity and full of the remains of monastic times. The wide extent of the mutilated abbey demonstrates by the Gothic wealth of detail the past riches and glories of its proud abbots and monks. A beautiful stone cross stands in the market-place ; and the two churches are St. Helen's with square embattled tower and lofty spire, by the side of which is Christ's Hospital ; and St. Nicholas, with a tower at the west end. The old bridge of Cullum dates from the time of Henry V. On February 16th, 1609, James granted a new charter to the borough, confirming the possession of certain properties to the Corporation, " in consideration of the sume of Fifty pounds nine shillings and four pence of good and lawful money of England." The rights and privileges granted by the charters of Philip and Mary, and Elizabeth, were further confirmed to the mayor, bailiffs, and burgesses, on the 3rd of March following, the town being made a Borough of the Peace, with Recorder and justices. Two annual fairs were to be held, and a market every Friday for corn, grain, victuals, and other commodities, also a wool market every Monday. The tolls taken were to be used for the discharge of public expenses and the relief of the poor. Another charter, dated June 21st, 1620, confirmed all previous charters, and the tolls on grain, corn and malt, fish, cheese, cloth, horses, etc.

In December, 1608, William Bennett, of Marl-borough, willed to his uncle, Thomas Tesdale, of Glympton, lands in Blunsdon, Wilts, for the relief and benefit of six of the poorest children in the town, who were to be brought up in John Royse's Free

Grammar School, for the space of six years. Two
months later, Thomas Tesdale gave to the Trustees
of Christ's Hospital his glebe lands and tithes in
Warwickshire for the maintenance of an Usher
at the Free School.

On July 12th, 1619, a pardon was given to Robert
Wrixham of Abingdon for killing John Baylie " in
a sudden fray."

Close to Abingdon is Drayton, its church dedicated
to St. Leonard, and a mile off on the left the village
of Culham is almost surrounded by the river. It
has a Church of St. Paul, and the manor-house was
formerly the occasional retreat of the Abbots of
Abingdon. On August 24th, 1623, Thomas Sutton
was drowned in his passage from Newcastle to
London. He was minister of Culham and Lecturer
at St. Mary Ovarie's, Southwark; and at both places
was much followed for his preaching.

A mile distant, on the right, is Sutton Courtney,
its Church of All Saints a mixture of Norman and
Early English, and the abbey-house was another of
the abodes of the Abbots of Abingdon.

In 1607, Edmund Bradstock bequeathed a house
and some land here for educational purposes. He
also founded and endowed a free school for the
education of twenty poor children, at the small
hamlet of Appleford, where is a Chapel of SS. Peter
and Paul.

Next comes Earls, or Long Wittenham, with a
Church of All Saints. The river now takes a wide
backward curve, and on the bend to the left is
Clifton Hampden, shewing a quaint old Church of
St. Michael.

We pass the little hamlet of Buscott, and reach
Dorchester, a market town of remote antiquity,

standing in the midst of rich pastures, near the confluence of the Thame, which flows under the picturesque town bridge. The Church of SS. Peter and Paul combines Norman with other Gothic styles, and the Priory of departed Black Canons is crumbling in desolate neglect.

On the other side of the river is the village of Little Wittenham gathered around its Church of St. Peter. Sinodun Hill, rising above a wood and surrounded by British and Roman entrenchments, is near at hand.

Warborough, on the left, is partially bounded by the Thame and Thames, and has an ancient Church of St. Lawrence.

Shillingford is a hamlet in this parish.

Next comes the old village of Bensington or Benson, with a square white tower to its Church of St. Helen. On July 23rd, 1606, a Commission was issued from the Exchequer to Sir Francis Stonor and others to make a survey of the manor of Bensington, which consisted chiefly of lands and tenements in Benson, Warborough, Shillingford, and Newnham-Murren. Bensington had two commons covering fifty acres, a common moor containing twenty acres, and a common marsh of twenty acres. Warborough had a common pasture of ten acres, and a common marsh of sixteen acres. There were cottages and other buildings on the commons of Bensington and Warborough. The fishery of the manor was in possession of a Robert Arnold. Bensington at the time of this survey was a very swampy place, and the ague common in the district was known as " the Benson shakes."

On one side the river overflows on to the Crow-marsh, which extends down the stream to the bridge connecting the county of Oxford to Berkshire at Wallingford. At Crowmarsh Gifford is a small Norman Church of St. Mary Magdalene, and the remains of fortifications going back to Stephen.

Wallingford, a borough and market town—returning two members to Westminster—on the road between Oxford and Reading, is approached from the river by a long stone bridge of high antiquity, consisting of nineteen arches. The quaint old town, grouped around its market-place, was formerly of great extent, and before its depopulation by the plague in 1348, contained, according to Leland, fourteen churches, four of which now exist—St. Peter's, St. Leonard's of Norman and Early English character, All Hallows, and a fine Church of St. Mary-le-More, near the market-house. And grimly overlooking all is the massive royal castle in a ruinous condition.

The river with a widened channel flows on past the village of Newnham-Murren and its Church of St. Mary, on the left ; and Mongewell, with a graveyard without a church.

Two miles on the river becomes broader and deeper opposite North Stoke, where the church is dedicated to St. Mary. A little way off is South Stoke with a Church of St. Andrew ; and a ferry across the river brings us to Moulsford and its Church of St. John the Baptist. On June 20th, 1616, a Licence was issued to Henry Samborne to hold a Court Leet in the manor of Moulsford and elsewhere in the county of Berkshire.

Still acquiring breadth the river flows placidly on to the beautifully placed village of Streatley, which has a Church of St. Mary and a deserted Dominican convent.

On the other side, where the Ikeneld Street crosses
the Thames, the village of Goring commands fine
extensive views of the river and country. Its
Norman Church of St. Thomas à Becket, with a
massive tower, was formerly attached to the empty
Priory of St. Augustine nuns. A medicinal spring
here, near the water, is held in high estimation for
diseases of the eye and cutaneous eruptions.

Basildon, a short distance from the river on
the left, is a village with an important past, and
a church dedicated to St. Bartholomew. The
next village, Pangbourn, with a Church of St.
James, is on a fine trout stream running into the
river. On the opposite side is Whitchurch and a
Church of St. Mary.

Purley on the left and its Church of St. Mary
repose in pasture and meadow ; and now both sides
of the river are covered with a splendid stretch of
woods. Peeping out of stately trees and green
foliage on the left is the village of Maple Durham and
its Church of St. Margaret, whilst near the water is
the fine Elizabethan hall of the Blounts. The
river here is broad and studded with numerous islets,
between which the water tumbles and foams over
weirs, giving life to the dreamy calm ; and a quaint
old mill, enveloped by the leafy overhanging shade,
adds picturesqueness to the delightful scene.

Tilehurst, on the right, shews a plain brick Church
of St. Michael. On the left is the neat and salubrious
village of Caversham, and its Church of St. Peter
on the high grounds commands wide views of
Reading and the beautiful country around. In
grounds adjoining the lower side of the churchyard
is an ancient mansion, with gardens extending to
the river, formerly belonging to the monks of Nutley

Abbey in Buckinghamshire. Lord Knollys lived
here at this time, and on April 27th, 1613, the Queen,
in her progress to Bath, spent the night at Caversham
House, and was entertained with revels and a
masque written by Dr. Thomas Campion.

From Caversham a stone and timber bridge
crosses the river to Reading, which looks exceedingly
quaint and mediaeval with its timbered and tiled
houses ; its Gothic churches with the majestic tower
of St. Lawrence's dominating all ; the ruins of its
castle, and the grey wide-spreading walls and
traceried windows of the magnificent Benedictine
Abbey of Henry I., now shorn of the pride of its
mitred Abbot, and partly demolished to build St.
Mary's Church in 1550. The ancient borough,
sending two members to Westminster, and carrying
on a large trade in woollen cloth, clusters thickly
around its market-place, Free Grammar School,
and Churches of St. Lawrence, St. Mary, and St.
Giles. Stow mentions that "in times past," the
place was called "Pontium," from the number of
bridges built over the Kennett, a small river running
through the town and falling into the Thames
about a quarter of a mile below. There are royal
stables in the Abbey dormitories at Reading, and in
January, 1604, James Braig was appointed keeper of
them, with a salary of £12 13s. 4d. James visited
the town in 1612, and his consort was there the
following year. The Abbey was settled on the
Queen, and a keeper of the house appointed with
a fee of £20 per annum. After the death of Queen
Anne in 1619 the Abbey was granted to Prince
Charles, and some members of the Knollys family
resided there. Dr. Laud, now rising into eminence,
was the son of a clothier in Broad Street, where he

was born in 1573, receiving his early education at the Grammar School.

In 1605, Sir Thomas White bequeathed money for providing loans, by election, to poor young men being clothiers of the town.

Fourteen apprentices were made free of the borough in 1608 ; nine in 1618 ; twelve in 1619 ; seven in 1621. In 1610 Thomas Deane gave £10 a year for two poor men and three poor children in the Hospital. James Pococke, in 1611, bequeathed £25 for the distribution yearly of sixteen shirts and smocks to sixteen poor people in Reading and Yattendon or Frilsham. On September 12th, 1612, the mayor and burgesses ordered that every burgess should, at his own charge, provide three leather fire buckets within his own house ; and each " subsidye " man should have in readiness two such buckets.

On the following December 18th, the Mayor and Corporation announced that an Aid from the Freeholders of the borough was required, and would be levied for marrying the King's daughter—the Princess Elizabeth to the Prince Palatine. In 1614 Edward Kernishe, a London merchant, left £50 for the relief of twenty-four poor householders of Reading for ever. On March 3rd, 1615, the Corporation directed that the posts of the well in the market-place should be used for whipping rogues and vagrants. In February, 1623, six prisoners were hanged at the Assizes. On the following March 5th, the Corporation " was informed by the cofferer, Mr. Brackston, that a great part of Caversham Bridge is in decaye and must of necessitye be forthwith amended ; and it was then agreed that the cofferers shall provide tymber and plankes, and cause it to be amended." About a year later information was submitted to the Corporation that the causeway and highway leading to the bridge was decayed and not passable, when " It was agreed that the Cofferers shall fourthwith repayre and amend the stone bridge and bridges in what is needfull ; and as touchinge the cawsey and highwayes there the parishe Surveyors shall doe what is needfull." Nine persons having been drowned in the river at Reading, a motion was made by William Kendricke, at a meeting of the Corporation on Monday, March 24th, 1623, for advice " concerning the goodes drowned by the drowninge of the boat in the ryver of Thems, when nine persons were drowned and lost their lives." It was resolved that the boatmen should petition the King's Almoner for " deodandes." On April 21st, Edward Hamblen complained to the Corporation that Margaret Terrant, wife of a bargeman of the town, and Mary her daughter, had stolen from him half a bushel or more of barley, " being in rickes and shockes in his growndes or feildes at Caversham, and the same did carry away with force."

In 1623, Dr. Swaddon bequeathed lands to the poor of Reading and other towns ; and in 1624, John Kendrick, an eminent clothier of the town, left £7,500, in trust to the mayor and burgesses, to be employed partly in building a house for the employment of the poor, which was named the " Oracle."

Winding slowly along, the river next passes Sonning on the right amidst diversified scenery. This village, of great note in early times, has a Church of St. Andrew with an ancient chapel at the eastern end dedicated to St. Sarick, to which pilgrims formerly resorted for the cure of insanity. A wooden bridge crosses to the left bank, on which, a short way on, is the hamlet of Shiplake, with an Early English Church of SS. Peter and Paul.

A little way farther, on the right, the river Loddon falls into the Thames, and then comes Wargrave in sight of well-wooded hills and verdant valleys. Its Church of St. Mary has an Early English tower.

Henley, on the left, is a very old incorporated market town, in an exceedingly pleasant position on an ascent from the bank of the river, which here takes a fine curve. Beech-clad hills and beautiful rustic scenery envelop the old-world, yet busy little town, with its Decorated and Perpendicular Church of St. Mary, to which an embattled tower erected by Cardinal Wolsey adds dignity. The ancient wooden bridge crossing the river leaves its passengers travelling London-wards at the foot of a steep chalk hill, which repays the labour of climbing by the unsurpassed scene of sylvan beauty obtained at the top.

There is a royal park at Henley, and the keeper received a fee of £9 2s. 6d. The park was in possession of Henry Alford, of Cotes, Gloucestershire, and he, in January, 1616, sold it to Sir Robert Mellor, of Dorset. In 1620 it was in the hands of Sir John Mellor, who in turn sold it to Sir James Whitelock. On December 14th, 1604, a grant of Incorporation was made at Oxford for the foundation of a Grammar School in the town, and it was endowed with the proceeds of certain church lands and other property partly bequeathed by Augustine Knapp. On October 28th, 1622, the Lord Mayor and Aldermen of London submitted an answer to the Privy Council, " on the petition of William Goade and other maltsters of Henley-upon-Thames, shewing that their complaints against the Billingsgate porters are unfounded, they being an established company under fixed rules, and not complained of by other parties, who use them much more than maltsters."

After passing Henley Bridge the river widens to a silvery expanse and flows by a densely-wooded islet in sight of the pretty village of Remenham, on the right, standing on a hilly surface around its Church of St. Nicholas. A little farther on is the hamlet of Fawley, with a small and simple parish church.

Turning a bold sweep of the river we come to Hambleden, shewing a handsome church. The banks here are undulating and well-wooded, and near the river the D'Oyley family built a house in 1604, afterwards known as Greenland Lodge.

Flowing each side of an island, the river then reaches Medmenham, on the left, a village half buried in a wealth of rich foliage, through which is seen, near the water, the Church of St. Peter, and the extensive remains of a Cistercian Abbey.

Now deviating to the left, we meander along to Hurley on the right, where the Church of St. Mary shews Norman features, and the Benedictine Priory has recently been dismantled to build a mansion for the Lovelace family, afterwards known as Lady Place.

A bold sweep to the right brings us within sight of luxuriant hanging woods, and the village of Bisham, on hilly ground. The noble church, near the weir, is dedicated to All Saints, and the Temple Mills are named after their ancient possessors, the Knights Templars, who also founded the fine old Abbey, afterwards given to the Augustine Friars, and now partly converted into the abode of the Hoby family. Sir Edward, the present possessor, and his wife entertained here at the end of 1605, a Madame de Hoboquens, who had recently been with the Queen at Hampton Court. The Queen herself visited the Abbey in the course of her progress in August, 1610 ; and King James passed the night here on September 3rd, 1612, and again on August 28th, 1616. The next year the King, returning from his Scotch journey, spent another night at the Abbey. As he approached the mansion, on September 12th, the bells of Great Marlow, the neighbouring parish, were pealed in welcome.

A little lower down on the left is Great Marlow, a borough town of two streets crossing at the market-place, where is the Church of All Saints. After sending representatives to Parliament during the reigns of the first two Edwards, the privilege ceased, but upon a petition submitted by the burgesses to the House of Commons, the right was restored in 1623. In 1609, John Brinkhurst devised to the town almshouses for six widows. In 1624, Sir William Borlase, of Medmenham built a school house and started a school at Great Marlow.

Little Marlow, almost adjoining, has a late Gothic Church of St. John with an embattled tower ; and here also is the shell of a small Benedictine nunnery.

On the right, near a ferry, is the picturesque church, with square tower, of Cookham, dedicated to Holy Trinity. Behind the church is the village, which had a market in the time of the Domesday survey, and now the tenants of its royal manor are toll-free in all markets, and exempt from jury calls.

Passing Hedsor and its Church of St. Nicholas on the left, and the heights and fine overhanging woods of Clieveden—in the midst of which George Villiers, Duke of Buckingham, built a summer mansion—

we reach Maidenhead by means of a timber bridge carrying the great western road over the river. This is a borough and market town of one long street, some distance from the water, and in the midst of its quaint buildings is a venerable chapel dating from the thirteenth century. On August 4th, 1604, a charter of Elizabeth was confirmed whereby the place was constituted a Free Town and its inhabitants a Body Corporate, under the name of " The Warden, Bridge Masters, Burgesses and Commonalty of the Town of Maydenheth." Two serjeants-at-mace were appointed to attend on the warden, and carry silver or gilt maces before him ; a fair was to be held on Whit Wednesday in addition to those on the Feasts of St. Mary Magdalen and St. Andrew ; and three oak trees from Cookham Wood were granted yearly for the repair of Maidenhead Bridge.

Bray appears next on the right. Its Church of St. Michael, a mixture of all Gothic styles, is associated with the recent memory of Symond Symonds, who changed with every change of religion from Henry VIII. well into Elizabeth's reign, and holding his living through all died " Vicar of Bray." On July 15th, 1616, the King granted a Licence to the Fishmongers' Company of London to found Jesus Hospital at Bray, pursuant to the will of William Goddard, fishmonger, of London, who gave for the purpose certain lands, messuages, etc., in the metropolis and Berkshire ; the wardens and assistants of the Fishmongers' Company were also incorporated as governors of the hospital.

The tenants of this royal manor have the same privileges as those of Cookham.

Opposite Maidenhead is the village of Taplow, with a Church of St. Nicholas. John Chamberlain wrote to Sir Dudley Carleton, on October 26th, 1616 : "Sir Henry Guildford hath had a great loss of late, at Taplow, near Maidenhead, to the value, they say, of six or seven thousand pounds, by the burning of his house, with all the movables of great worth, besides plate, money, and jewels, and, which is worst of all, the greatest part of his evidences. The fire was so serious, that the house is said to be burned down to the ground, though it were of brickwork, and, coming in the night, they had scant leisure or means to save themselves."

Some way back from the water on the left is Dorney and a Church of St. James with a handsome tower.

On rising ground two miles inland the village of Burnham is seen, with a fine Church of St. Peter, and a dismantled abbey of the Order of St. Augustine.

Boveney, near the river, is a hamlet with a chapel dedicated to St. Mary Magdalene.

Passing Clewer on the right, and its ancient Church of St. Andrew, we come to the royal borough and market town of New Windsor—under the shadow of the grand old castle—a place of quaint timbered houses and old inns, with a Church of St. John the Baptist in the midst. In the early autumn of 1604, a fire damaged the town, and on September 21st, a royal warrant ordered the payment of £100 to the mayor for distribution among the sufferers. On several occasions the burgesses of the town stoutly and successfully defended their privileges against the encroachments of the King.

On the other bank, reached by a wooden bridge, stand Eton and its Churches of St. Mary and St. Nicholas, with the college and school in meadows

C

beside the river. The Plague appeared here in
1603, and two or three years later. Again, after
four years, when the pestilence was at Windsor,
Robert Keyne, of Eton, was paid a sum " towards
the ¦charges of them that watched in Eton in
the tyme and sickness in Windsor." This was
probably for men placed at the bridge to prevent
any communication between the two places. James
I. visited Eton from Windsor on September 21st,
1604, when he partook of a banquet at the college
and knighted Sir Henry Savile the Provost. Sir
Thomas Edmonds wrote on this occasion to Secretary
Winwood : " The gentlewoman (Lady Savile), your
friend, saith that the favour cometh now too late,
and therefore now not worthy of her." Lady Savile
was jealous of her husband's devotion to study and
once said : " Sir Henry, I would I were a book too,
and then you would a little more respect me."

The King visited Eton again in 1611 or 1612, when
some slight alterations were made in the church.

Adam Robyns, a fellow of the college, left at his
death in 1613, £100 for the purchase of a silver
ewer and dish, and of tapestry for the hall.

Among the pupils at this time, Lord Wriothesley
(afterwards Earl of Chichester) kept a page. Philip
Lytton, a younger son of Sir Rowland Lytton, of
Knebworth, was another, of whom Dudley Carleton
wrote in December, 1608 : " His schoolemaster made
a complaint unto me that he was too daintie
mouthed, and could eat no beefe, but he answeares
the matter well, ' Verum est ! When I was at Mr.
Alden's I had better meat.' " Alden was a fellow
who lodged some of the boys.

Con O'Neil, a younger son of the " arch-rebel "
Hugh, Earl of Tyrone, was sent to Eton in 1615,

by order of the King, and maintained there at his expense for more than two years. The young man was afterwards removed to the Tower of London, and died there in confinement.

In February, 1621, Sir Henry Savile died at Eton, to which beloved place he had returned a few days previously " resigned for death," and was buried at night, by torchlight, in the church ; so that no unnecessary expense should be incurred, although he left £200 for his funeral. Thomas Murray, a Scotchman, who had been tutor and secretary to Prince Charles, succeeded as Provost on February 23rd.

On August 10th, 1622, John Chamberlain wrote to Sir Dudley Carleton, " The Prince and Buckingham swim every evening at Eton."

Lord Keeper Williams wrote on April 11th, 1623, to the Marquis of Buckingham : " Mr. Murray, the Provost of Eton, is now dead ; and the place stayed by the Fellows and myself, until your lordship's pleasure be known. Whomsoever your lordship shall name, I shall like of, even should it be Sir William Beecher, though the provostship never descended so low. The King named unto me yesterday morning Sir Albertus Morton, Sir Dudley Carleton, and Sir Robert Ayton, our late Queen's secretary ; but, in my opinion, though he named him last, his Majesty inclined to this Ayton most. It will rest wholly with your lordship to name the man. It is somewhat necessary to be a good scholar, but more that he be a good husband and a careful manager, which no man can be that is so much indebted to my Lord St. Albans " (Bacon).

On July 24th, 1624, Sir Henry Wotton, called " the most widely cultivated Englishman of his time," was elected to the Provostship.

This poet, diplomatist, and scholar was the friend of Isaak Walton, author of the " Compleat Angler " ; and it has been said : " The bend in the river just below the Playing Fields, known as Black Potts, must always remain classical ground for anglers— for there Wotton and Walton used to fish together, and there perhaps Wotton wrote these lines ' on a bank as he sate a-fishing ' :

> " ' And now all nature seemed to love ;
> The lusty sap began to move ;
> New juice did stir the embracing vines,
> And birds had drawn their valentines ;
> The jealous trout that low did lie,
> Rose at a well dissembled fly ;
> There stood my friend with patient skill,
> Attending to his trembling quill.' "

During this same month the King, from Theobalds, recommended to the Provost, the son of John Smith, his shoemaker, for admittance into the sixth, seventh, or eighth place in the college at the next election.

Sweeping round a bend we come to Datchet, opposite the Little Park of Windsor. Here the church is dedicated to St. Mary. The site of Old Windsor and its hoary old church is passed on the right ; and then on the left, facing Runnymede and the island on which Magna Charta was signed, is the village of Wyrardisbury, standing away from the river, and shewing a Church of St. Andrew and an empty Benedictine nunnery. Egham, on the right, has a Church of St. John the Baptist, and is inter- sected by a Roman road. In November, 1613, the Earl of Suffolk wrote in a letter from Whitehall to Sir Thomas Lake : " Order has been taken with the keeper of Egham Walk, for the King's six wild

pigs, until they are fit to be turned out." In 1624,
Chief Baron Denham built an almshouse of brick,
on the West Hill, Egham, and endowed it for the
maintenance of five poor aged women not relieved
by the parish. He also left by his will money for
each of these poor women to have a new gown,
costing fourteen groats a yard, every Christmas,
and stockings and shoes costing fourteen pence
twice a year.

The market town of Staines is next approached
on the left. Near the Church of St. Mary is an old
house which somehow became locally known as a
palace of King John. By the river here is the
stone, with the inscription round the top, " God
preserve the City of London, A.D., 1280," marking
the limits of the jurisdiction of the Lord Mayor as
Conservator of the Thames. On February 2nd,
1618, Lord Chancellor Bacon wrote to the Lord
Mayor and Court of Aldermen of London with
respect to the repair of Staines Bridge and the
Causeway at Egham. On June 28th of the following
year he stirred them up with another letter complaining of the delay in raising money for this
urgent work, and demanded a return of the
names of such " as shall make default of their
speedy payment."

On the previous February 18th, a Brief had been
proclaimed for collections throughout Middlesex
and the Western Counties for repairs to the bridge
and maintenance of the causeway. The reason
given for this was that as the tolls only brought in
£24 yearly the inhabitants could not meet the
expense of the work, estimated to cost £1,000,
without help.

On November 27th, 1624, the Solicitor-General

Heath sent to Secretary Conway " on behalf of his countrymen of Egham and Staines, a Warrant for repair of Staines Bridge and Egham Causeway."

A Licence was granted on January 7th, 1625, to Thomas Clarke and other inhabitants of Staines and Egham, " nominated Bridge-masters by the Lord Keeper," to receive tolls for the repair of the bridge and causeway, and they were instructed to yield up their accounts to him.

Some distance on is Laleham, intersected by a branch of the small river Colne, and with a Church of All Saints dating from Norman times.

Chertsey, in meadows on the right, is a very old market town, with a Church of All Saints. The fine dismantled abbey, coming down from the Saxon period, is said to have " covered four acres and looked like a town " ; but the monks and their mitred abbot have departed for ever. The abbey domain extended for a long stretch of fine meadows along the river. A cut at the upper end of it took in the river water, and when approaching the abbey gained sufficient fall for a large mill, which was surrounded by farm buildings, barns, and granaries. The manorial mansion here is a venerable stone and brick structure, in which Henry VI. resided when a child.

In the course of November, 1608, the King granted the Rectory of Chertsey and the advowson of the Vicarage to Richard Lyddall and Edmund Bostock, " except to the King the tithes of sheaf and wood there ; and a stable, garden, a moor, and a field called the ' Knights Borewaie,' and straw there for litter for the King's horses."

In January, 1610, Dr. John Hammond, physician-in-ordinary to the King and Prince Henry, was granted, in consideration of £16 3s. 4d., the " house, site, and circuit of the late monastery of Chertsey." On July 2nd, Dr. Hammond expressed to the Earl of Salisbury his willingness to pay as much as the contractors for Chertsey Mills, and would purchase the reversion of the lease.

A Letter was sent to the Dean and Chapter of Windsor, in September, 1614, instructing them to grant Dr. Hammond a lease of Ham Farm, Chertsey.

On July 10th, 1620, a Warrant was issued from Westminster for the payment of sums not exceeding £430, to be used for rebuilding Chertsey Bridge.

James Johnstone received a Licence, on September 30th, 1624, " to set up and keep a Wharf at Chertsey, on the river Wey, for convenience in carrying goods on that river and the Thames, reserving a rent of 10s. to the Crown."

Some way lower down, on the opposite bank, is the village of Shepperton, with a Church of St. Nicholas and a stretch of common or waste land. Here is the parsonage house where the learned Erasmus spent some of his earlier days with his preceptor, the then incumbent, William Grocyn. On September 11th, 1621, Thomas Reynell and Katherine, daughter of Sir Henry Spiller, were married in the church ; and on July 14th, 1624, Dorothy, the wife of Sir Henry, was buried there.

Contiguous is the hamlet of Halliford, the haunt of fishermen. On the right is the royal park of Oatlands, with the village of Weybridge, about a mile from the water, on the upper bounds. The Wey runs into the river near here, and is crossed by a wooden bridge. The village of Walton is separated from Oatlands by a smaller park, containing a mansion probably built by Cardinal

Wolsey. The ancient church is dedicated to St.
Mary. Sunbury and its Church of St. Mary are on
the left, and then comes the very old village of
Hampton, where a ferry crosses the river. A
venerable Church of the Blessed Virgin Mary, and
a Free Grammar School, founded in 1556, are seen.
People of high rank, mostly attached to the Court,
live in and around the village, and about a mile and
a half distant is Wolsey's magnificent palace of
Hampton Court, surrounded by a large chace or
park stocked with deer and game. This is now a
favourite residence of the King, and the royal life
here is portrayed in the section headed " Court
Life."

Opposite is the village of Molesey (Moulsey), intersected by the river Mole, and with a long line of
common along the water side. Here the Heneage
family have a sumptuous mansion. One of Queen
Elizabeth's last grants was made on February 22nd,
1603, to Lady Dorothy Edmonds of a water mill
and granary in the Manor of Moulsey, with the
fishings attached, " from Michaelmas last for forty
years, rent 26s. 8d., being valued at £2 a year."
On February 13th, 1607, Lady Dorothy obtained
a grant of wood, underwood and woodlands, called
" Horsecopps," in Moulsey, " containing 14 acres,
from Michaelmas then last, for thirty-one years, at
a rent of 21s. 8d., and delivering two loads and an
half of wood and two loads and an half of faggots
for the King's use at Hampton Court or Oatlands,
it being of the annual value of £3."

A little farther on, facing the chace of Hampton
Court, is Thames Ditton, and near the water is
a chapel-of-ease to Kingston, dedicated to St.
Nicholas.

Next is the borough and market town of Kingston, with a Decorated cruciform Church of St. Nicholas, having tower and spire at the intersection ; and near it the venerable Chapel of St. Mary Magdalene, in which some of the Saxon kings were crowned, and others on the weather-worn stone near the town-house.

The chapel is now used as a Free Grammar School, founded by Queen Elizabeth. A wooden bridge carries the old highway over the river, and so through the hamlet of Hampton Wick. On November 17th, 1603, a charter was given at Westminster to the bailiffs and freemen of the town, granting divers privileges and a weekly market on Saturday. One prison or gaol was allowed within the town, or the precincts of its liberties for the safe custody of offenders. Further, in 1623, the King renewed the grant of Edward IV. to hold a weekly court of record at Kingston, before the bailiffs and high steward ; and ordained that the bailiffs, high steward, and recorder for the time being should have the authority of Justices of the Peace ; that the bailiffs and freemen might have a jail within the vill ; that they might hold a weekly market on Saturdays, and also that they might levy and receive from all tenants all manners of fines, etc., for their own use and profit. On September 20th, 1619, an entry was made in the Churchwardens' Accounts of Croydon that that town, " being oppressed in the carriage of saltpetre to Kingston-on-Thames," had had the road measured " and found it ten miles sixty-two roods." About 1611 John Dolling willed money to be used for the benefit of the poor of the town. In 1618, Edward Buckland left a wharf and money to buy coals " at the best hand " and sell them at reasonable rates to the poor of the town. John Ramsay, Earl of Holderness, of Norbiton Hall, was granted, in April, 1622, the patronage of the vicarage ; and the next year the advowsons, etc., of the rectory were granted him. On June 11th, 1624, Henry Smith gave by deed to the town, money for the relief, maintenance, and setting to work of the poor, and for putting out apprentices.

Teddington, on the left, is a village, a little way from the water, with a Perpendicular church dedicated to St. Mary.

The river now with expanded current sweeps on to Twickenham, a village between two brooks flowing at each end into the river. The Church of St. Mary stands up from the quaint houses and mansions of the nobility and gentry peeping from masses of foliage within and around the charming place. Here is Twickenham Park, containing a fine mansion, and the reversion of the lease of the place, which had been the home of Sir Francis Bacon, came into the hands of Sir Henry Goodyer and Edward Woodward in 1607. In the course of the next year the lease was transferred to George, Lord Carew, and George Croke, in trust for Lucy, Countess of Bedford, who, when the Princess Elizabeth removed to Kew, " took up her own residence close by at Twickenham, and lived there till 1618 . . . ." The Countess was a wealthy woman, both in her marriage and as co-heiress with her brother, John Harrington, of Exton. " She was just setting up at Twickenham Park a household maintained on so generous a footing, that it seemed a small repetition of the Lady Elizabeth's establishment, and was even compared with it." The Countess was known as the " favourite of the

Muses," and she attracted to Twickenham John Donne, Samuel Daniel, Michael Drayton, and other poets of the time ; and gathered around her, in the mazes of her garden, a graceful and brilliant little court. About the same time, the artist David Vinkenboom sketched from the Park, and produced a well-peopled painting, with boats, swans, and horses drinking in the river, the ferry boat conveying a few passengers, and a view of Richmond Palace, whilst in the Park were the morris-dance and hobby-horse. On January 4th, 1609, the widowed Lady Bridget Markham, one of the Ladies of the Bedchamber to the Queen, and first cousin of the Countess, died at Twickenham Park, and was buried in the parish church. John Donne wrote an impressive elegy on the sad occasion, and on a monument erected in the church, Francis Beaumont celebrated her virtues in verse. On February 27th, 1614, Lord Harrington, an amiable and accomplished young nobleman of twenty-two, the particular friend of the late Prince Henry, died at the house of his sister, the Countess, from the effects, it was supposed, of poison taken while travelling in France and Italy. John Donne, who had a great affection for the young man, wrote the longest and best of his minor funeral poems, " Obsequies," on the mournful occasion. On November 11th, 1615, Charles, son of Sir Philip Stanhope, was baptised by the special dispensation of the Bishop of London, at the house of the Countess.

In 1618, Countess Lucy gave Twickenham Park to her relative, Sir William Harrington, and he sold the place, in 1621, to Mary, Countess of Home.

Among the baptisms in Twickenham Church

during the reign were—John, son of John Suckling, prebendary and poet, in 1609; Henry, son of Sir Thomas Savage, afterwards Earl Rivers, in 1610; and the daughters of Sir Humphry Line—Margaret in 1618, another Margaret in 1620, and Katherine in 1621. Katherine, the wife of Mr. Rowland White, was buried there in 1604, and Sir John Fitz, of Fitzford, Devon, was interred in the churchyard in 1605.

In the course of May, 1607, an Order was issued for paying to Thomas Ride " the sum of £40 in recompence and satisfaction of a farm-house and eight acres of land, which he holdeth of his Majesty for certain years yet to come, lying in the parish of Twickenham, and appointed by his Majesty for a dwelling-place for the keeper of the game there." On October 11th, 1618, the sum of thirty pounds, which had been willed by Andrew Johnson to the poor people of Twickenham, was paid in, and by consent of the vestry the money was left in the trust of Mr. Lewis Owen.

At a Vestry meeting held at Twickenham on October 6th, 1622, it was agreed and covenanted " that Mr. Robert Bartlet should keep still in his possession the three acres and a half of parish land with the bull meads, paying the same rent as he did formerly, with the condition that he, receiving now a bull of the Churchwardens, shall keep the said bull at his own charge, and if the bull do fortune to dye or miscarrye any other way the said Robert Bartlet promiseth to make it good, so that the parish shall not at any time want a sufficient bull for their use, but he will provyde one at his own costes and charges so long as he shall live and holdeth the aforesaid land at the same rate, and he promiseth also to leave the parish as sufficient a bull as he now receiveth."

Ham, a pretty hamlet, stands back from the water, on the opposite shore. A short distance on, after passing a park skirting the river, containing the noble mansion of Ham House, built by Sir Thomas Vavasour in 1610, is the village of Petersham, in the midst of woods, parks, and gardens, shewing a brick Church of St. Peter. In 1624, George Cole left by will money to be invested in land for the poor of the village.

Richmond now comes into view, with the noble prospect of the richly wooded hill and the fine palace of Henry VII. by the margin of the river. The place is still more commonly known as Sheen, and was so called till, as Aubrey wrote, Henry built his palace on the ruins of the ancient one destroyed by fire, " after the most exquisite way of architecture of the age, and gave it his own name of Richmond." In the town is the brick church of St. Mary Magdalene, and almhouses were founded in 1606 for eight poor women, on the lower road beneath the Hill.

A quarter of a mile from the palace at West Sheen is a decaying Carthusian Convent called the House of Jesus of Bethlehem.

On March 9th, 1622, letters-patent, dated at Westminster, granted and demised " the passage of water, called Richmond Ferry, with all and singular profits, commodities and advantages thereunto belonging or appertaining unto Edmund Coke and Edmund Sawyer, of London, gentlemen, for 40 years, paying 13s. 4d. twice a year into the Exchequer."

On the other side of the river is the village of

Isleworth of one street, in which is the Early English Church of All Saints. Near the water are the fine monastic buildings of Sion House, which was granted on July 4th, 1604, with the Manor of Isleworth, in fee farm, to Henry Percy, 9th Earl of Northumberland, and his heirs for ever, in whom were already vested the various leases, made by Queen Elizabeth, of the demesne lands.

Among the baptisms in Isleworth Church at this time were various children of Sir Thomas Savage, afterwards Earl Rivers—Henry in 1606, Jane in 1607, Francis in 1608, and James in 1609. Others were Henry, son of Sir Ralph Winwood in 1614, and Dorothy (Waller's "Sacharissa"), daughter of Sir Robert and Lady Dorothy Sidney, on October 5th, 1617. Dorothy, daughter of Sir William Lower, was buried there in 1606, as was Dorothy, Countess of Northumberland, on August 14th, 1619. This latter lady was the grandmother of Waller's "Sacharissa." Among the marriages were those of Henry Leegh and Lady Scudamore in 1616, and Sir John Waters and Lady Anne Biggs in 1622. In 1612, Richard Wyat gave the Stone-house in the churchyard and some lands to the poor. Margaret Wyat of Isleworth, in 1619, gave the moiety of a house and land at Laleham to the poor. On October 12th, 1624, Lord Strafford, writing to George Calvert, Lord Baltimore, Secretary of State, said "he took it for granted that he had quitted Isleworth at that season of the year and gone to town." Calvert had a country seat at Isleworth.

On the left is Brentford, an ancient market town of one long street running parallel with the river. Here is a chapel dedicated to St. George, and a ford across the Brent above its junction with the river.

In the course of 1610, the King granted the profits
of the market and fair at Brentford—held since the
dissolution of the monasteries by the Crown—to
James Hawley, whose family had been lessees under
the Priory, reserving a rent to the Crown of 20s.
per annum. On August 12th, 1621, the following
entry was made in the Parish Book of Brentford :
" Paid to her that was Lady at Whitsontide, by
consent, 5s. od. ; paid for a beast for the parish
use, £2 6s. 8d." " The Whitsuntide holidays were
celebrated by various pastimes commonly practised
upon other festivals ; but on the Monday after
Whitsun week at Brentford, a fat ox was provided,
and the maidens of the town, having their thumbs
tied behind them, were permitted to run after it ;
and she, who with her mouth took hold of the ox,
was declared Lady of the Ox, which being killed and
cleaned, but with the skin hanging upon it, was
carried on a long pole before the Lady and her
companions to the Butts Common, attended with
music, and a morrice-dance of men, and another of
women. The rest of the day was spent in mirth
and merry glee. Next day the beast, partly baked and
partly boiled, was served up for the lady's feast,
where she sat majestically at the upper end of the
table, and her companions with her." On July 9th,
1623, this entry was made : " Received for the
May Pole £1 4s." " The celebration of the May
Games took place on the first of May ; the juvenile
part of both sexes were accustomed to walk to some
neighbouring wood, accompanied with music, where
they broke down branches from the trees, and
adorned them with nosegays and crowns of flowers,
and returned with their booty homewards, and made
their doors and windows triumph with their spoils,

and the after part of the day was spent in dancing round a tall pole, called a May Pole, which, being placed in a convenient part of the village, stood there, as it were, consecrated to the Goddess of Flowers. In the celebration of May Games, the youth divided themselves into two troops, the one in livery, the other in the habit of the spring."

Facing Brentford is the royal domain of Kew, and here are a Chapel of St. Anne, and a large mansion where the King's daughter Elizabeth often resided before her marriage with the Prince Palatine. In February, 1605, a lease was granted to Walter Hickman of the Ferry over the river at Kew. In 1619 Lord Chancellor Bacon spent a great deal of time at his house at Kew.

Next comes the village of Mortlake, on the road from London to Richmond, with market gardens abounding in the flat country around. The sixteenth century church has a much older embattled tower of stone and flint. The Archbishop of Canterbury has a house here, and about 1616 or 1619 a manufactory of tapestry was established in the village by Sir Francis Crane.

On June 8th, 1615, a grant was made, for life, to Sir Charles Howard, junior, of the office of Keeper of Mortlake Park, etc.

On the same side is Barnes, a village with a long flat stretch of common or waste by the river. The Early English Church of St. Mary, of flint and freestone, has a later square brick tower. The manorhouse was the residence of Sir Francis Walsingham, and later of the Earl of Essex. A stately row of elms mark Barn Elms, where is a mansion called " Queen Elizabeth's Dairy."

The village of Chiswick, on the left, stands near

the margin of the stream, and besides the Church of
St. Nicholas and its churchyard of old tombs, has
many mansions of nobles and the gentle, standing
amidst masses of foliage and stately gardens. In
1609 a north transept was added to the church.
On July 26th, 1615, John Chamberlain wrote to
Sir Dudley Carleton : " Your nephew Carleton,
on Monday last, married the Lady Cotton, a fresh
widow, at Chiswick, and kept their wedding dinner
in a tavern at Putney." Sir Thomas Chaloner,
who died here in 1615, was the first discoverer of
alum mines in the kingdom, on an estate of his near
Gisborough in Yorkshire. In 1623 and after, Baron
Chichester, of Belfast, late Lord Deputy of Ireland,
was living at Chiswick ; and when the late favourite,
the Earl of Somerset, was released from the Tower
in October, 1624, he retired to a house he had taken
in the village. On January 1st, 1625, Lord William
Russell wrote to the Council from his house at
Chiswick.

Near at hand is Hammersmith, with a chapel
dedicated to St. Paul, and several fine mansions.
In 1624 Edward Latymer founded here a school
for boys, and gave thirty-five acres of land for its
support.

Some distance on is Fulham, an irregular village
on the left, the Church of All Saints shewing a handsome tower at the west end. The manor belongs
to the See of London, and in a park shadowed by
stately trees is the summer dwelling-place of the
Bishops. In September, 1621, a Brief was dated
on the cause between George Montaigne, then
Bishop of London, and Joan King, widow and
administratrix of the late Bishop, whose average
yearly revenue was estimated at £1855—relative

D

to repairs required at Fulham House, Much Haddam House, Stortford Gate House, the Bridges of Fulham, Acton, and Ealing, and other properties belonging to the See.

On April 7th, 1609, Sir Dudley Carleton wrote in a letter from London to Sir Ralph Winwood : " I have here in my poor habitation a special benefit of near neighbourhood to Sir Thomas Bodley, from whom I receive many favours, and yesterday my wife was invited by him to Fulham, whither we went, and Mr. Chamberlain in company." In 1615 Thomas Walkington was presented to the Vicarage of Fulham. He was the author of " Rabboni," " Mary Magdalen's Tears of Sorrow and Solace," and another sermon. When Sir Francis Bacon was liberated from the Tower on June 4th, 1621, he went to Sir John Vaughan's house at Fulham.

On the opposite bank, across a ferry, is the quaint village of Putney, with its Church of St. Peter near the river. Tradition says that this and Fulham Church were built by twin sisters.

There are many fine houses and gardens here. In 1603 Mr. Lacey, the merchant friend of Queen Elizabeth, lived in the village, and King James visited him on his way from Hampton Court to his Coronation. In February, 1608, Sir Julius Cæsar instructed Sir Thomas Lake to procure a Privy Seal for £128, to be paid to Sir Edward Cecil, Keeper of Putney Park, for expenses in repairs there, according to a certificate by Michael Haydon.

A short distance brings us to Wandsworth, a village of one street, on the declivity of two hills, standing where the Wandle falls into the river. Here are mansions and gardens, and besides the Church of All Saints, there is the only Presbyterian congregation in England at this time—established here since 1572.

On January 29th, 1618, the body of Sir William Foster was buried at Wandsworth and his bowels at Lambeth.

A stretch of gardens and fields brings us to Battersea, where there is a venerable Church of St. Mary, and a mansion near the river belonging to the family of St. John.

The riverside village of Chelsea stands some feet above the other bank, and its Church of St. Luke, near the water, was built in the previous century. The taverns and gardens here are the resort of the courtly, and there are residences of people of rank, notably the mansion where Sir Thomas More had lived, with its garden extending to the waterside ; and the manor house where Queen Elizabeth had lived as a girl of thirteen with Queen Katherine Parr and her second husband, Lord Thomas Seymour.

On June 10th, 1604, the Countess of Nottingham was granted the manor and mansion house at Chelsea ; and in November, 1609, James Howard, the son of the Countess, was granted a lease of Chelsea Place and Manor. From letters written by the Earl, who was Lord High Admiral, we gather that his house faced the river, and he was very jealous of any encroachments on the stream at this point. Later the manor came into the hands of Lord Cheyne. In the village was the house of Sir Thomas Mayerne, Physician to King James, on the site of which Inigo Jones afterwards built Lindsey House, for Bertie, Earl of Lindsey. On October 26th, 1604, John Stewart, Lord of Orkney, was married in the Church to the widowed Lady Elizabeth Southwell. In January, 1605, the Dean

and Chapter of St. Paul's were instructed to lease
to Bernard Lindsay the farm and parsonage of
Chelsea. In the course of 1609 the short-lived
Theological College was founded here ; and in 1622
Isaac Barrow was appointed to a Fellowship for life.
On August 12th, 1619, Sir Robert Lane and Mrs.
Dudley Gorges were married in the church ; and
just a year later, Katherine, daughter of John, Earl
of Northumberland, and widow of Henry, Earl
of Huntingdon, was buried there. On January
4th, 1622, John Chamberlain wrote to Sir Dudley
Carleton : " Great christening of the Lord
Treasurer's (Earl of Middlesex) son at Chelsea ;
the King, who was godfather, gave the child 1000*l.*
in land." On the following May Day the King
supped with the Lord Treasurer at his house in the
village ; but in 1623 the Earl was living here in
disgrace, and was busy corresponding with his
influential friends. In the following March he was
waiting in uneasy expectancy for the Council's
proceedings against him, and in May he was fined
heavily and sent to the Tower for neglect of his
duties as Lord Treasurer. This confinement lasted
till June, when he was liberated and returned to his
house.

In 1610 the Manor of Vauxhall was settled on
Prince Henry. In 1615, Vauxhall Gardens were the
property of Jane Vaux.

Round a bend of the river now appears Lambeth
nestling up to the Archbishop's palace, and
the Church of St. Mary adjoining. The village,
like Chelsea, is the home and resort of people
of quality. The Duke of Norfolk had a garden
on the banks of the river, afterwards " Cupar's
Garden." The Duck and Drake tavern gardens

dated from 1617. The country close to the village
is swampy and feverish, and at times was completely
under water. Lett's Timber Wharf, dating from
Queen Elizabeth's time, laid amidst ponds and marsh
streams. The only horse-ferry permitted on the
Thames at London was between here and Westminster, and near the Archbishop's gates were two
inns for the accommodation of travellers arriving
at night and not caring to risk the crossing in
the darkness. When Parliament was sitting the
Archbishop's superb barge carried him over to
Westminster.

In a list of Crown officials compiled in 1607 the
following item occurs, headed "Stockwell and
Leadhurst in Lamheath (Lambeth) Deane":
"Keeper of the mansion house at Stockwell, with
gardens and orchards, fee 4d. per diem." Com-
menting on the mildness and dampness of the winter,
John Chamberlain wrote on February 8th, 1616:
"We have all the signs and shows of a warm spring,
as well in all manner of herbs and sweet flowers,
as in beds of roses and blossoms of apricot and peach
trees, which have been usually worn any time these
three weeks. But, among the many wonders that
are spoken of in this kind, the greatest in my judg-
ment is that my Lord of Canterbury had a nest
of young blackbirds in his garden at Lambeth about
twelve days since, and another sent him from Croydon
four days after." Sir Thomas Parry lived at Lambeth, and in 1610 he had the Lady Arabella Stuart
a prisoner in his house for a time, after her un-
authorised marriage with Lord William Seymour.
A resident of the village at the beginning of the
reign was Dr. Simon Forman, who had settled
there and carried on the joint occupations of

physician and astrologer. Lilly wrote: "Here
he lived with good respect of the neighbourhood,
being very charitable to the poor, and was very
judicious and fortunate in horary questions and
sicknesses." The wicked Countess of Essex was
introduced to him by Mrs. Turner, and obtained his
assistance in her nefarious designs, especially before
the murder of Sir Thomas Overbury in the Tower,
and it was said that Forman frequently locked
himself in his study to avoid her. He died in
September, 1611, and was buried in the village.
He had foretold his wife on the previous Sunday,
so it was related, that he would die on the coming
Thursday. "Thursday came, and dinner was
ended, he very well; he went down to the water
side and took a pair of oars to go to some buildings
he was in hand with in Puddle Dock. Being in the
middle of the Thames, he presently fell down, only
saying, 'an impost, an impost,' and so died. A
most sad storm of wind immediately ensued."
In "Sir Thomas Overbury's Vision," 1616, are these
lines:

> "So over Thames, as o'er th' infernal lake,
>   A wherry with its oars I oft did take,
>   Who Charon-like did waft me to that strand,
>   Where Lambeth-town to all well-known doth stand:
>   There Foreman was, that fiend in human shape,
>   That by his art did act the devil's ape.
>   Oft there the black enchanter, with sad looks,
>   Sad poring over his blasphemous books,
>   Making strange characters in blood-red lines;
>   And, to effect his horrible designs,
>   Oft would he invocate the fiends below
>   In the sad house of endless pain and woe!"

In 1615, Lambeth Parish Church was repaired
and ornamented by voluntary contributions. A

gallery was constructed at the expense of a parishioner, Roger Jeston, haberdasher, of London. Mr. Hart gave a new marble font. Two years later Sir Noel Caron, Ambassador from the States of Holland, gave £100 towards repairing the church, and £50 for the poor of the parish. In 1620, Sir Noel gave seven messuages at Lambeth as habitations for seven poor widows, aged sixty years and upwards : also a messuage and land for the maintenance of these widows in his almshouses.

This philanthropic Dutch Ambassador died in the beginning of 1625, and was buried in the church on January 25th.

" Hog's Tide," or " Hock Tide," was kept at Lambeth as late as 1618, and was the survival of a popular holiday celebrated for generations to commemorate the death of the Danish King Hardicanute at a wedding feast here. The sums gathered at these festivals were used in repairing the parish church. An Annual Fair, lasting fifteen days, came down from the time of King John.

In June, 1620, a widow named Elizabeth Grub presented a petition to Lord Zouch " for his influence in Council on her behalf, touching rent due to her for the Glasshouse at Lambeth." In 1622, Roger Jeston gave land at Lambeth to aid in the relief of the poor.

Lambeth Churchyard was enlarged in 1623, and in pursuance of an Order from the Ecclesiastical Court, an assessment was made to defray the charge of building a new wall, and of other needful repairs. Four days before the death of King James the Privy Council met at Lambeth, on March 23rd, 1625.

Westminster, on the left, with the irregular mass

of the old palace buildings next the river, and St. Margaret's Church and the magnificent Gothic wonders of the great Abbey behind, presents a wide cluster of ancient and picturesque structures of all ages and degrees. The more crowded quarter, which in the time of Elizabeth was the haunt of " masterless " men, felons, and cutpurses, is still of very evil fame, and it was said " almost every fourth house was an alehouse, harbering all sorts of lewd and badde people."

A tower and water gate next the river is called the " Long Staple," and the Wool Staple here was appointed in 1353, for weighing all wool brought to London. On August 3rd, 1604, letters-patent defined the limits of the franchise of Westminster to extend along the Strand to the " Barr of the Temple," the Liberties of the Duchy of Lancaster and the Savoy. In 1618, William, Earl of Derby, built a mansion in Cannon Row, and the gardens ran down to the river. Sir Francis Nethersole wrote, on May 24th, 1624, to Sir Dudley Carleton : " A Bill has passed the Lords to remove all brewhouses between the Bridge (London) and Tuttle Fields. . . . The Commons hesitate to pass it, as it will damage the estates of many, but they may do so to please the Prince (Charles), who, in St. James's Park, is annoyed with the Tuttle Street Brewhouses."

Passing the huge jumble of the royal riverside palace of Whitehall, we come to the splendid mansions of the nobles stretching along the Strand, and with gardens sloping down to the river. Their upper windows look across a wide expanse of open country, backed by the Surrey hills.

Northumberland, or lately Suffolk House shews a square mass with corner turrets, built around a courtyard, on or near the site of a former hospital called St. Mary Rouncival. When the Gunpowder Plot was being hatched in 1605, the Earl of Northumberland largely rebuilt the house, and at this time or later Inigo Jones erected on the garden side a range of State rooms.

York House, its main front and turrets facing the river, was built by Archbishop Heath, of York, and leased by his successors to the Lord Keepers of the Great Seal. The mansion was occupied by Nicholas Bacon, when, in 1561, was born here his famous son, Francis, who spent his childhood under its palatial roof or in the garden gently falling to the water stairs. He spent his youth and early manhood at Twickenham, and was already a knight in 1607, when, sumptuously clad in Genoese purple velvet, he rode from the Strand along the lanes to Marylebone Chapel and wedded Alice Barnham, the handsome daughter of a rich London alderman. The next day Dudley Carleton wrote in a letter to John Chamberlain : " Sir Francis Bacon was married yesterday to his young wench in Maribone Chapel. He was clad from top to toe in purple, and hath made himself and his wife such store of fine raiments of cloth of silver and gold that it draws deep into her portion. The dinner was kept at his father-in-law, Sir John Packington's lodging over against the Savoy, where his chief guests were the three knights, Cope, Hicks, and Beeston." In 1617, Bacon watched, in one of the chambers of York House, by the sick couch of Lord Ellesmere, and on the dying Chancellor surrendering the seals, presented him with the coronet of Brackley. After the death of Ellesmere, Bacon bought the lease of the house from the late Chancellor's son,

and finding the rooms vast and naked, his army of
friends gave him for their adornment books and
drawings, stands of arms, cabinets, jewels, rings, and
boxes of money. As Lord Keeper and Chancellor
he lived here, feasting poets and scholars in its
banqueting-hall, and dating from it his great
Instauration. It is related that as the Chancellor
once stood looking from the garden at the fishermen
below him throwing their nets, he made them a
speculative offer for their coming draught. This
was refused, and when the net was hauled in with
only two or three little fishes in it, he told them that
" hope was a good breakfast, but an ill supper."
On January 22nd, 1620, when nearing the publica-
tion of his " Novum Organon," he gave a grand
banquet here to his friends. Ben Jonson was one
of the guests, and is said to have recited a set of
verses, in which he said :

> " Hail th' happy genius of the ancient pile !
>   How comes it that all things so about thee smile,
>   The fire, the wine, the men ?—and in the midst
>   Thou stand'st as if some mystery thou didst."

A year later came the terrible crash of his fall,
and in one of the bedrooms of the mansion he wrote
his submission and confession, received the Earls
of Arundel, Pembroke, and Southampton as
messengers from the House of Lords, and surrendered
the Great Seal. On November 17th, 1623, the
favourite Buckingham feasted the King, Prince
Charles, and the Spanish Ambassador at York House.
Buckingham coveted the possession of the house,
and early in 1624 this was effected by passing a Bill
through Parliament for enabling the King to exchange some lands for the property. The haughty
favourite at once partly demolished the old house, and

lining the walls of the temporary structure he erected on the site with huge mirrors, lavishly entertained foreign ambassadors and other gay company. The fond and foolish King contributed 2,000 tons of Portland stone, at a cost of £1,800, towards the rebuilding scheme, but no permanent structure arose from the wasteful expenditure.

Durham House, the imposing building erected in the middle of the fourteenth century by Bishop Thomas de Hatfield, of Durham, has its private apartments looking on to the river. The noble mansion was bestowed by Queen Elizabeth on the gallant Sir Walter Raleigh in 1583. Aubrey well remembered Raleigh's study, " which was on a little turret that looked into and over the Thames and had a prospect which is as pleasant, perhaps, as any in the world."

When the misfortunes of the knight commenced with the accession of King James, and he was committed to the Tower in 1603, the then Bishop of Durham claimed the house for his See, but it was never again occupied, and soon after the stables came down to make way for the New Exchange.

In October, 1618, was dated an Indenture of Sale, " from Sir Thos. Wilson, of Hertford, now residing in St. Martin's-in-Fields, London, of a dwelling-house, garden, etc., in St. Martin's-in-the-Fields, between Durham House, Britain's Burse, York House, and the river, to Wm. Roo, of London, for £374."

Exeter, or Burleigh House, the abode of Thomas Cecil, Earl of Exeter, is close to the fine new mansion of Salisbury House, built by Sir Robert Cecil, who figured so largely in State affairs as Earl of Salisbury during the first part of the reign.

The next is Worcester House, which, before the Reformation, was the Inn of the Bishops of Carlisle,

Afterwards it belonged to the Russell family as Bedford or Russell House, and then passed to the present possessors, the Earls of Worcester.

Near at hand, and close to the water, the high tide washing its walls, is the old royal Savoy Palace, now shorn of its former glory, and its ruinous apartments used as an hospital for the poor. Stow wrote that there were in the Savoy precincts, " parish churches twain, sometime three." On October 30th, 1605, George Clifford, third Earl of Cumberland, died at the Savoy. He was one of the first of the adventurers who formed the East India Company in 1600.

Somerset House, the Queen's residence, is only separated from the Savoy by a narrow lane, and has large and fair gardens bordering the stream.

Arundel House is a dignified baronial building, the home of the Earls of Arundel, who acquired it from the Bishops of Bath.

Essex House has a fine garden, also a water-gate and stairs, from which the Earl, the proud favourite of the late Queen Elizabeth, embarked on his rash and fatal act of rebellion.

The green lawns and shady gardens, and old church and buildings of the Temple come next. On August 13th, 1609, the King, by letters-patent, made an absolute conveyance of the Inner and Middle Temples, with their respective precincts and appendages, to the Treasurer, Benchers, etc., of these houses and their assigns for ever, for the " lodging, reception, and education of the professors and students of the law of this realm," each house " yielding and paying " to the Crown £10 yearly. About April, 1618, the sheriffs of London sent a letter to the Lord Chief Justice, " acquainting him that at Whitsuntide last one Thurston Hunt, a prisoner in the Poultry Compter, was removed by Habeas Corpus, returnable before Mr. Justice Warburton, at his chambers in Serjeants' Inn. Being brought there in the custody of one of their officers, Hunt escaped into the Temple, where he was rescued by the gentlemen of those houses. The officer was violently taken and cast into the Thames, and there drawn along through the stream in peril of drowning. They thought it their duty to acquaint his Lordship and the rest of the Judges of the matter, and requested that some order might be taken for reformation of such insolencies too often practiced by the gentlemen upon their officers, which could but bring an evil and dangerous consequence such as they knew their Lordships (out of their love for those fellowships), had rather prevent than punish."

Next the Temple and bordering on the river is Whitefriars, a district on the site of the house and gardens of a Convent of Carmelites or Whitefriars. There were built here in Elizabeth's time, after the demolition of the religious buildings, "many fair houses, lodgings for noblemen, and others." The precincts of the district possessed the privileges of sanctuary, and these were confirmed by royal charter in 1608. In this reign Whitefriars gradually descended from the dwelling-place of nobles and gentry to an asylum of the hopeless and criminal, and its streets, lanes, and alleys, narrow and crowded with fine structures debased by squalor and neglect, swarmed with a mob of unscrupulous debtors, cunning cheats, desperate gamblers, lewd women, and even murderers. The place became known as " Alsatia," and here the worst of offenders swaggered safe from arrest. The contiguous theatre in Dorset-gardens also attracted to Whitefriars poets, players, and dancing-masters, and in one of its mixed resorts Turner, the fencing-master, who had put out Lord Sanquhar's eye during a fencing lesson some years before, was brutally murdered by two assassins hired by the revengeful nobleman. The two ruffians were hanged opposite Whitefriars gates in Fleet Street, and Lord Sanquhar was hanged in Old Palace Yard.

Bridewell, the palace built by Henry VIII., stands in the parish of St. Bride's, by the river Fleet, where the city wall ends by the water. It is now used as a place of confinement for idle and lawless vagrants. Dissolute and worthless apprentices also made the acquaintance of its unsavoury confines.

Blackfriars, on the city side of the Fleet, and the site of the ancient monastery of Black or Dominican Friars, has its extensive precincts, walled in and with four gates, and possessed the privileges of sanctuary. Many persons of quality had houses in the district, and a theatre existed here till on the complaint of the inhabitants of the objectionable rabble it attracted, it was demolished. A glimpse into the amenities of social life in Blackfriars is furnished by a letter written on June 24th, 1613, by William Gouge, minister of the parish, to Sir Robert Harley, in which he said : " I know not whether you have heard the great ado about Lady Savile's bond. Mr. Emerson has been arrested for it. I should counsel you to use some means to satisfy the lady and Mr. Emerson. It has pleased God to settle our little state in the Blackfriars ; the disturber of the peace, that busybody Neale, will now never trouble us any more in this world. His head is at rest."

The house that William Shakespeare bought of
Henry Walker, in Blackfriars, was described in the
conveyance, dated March 10th, 1613, as " abutting
upon a streete leading down to Puddle Wharfe in
the East part right against the Kinge's Majesties
Wardrobe."

In premises here the " distinguished scholars,"
ordered by King James to translate the Bible, met
to review the whole work, and it was here finally
revised by Dr. Smith and Dr. Bilson, Bishop of
Winchester, prior to being printed in 1611.
Cornelius Jansen, the portrait painter employed by
King James, resided here.

The parish Church of St. Anne's is a large Gothic
structure, and the minister during the reign (he
held the living for forty-six years) was William
Gouge, whose children were baptized at its font—
Ezekiel in 1610, Elizabeth in 1612, Mary in 1615, and
another Elizabeth in 1624. Other baptisms were—
in 1605, Robert, son of Sir Edward Wynter; Anne,
daughter of Sir Thomas Vavasor; Cicely, daughter
of Lord de la Warre; Anne, daughter of Sir Edward
Onslow; and Richard, son of Sir Richard Haughton.
In 1609, Henry, son of Sir Robert D'Arcy, and
Elizabeth, daughter of Sir Henry Hobart, the
Attorney General. In 1610, Edward, son of Sir
Robert D'Arcy and Burrow, son of Sir John Scow.
In 1611, Robert, son of Sir Richard Browne. In
1613, Katharine, daughter of Lord D'Aubigny. In
1614, Francis, son of Sir Edmond Horrell; Anne
Steward, daughter of Lord D'Aubigny; and Charles,
son of Sir Robert D'Arcy. In 1616, Francis, son of
Sir William Smith. In 1622, Peter, son of Dr. Paul
Delaune, and James, son of Sir Nicholas and
Dorothy Smith. In 1623, Henry, son of Lord John

and Lady Elizabeth Morden ; and, in 1624, Henry,
son of Sir William and Anne Andrews. Among the
marriages in the church were—in 1607, Sir Robert
Crane, of Chilton, Suffolk, and Dorothy Hubbard ;
in 1608, Lord Robert Sanker and Mary Farmer ;
in 1614 Sir Edward Hoby of Bisham ; in 1615,
Thomas Shirley and Elizabeth Stevens, and Sir
Allen Apslie and Lucy St. John ; in 1618, Sir
Thomas Savile and Lady Frances Lewson, and on
February 2nd, 1625, Sir Samuel Luke and Elizabeth
Freeman. Among the burials in the church were—
in 1617, Isaac Oliver, the miniature painter ; in
1621, Lady Ann Finch ; and, in 1622, Charles, son
of Lady Susan D'Arcy.

On Sunday, October 26th, 1623, at about three
o'clock in the afternoon, as Father Drury was
preaching to nearly four hundred English and Irish
Catholics, secretly assembled in a room on the third
or top story, over the entrance to the French Ambassador's house, in Blackfriars, the great weight of
the company snapped the main beam of the floor,
which crashed down with the struggling crowd to
the floor below, which was also broken and fell
through into the French Ambassador's drawing-
room. Part of the top floor held, and the frightened
few on it, momentarily expecting to be precipitated
into the yawning gulf, desperately drew their knives
and cut a way through a plaster partition into an
adjoining room. Ninety-four persons were killed
outright, and many injured. The preacher had his
brains scattered, and his bowels crushed out.
Malcolm wrote : " Several people escaped in a very
extraordinary manner, particularly Mrs. Lucy Pen-
ruddock, who was preserved by a chair falling
hollow over her ; and a young man who lay on

the floor overwhelmed by people and rubbish, yet untouched by them, through the resting of fragments on each other, and thus leaving a space round him. In this horrible situation he had the presence of mind to force his way through a piece of the ceiling, and he shortly after had the indescribable happiness of assisting in the liberation of others."

Henry Banister, writing on the 27th, from Hackney, to Lord Zouch, said : " A house, formerly Lord Hunsdon's, in Blackfriars, fell on Sunday last, when a number of Papists were assembled to hear mass. A priest, formerly a Protestant, who preached and eighty other persons were killed."

In another account of these fatal Blackfriars Vespers appears this : " A few chairs were occupied by the superior classes of the congregation before the priest, who had a table near him, and a chair something elevated ; but the remainder stood literally wedged together. Drury made his appearance in a surplice and scarlet stole, and a person who officiated as clerk placed a book and hour-glass on the table. The priest then kneeled and repeated a silent ejaculation, and rising crossed himself. He then read his text from the servant and 10,000 talents. In the progress of this exposition he vehemently insisted on these words, ' I forgive thee all thy debt, shouldest not thou also have had compassion on this fellow, even as I had pity on thee.' About half an hour had elapsed when the dreadful catastrophe occurred, which in one moment precipitated the whole mass of wretched sufferers through a floor beneath them, down to the arch of stone ; where they were ingulfed in a torrent of timber, lath and dust, after a descent

E

of twenty-two feet. . . .   The Recorder of London, Serjeant Finch, ordered with the greatest prudence, that every avenue to the scene of misery should be immediately closed, in order that it might not be increased by the impetuosity of an inquisitive crowd ; and employed persons to extricate the living, which could not be accomplished in any other way than through an upper window, so completely were the lower passages choked."

Among the dead were Dorothy, wife of Mathew Somers, and Mary Clement, her waiting-woman ; and they were both buried, on the 28th, in St. Anne's Church, Blackfriars.

Dudley Carleton wrote to Sir Dudley Carleton that those killed were " buried where they died, the Bishop of London refusing them burial in churchyards."   John Chamberlain stated that " the barbarous multitude rather railed and taunted the sufferers than helped them.   The dead were buried in two pits behind the house and black crosses erected, which were taken down by order of the Council."

Immediately adjoining Blackfriars, the water lapping its base, stands Baynard's Castle, as repaired or rebuilt by Henry VIII., and the memory is almost lost of its massive ancient splendour, when the standard of a powerful steel-clad baron flew from its battlements. Stow recently wrote that " It was not embattled or so strongly fortified castle-like, but far more beautiful and commodious for the entertainment of any prince or great estate." On June 4th, 1606, Thomas Morgan was granted the reversion of " the Mansion House called Baynard's Castle." The Earl of Pembroke occupied it as his town house, and it was here that, early in 1617, he was invested by the Vice-Chancellor of Oxford, accompanied by fifty bishops, doctors, and graduates, with the Chancellorship of the University.

The Church of St. Andrew's, near the Castle, registered on June 19th, 1610, the marriage of Sir Samuel Payton and Mary Austen. Many baptisms took place here, and among these were—Mary in 1615, and Margaret in 1617, daughters of Sir George Goring; in 1618, Rebecca, daughter of Sir George Southcote; in 1619, Robert, son of Sir John Cook, and his daughter Mary in 1621.

Paul's Wharf and other landings and buildings, with St. Peter's and St. Bennet's Churches behind, bring us to Queenhithe, a harbour described by Stow as " the very chief and principal water gate of this city, equal and of old time far exceeding Belinsgate " (Billingsgate). He further stated that customs and dues were exacted from ships and boats laden with " salt, wheat, rye, and other corn from beyond seas ; or other grains, garlic, onions, herrings, sprats, eels, whiting, plaice, cod, mackerel, etc." Corn is the chief trade, from whence the quay is sometimes called Cornhithe. Stow also described a corn-mill here between two barges or lighters, which " ground corn, as water-mills in other places, to the wonder of many that had not seen the like." Among the burials entered in the Register of St. Bennet's Church, were : in 1619, Dr. Burley, parson of the parish, and Richard Stokes, Archdeacon of Norfolk ; in 1620, George Lackstone, a stranger, who was drowned " by misfortune "; in 1623, " A poore man that dyed in the streete "; in 1624, Edward Tomlison, " dyed in the cage," and on January 24th, 1625, John Smith, chaplain to the Earl of Pembroke.

Vintners' Hall stands on the river-side near Queenhithe. All wines coming to London are unloaded at the Vintry, where the King's bottlers and gaugers take custom. King James, in his ninth year, granted the Vintners their acting Charter.

From here, on the river front, stretches a crowd of warehouses and dwellings with wharfs and stairs. The " Three Cranes " Stairs is the principal landing-place for the City, and it is from here that the new Lord Mayor embarks on his water procession to be sworn in at Westminster. The " Three Cranes " Tavern in the rear was much frequented by Ben Jonson and the wits of his time. In his play " The Devil is an Ass," he makes Iniquity say :

" Nay, boy, I will bring thee to the sluts and roysters
   At Billingsgate, feasting with claret-wine and oysters ;
   From thence shoot the bridge, child, to the ' Cranes,' in the Vintry,
   And see there the gimblets how they make their entry."

The old Steelyard is no longer a scene of very active commercial life, as the establishment was closed and the German merchants sent away as recently as 1597. Holbein's two famous pictures in distemper, representing the triumphs of " Riches and Poverty," in the Company's Hall, were presented by the representatives of the Steelyard merchants to Henry, Prince of Wales. Close to the Steelyard in Thames Street is the Church of All Hallows. On January 5th, 1625, Thomas Dawes and Judith, daughter of Alderman Cuthbert Hackett, were married here.

Cold Harbour, the ancient princely residence of merchants and nobles, stands by the waterside : and near by is the Hall of the Watermen's Company.

And then, after passing the Old Swan Stairs—where people coming down the river by boat landed to avoid the swift current between the starlings in shooting the bridge—we come to the Stock Fishmongers' Hall, which was in 1615 reported to be in a dangerous state and ordered to be repaired. After this part of it was inhabited by the widow of a John Ducane, who had leased from the Fishmongers' Company the lower part of a house " with the garret at waterside," and " a right of way to the privy," which stood on a Mr. Ware's wharf. These latter general conveniences were now (and until the Great Fire) a common nuisance along the river-side.

Passing a few other buildings, with balconied terraces and stairs to the water, we arrive at the Water Works and London Bridge.

From the mouth of the Fleet river at Blackfriars to the bridge, the City stretches back a huge picturesque mass, dominated by the superb Gothic Cathedral of St. Paul's. At this period the view of London from the river on a clear night, gave black masses of buildings, with outlines of gables, turrets, towers, and spires against the star-lit sky. Spots of glaring yellow dotted these masses from the windows of lighted rooms, and the flicker of a few lanterns hung out from houses, in the narrow streets. In 1607 Nicolo Molin, the Venetian Ambassador, wrote in a comprehensive Report on England to his government : " The river is the Thames, which besides its beauty is of the highest service for the large number of ships from three to four hundred tons burden, which come in upon the tide from all parts of the world, although the City lies upwards of sixty miles from the sea. Not only is the City flourishing in trade and commerce, but it is especially rich in the privileges enjoyed by its inhabitants, the merchant-burgesses and craftsmen, from among whom about twenty-five are elected, called Aldermen, who govern the City absolutely, almost as though it were an independent Republic, and neither the King nor his ministers can interfere in any way." The occasion of the royal visit to St. Paul's on March 26th, 1620, for the purpose of encouraging a fund for the restoration of the Cathedral, was commemorated by a picture painted on a board by John Gipkyn for Henry Farley, giving not only a view of the procession to the church, but an accurate impression of the then appearance of the quaint old metropolis as seen from the river. It has been thus described :

" The painting is on two leaves of wood, made to shut together like the ancient altar pieces. Each leaf or flap is 4 feet 2 inches to the point of the pediment by 3 feet 4 inches. On the outside of the right-hand leaf is a view of London, Southwark, and the river. Among five churches on the Surrey side, St. Saviour's is the most distinguished, and before it appears the Bishop of Winchester's palace, out of which the procession hereafter mentioned proceeds. Under the gates of this palace are two men in gowns and white sleeves. The trumpeters come out before them, preceded by a number of men in black gowns with white sleeves, who advance after another numerous train over London Bridge, which appears sided by houses, and crossed by a gate with a pointed pediment, surmounted by a cross.

" On the right hand of this is thrown by the perspective the heavy tower of St. Magnus' Church, with its pyramids at the corners. Beyond the bridge, along Watling Street, walk men in black gowns, three and three ; then nine Aldermen, three

and three, in red gowns and chains, preceded by the
Lord Mayor in his gown, and the sword-bearer :
before these go twelve clergymen in black gowns,
following twelve bishops in lawn sleeves, with the
archbishop at the head, holding his cap in his hand,
and preceded by nine noblemen, some in black,
others in red doubtlets, who are preceded by twelve
ladies in black and red gowns, with stiff ruffs, five
pages walking before them in cloaks. These are now
arrived at the West door of St. Paul's Cathedral,
under which is the King in a red doublet, trimmed
with ermine, the crown on his head. On one side
the door stands a page lifting up a scroll in his right
hand, his cap in his left, and opposite to him a little
girl full dressed in a ruff, etc. On the left, just
without the gate, stands a bishop, probably the
Bishop of London, who seems to have given way to
the King. Over the gate is this inscription in
Roman capitals : ' Behold, the King cometh with
great joy.' Twenty churches appear in the city ;
and on the river side we see Baynard's Castle and
the Tower : the latter a square fort, surrounded by
an embattled wall, with round towers in the corners,
a gate to the water, and in the centre of the south
side a large building as the Tower of Babel
is commonly represented, with a lofty cross on it.
In the Borough are five churches besides St. Saviour's :
that in the left corner has a lofty steeple, seemingly
round, surmounted by a small spire. The Thames
is covered with ships, which have a Union flag.
The hills appear beyond London, and some very
high to the right. From the sky proceed these
two lines in capitals :

" ' For thy Temple's sake I will wish thee all prosperity.'
' Many good things are done in thee, O thou fayre citie.'"

Round the black frame of this leaf is written in gold capitals :

" ' And when it came into the Kinge's minde to renew the house of the Lord, he assembled the Priests and Levites, and said unto them, Go into the cities of Judah, and gather of all Israel money to repair the house of God from yeere to yeere, and haste the thinge ; and they made a proclamation throughout Judah and Jerusalem. 2 Chron. xxiv. 4, 5, 9.' "

At various times in 1618, Horatio Busino, Chaplain to the Venetian Ambassador, set down in his diary the following interesting impressions of London and the river :

" The City of London renders itself truly worthy to be styled the metropolis of the Kingdom, and the abode of royalty.   It is handsome and very extensive with a circumference of seven miles.   It is three miles long and very densely populated.   Two-thirds of its extent consist in the suburbs where the nobility and the people also reside, and where all the royal palaces, parks, and gardens are situated.   In the third part are the warehouses of the principal merchants, from whom they select the chief magistrate of the City, called the Lord Mayor, and the officials.   It is situated, as I have perhaps already mentioned, on the banks of the Thames, which flows from west to east, so that the greater part of the City stands along the banks of the stream, and has a southern aspect.   There are also some good dwellings on the opposite shore, but less numerous. They are connected by a very noble stone bridge of nineteen very lofty arches, on each side of which are convenient houses and shops, so that it has rather the air of a long suburb than a handsome structure such as a bridge.   The parishes are large, each

having its church and belfry intact, but bare
of altars, save one in the choir. Two boards
with the ten commandments are inserted instead
of an altar piece. The Cathedral is St. Paul's,
which towers loftily above the others. The
streets are commodious and wide, with their
shops furnished in every direction. There are
very handsome stone fountains, especially in
the heart of the City. . . . I know not what
to commend in their buildings as for the most
part they employ timber, driving posts in very
deeply like a rough scantling, which they coat
with mortar mixed with the hair of animals ; instead
of which the poor use very finely chopped straw.
The staircases are almost all spiral, and the distribu-
tions of the rooms sorry and irregular. The windows
project, their glass being in large panes, though
they have only certain wickets not large enough
to admit even the head, so a Genoese gentleman
exclaimed smartly the other day : ' O luckless
windows, it is impossible to open you by day or to
shut you at night, as you have no shutters.' The
timber used by them for building is for the most
part oak, but they have a great quantity of elms
which they plant along the public roads and walks,
and even by the side of the field ditches and cause-
ways. . . . On last Bartholomew's day the fair
was held in London. There was nothing very
surprising, except a quantity of woollen cloths,
hides, etc., but we saw an infinite number of cattle,
which filled the meadows near London, and were
all disposed of in one day or a little more. . . . The
natives are all fond of dwelling in this City, or at
least very near it, so they would fain be constantly
building new houses, abandoning both the country

and husbandry, were it not by law prohibited to multiply them. Around the liberties of London there is such a patchwork of suburbs that they look like so many monsters who have been converted after being lured by the Goddess Circe, the greater part being inhabited by an inept population of the lowest description. The villages in like manner teem around London, being situated in the midst of meadows and woods, and here and there one sees trim pleasure residences belonging to the citizens and merchants and to the gentry, with such delights as flower and fruit gardens and orchards. . . . The neighbouring suburbs and villages are dependent upon other magistrates than the Lord Mayor, who has enough to do in governing the inhabitants of the City and adjoining liberty. A few days ago, when his Majesty knighted the late Mayor (George Bowles), as usual, he praised him greatly for his good government, giving him some hints, however, two of which were really amusing. He said : ' You will moreover see to two things, that is to say to the great devils and the little devils ; by the great ones I mean the carts which in passing along the streets, whether narrow or wide, do not choose to yield or give way as due to the coaches of the gentry, when they meet them. The imps are the apprentices, that is to say shop boys, who on two days of the year, which are fatal for them, namely Shrove Tuesday and the 1st of May, display such unbridled will and are so licentious, that in a body three or four thousand strong they go committing outrages in every direction, but particularly in the suburbs outside the city, killing people and demolishing houses, especially those of correction, which are a sort of prison, beginning the work of destruction with the roof. They also commit many other iniquities which the city train-bands are unable to prevent, for like a sudden flash of lightning they change from place to place, and never cease giving annoyance until the day of their furious misrule and impetus comes to a close.

" 'To return to the carts of London, there is such a multitude of them, large and small, that is to say, on two wheels and on four, that it would be impossible to estimate them correctly. Those which circulate in the city are for the most part on two broad and high wheels like those of Rome, and serve for the conveyance of sundry articles such as beer, coal, wood, etc. ; but among them are some very filthy ones, employed solely for cleansing the streets and carrying manure, and it is precisely the drivers of these who are usually the most insolent fellows in the world. The other four-wheeled waggons come up from the country bringing goods and passengers higgledy-piggledy, precisely like Marghera boats, and they are drawn by seven or eight horses in file, one behind the other, with plumes and bells, embroidered cloth coverings, and their stamping in the centre of the deep rut renders travelling on narrow roads in the country so inconvenient that it is impossible to get on with a coach and four. So we, who lately took a distant journey, broke the carriage and harassed the mares cruelly, although they were very fresh and spirited. . . .'

" I also deem it a marvel to see such quantities of butchers' shops in all parishes, the streets being full of them in every direction. The very fat meat is exhibited at the gratings from the top of the windows to the bottom, precisely in the same way as the unique Bartholomew dal Calese used to do at

Ascensiontide in Venice, framing, as it were, his rich gold stuffs. There are endless inns and eating-houses, for board alone or for board and lodging, beer and wine shops, wholesale and retail—for every imaginable growth, alicant, canary, muscatels, clarets, Spanish, Rhenish, and from hundreds and thousands of other vineyards, all excellent, though one must drink them, forsooth, out of a silver cup, as they are very dear. Thus they hold their very hiccoughs in account, nor is it considered impolite to discharge them in your neighbour's face, provided they be redolent of wine, or of choice tobacco.

" Let us go back to the river for some water to wash or remove this stench from our minds. They are very badly off for water, although they have an immense supply. They raise it artificially from the stream, even by windmills, and force it into all the fountations throughout the suburbs, but it is so hard, turbid, and stinking that the odour remains even in clean linen. In the heart of the city, however, they have fountains supplied by conduits, where the water is clear and tolerably good. Thither flock great crowds of women and porters, who for hire carry it to such houses as desired in long wooden vessels hooped with iron. . . . One sees pastry-cooks without end, and innumerable poulterers, especially of those who sell rabbits also, of which every shop has hundreds, and there are customers for all. Then there are the bird-fanciers' shops, where they train and sell falcons, hawks, and other birds of prey. One day in his Majesty's ante-room, the Master of the Ceremonies told his Excellency that he himself saw a fine feat performed by a falcon, who seized a large fish in the air. He was flying

at a heron, who, in the strife, by instinct, threw the
fish which he had in his claw, into the falcon's face,
and thus escaped the enemy's talons. . . . There
is one particular quarter full of apothecaries' shops
on either side of the way, besides others scattered
here and there about the City ; another is entirely
inhabited by booksellers, who, however, do not
possess a single missal. Then there are the other
streets of feather-sellers, while certain mechanics
make horn flowers and rosettes, as delicately wrought
as if they were of the finest cambric. They paint
them various colours. There is a suburb of gun-
smiths ; others only make bows and arrows. Some
manufacture very handsome proof-corslets, for the
wear of the pikemen. There are several falconers'
shops, whose proprietors do nothing at all but
train birds of every sort for such as are fond of
sport."

Some of the common cries heard from the river-
side in the streets of London are thus embodied in
ballads in vogue about 1622 :

" My masters all, attend you,
    If mirth you love to hear,
And I will tell you what they cry
    In London all the year.
I'll please you if I can ;
    I will not be too long :
I pray you all attend a while
    And listen to my song.

" The fish-wife first begins :
    Any mussels lily white !
Herrings, sprats, or plaice,
    Or cockles for delight.
Any welflet oysters !
    Then she doth change her note :
She had need to have her tongue be greas'd
    For she rattles in her throat.

" Mark but the waterman
    Attending for his fare,
Of hot and cold, of wet and dry,
    He always takes his share :
He carrieth bonnie lasses
    Over to the plays,
And here and there he gets a bit
    And that his stomach stays.

" Ripe, cherry ripe !
    The costermonger cries ;
Pippins fine or pears !
    Another after hies,
With basket on his head
    His living to advance,
And in his purse a pair of dice
    For to play at mumchance.

" Hot pippin pies !
    To sell unto my friends,
Or pudding pies in pans,
    Well stuft with candle ends.
Will you buy any milk ?
    I heard a wench that cries :
With a pail of fresh cheese and cream,
    Another after hies.

" Oh, the wench went neatly ;
    Methought it did me good,
To see her cheery cheeks
    So dimpled o'er with blood ;
Her waistcoat washed white
    As any lily flower ;
Would I had time to talk with her
    The space of half an hour."

Sir Walter Scott, in his historical romance, " The Fortunes of Nigel," sketched some vivid glimpses of the London of James I., and among these the following are closely connected with the scope of this work :

In describing the shops within Temple Bar eastward of St. Dunstan's Church, he wrote : " The shop of a London tradesman at that time, as it may be supposed, was something very different from those we now see in the same locality. The goods were exposed to sale in cases, only defended from the weather by a covering of canvas and the whole resembled the stalls and booths now erected for the temporary accommodation of dealers at a country fair, rather than the established emporium of a respectable citizen."

" Stout-bodied and strong-voiced apprentices kept up the cry to the passers-by of ' What d'ye lack ? What d'ye lack ? ' accompanied with the appropriate recommendations of the articles in which they dealt.

" This direct and personal mode of invitation to customers became, however, a dangerous temptation to the young wags who were employed in the task of solicitation during the absence of the principal person interested in the traffic ; and confiding in their numbers and civic union, the 'prentices of London were often seduced into taking liberties with the passengers and exercising their wit at the expense of those whom they had no hopes of converting into customers by their eloquence.

" If this were resented by any act of violence, the inmates of each shop were ready to pour forth in succour ; and in the words of an old song which Dr. Johnson was used to hum :

> " Up then rose the 'prentices all,
> Living in London, both proper and tall."

" Desperate riots often arose on such occasions, especially when the Templars, or other youths connected with the aristocracy, were insulted, or conceived themselves to be so. Upon such occasions

bare steel was frequently opposed to the clubs of
the citizens, and death sometimes ensued on both
sides. The tardy and inefficient police of the time
had no other resource than by the Alderman of the
Ward calling out the householders, and putting a
stop to the strife by overpowering numbers, as the
Capulets and Montagues are separated upon the
stage."

The house of John Christie, the ship-chandler,
at which the hero, Nigel, lodged, " was situated near
to Paul's Wharf, at the end of one of those intricate
and narrow lanes, which, until that part of the
city was swept away by the Great Fire in 1666,
constituted an extraordinary labyrinth of small,
dark, damp, and unwholesome streets and alleys,
in one corner or other of which the plague was then
as surely found lurking, as in the obscure corners
of Constantinople in our own time. But John
Christie's house looked out upon the river and had
the advantage, therefore, of free air impregnated,
however, with the odoriferous fumes of the articles
in which the ship-chandler dealt, with the odour
of pitch, and the natural scent of the ooze and sludge
left by the reflux of the tide."

Dame Nelly, the wife of Christie, once remarked
of the King : " And this good gentleman goes as
often down by water to Greenwich, and employs
as many of the barge-men and water-men of all
kinds ; and maintains in his royal grace, John
Taylor, the water-poet, who keeps both a sculler
and a pair of oars. And he has made a comely court
at Whitehall, just by the river."

George Heriot, the goldsmith, was frequently
summoned to Court by the King on financial
matters, and in journeying from the City " it

may be worth while to remind our readers that the Temple Bar which Heriot passed was not the arched screen, or gateway of the present day ; but an open railing, or palisade, which, at night, and in times of alarm, was closed with a barricade of posts and chains. The Strand also, along which he rode, was not as now, a continued street, although it was beginning already to assume that character. It still might be considered as an open road, along the south side of which stood various houses and hotels belonging to the nobility, having gardens behind them down to the waterside, with stairs to the river, for the convenience of taking boat ; which mansions have bequeathed the names of their lordly owners to many of the streets leading from the Strand to the Thames. The north side of the Strand was also a long line of houses, behind which, as in St. Martin's Lane, and other points, buildings were rapidly arising ; but Covent Garden was still a garden, in the literal sense of the word, or at least but beginning to be studded with irregular buildings. All that was passing around, however, marked the rapid increase of a capital which had long enjoyed peace, wealth, and a regular government. Houses were rising in every direction ; and the shrewd eye of our citizen already saw the period not distant, which should convert the nearly open highway on which he travelled into a connected and regular street, uniting the Court and the town with the City of London.

" He next passed Charing Cross, which was no longer the pleasant solitary village at which the judges were wont to breakfast on their way to Westminster Hall, but began to resemble the artery through which, to use Johnson's expression,

F

' pour the full tide of London population.' The
buildings were rapidly increasing, yet certainly
gave not even a faint idea of its present appearance.
At last Whitehall received our traveller, who
passed under one of the beautiful gates designed by
Holbein, and composed of tesselated brickwork,
being the same to which Moniplies (Nigel's retainer)
had profanely likened the West Port of Edinburgh,
and entered the ample precincts of the palace of
Whitehall, now full of all the confusion attending
improvement.

" It was just at the time when James—little
suspecting that he was employed in constructing
a palace, from the window of which his only son was
to pass in order that he might die upon a scaffold
before it—was busied in removing the ancient
and ruinous buildings of De Burgh, Henry VIII.,
and Queen Elizabeth, to make way for the superb
architecture on which Inigo Jones exerted all his
genius. The King, ignorant of futurity, was now
engaged in pressing on his work ; and, for that
purpose still maintained his royal apartments at
Whitehall, amidst the rubbish of old buildings, and
the various confusion attending the erection of the
new pile, which formed at present a labyrinth not
easily traversed."

On one occasion Nigel was taken to Court by the
Goldsmith.

" At the appointed hour, the barge of Master
George Heriot arrived, handsomely manned and
appointed having a tilt with his own cipher, and the
arms of his company painted thereon. . . . On
they glided, by the assistance of the oars of four
stout watermen, along the Thames, which then
served for the principal high-road betwixt London

and Westminster ; for few ventured on horseback through the narrow and crowded streets of the City, and coaches were then a luxury reserved only for the higher nobility, and to which no citizen, whatever was his wealth, presumed to aspire. The beauty of the banks, especially on the northern side, where the gardens of the nobility descended from their hotels, in many places, down to the water's edge, was pointed out to Nigel by his kind conductor. . . . They landed at Whitehall Stairs and entered the Palace after announcing their names—the guards paying to Lord Glenvarloch the respect and honours due to his rank."

The hero's return from a night adventure was concluded with : " The generation of linkboys, celebrated by Count Anthony Hamilton, as peculiar to London, had already, in the reign of James I., begun their functions, and the service of one of them, with his smoky torch had been secured to light the young Scottish lord and his follower to their lodgings."

Of London Bridge, Nicolo Molin, the Venetian Ambassador, wrote in his Report beforementioned : " There is London Bridge of nineteen arches spanning the river. The bridge is covered with shops, which make it very narrow and spoil its beauty, and if two carriages meet there they can hardly pass one another." The appearance of the bridge in 1624, is very accurately portrayed in a view published this year by John Norden, Surveyor to the Prince of Wales. Quaint old buildings, with the Chapel of St. Thomas and Nonsuch House, fill the structure, while the gate from the Borough is surmounted with the heads of traitors. Above the houses at the north end is seen the " Water-Work." From the

windows of some of the buildings buckets are being
let down by long ropes into the water, which is
rushing through the old Gothic arches with extreme
impetuosity, although no fall is shewn.   To the right
is seen an overturned boat, with oars afloat, and a
drowning man.   Another boat is saving two persons
from the water.   Two or three vessels and other
craft are in other parts of the picture.   On
November 28th, 1624, the King commanded Sir
Thomas Bennet and other Commissioners for the
Estates of London Bridge, " to renew the lease of a
tenement on reasonable conditions to Thos. Taylor."
In a summary of Accounts of the Bridge, under
this same year, appeared the following : " To
John Langley and Richard Foxe, Bridgemasters,
half a year's fee at our Lady-day £50 ; and for the
other half year augmented by order of the Court
of Aldermen £66 8s. 4d. ; and for their Liveries
etc., £6.   Total, £122 8s. 4d.   Rental, £2,054
4s. 2d."

Passing over the bridge we enter, through a
massive stone arched gateway, with rotting heads
above, into the borough of Southwark, and
close at hand on the right is the stately Church of
St. Mary Overy (St. Saviour's).   In 1624 the Chapel
of the Virgin Mary in the church " was restored
to the Parishioners, being let out to Bakers for
above sixty years before, and £200 laid out in
repairs."   Among the burials in the church were—
in 1605, Elizabeth, wife of Sir Edward Parham,
and Francis, son of Lord Decies ; in 1607, Edmond
Shakespeare, player ; in 1609, Richard Johnson,
Coroner of the King's Household and of the Verge ;
in 1614, Sir George Browne ; in 1616, Richard
Humble, Alderman of London—a stately monument

was erected in the church to the Alderman, by
Peter Humble, and on the north side of it were these
lines :

> " Like to the Damask Rose you see,
> Or like the blossom on the Tree,
> Or like the dainty Flower in May,
> Or like the Morning of the Day,
> Or like the Sun, or like the Shade,
> Or like the Gourd which Jonas made,
> Even so is Man, whose Thread is spun,
> Drawn out, and cut, and so is done :
> The Rose withers, the Blossom blasteth,
> The Flower fades, the Morning hasteth,
> The Sun sets, the Shadow flies,
> The Gourd consumes, and Man he dies."

and in 1622, Dr. Thomas Sutton, who the previous
year had delivered a sermon in the church before
the Judges. The bequests to the parish were—in
1617, Richard Humble and his son Peter, a rent-
charge on messuages near Crown Court for the poor
and for cleaning the former's tomb ; and Stephen
Scudamor, £1 per annum for the poor ; in 1618,
Elizabeth Paget, the annuity of £50 for paying
3d. a week each to four poor women, and a Mr.
Lenthall, £2 to the poor ; in 1620, Thomas Emerson,
£50 for the poor, and the charge on a garden plot
in Maid Lane for paying 1s. per week each to two
poor men ; in 1621, Mr. Drinkwater, £2 to the poor ;
in 1622, Edward Hewlett, the rent-charge of £20
per annum on a messuage called " The Swan with
the two Necks," and another adjoining for the poor
in general ; and in 1624, John Bingham, £50 and £1
per annum for the poor. On April 10th, 1618,
Mr. Francke was elected—out of seven competitors
—first Master of the School of St. Mary Overy's,
under the new Statutes framed in 1614.   On January

23rd, 1624, Davidge, the usher in the School, told the Governors he had been beneficed in Somersetshire, " and soe with weepeing teares took his leave, and had the Governor's good words, and so parted."

Among the burials registered in 1618, at St. Olave's Church, below the bridge, were Thomas Frith, a prisoner in the King's Bench, who shot himself, and Roger Damby, who hanged himself in the same prison. On June 18th, 1623, the Governors of St. Olave's School decided " to take counsell about their difference " with Nathaniel Bugg, the then master. Bugg, dissatisfied with his pay, asked that " he might with their loves and leave depart and rezine." The Governors promised a " gratuitie towards his better preferment," but he apparently left, as at the end of July Richard Vaughan was elected Master. In February, 1606, George Swain left two rent-charges in St. Olave's for the general relief of the poor ; and Henry Browker left £10 obtained from a messuage in Red Lion Street, one moiety to the Grammar School, the other to the general poor of the borough.

St. George's Church is more remote from the bridge. The register recorded on June 28th, 1610, the burial of Michael Banks " who was executed out of the King's Bench, and did revive again, and was in the old Vestry three hours at the least, and then was carried back and was executed again." On May 2nd, 1622, William Cooper gave a messuage in Priest's Alley, Tower Street, for the benefit of eight poor men and women at the discretion of the parson and Vestrymen of St. George's.

In 1607 John Palin left generally for the poor of Southwark, the annuity from £20 : John Taylor also willed to the poor, tenements in the Ship Inn, and David Newman left £10 for an annuity to buy coals for the poor of the borough ; and in 1616 Edward Alleyn built alms-houses in Soap Yard, Deadman's Place, for ten men and women, with an allowance of 6d. a week each.

Adjoining St. Mary Overy's Church are the fine old Gothic monastic buildings on the Bankside, now used as the palace of the Bishops of Winchester, and attached are gardens, fountains, fish-ponds and an extensive park. Stow mentioned the place as " a very fair house, well repaired, with a large wharf and landing-place, called the Bishop of Winchester's Stairs." John Chamberlain wrote to Sir Dudley Carleton, on November 8th, 1617 : " The Bishop of Winchester hath bestowed great cost in repairing and beautifying his house at St. Mary Overies, and on Monday to warm it, he made a great feast to all the lords and others of quality that went the Scottish journey."

From Winchester House westwards along the Bankside, stretch a varied assortment of buildings— houses, taverns, the bull and bear baiting pits in Paris Garden, the Globe, the Swan, the Rose Theatres and a mass of low dwellings in which are herded a festering swarm of the dregs of the populace.

On January 31st, 1619, an Order in Council ran : " Upon consideration of a difference between the City of London and the Borough of Southwark on the one part, and the inhabitants of the Liberty of Paris Garden, the Clink, and the Bankside on the other part, concerning a way leading through some part of St. George's Field into some part of the Liberty and Manor of Paris Garden, and so to the Thames side, directing, for preservation of the peace, that both parties should join in a course for speedy trial of the right to the way by law, and that in the meantime there should be no alteration of possession on either side." On the following March 16th, Sir Sebastian Harvey, the Lord Mayor, and the Aldermen of London recommended to the Privy Council, a petition of the inhabitants of Southwark against a road leading from their district to two new Inns on the Bankside : " The road, proving a ready escape for malefactors out of the City, and injurious to the borough, was closed but reopened on their Lordship's order, given on a petition from the two innkeepers in question, and a few other."

Below the bridge, past Bermondsey and Rother-hithe to Deptford, the carpenters, boatbuilders, and ropemakers are busy among great stacks of timber and other stores, and the framework of many crafts in all stages of construction. On the other side, below St. Magnus' Church are store and ware-houses, the Elizabethan Custom House, numerous ships of all sizes and nations and a forest of masts. A swarm of busy men crowd the Quays and Wharfs of the Custom House, Billingsgate, and the Tower, over which looms the grim and frowning mass of the great fortress prison and palace, with a wide cluster of citizens' houses on Tower Hill in the rear.

The very ancient harbour of Billingsgate is at this period as Stow described it : " a large water gate, port or harborough for ships and boats, commonly arriving there with fish, both fresh and salt, shell fishes, salt, oranges, onions, and other fruits and roots, wheat, rye, and grain of divers sorts, for the service of the City." On Easter Monday in April, 1617, the Archbishop of Canterbury, the Lord Keeper, the Lord Chamberlain, the Earl of Worcester, Lord Carew, the Bishop of London and other persons of distinction, accompanied the Lord Mayor, Sir John Leman, to hear the Spital sermon, and then proceeded with him on horseback to his house near Billingsgate, and were, with their attendants, most sumptuously regaled.

The Tower of London is used as a state prison, although certain apartments overlooking the river are occasionally used on special occasions as a lodging for the King and Court. In 1607, Nicolo Molin, the Venetian Ambassador, wrote in a comprehensive Report on England to his Government : " Then there is the Tower, a right noble pile for age, but not for strength, as it has neither bulwarks nor bastions nor other fortifications. The royal treasure, which I shall presently describe, is kept there ; there is also an arsenal of arms ; but its chief use is as a ward for prisoners of state." On July 10th, 1618, a Commission was issued at Westminster, to the Earl of Suffolk, High Treasurer ; the Earl of Worcester, Lord Keeper ; the Earl of Nottingham, Lord High Admiral ; and four others ; for making an inventory of the jewels in the Jewel-house at the Tower. In the course of 1621 a Report was made by Sir Robert Johnson and other officers of the Ordnance, " on a petition by the assignees of Sir Roger Aston, that they are wronged by the appropriation to the private use of the officers of the Tower of part of the Wharf granted to him— denying that it is used by the ordnance officers. State the present ruinous state of the Tower Wharf, by injuries from ships and land carriages, so that the pieces of ordnance are half buried in mud and rendered unserviceable, and suggest remedies there-fore." On June 12th, 1623, a warrant was issued for the delivery at Tower Wharf of 1,000 tons of

Portland stone, for the use of the Duke of Richmond in the erection of Richmond House in Holborn.

Many persons of quality lived in the houses on Tower Hill. In 1609, John, last Baron Lumley, died at his residence there. During this reign Lumley, who had conveyed Nonsuch palace and park to Queen Elizabeth, was appointed their keeper. Camden wrote that he was a person of entire virtue, integrity, and innocence, and in his old age a perfect pattern of true nobility. On August 16th, 1624, Sir Robert Shirley communicated with the Privy Council concerning Persian affairs, from his house on Tower Hill.

The Hospital of St. Katherine near the Tower is one of the few houses of charity existing from monastic times. Originally founded by Matilda, Queen of Stephen, it was, after a series of lawsuits, re-established about 1273 by Eleanor, Consort of Henry III., "for a master, three brethren, and three sisters, ten bedeswomen, and six poor scholars." On April 29th, 1604, Thomas Sanderson, of Lincoln's Inn, was appointed Steward of the Hospital. The next Steward, in 1608, was Thomas Cæsar, the brother of Sir Julius Cæsar, Master of the Hospital. In 1611 Francis Williamson, of Lincoln's Inn, was Steward, and in 1618 Michael Brooke. Richard Verstegan, the antiquary, who published in 1605, his "Restitution of decayed Intelligence concerning the Antiquities of the noble and renowned English Nation," was born of Dutch parents in the precincts of St. Katherine's. On January 20th, 1623, the officers and inhabitants of the precincts certified to Sir Robert Heath of the good conduct and character of Bartholomew Van Crombrougghe, free denizen and tallow-chandler, who had been resident in the parish for thirty years.

On the other side of the river, adjoining Southwark, is Bermondsey, insulated with water-courses, where tanners and leather dressers are beginning to settle. Groups of dwellings cluster around the parish Church of St. Mary Magdalene, and the empty Priory of St. Saviour's, now falling into ruin. In May, 1603, Sir Richard Thekeston was made King's Bailiff and Collector of the Lands of the late Monastery. A panic occurred in the church in March, 1619; and in 1625, James Herriott, one of the forty children of a Scotchman, was married there to Elizabeth Josey. The benefactors of the parish were: Stephen Skidmore, who bequeathed money, in 1606, to buy firing for the poor; Robert Pratt, who left money, in 1607, for the poor; Francis Tirrell, who in 1609, left six chaldrons of coal yearly, for ever, to the poor; and Richard Archden, who in 1614, left money to buy bread for the poor.

Rotherhithe, called Redriffe, between Bermondsey and Deptford, is a marshy village, where a haven has existed since Saxon times, and is now the abode of watermen and sea-faring men.

Gataker, the erudite Latin critic, was, in 1611, rector of the Church of St. Mary. In 1612, Peter Hills gave by deed the Free School and £3 a year to the Master, to teach eight children, sons of sailors, in the parish.

Crossing the river again to the Middlesex shore, a little below the Tower is Wapping, a distinct village till 1609, when owing to the increase of resident mariners, it was connected to Tower Hill. The church, dedicated to St. John the Evangelist, and built by the subscription of the inhabitants,

was consecrated on July 16th, 1617. Only as
recently as 1571, the village was secured by walls
from the encroachments of the river, and the district
is still remembered as a great Wash, called,
" Wapping in the Wose or Wash." It is a growing
and busy place, noted for nautical sign-makers,
ship and boat builders, rope-makers, biscuit-bakers,
and provision dealers ; mast, oar, and block makers,
ship-chandlers and sail-makers. Here, at low-water
mark, is the execution place of pirates, where they
remain, hanging in chains, till three tides have
overflowed them. In March, 1617, one of the
gibbets received Sir George Sandys, who was hanged
for taking purses on the highway, whilst his wife
and son were in prison as accomplices. The Knight
had been formerly pardoned for like offences.

Ratcliffe is a mariners' hamlet adjoining, and
Stow said the highway running through it " with
fair elm-trees on both sides," had in his time been
built along almost to Limehouse, a mile distant.
About November, 1623, Richard Moore requested
the influence of Secretary Conway with the Lord
Keeper and others " for remission of his fine for
building six tenements in Ratcliffe Highway, they
being taken from him and given to the poor."

On January 3rd, 1624, John Chamberlain wrote
in a letter to Sir Dudley Carleton : " Two nights
ago a small vessel that came from Dunkirk and lay
at Ratcliffe, was surprised by sixteen conscionable
sailors, or thieves, that took away only a case of
taffetas, a bale of black Naples silk, and a pack of
linen cloth, of a great quantity of such like goods
that were in her ; and when some would have had
more the major part urged it was enough ; and so
went their way, and are not yet heard of."

Shadwell is a small hamlet of Stepney, with rope-walks and makers of ships' outfits. In 1615 two Roman coffins of stone and lead, containing bones, lachrymatories, and two ivory sceptres, were found here, in Sun Tavern Fields.

A short distance on brings us to the populous village of Stepney and the adjoining hamlet of Limehouse. Some years before, Sir Thomas More in a letter to Dean Colet, had remarked on the pleasant situation of Stepney, and the beauty of its scenery ; and at this time the village and Limehouse were not only favourite places of residence for persons of distinction, such as Sir Thomas Lake, Secretary of State, but were used as health resorts by the nobility and gentry. Evidence of this is furnished in a letter of condolence written at Salisbury, on July 3rd, 1605, by E. Reynoldes, to his sick friend, Thomas Rawlins, High Sheriff of Essex, recommending the pure air of Limehouse. In the following November Sir Edward Hoby of Bisham Abbey, wrote that his wife " lieth so far off at Stepney, as this winter weather it is a great toil to go to her."

In January, 1605, " Hickman's landes " at Stepney, lately belonging to the Hospital without Bishopsgate, were valued on their passing in fee-farm to the Earl of Sussex. There is a Church of All Saints, but the large Church of St. Dunstan is a favourite one for marriages, and the contracting parties come not only from Stepney, but Limehouse, Ratcliffe, Shadwell, Poplar, Wapping, and other parishes, and many of the bridegrooms are water-men, mariners, shipwrights, and other waterside craftsmen. Among the marriages registered were : in 1609, Sir Roger Nevinson, of Kent, and Mary, daughter of Sir Thomas Bludder, of Mile End ; in 1610, Sir Roger Millicente of Linton, Cambridge, and Amphillis, daughter of George Grymes, of Folkham, Norfolk ; and Thomas, eldest son of the same George Grymes, and Bridget, daughter of Sir Edward Butler, of Birch-hanger, Essex ; in 1611, Montague Watts, of Lambeth, and Dorothy, daughter of Sir George Paule, biographer of the late Archbishop Whitgift ; in 1617, Sir John Doddridge, of Mile End, one of the Justices of the King's Bench, and Anna Newman of St. Matthew's, Friday Street ; and Sir Francis Leigh, of Newnham Regis, Warwick, and Susanna Banning, a widow ; in 1618, Walter Rolfe and Frances, daughter of Sir Wolstan Dixey, of Blisworth, Leicester ; and in 1623, Francis Theobald, of Gray's Inn, and Judith, daughter of Sir Henry Conquest ; and Sir Percival Hart, of Lullingstone, Kent, and Mary Harrison, a widow. Among the baptisms were—in 1606, George, son of Sir Hugh Woorall ; in 1607, Martha, daughter of Sir Thomas Bludder ; in 1609, on St. Stephen's day, Afra, daughter of Sir Roger Nevinson, of Mile End ; in 1611, Margaret, daughter of Sir Thomas Bludder ; and Elizabeth, daughter of Sir Roger Nevinson ; in 1615, Charles, son of Sir James Murrall, of Poplar ; and in 1620, Rachel, eldest of triplets, daughter of John Todd, a mariner, and Elizabeth, his wife, of Limehouse. Among the burials were : in 1608, Richard Lacy, a " stubborn " Brownist tailor ; in 1609, Elizabeth, daughter of Sir Jervis Elloway ; Henry, infant son of Sir Henry Hobart, the Attorney-General, and Hugh Goffe, late servant of the Archduke's Ambassador, who was " by his own men slain before his door at Stepney " ; in 1612, John, son of Sir Alexander

Barlow; and on April 2nd, 1618, Edward Parker, Lord Morley.

In a bold curve of the river, between Limehouse and Blackwall, is the Isle of Dogs, on which is the ruin of St. Mary's Chapel, stated to have been a hermitage, where in former times masses were said for the souls of mariners. The island is now a rich feeding ground for oxen.

Deptford, a busy town on the Kentish shore, is called Deptford Stronde, from a deep ford on the river Ravensbourne, the mouth of which forms a small estuary (Deptford Creek). The place is surrounded by marshes, where large herds of cattle feed when the floods are not out. The town is full of shipwrights and other trades and businesses connected with the construction, outfitting, and victualling of ships ; and is a favourite residence for old retired naval captains and officers. Besides the King's dockyards and storehouses, the East India Company has docks and extensive premises here. The church is dedicated to St. Nicholas, and in 1621 John Brent left £20 towards erecting a new pulpit. Among the baptisms here were : in 1615, Richard, son of Sir James Sandalan ; in 1616, Benjamin (afterwards an eminent physician and author of a treatise on gout), son of John Wells, Paymaster of the King's Navy ; and the children of Sir William Russell, Treasurer of the Navy— Anne in 1619, Gerrard in 1620, Edward in 1621, and Robert in 1622. Among the marriages were : in 1613, William Bright, one of the master shipwrights of Deptford, and Mary Backster ; in 1617, Sir Thomas Shirley, and Judith Taylor, a widow ; in 1622, Andrew Burrell, one of the master shipwrights at Deptford, and Alice, daughter of Captain

Pring, of Bristol. Among those buried in the church was Henry Boyle, son of the Earl of Cork, who died in 1615 at a Deptford School.

On May 4th, 1617, the Queen was entertained at Deptford, by the girls of " Ladies Hall," then one of the principal boarding schools of the period. A masque was performed, called " Cupid's Banishment," in allusion to the King's absence in Scotland ; and the part of Diana was taken by the twelve years old Master Richard Browne, of Sayes Court. In January, 1619, the Rev. Thomas Lorkin, in a letter from London to Sir Thomas Puckering, said : " We have been lately not a little frighted by another fire at Deptford, threatening not a private, but a public calamity ; for it fixed upon, in a furious manner, a certain house of Sir Thomas Smith, adjoining upon the store-house of shipping for the King. But the wind blew a contrary way ; and although that were in a short time burnt down to the earth, yet this remained untouched."

On December 10th, 1623, the Court of the East India Company considered a letter from the Countess of Kildare, wishing to borrow their house at Deptford, for the purpose of entertaining her poor neighbours there at Christmastide. The Court, recalling some favours received from the Countess, decided to lend her the house until Candlemas, but directed that an inventory should be taken of the goods left on the premises. The benefactions bequeathed were : in 1606, Mr. Ady, master shipwright in the King's Yard—who was buried in St. Nicholas' Churchyard—willed to the poor of the parish a piece of land called the " Gravel-pit " ; and, in 1610, Philip Ellis, Clerk of the Prick and Cheque at Deptford Dockyard, left 20s. per annum for four years after his decease to the poor. It was said that he had been a great reliever of the destitute all his life.

Sayes Court at Deptford had been held for many years by the family of Sir Richard Browne, who died there in May, 1604. In a Rental Survey, dated July 27th, 1608, the lands and tenements belonging to the Manor of Sayes Court, now held by Christopher Browne, the mansion was described as containing eighteen rooms, " and is two storeys high and nine bays ; gardens and orchards 2½ acres, with stabling, etc." On January 17th, 1610, a grant was made by letters-patent, " in consideration of services done by Christopher Browne, as well as of the charges he had been at in repairing the mansion-house at Sayes Court, and its appurtenances," of the mansion-house " lying in Bromefield, Deptford, with the orchards, gardens, and two closes of four acres, now in his possession, and also sufficient hay and pasture for the keeping, feeding, and pasturing twelve kine, one bull, and two horses, in winter and summer, upon the grounds of Sayes Court, for the term of forty years, without any rent." On the following June 11th, Christopher Browne, who was Marshal of the Hall, was granted, under certain conditions, the custody of the King's pastures at Sayes Court, and of a mansion-house there.

Some distance lower down is Greenwich, a town pleasantly placed at the base, and on the declivity of a range of heights forming the southern boundary of the vale of the Thames. A royal residence and park have existed here since the time of Edward I. The church is dedicated to St. Alphage, and among the baptisms registered there were : in 1619, Francis, son of Samuel North—this child was born without arms, his hands growing out of his shoulders; in 1622, Robert, son of Sir Robert Varne; and in 1624, Humphrey, son of Sir Humphrey Paiton and Elizabeth, daughter of Sir Leonard Boswell. On July 16th, 1623, Sir Henry Harley and Brilliana, daughter of Edward, Viscount Conway, were married in the church. In 1618, Sir James Sandalen, and John Rowell, the Queen's coachman, were buried at Greenwich. Trinity Hospital, or Norfolk College, was established here in 1613, by Henry Howard, Earl of Northampton.

John Chamberlain wrote to Sir Dudley Carleton, on January 4th, 1616: "Yesterday there fell a great mischance to the Earl of Arundel, by the burning of his house, built and left him by the Earl of Northampton, at Greenwich, where he likewise lost a great deal of household stuff and rich furniture, the fury of the fire being such, that nothing could be saved. No doubt the papists will ascribe and publish it as a punishment for his dissembling and falling from them."

On November 20th, 1618, a note was made by Sir Lionel Cranfield that the King had promised not to licence more than four retailers of wines in the town. Dr. James Montague, Bishop of Winchester, died at Greenwich in 1618. This virtuous and orthodox prelate was only forty-nine years old, and died of a dropsy.

Again crossing the river we come to Poplar, which obtained its name from the number of poplar trees growing at this spot, near the water.

Blackwall, a hamlet adjoining near the influx of the River Lea with the Thames, is a growing commercial district and here the East India Company has docks, storehouses, and other premises.

The river, broadening to a noble width, now brings us to Woolwich on the Kentish shore, on slightly elevated ground rising from the water. The place, with a Church of St. Mary Magdalene, is increasing from a small fishing town to more important dimensions around the King's dock, stores, and shipbuilding yard. On November 14th, 1617, a licence was granted at Westminster to Sir William Barnes and Hugh Lydyard for them to hold a weekly market and two yearly fairs at Woolwich, " at the request and for the benefit of the inhabitants."

Plumstead is an old market town, possessing a Charter for fairs. The church is dedicated to St. Nicholas. Along this part of the river are extensive marshes.

Erith, a market town standing on a haven, shews an old Church of St. John the Baptist, and a desolate Abbey of Canons Regular.

Purfleet, an Essex village pleasantly placed on rising ground at the mouth of a rivulet, with large tracts of woodland behind, has a chapel belonging to West Thurrock. The chalk pits in the district are in active operation.

Opposite, in Kent, is the village of Northfleet, with the country behind diversified by gently rising hills and small valleys, and to the north-west are lowlands overflowed by the high tides. Here are chalk pits. The Church of St. Botolph, five miles distant, is of several styles of Gothic architecture, and near the village is Nursted Church of St. Mildred, a small building with a tower.

The village of West Thurrock on the Essex side, has an ancient stone Church of St. Clement, with a massive square tower.

Thurrock Grays, an irregularly built market town, stands on a navigable creek for small craft, running in from the river. The church is dedicated to SS. Peter and Paul. Here are chalk pits and lime burning. Adjoining is Little Thurrock, a village by the river, with a Church of St. Mary.

Greenhythe is a hamlet pleasantly placed on the Kentish bank opposite, and its chapel dates from the time of Edward III. Lime and flint works are carried on.

Gravesend, with a Church of St. George, is a corporate town, pleasantly seated on a declivity rising from the bank of the river, on which is a blockhouse or fort. Here is the landing-place for all people coming up the river from abroad, and the town is full of capacious inns for the accommodation of travellers. One of the principal of these is the " Post " Inn, where foreign ambassadors and other persons of distinction lodge on landing. A service of barges, tilt-boats, and wherries, called the " Long Ferry," ply between here and London. In March, 1617, the Virginian Princess Pocahontas, wife of Mr. Rolfe, died on board ship off Gravesend, when just on the point of sailing for America. Her body was brought ashore and buried in the chancel of the church. She was born in 1595, the daughter of a great Indian chief. Ripening to a rare beauty of person and intelligence, she learnt English, became a convert to Christianity, and married Mr. Rolfe, a settler. The previous year she had been brought to England, and was graciously received at Court, but her unusual surroundings and the harsher climate seriously affecting her health, a rapid consumption swiftly carried her off. In 1619, three gentlemen of Gravesend only were entitled to bear arms, and their names were Bere, Robinson, and Tucker. Richard White, of Chalk, left by his will in 1622, forty shillings yearly, for ever, to the parishes of Gravesend and Milton, to be received from the rent of a marsh called Eastwick, in the parish of High Halstow; and in 1624 Henry Pinnock left several tenements, to be called "St. Thomas's Houses," for the reception of decayed people of the parishes of Gravesend and Milton.

Milton, a hamlet close to Gravesend, has a fine old Church of SS. Peter and Paul, wherein are painted the crests of the Kings of England from Edward III. to James I. Assizes for the county of Kent were held here in 1609, and again in 1615.

On the opposite side is Tilbury, from whence a ferry crosses to Gravesend. The church is dedicated to St. Margaret, and the manor-house has a lofty tower. The Fort here was the scene of lively preparations at the time of the attempted Armada invasion.

Some distance lower down on the same side, and near the mouth of the river is Canvey Island, with a chapel dedicated to St. Catherine. In 1622 Sir Henry Appleton and other proprietors of the island agreed to give one-third of their lands in fee-simple to Joas Croppenburgh, a Dutchman, in consideration of his securing the island from the overflowing of the tides and the encroachments of the sea. Burfleet is separated from the island by a creek, and others enter the village from the river. Here is a large stone Church of St. Mary.

Open and low banks now extend to the open sea. On the Essex side is the village of Leigh, from which the country rises to a considerable elevation, affording to view a variety of scenery. On a hill is the Church of St. Clement, and the cottages of shrimpers and fishermen cluster around.

On the Kentish side is Queenborough, standing on the isle of Sheppey, where the River Medway joins the outfall of the Thames. This old corporate town and staple for wool sends two members to the Parliament at Westminster; and two weekly markets and two annual fairs are held here. The Church of Holy Trinity has a very old tower at the west end, and the Castle was repaired by Henry VIII. In 1607 the fee of the Keeper of the Castle was given at £29 2s. 6d.; and in March, 1617, a grant was made to Philip, Earl of Montgomery, of the office of Constable and Porter of the Castle, void by the death of Sir Edward Hoby.

1603. At the accession of James I. there were eight royal residences along the river—at Windsor, Hampton Court, Oatlands, Richmond, Westminster, Whitehall, the Tower of London, and Greenwich. A ninth was added when Queen Anne was granted, as a separate residence, Somerset House, which she renamed Denmark House, after her native country.

Windsor Castle, the grandest of the royal homes, with the massive foundations of William the Conqueror, and the fine architecture of William of Wykeham, was only used occasionally by James and his Court. In a list compiled in 1607 of officials on the various royal estates Windsor is thus given : Constable of the Castle, fee £20 ; Lieutenant, fee £10 ; Keeper of the Keys of the Castle, fee £9 2s. 6d. ; Keeper of the Great Park, fee £12 13s. 4d. ; Porter of the Outer Gate of the Castle, fee £4 11s. 4d. ; Keeper of the Leads, fee 60s. 8d. ; Clerk of the Castle, fee £9 2s. 6d. ; Rod Bearer in the Castle, fee £8 13s. 4d. ; Keeper of the Warderop, fee £13 13s. 4d. ; Ranger of the Forest, fee £9 2s. 6d. The Keeper of the Park of Bagshot, in Windsor Forest had a fee of 100s. ; and " harbage paienige " (probably herbage and pannage) is given as £11.

In 1610 William Suthis was granted for life the office of Master Mason of the Castle. The park and forest were surveyed in 1605 ; and on May

20th, 1609, a Survey was dated of the decayed state of the foundation walls and keep of the Castle, and an estimate prepared for their repair. In September, 1619, a grant was made to Sir Charles Howard of the office of Steward of the Castle and Keeper of the Seal for causes arising in Windsor Forest, " which office he now holds by grant from the Earl of Nottingham as Constable of Windsor Castle." An Order was issued on February 11th, 1625, for paying £300 to William Taylor, Surveyor of the Honour and Castle of Windsor, " by way of imprest, for satisfying the surplusage of the monies due for trenching and draining his Majesty's great park at Windsor, the making of bridges, cleansing the river, and other necessary businesses about the said park, and for paying the workmen for grubbing and digging up the paddock, or piece of ground, within the little park of Windsor."

Hampton Court—Wolsey's magnificent pile— is the newest and most extensive of the monarch's abodes. In 1603 the Venetian Ambassador wrote : " They say that Hampton Court has one thousand eight hundred inhabitable rooms, or at least all of them with doors that lock. The furnishings of the royal apartments are the richest that the crown possesses. Each of the eight palaces has its own furniture, which is never taken to furnish another." Horatio Busino, Secretary to the Venetian Ambassador, wrote in his diary on July 19th, 1618 : " We went lately to Hampton Court, a place which also belongs to the King. It is the largest and most magnificent which we have hitherto seen, both from its variety of buildings and from the extent of its gardens, orchards, and parks, which are all surrounded by a good and strong wall. It is adorned with every convenience and luxury that can be desired." In the list compiled in 1607, of royal officials, Hampton Court is thus given : Keeper of the Park, fee 4d. per diem ; Paler of the Park, fee 4d. per diem ; Keeper of the Orchard, fee £10 ; Keeper of the Garden, fee £6 13s. 4d. ; Keeper of the House, fee £6 13s. 4d. ; Walker about the Pales and Chase, fee £6 20d.

On October 26th, 1607, instructions were sent to the Master of the Horse " to cause all buildings to be removed within the precincts of the Mews at Hampton Court." A Warrant was issued on July 24th, 1611, for paying £45 to William May, for erecting a lodge in the Great Park ; and on the following December 24th, an Order directed the payment of £100 to William Hogan, Keeper of the Stillhouse and Garden, " for planting the walls of the said garden with apricot trees, peach trees, plum trees, and vines of choice fruits." On September 21st, 1620, a grant was made to the Vicar of Hampton and his successors, " of forty marks per annum, in lieu of certain glebe lands enclosed for the King's park at Hampton Court."

Oatlands, the smallest of the royal residences, stands in a park, between Walton and Weybridge; and the palace, built on an eminence, commands a fine sweep of the river. At the beginning of the reign the mansion was converted into an establishment for the young heir, Prince Henry, and his brother and sister ; and Sir John Trevor, who earlier had been appointed Steward and Receiver at Windsor Castle, was made Keeper of the House and Park. In the list compiled in 1607 of royal officials, Oatlands is thus given : Keeper of the House, fee 60s. 8d. ; Keeper of the Warderop, fee

£9 12s. 6d. ; Keeper of the Garden and Orchard, fee £12 13s. 4d. ; Keeper of the Park, fee 60s. 8d. ; "harbage paieinge" (probably herbage and pannage), £11. In February, 1609, Sir John Trevor was paid £900 for the purchase of lands, from those agreeing to sell of their estates, for the enlargement of the park. In May a Warrant ordered £200 to be paid to Edward Forsett for repairs about the park. On August 29th, 1611, the Queen, who was in residence at the time, was granted the manor and park of Oatlands. An order, dated July 23rd, 1619, directed the payment of £71 9s. to John Bonnall, disbursed by him in "providing and planting of new and rare fruits, flowers, herbs, and trees, in his Majesty's gardens at Oatlands ; for dressing and keeping the vines and other works there."

Richmond Palace, built by Henry VII. in 1499, on the charred ruin of Henry I.'s palace of Sheen, is a stone Tudor turreted structure. The buildings occupy a space of ten acres, extending between the Green and the river. The palace was the favourite residence of Queen Elizabeth, and after her death was only occasionally used by the monarch as a lodging between one or other of the more favoured royal abodes. Prince Henry, and after his death, Prince Charles, spent much time there.

In June, 1603, Sir Thomas Gorges and Helena, Marchioness of Northampton, were created Joint Keepers of the Palace and Park ; and the Keepership was regranted to them for life in February, 1605.

In the summer of 1604 John Tavernor's estimate of £661 18s. 4d. was paid for the erection of a new lodge. Of this sum, William Christmas, Woodward of Hampshire, received £231 18s. 4d. for the felling and carriage of trees, and the balance went to Sir Thomas Gorges for other materials, labour, and superintendence.

In the list compiled in 1607 of royal officials, Richmond is thus given : Keeper of the House, fee 6d. per diem ; Keeper of the Park, fee 3d. per diem ; Keeper of the Garden, fee 60s. 10d. ; Keeper of the Library, fee £16 0s. 2d. ; "harbage paieinge" (probably herbage and pannage), £11 ; Keeper of the Warderop, fee £9 2s. 6d. ; Keeper of the Orchard, fee £6 20d.

In February, 1608, a grant was made to Sir Edward Gorges, in reversion after Sir Thomas and the Marchioness of Northampton of the Keeping of the Palace, the Wardrobe, the Gardens, and the new Park. In April, Sir Thomas was paid by Warrant certain sums for expenses at the new park and for keeping the deer there. As shewing the nature of the royal game preserved at Richmond an Order of this year, dated July 3rd, ran : " to pay £61 11s. 10½d. to William Risbrooke, Under-Keeper of his Highness's House at Richmond, parcel of his allowance at 4s. per day for himself and 6d. per day for his servant, for keeping, breeding, feeding, and other necessaries fit for the pheasants, partridges, and other fowls there under his charge."

On March 11th, 1609, Walter Meek was granted, in reversion after Edward Lovell, the office of Overseer and Keeper of the King's orchard, gardens, lodge, etc., at Richmond.

By a deed of September 1st, 1610, the manor of Richmond (Sheen) with the palace and park, together with the manors of Ham and Petersham, were settled on Prince Henry. After his death the royal estate of Richmond, Ham, and Petersham was vested in Sir Francis Bacon and other trustees for Charles, Prince of Wales.

George Gerrard wrote to Sir Dudley Carleton, on July 22nd, 1617 : " Lord Hay has returned from Scotland, and lives in a little house in Richmond Park to be near Syon, where his fair mistress stays."

On May 4th, 1618, an Order was issued for paying the Marchioness of Northampton the sum of £61 6s. 3d., " parcel of her yearly allowance or annuity of £245 5s. for rent of Sheen (Richmond) House, which said house, park, meadow, ferry, and other small parcels thereunto belonging to his Majesty, thinking fit to retain, payable quarterly during her life."

Westminster Palace, the home of Edward the Confessor, is now declined from its ancient dignity and extent. St. Stephen's Chapel has been the meeting-place of the Parliament since it was granted for that purpose by Edward VI., and the grand old Hall of William Rufus has been the permanent seat of the English Law Courts since 1224. In the list compiled in 1607 of royal officials, Westminster is given with a Keeper of the Park, bowling-alleys, tennis court, and pheasant court, fee £12 13s. 4d. In November, 1609, a Warrant ordered the payment of £935 to William Stallenge for clearing, levelling, and enclosing with a wall four acres of ground near the Palace, and planting with mulberry trees.

On June 12th, 1611, the favourite, Robert Carr, Viscount Rochester, was granted the Office of Keeper of Westminster Palace for life.

The confused jumble of buildings of all dates from the thirteenth century onwards, sprawling along the river front, and making up the palace of Whitehall, is the York Place that Wolsey resigned to

Henry VIII. in 1530. The King's lodgings overlook the river, and between them and the royal chapel is a perfect wilderness of small and inconvenient chambers partly occupied by the Queen and her maids of honour ; and westward of these is the Great Stone gallery looking on to the garden and bowling-green. The only large and handsome room in the palace is the Great Hall, and Paul Hentzner, in Elizabeth's time, praised the Library. In the early years of the reign the Great Hall frequently resounded with the festive merriment of the masque. Ben Jonson exercised his poetic talent in composing the words, and Inigo Jones employed his subtle ingenuity in devising the best machinery and setting for their exhibition in the comparatively confined space at his disposal. In the chapel King James listened to many discourses from the plain-spoken old Bishop Andrewes and other divines. Among the baptisms here were : on February 12th, 1613, Anne, first daughter of Robert Cecil, second Earl of Salisbury, the Queen and the Countess of Derby standing as godmothers, and Gilbert, Earl of Shrews-bury as godfather ; on April 2nd, 1616, Henry, son of Lord D'Aubigny ; and on May 17th, 1618, Charles, second son of Sir James Ramsay, by the Bishop of Durham. On March 31st, 1604, Andrew Bright and Edmund Doubleday were jointly granted the office of distilling herbs and sweet waters at the palace, and were also made Keepers of the Library. About the same time Orlando Gibbons was appointed Organist of the Chapel. At Royston, on July 21st, 1614, a grant was made to John and Francis Bonwall of the office of Keeping silkworms at Whitehall and Greenwich.

On Tuesday, January 12th, 1619, at about eleven

o'clock in the morning, a fire broke out in Whitehall Palace. John Chamberlain said that it commenced in the Banqueting House, and quite consuming it, " put the rest in great danger, but that there was so much help at hand, besides that which was sent out of London on all sides, and so good order taken, by the presence of the Lord Chancellor, the Duke (of Lennox), and the Earl of Arundel, that all passed with as much quiet as was possible in such a confusion ; and the fire, though it was exceeding furious, kept from spreading further than the limits of that building, saving only, that the vehemency of the heat burnt down one of the rotten terraces or galleries adjoining, and took hold of the pulpit place, which was soon quenched. One of the greatest losses spoken of, is the burning of all, or most of the writings and papers belonging to the offices of the Signet, Privy Seal, and Council Chamber, which were under it." Some said the fire was caused by a joiner, engaged in mending part of the property of the masque, heating his glue-pot on a false hearth of dry deal boards, which were ignited in his absence, and the flames caught the device of the masque, composed of dry fir, oil paper, and other inflammable materials. Another account said that the blaze was occasioned by a person carrying a candle under the scaffolding. G. Gerard wrote that " all the pilferers in the town got in and stole many of the King's things ; the Signet Office lost most of their papers."

Sir Gerard Herbert writing to Carleton on the same subject said : " The whole palace would have been burnt, but for the providence of the Lord Chamberlain in having some place broken down ; it might have been saved, but two fellows, who first saw the fire went away, and said nothing, for fear of being blamed for it ; they are committed."

On the following April 19th, an Estimate was dated amounting to £9,850 by Inigo Jones and others, of the whole charge for rebuilding the Banqueting House, 110 feet long by 55 feet broad. Sir Simon D'Ewes in his autobiography wrote that on Saturday, October 14th, 1620, in the afternoon, " I had time to ascend the top of St. Paul's steeple, which I had never done before, though I had lived long in London ; and in the forenoon of the Monday following, to view the monuments at Westminster ; observing also in my passage thither the stately new banqueting house now building at Whitehall, in the place of the old one burnt down the last year."

On St. Peter's Day, June 29th, 1624, Orlando Gibbons, organist at Whitehall, had a dispute with one, Eveseed, a gentleman of the Chapel Royal, when the latter " did violently and sodenly without cause runne upon Mr. Gibbons, took him up, and threw him doune uppon a standard whereby he receaved such hurt that he is not yett recovered of the same and withall he tare the band from his neck to his prejudice and disgrace."

The Somerset House of this time was commenced by the Protector Somerset in March 1547, and was the first specimen of Italian architecture erected in this country. James I. assigned the mansion as a separate residence for his consort, Anne of Denmark, who renamed it Denmark House. The grounds and gardens stretch from the Strand to the river, and on August 14th, 1604, the Queen granted John Gerard, the King's surgeon and herbalist, the lease of a garden plot adjoining the House, on condition that he supplied her with herbs, flowers, and fruit. On

June 22nd, 1608, the Earl of Salisbury was granted the office of Keeper of Somerset House and garden during the Queen's life. In February, 1609, William Goodrowse, Serjeant Surgeon, received £400 for laying out the gardens. On the death of Queen Anne, in 1619, the House was given into the keeping of the favourite Buckingham.

William the Conqueror's fortress of the Tower of London was first used as a royal palace by Stephen in 1140; and since that time has been used by the English monarchs, not as a permanent home, but a place of refuge when pressed hard by rebellious troubles. A set of apartments was maintained for the ruler's use, and he spent the night before his coronation here. This custom was not observed in the case of James I. on account of the Plague in the City. In the list compiled in 1607 of royal officials the Tower is thus given : Constable, fee £100 ; Lieutenant, fee £200 ; Keeper of the Lions and other Beasts, fee £30 14s. 6d. ; Carpenter, fee £12 13s. 4d. ; Porter, fee £9 2s. 6d. ; Yeomen, fee £9 2s. 6d. apiece ; fuel allowed the said Yeomen, 53s. 4d.

The royal palace or " plaizance," near the river, at Greenwich, is a collection of buildings of various dates, certainly from the time of Edward I., and probably earlier ; and the park was commenced by Humphrey, Duke of Gloucester, in 1433. Several English sovereigns had here gleaned their first glimpses of the world from the life of the river, and had looked their last from its windows on its busy movement. Horatio Busino, the Secretary to the Venetian Ambassador, wrote in his diary on June 29th, 1618 : " on another occasion, through the opportunity afforded by his Excellency going to visit the Queen at a place called Greenwich, on the river, four miles from London, we saw the fabled tower of Oriana, on the top of a hill there. The palace is very large, big enough indeed to accommodate the whole Court, but it is not very well arranged, having originally been a Monastery. We did not observe anything remarkable there, except a large and handsome aviary with a quantity of birds, covered with lead, and surrounded by a balustrade. It has tall windows of copper network in front and at the sides and above the roof itself, with a handsome fountain, rising from the ground. It is situated at the end of some flower beds, not very far from the palace, and purposely, so that the song of these numerous warblers may be heard there." In the list compiled in 1607 of royal officials, Greenwich is thus given : Keeper of the Manor and Park, with park of pheasants, fee £17 4s. 2d. ; Keeper of the Garden, fee 60s. 8d. ; Keeper of the Warderop, fee £20 5s. ; Keeper of the Lodge, Orchard, and Garden, fee £18 5s.

In April, 1604, Lord Treasurer Dorset ordered payment to be made for urgent repairs to the dilapidated stables at Greenwich, Hampton Court, Oatlands, and elsewhere. At Westminster, on July 17th, 1612, William Glover, of Westminster, and Samuel Evans, of East Greenwich, were granted a pardon for a robbery committed at the Palace.

John Chamberlain wrote in a letter to Sir Dudley Carleton, on November 25th, 1613 : " Greenwich is added to the Queen's jointure by her late pacification." On the following December 9th, the Earl of Northampton wrote in a letter from Whitehall to Sir Thomas Lake : " Fear that her Majesty will displace him from his office of Keeper of the Game, in Greenwich Park, with possession of the Lodge.

Was brought up in the place from a child; has expended upwards of £2,000 there, and desires to lay his bones there. Requests the King, in passing the grant of it to the Queen, to provide for his remaining, otherwise he will be at the mercy of a wrathful mistress, and his expulsion will be inevitable." Four days later he further wrote: "Thanks for the King's request to the Queen not to thrust him out of Greenwich Park. She professes that she does not intend it; but his security depends upon an express provision in the grant, without which she would have power to do it as soon as her patent is passed." On the 20th the Earl was finally confirmed in his office of Keeper of Greenwich Park, " and the herbage and pannage of the same." The Grant, dated February 19th, 1614, gave the Queen, " the capital messuage of Greenwich House and other things, for a hundred years if she should live so long." In June, 1617, Queen Anne was having some building work executed at Greenwich, of which John Chamberlain wrote: "It is said to be some curious device of Inigo Jones, and will cost about £4,000." Chamberlain wrote to Carleton, on September 11th, 1619: "There is a brick wall making round Greenwich Park that will prove a matter of no small charge." This wall enclosed a park of 200 acres.

On May 30th, 1623, the Rev. Joseph Mead said in a letter: "Yesterday sennight, his Majesty required my Lord of Winchester forthwith to cause Greenwich Chapel to be new repaired and guilded, being much decayed, as not having been new furnished since Queen Mary's days."

COURT LIFE ALONG THE RIVER.

1603. When in the early spring of 1603 that great sovereign, but vain and wretched woman, Queen Elizabeth breathed her last in her river-side palace at Richmond, the virile Tudor dynasty expired, and the busy stream of life on and along the Thames paused to mourn a monarch, who, despite her tyrannical temper, possessed the respect, and a large share of the love of all her subjects. Much uncertainty and dread filled men's minds regarding their new Scottish ruler, who they had reason to fear would hold the nation to blame for the violent death of his mother.

The people of the capital were at the same time oppressed by another and nearer danger in the rapid spread of the Plague, then threatening a terrible and sudden end to all.

Only a few weeks had elapsed since their late ailing mistress had, for the last time, passed along the river in royal state from Whitehall to Richmond, when she paused to dine with Mr. Lacey, her old merchant friend, at Putney. Her sickness rapidly assumed so serious an aspect that the Bishop of Chichester, the Lord Almoner, composed a special prayer, entreating that the sins of the nation might not provoke God to shorten its happiness under the Queen, who was " the safety of Thy people, the peace of the Church, and the very lives of Thy Saints."

She died on March 24th, and late in the day the Council and the nobility at Court proceeded to London, and before ten o'clock at night James VI. of Scotland had been proclaimed King. At Kingston five shillings were paid to a trumpeter " for sounding a proclamation."

On Saturday the Council returned to Richmond, and at night a water procession escorted the royal barge bearing the remains to Whitehall, where they laid in state till April 28th, when the last of the countless progresses of the lion-hearted Elizabeth moved in solemn magnificence to Westminster Abbey, and she was left to a final rest canopied by the architectural glories of Henry VII.'s chapel.

A Chronicler recorded that on the occasion Westminster " was surcharged with multitudes of all sorts of people in their streets, houses, windows, leads, and gutters, that came to see the obsequie ; and when they beheld her statue or picture lying upon the coffin, set forth in royal robes, having a crown upon the head thereof, and a ball and sceptre in either hand, there was such a general sighing, groaning, and weeping as the like hath not been seen or known in the memory of man."

James, met at Sir Robert Cecil's splendid seat of Theobalds, in Hertfordshire, by the Privy Council, approached his greater capital in leisurely state, and on May 7th, escorted by the Lord Mayor, the Aldermen wearing scarlet robes and chains, and five hundred of the principal citizens on horseback, passed through the tumultuous welcome of the Londoners to the Charterhouse, where for four days he was royally entertained by Lord Thomas Howard.

On Wednesday, the 11th, for fear of the Plague ravaging the city, he rode quietly on horseback

to Whitehall, and there taking barge shot the
bridge, and rested on the water before the grim
prison fortress to view the great ordnance of the
White Tower and on Tower Wharf, and to hear it
discharged with a mighty peal in his honour. Landing at the Tower Stairs, the King, attended by a
brilliant crowd of great officers of state and nobles,
was presented at the top with the sword, which was
then borne before him by the Duke of Lennox.
The Lieutenant humbly delivered the keys of the
Tower, and James, acknowledging the faithful
loyalty and trust reposed in him, took the officer
about the neck, and gave them back into his charge.
Some hours of repose followed, and then after
visiting the Armoury, Wardrobe, the Artillery, and
the Chapel, and walking in the garden, the King
retired for the night.

Scaramelli, Secretary to the Venetian Embassy,
describing these happenings in a despatch to his
Government, wrote : " The King had not been two
hours in the Tower of London—in sight of which,
and hard by, I have my lodging in a house in the
borough, quite new, with a great Italian garden,
belonging to a merchant of Lucca—when his Majesty
sent one of his gentlemen to wait on me with expressions of great affection for your serenity, and
kindliness towards your Secretary and servant."

The next day the Ordnance and Mint Houses were
inspected, and a visit paid to the lions. On Friday
various Lords and Knights were created in the
Presence Chamber, and then James embarked in
his barge, and proceeded to Greenwich palace.
Meanwhile, six men-of-war and two armed pinnaces,
which at the moment of Elizabeth's death were in
commission for a cruise to harass the Spaniards,

received orders to move down the river to Greenwich for the King's inspection.

During the following days several knighthoods were conferred, and on the 22nd a triumphal display of fireworks was exhibited on the river.

The next morning the King went back to Whitehall, but soon returned to Greenwich, and on the 27th gave audience to the Venetian Secretary, who in a despatch the next day to the Doge and Senate, wrote : " I was received in audience yesterday at two o'clock, at Greenwich. I went there and found such a crowd that I never saw the like, even in Constantinople in time of peace. There were upwards of ten or twelve thousand persons about. All the efforts of the guards hardly enabled me to reach the first, let alone the inner chamber, owing to the throng of nobility. At length, having arrived at the chamber where the King was, I found all the Council about his chair, and an infinity of other Lords almost in an attitude of adoration. His Majesty rose and took six steps towards the middle of the room, and then drew back one, after making me a sign of welcome with his hand. He then remained standing up while he listened to me attentively. At the opening and at the close he held his hat in his hand awhile. He was dressed in silver-grey satin, quite plain, with a cloak of black tabinet reaching to below the knees, and lined with crimson ; he had his arm in a white sling, the result of a fall from his horse when out hunting, which occasioned more danger than damage ; from his dress he would have been taken for the meanest among his courtiers, a modesty he affects, had it not been for a chain of diamonds round his neck and a great diamond in his hat."

Sir Anthony Welldon wrote of the King's person at this time : " He was of a middle stature, more corpulent through his clothes than in his body, yet fat enough, his clothes being made large and easy, the doublets quilted for stiletto proof, his breeches in great pleits and full stuffed. He was naturally of a timorous disposition, which was the reason of his quilted doublets ; his eyes large, ever rolling after any stranger that came into his presence, insomuch as many, for shame, have left the room, as being out of countenance ; his beard was very thin ; his tongue too large for his mouth, which ever made him speak full in the mouth, and made him drink very uncomely, as if eating his drink, which came out into the cup of each side of his mouth ; his skin was as soft as taffeta sarsnet, which felt so because he never washed his hands, only rubbed his fingers' ends slightly with the wet end of a napkin ; his legs were very weak, having had (as was thought) some foul play in his youth, or rather before he was born, that he was not able to stand at seven years of age, that weakness made him ever leaning on other men's shoulders. His walk was ever circular, his fingers ever in that walk fiddling about."

During the greater part of June the Court resided at Greenwich, and the King paid brief visits to Sion House at Isleworth, some other of the principal mansions in Surrey and Middlesex, and for a short time was driven by the Plague to the Earl of Pembroke's seat at Wilton, near Salisbury. On Whit Sunday, the 12th, Mons. de Rhosney, Ambassador from France, accompanied by a train of richly bejewelled gentlemen, went to an audience at Greenwich, where, on the Tuesday,

Dr. Anthony Rudd, Bishop of St. David's, preached to an assembled Court.

Later in the month James journeyed to Windsor, and on the 27th, Queen Anne, with Prince Henry and Princess Elizabeth, arrived at the Castle, in the midst of a train of two hundred carriages and more than five thousand horses, " her retinue having grown greatly on her journey."

The Feast of St. George was celebrated on July 2nd, when, in the presence of the King, the Prince, the Duke of Lennox, and the Earls of Southampton, Pembroke, and Mar were invested with the Order of the Garter.

At this time the Venetian Secretary wrote in a despatch : " The Ambassadors of Brunswick and Lorraine have arrived, and, on account of the Plague, they passed straight on to Court at Windsor, where the crowd is so great and the dearth so excessive that the King will be forced to move."

Influenced by the increasing terror of the Plague, the young Prince Henry was taken to a hastily established household set up for him in the seclusion of Oatlands near Weybridge.

Meanwhile the Court remained at Windsor, and busied itself with preparations for the approaching Coronation.

The King, during a visit to Hampton Court, issued a general summons to all persons who had £40 a year in land, or upwards, to come and receive knighthood, and pay the obligatory fees. Three days later, John Gammes, of Radnorshire, and William Cave, of Oxfordshire, presented themselves at Hampton Court, and were the first under these conditions to receive the accolade at the hands of the King.

A Commission for considering the Coronation proceedings and claims reported that as the sovereign could not pass through the stricken City from the Tower, all the customary services rendered should be performed between Westminster Bridge and the Abbey. A Proclamation was issued forbidding the citizens to repair to the ceremony, with the exception of the Lord Mayor and a few chief men of London, who by virtue of the ancient claim were to assist the Chief Butler at the State banquet. To guard against tumult and disorder, five hundred soldiers were levied for two days in Westminster, the Strand, and other places in the Liberties. The trains of nobles and bishops were limited ; and the fear of the spread of infection attending a great concourse of people caused the date of St. James's Fair at Westminster to be altered.

Towards the end of July, the Court departed from Windsor, and, leaving the royal children at Oatlands, passed on to Hampton Court, where, on the 20th, the King conferred knighthoods, and the next day created eleven new peerages, in the Great Hall of the Palace.

Lady Anne Clifford wrote in a letter to a friend : " My mother and I lay in one of the Round Towers, round which were tents, where they died two or three a day of ye Plague. . . . My Aunt Warwick sent us medicines from a little house near Hampton Court, where she then lay with Sir Moyle Finch and his lady."

On the 22nd, the King and Queen set out by road for the capital, the Court proceeding in two divisions, each with a guard of five hundred men. The journey was broken by a visit to Bishop Bancroft at Fulham, and a call on Mr. Lacey, the late Queen's merchant friend, at Putney. Arrived at Whitehall, James constituted a Court of Claims, and the next day dubbed three hundred knights in the royal garden— amongst the number being judges, serjeants, doctors- at-law, and George Somers, or Summers, afterwards one of the chief founders of the Virginia Company. Seven more knights were made on the Sunday.

Monday, the 25th—St. James's and the Coronation day—opened with the gloom of death hanging in the air, and the pomp and circumstance of the customary City pageant had no place in the gorgeous ceremonial. Early in the morning the Lord Mayor, Sir Robert Lee, in a gown of crimson velvet, the Aldermen in gowns of scarlet, and twelve principal citizens, entered the Mayor's barge at Three Cranes Stairs, and were rowed to Westminster in silent state. All other citizens attempting to go West were sternly turned back, strong bodies of guards being placed for the purpose at the gates of London ; while a penalty of death threatened people coming in boats from Citywards.

The King and Queen Anne—" with her hair hanging down "—accompanied by the Council and their respective Courts, embarked in barges at Whitehall, and landing at Westminster proceeded to the Abbey, where they were crowned by Archbishop Whitgift.

At the conclusion of the ceremony the principal company retired to chambers behind the altar, where the King exchanged his heavier for a lighter crown, and the Queen, doffing her crimson mantle, appeared in black. Some refreshments were con- sumed, and then the procession, returning in the order of coming, re-embarked on board the royal barges. The King and Queen, after exhibiting themselves to their subjects for some time on the river, retired to Whitehall, where on the following day James knighted all the Aldermen of London, who had not already received that honour. After a brief stay, the Court returned to Hampton Court, but in the course of the visit Queen Anne was entertained by the freshly liberated Earl of Southampton at Southampton House. He engaged Burbage and his Company of actors, of whom Shakespeare was one, to perform " Love's Labour Lost " in her presence.

The Venetian Secretary Scaramelli gave the King and Queen great satisfaction about this time by visiting the royal children at Oatlands ; and the Italian, in a despatch to his Government, wrote of Prince Henry : " The Prince is ten years old, little of body and quick of spirit. He is ceremonious beyond his years, and with great gravity he covered and bade me be covered. Through an interpreter, he gave me a long discourse on his exercises, dancing, tennis, the chace. He then himself conducted me down one flight of stairs and up another to visit the Princess. I found her surrounded by her Court, under a canopy. They both said they meant to learn Italian."

The King now spent some days busily knighting more gentlemen, and feasting the Ambassadors of several countries. The Danish Ambassador and his train of over one hundred and forty persons were lodged at the palace of Richmond ; and his Excellency of Brunswick and his following of more than twenty were boarded and entertained at Kingston. Lord Danvers and Sir Lewis Lewkenor made an arrangement at Kingston for bringing a new Spanish Ambassador to meet the King at

Oxford, in the course of an extended royal progress, which started from Hampton Court on Wednesday, August 10th.

Towards the end of August the Plague attacked a groom of the Wardrobe at Oatlands, with fatal results, and the Princes were hastily moved to Nonsuch Palace in Surrey. The appearance of the pestilence also drove the Earl of Northumberland from Sion House to lodgings at Richmond.

In the early part of September, the King and Queen, after being entertained by Mr. Tanfield, at Burford Priory, went to Woodstock.

A jest-book of the period tells an amusing story of the King, that may possibly apply to this visit, as follows : " King James being in his progress at Woodstock in Oxfordshire, the King, finding it to rain so one morning that he could not ride a-hunting, had got some nobility and gentry together, resolving to be merry.   And one humour was, that the King having that morning a fine curvetting horse given him, which kind of horse he never lik'd in his life, told them that he that could tell the greatest lie should have that horse.   So one told one lie, and another, another ; and several had told others, that there was great laughing ; and just in the midst of this mirth in comes a country fellow, complaining to the King that some of his servants had wrong'd him.   'Well, well,' says the King, 'we'll hear you of that anon; come, come hither amongst us, and you must know that he that can tell the greatest lie shall have that horse.'   'Truly, Sir,' says he, 'an't please your Grace, I never told a lie in all my life.'   With that says the King, 'Give him the horse, give him the horse, for I am sure that is the greatest lie that has been told to-day.' "

As a royal visit to Oxford was now expected, the new Spanish Ambassador was brought to the City for an audience, but one of his train dying here not without suspicion of the Plague, he was taken to Southampton, there to await the coming of the King to Winchester.

In December Prince Henry was brought from Nonsuch to Hampton Court, where a day or two before Christmas the King received the congratulations of the Ambassadors of Holland and Savoy on his accession.

1604. On Sunday evening, January 8th, 1604, the Queen, with eleven ladies of honour in attendance, personated, in the Great Hall of the palace, the chief character in Daniel's masque, called "The Vision of the Twelve Goddesses."

On February 13th the bells of St. Margaret's, Westminster, greeted the arrival of the Court at Whitehall, where James was met by his Privy Council.

Early in March the time was deemed fitting for the long-contemplated triumphal progress through the City of London, and the King and Queen, with Prince Henry, the Council and Court, left Westminster in state barges and, surrounded by a large number of boats, were rowed to the Tower, where the landing stairs were with difficulty climbed, owing to the pressure of the crowd, which had gathered to get a sight of the royal party.

On Monday, the 13th, the baiting of a lion by three fierce dogs from the Bear Gardens was witnessed, while all the dungeons of the Tower were opened and the prisoners liberated. Sir Walter Raleigh, not sharing in the royal clemency, was temporarily removed to the Fleet Prison.

The next day, James, after making the Lord Treasurer Earl of Dorset, and Lord Henry Howard Earl of Northampton, and conferring thirty knighthoods, watched a new vessel, just built for the Prince, as it sailed up from Limehouse and anchored opposite the royal lodgings. The Prince, accompanied by the Lord Admiral and other noblemen, viewed the ship, gay with ensigns and pennants, and expressed unbounded delight with it.

Gilbert Dugdale, in describing the rejoicings on this occasion, in a tract named " The Time Triumphant," wrote of the spectacle on the river as seen from the Tower : " Upon the Thames, the waterworks for his entertainment were miraculous, and the fireworks on the water passed pleasing. As of a castle or fortress built on two barges, seeming as a settled fort in an island, planted with much munition of defence ; and two pinnaces ready rigged, armed likewise to assault the castle ; that had you beheld the managing of that fight, with the onset on the castle, repulse from the castle, and then the taking of it, it was a show worthy the sight of many princes. Being there placed at the cost of the Cinque Ports ; whereat the King, all pleased, made answer that ' their love was, like the wild-fire, unquenchable.' "

On Wednesday the King, in company with his Consort and Prince Henry, set out from the Tower, at eleven o'clock in the morning. At the head of the procession went the City magistrates, the Court functionaries, the bishops and clergy, and nobles and knights superbly clad in silk of gold with pearl embroideries. The Prince was on horseback ten paces in front of the King, who rode a white gennet under a rich canopy borne aloft by eight splendidly dressed gentlemen of the privy chamber. The Queen, twenty paces in the rear, seated on a royal throne drawn by two white mules, and followed by Lady Arabella Stuart in a richly-furnished carriage, was attended by maids-of-honour, and by seventy beautifully-arrayed ladies on horseback. A vast multitude acclaimed the gorgeous procession as it passed, under seven arches of triumph, through the City to Westminster. In celebration of this event, the poet Michael Drayton wrote " A Pæan Triumphall : composed for the Societie of the Goldsmiths of London, congratulating his Highness magnificent entring the Citie."

On Good Friday, April 6th, Dr. Lancelot Andrewes, Dean of Westminster, preached before the King in the Chapel of Whitehall Palace. This divine impressed James with his discourse, and throughout the reign was his favourite preacher. Born in the parish of All Hallows, Barking, he was the son of a merchant who became Master of the Trinity House.

The Court remained at Whitehall till June, when it removed to Greenwich ; and on a Tuesday early in July, the King left for the chase, intending to review his fleet at Rochester on the Thursday, but, according to the Venetian Ambassador, " as he and the Queen were riding, the King wished to pass her Majesty, but he received a kick on the leg from her horse. They had all to go home, and the King was in bed for two days. The naval review at Rochester is put off."

In the first part of July, the King held meetings of the Privy Council and dubbed numerous knights at Whitehall, and then proceeded to Oatlands, from whence, in the middle of the month, a Commission of great state and household officials was constituted to regulate the supply of wood and coals for the royal households within twelve miles of the Thames. Their Commission ran : " We understand that the expense of wood and coal in our house is so great, and the burden thereof to our subjects so grievous, as that it has been the cause of pitiful complaints. To ease our subjects we are pleased to lay part of the charge upon ourself, by making provision of wood and coal for our house out of such woods of our own inheritance as lie convenient. We therefore give you our full lawful power to call before you all persons enjoying any interest in any of our woods within twelve miles of the Thames, or any other river or creek upon which boats may pass, and which are running into the Thames, and compound with them for their interest in such woods ; and after payment to take into our hands the said woods and coppices, and deliver them to the officers of our household, to be employed towards provision of wood and coal for our household."

At the same time a Warrant authorized the Lord Treasurer and others to make composition with all persons having interest in the King's woods within twelve miles of the Thames.

A brief visit was paid to Windsor, and then the King and Queen returned to Whitehall, where meetings of the Privy Council were held in August. Many new knights swelled the list during this month, and early in September the Sovereign and his Consort, after spending two days with Prince Charles at Oatlands, again moved to Windsor, where they remained till October, when the King went to Hampton Court to meet the Scottish Commissioners for treating of the Union between the two kingdoms. On the 16th the ringers of St. Margaret's, Westminster, were paid 2s. 6d. for pealing the bells on the royal return to Whitehall.

After a short trip to the royal hunting seat at Royston, James came back to Whitehall on Wednesday, November 7th, and during this month and December another large batch of knights appeared.

The Court spent the Christmas festivities at the London riverside palace, and Sir Dudley Carleton wrote, in a letter to Ralph Winwood: " On St. John's Day we had the marriage of Sir Philip Herbert and the Lady Susan performed at White-hall, with all the honour could be done a great favourite. The Court was great, and for that day put on the best bravery. The Prince and Duke of Holst led the bride to church, the Queen followed her from thence. The King gave her, and she, in her tresses and trinkets, brided and bridled it so handsomely, and indeed became herself so well, that the King said " if he were unmarried he would not give her, but keep her himself."

The marriage dinner was consumed in the great chamber, where the Prince and the Duke of Holst and the great lords and ladies accompanied the bride. The Ambassador of Venice was the only bidden guest of strangers, and he had place above the Duke of Holst, which the Duke took not well. But after dinner he was as little pleased himself; for being brought into the closet to retire himself, he was there suffered to walk out his supper un-thought of. At night there was a masque in the hall, which for conceit and fashion was suitable to the occasion. The actors were the Earl of Pembroke, the Lord Willoughby, Sir Samuel Hays, Sir Thomas Germain, Sir Robert Cary, Sir John

I

Lee, Sir Richard Preston, and Sir Thomas Bager. There was no small loss that night of chains and jewels, and many great ladies were made shorter by the skirts, and were well enough served that they could keep cut no better. The presents of plate and other things, given by the noblemen, were valued at £2,500, but that which made it a good marriage was a gift of the King's of £500 land for the bride's jointure. They were lodged in the Council Chamber, where the King, in his shirt and night-gown, gave them a ' reveille matin ' before they were up, and spent a good time in or upon the bed, choose which you will believe. No ceremony was omitted by bride-cakes, points, garters, and gloves, which have been ever since the livery of the Court ; and at night there was sewing into the sheet, casting off the bride's left hose, with many other petty sorceries."

1605. With the Plague still prevalent in London, little of interest marked the beginning of 1605. Early in March, the Queen, accompanied by Princes Henry and Charles, was conveyed by the Council and great ladies to Greenwich, where, as Viscount Cranborne informed Sir Thomas Lake, " she is pleased with the Earl of Suffolk's order of her lodgings." An increase in the royal family was now expected, and on the 28th, Samuel Calvert wrote to Ralph Winwood : " The King, Queen, and all are now at Court, and there purposed to be some time. The Queen expects delivery in a month. There is great preparation of nurses, midwives, rockers, and other officers, to the number of forty or more."

On Easter Sunday, April 2nd, William Hericke, a goldsmith of Cheapside, was knighted for making, much to the royal satisfaction, a hole in the great diamond worn by the King.

A Princess was born on the 8th, and the citizens of London celebrated the joyful event by lighting bonfires and ringing all the bells in the City. Many new knights appeared this month, and then on Saturday, May 4th, the King, celebrating the Feast of St. George, dubbed two gentlemen, and in the hall of the palace, surrounded by the princes and great nobles, created three Earls, one Viscount, and four Barons. One of the new peers was Sir Philip Herbert, the new year's bridegroom, made Baron Herbert of Shurland, in the Isle of Sheppey, and Earl of Montgomery. Sunday's dawn saw the stirring of unusual bustle at Court, and later in the day the infant Princess was christened in the chapel, receiving the name of Mary.

Knighthoods rained thick during the rest of the month ; seven were made at Richmond, and sixteen at Greenwich.

In the opening days of July the Court moved to Windsor, calling at Whitehall on the way, and giving James the opportunity of producing at least one knight. On the 8th, a proclamation and other state orders were issued from the Castle, and a few days later the King journeyed to Whitehall, where he gave audience to and entertained the Emperor's Ambassador. The Venetian Envoy, in writing a despatch to the Doge and Senate, describing this visit of the Imperial Ambassador—who was the Landgrave of Lichtenberg—said that he was met at Gravesend by three Earls, four Barons, and many gentlemen ; and, " he was conducted to London, where a house was provided for him, but it was empty and unfurnished with any of the necessaries ;

and he was, moreover, informed that he would have to bargain with the proprietor about the rent. The Ambassador showed his amazement, and said that he was to be here for eight or ten days only, he would put up in some tavern, as he did, declining the arrangements made for him, and complaining bitterly of being so meanly received, and he did so to me also on the occasion of my paying him a visit. The Duke of Lennox, the Earl of Pembroke, and other gentlemen conducted him to audience."

In another despatch, on the 13th, he wrote : " The Queen had been kept in town by a toothache, which had caused her great pain ; and that the King, when stag-hunting in the neighbourhood of Oatlands, had been thrown with his horse under him, and ' by God's grace ' he took no other harm than a blow on the knee, which has kept him in bed two days. He is all right again, and goes a-hunting more than ever."

On Monday, the 15th, the Imperial Ambassador, after being feasted, was entertained at a bull-and-bear baiting. The next day a royal progress was commenced. Several of the western counties were visited, and on August 27th, the King, Queen, and Prince Henry arrived at Oxford, where they were received with great solemnity by the Chancellor, (the Earl of Dorset), the Vice-Chancellor and the Doctors of the University in their scarlet gowns, and attended by the " bedells," all on horseback. Both the heads of the University made a speech, and the King was presented with a Greek Testament in folio, and two pairs of Oxford gloves, " with a deep fringe of gold, the turnovers being wrought with pearls." The Queen and Prince were also presented each with a pair of very similar gloves.

The Mayor and Corporation having overtaken and passed the University procession, a dispute arose, which was ended for the moment by the City body falling into the rear. Moving through the quaint old city, the streets of which were lined with scholars and citizens, the royal visitors were conducted to lodgings—the King and Queen at Christ Church, and the Prince at Magdalen College.

The next day James and his son listened to sermons and disputations on Divinity and Civil Law in St. Mary's Church ; and after supper watched the performance of three plays—the scenery and devices contrived by Inigo Jones—in the Hall of Christ Church.

The following day, after a continuation of the disputations on medical questions, tobacco, and philosophy, the Earl of Dorset entertained the royal party to a dinner at New College. Supper over, Dr. Gwynn's comedy, called " Vertumnus," was performed, but the weary King was sleepy and in-attentive. Another day saw James visiting the Library founded by Sir Thomas Bodley, the Schools of Divinity and Arts, and the Colleges of Brazenose, All Souls, Magdalen, and Queen's ; and on Saturday, the 31st, the Court was back again at Windsor.

Nearly all September was spent quietly at the Castle, and little is recorded beyond a meeting there of the Privy Council, on the 10th, and the swearing in of Archbishop Bancroft as a Privy Councillor, at Hampton Court, on the 29th.

On October 26th, the Venetian Ambassador wrote in a despatch : " The King is in the country at the chase ; the Queen at Hampton Court. But they are beginning to get the royal apartments ready (at Whitehall) for the time for the meeting of Parliament is coming on. That is settled for the fifteenth (fifth O.S.) of next month."

The discovery of the Gunpowder Plot followed, and having opened and prorogued Parliament amidst intense popular excitement, the King and his family returned to Hampton Court.

At this time Sir Edward Hoby, who lived at Bisham, wrote in a curious letter to Sir Thomas Edmondes, English Minister at Brussels : " I hear that Madame de Hoboquen was with the Queen at Hampton Court, where she did excellently carry herself, to her great commendation. I have not yet seen her, but will do with the first opportunity I can, and will do her all the honour and service I can, purposing, when my wife shall come to the town and settled, solemnly to invite her."

The King, with uneasy energy, continually moved in November and December between his palaces of Hampton Court, Windsor, and Greenwich, and the Christmas festivities were celebrated at Whitehall.

On December 8th the Venetian Ambassador wrote in a despatch : " On Monday the King went to Richmond, intending to go on to Hampton Court, where he proposes to stay six or eight days for his usual amusement of the chase. This journey is disapproved by the Queen and by all who have the King's interests at heart ; for it seems unwise, in a time of such turbulence and commotion, that the King should go into the country attended by few persons, and, as often happens, when lured on by the pleasure of the chase, should stay out late into the evening, thus offering an easy occasion for any who desires to injure him to do so. These and similar considerations have been laid before his Majesty, but he, though he recognises their truth, is resolved to rely on the Divine mercy, and to place his pleasure above his peril."

1606. The first Sunday in 1606 (January 5th) saw a brilliant company gathered at Whitehall for the celebration of the marriage of Robert Devereux, Earl of Essex (son of Queen Elizabeth's decapitated favourite, and who had been restored to his father's forfeited titles and estates the previous year), with Frances, second daughter of the Earl of Suffolk; and on the gay occasion Ben Jonson and Inigo Jones united in devising an entertainment called "Hymenæi: or the Solemnities of the Masque and Barriers." The bride was about thirteen years and the bridegroom scarcely fourteen years old. They separated after the ceremony, and four years elapsed before they started their short, unhappy married life.

The next night, being Twelfth Night, Ben Jonson's "Masque of Blackness" was performed at the Court, in honour of the creation of Prince Charles, now five years old, as Duke of York. This was the first of the many brilliant entertainments given by the Queen, and the subject of the masque was a suggestion of her own. Jonson wrote that she insisted on having all the performers "blackmoors."

On Good Friday, March 29th, Bishop Andrewes preached before the King at Greenwich, and on Easter-day the prelate delivered another discourse at Whitehall.

The bells of St. Margaret's were rung on May 16th, when the King and Queen moved to Greenwich. For this journey of the Court, the Lord Mayor was ordered by the Council to supply two hundred two-horse carts and his barge for the removal of the royal effects. These were not very willingly supplied, the Lord Mayor calling attention to the serious

inconvenience the trade of the City would suffer by
the temporary withdrawal of so many carts ; and
with regard to the barge, it had been lent some
time previously to the Lord Chancellor for the conveyance of the Guards, but was not fitted to carry
luggage.

A short royal trip was taken to Windsor, where
on Tuesday, the 20th, Robert, Earl of Salisbury,
and Thomas Howard, Viscount Bindon, were installed Knights of the Garter.   Returning to Greenwich, James created several knights, and then, on
the 27th, the bells of St. Margaret's were again
welcoming him, when he came to Westminster and
adjourned Parliament.

Bishop Andrewes preached at Greenwich on
Whitsunday, June 8th.

The King was at Richmond dubbing a knight on
the 19th ; and then on Sunday, the 22nd, the Queen
gave birth to a princess at Greenwich.   The infant,
named Sophia, died the next day, and on the following Thursday the remains were conveyed by
barge, covered with black velvet, accompanied by
three other barges draped in black cloth, and
interred in the Royal Chapel at Westminster.

Wednesday, July 15th, saw the King making two
knights at Oatlands ; and the next day Christian IV.
of Denmark arrived with a fleet of ships at Tilbury
Hope, and landed at Gravesend.   When intelligence
of the unexpected arrival of his brother-in-law
reached James he hastened to Greenwich, and,
accompanied by Prince Henry and such of the
nobility as could be hurriedly assembled, embarked
in the Parliament barge, and, followed by a great
retinue in thirty-five other barges, was welcomed by
the Danish King at Gravesend, and magnificently

feasted on board his ship. The vessels of the English fleet in the river, including the " Elizabeth," " Jonas," and " Bear," were all in warlike trim, and when the monarchs met, " the tacklings, tops, and every part of the ships were so replenished with men that hardly might you discern the ropes, or see the ships' sides." After spending an hour on board the Danish ship, the two Kings and the Prince entered a barge, while the visiting noblemen and gentlemen were taken on board the barges of the courtiers. The royal barge was built like a tower, or little castle, with glass windows and casements " fair carved and gilt," and the roof had battlements, pinnacles, and pyramids, and was covered with fine symbolic carving. Upon this occasion it was towed by another barge of thirty oars. As the rowers moved away the ships, following the Admiral's lead, discharged a thundering peal of heavy ordnance and the blockhouses at Gravesend joined in the salute as the royal procession passed up the river to Greenwich, where the Danish sovereign landed at the palace steps, and was greeted by the princess and the little Duke of York. On Monday, the two Kings and Prince Henry, attended by a richly mounted retinue, hunted in the Park, killing two bucks. On Thursday morning, at about eleven o'clock, the monarchs and Prince Henry, on the way to Theobalds, entered their barges, and were rowed to Blackwall, where their trains and coaches waited. Landing amidst the shouts of a large multitude of people and the discharge of guns from the merchant vessels anchored in the road, they set forward towards Stratford.

The royal party returned to Blackwall on the following Monday, and took barge for Greenwich.

On Thursday, the 31st, the Danish King started to visit the City of London. The tide serving about two o'clock in the afternoon, the two Kings and the Prince, attended by the Privy Council, the nobility and a numerous company of knights and gentlemen, embarked in the royal barges, and as they were rowed towards London, salutes were fired from the flag-bedecked ships riding in the river, drums were beaten, trumpets sounded, and people shouted and waved hats and arms. Welcomed at the Tower Wharf by the pealing ordnance, they set forward with a great train, and were received and entertained by the Lord Mayor, Sir Leonard Holliday. After a splendidand gratifyingreception the royal visitorsproceeded to Somerset House, and there passed the night.

On the morning of August 1st, the bells of St. Margaret's were rung, when the Danish ruler visited the Abbey; and later his brother-in-law exhibited the Tower of London to him, finishing with a review of the ordnance at the Wharf, which delivered a thundering peal as the monarchs re-entered their barge, and the tide serving, shot the bridge, and were rowed to Whitehall.

The next day, after hunting in St. James's and Hyde Parks, they left the Privy Stairs, about four o'clock in the afternoon, and went by water back to Greenwich.

On the 6th, the Kings hunted at Richmond, and passed the night at the palace. In the morning, the royal cavalcade, greeted by the merry ringing of bells at Twickenham and other places, proceeded to Hampton Court, where a halt was made for dinner; a deer hunt followed, and the day concluded at Windsor.

Friday, the 8th, was largely spent in hunting at

Windsor, and in the evening they again reached Greenwich.

Saturday morning saw busy preparations for departure, and after taking leave of the Court, the Danish monarch, with the King and Queen and Prince Henry, entered barges, which carried them down the river to a point near Northfleet, where their trains and coaches were awaiting them. Immense crowds of people shouted greetings as they passed on the way to Rochester, where the night was spent in the bishop's palace. On Sunday morning the royalties heard a Latin sermon in the Cathedral, from Dr. Parry, Dean of Chester; and then taking their barges at Rochester Bridge, they were rowed along the Medway, reviewing the galleys, ships, and pinnaces lying in the river, till they came opposite Upnor Castle. At this point the description of Mr. Pory, contained in a letter to Sir Robert Cotton, may be quoted: "There they mounted the 'Elizabeth James,' in which their dinner was provided. This ship was joined by a bridge founded upon masts, and railed on each side, being two hundred feet long, to the 'Bear,' which was fitted in all points for the entertainment of the Danish lords and others. Between both these royal ships lay a hulk, which served for a kitchen to both. In the 'Elizabeth,' the great chamber, being part of the upper deck abaft the mainmast, contained a long table for my lord chamberlain and other of our English lords. The same deck before the mainmast had a table for the ladies. From whence, up a pair of stairs, there was a passage unto the 'Orelope,' where was a fair tent set up, lined and hanged, the inside with silks and cloths of gold; at the upper end whereof, under a rich cloth of state, sat the Kings, the Queen, and Prince at dinner. Some hour after they had dined, they took coach at Upnor Castle, on the shore towards Gravesend ; and, having gone some three-quarters of a mile, they made a stand upon a Windmill Hill, whence they might perfectly view all the whole navy. Then began the galleys next the bridge to discharge, and after them all the pinnaces and ships in order as they lay, to the number of 1,008 great shot. This thunder made such music in the King of Denmark's ears, as he told the King, if he had spent half his kingdom in a banquet, he could not have contented him so well ; and farther, that in requital he gave himself and his heart to do the King, as long as he lived, all friendly offices, both in word and deed. Whereto the King answered that never any man was to him so welcome as the King of Denmark, nor ever should any till he came again."

Early on Monday morning, the 11th, the royal party returned to Gravesend, where the port-reeve of the town and his brethren presented themselves to the King, and were graciously received. Meanwhile Christian IV. returned to his ship in the river to make ready for the reception of the English King and Queen, and as they ascended the " Admiral of Denmark," followed by a train of about fifty persons, the whole Danish fleet fired a mighty salute, which was answered by the two blockhouses of Tilbury and Gravesend ; and at the banquet, as each health was drunk, great volleys were discharged from the ships and forts.

About four o'clock in the afternoon, the King of Denmark exhibited to his royal relatives a beautiful and well-contrived firework. "It stood upon a lighter, being in form of a square conduit or cube, with four pillars answering the four corners. Upon the top of this cube stood a lion, with a chain in his hand, which fettered eight capital vices, that sat underneath upon the angles and sides of this cube or 'arc.' This firework very methodically, one part after another, continued burning and cracking for the space of three-quarters of an hour."

The tide now serving for going up the river, King James and his Consort, having taken a hearty and solemn farewell of their brother, embarked in the barge to the sound of another heavy salute, and returned to Greenwich, accompanied by the Prince.

Sir Robert Mansell was left with the "Vanguard" and the "Moon," to attend the departing monarch on his homeward way.

The Danish King had with him eight ships, and his own, the "Admiral of Denmark," the largest, was built very high and narrow, with the beakhead, stern, and her three galleries finely gilded, and the waist and half-deck adorned with arras and other rich ornaments. His Vice-admiral and best fighting ship, with a valuable rapier and hanger, he presented, on his departure, to his nephew, Prince Henry.

Henry Robarts, who probably had a place about Court, and saw much of the ceremonies and entertainments he pictures, described the visit of Christian IV. in a Tract, wherein he wrote : " The 'Admiral,' wherein his own person came, being a most huge ship, is esteemed of 1,500 tons ; which ship is so adorned with rich gold, and very excellent workmanship, as many thousands (upon report thereof) of purpose have gone to Gravesend, where she doth ride, to view her. Besides the beauty and richness of this great ship, she is appointed with most huge ordnance, men and victuals, fit for so kingly a presence. The rest, likewise, accordingly complete; all rich in ordnance, men, and ammunition. The kingly attendants of his person, and all others of his train, furnished in apparel very rich and most beautiful, every one in his estate and place; his council and chief men very decent, after their country fashion richly decked in silk, with gold and silver lace, jewels, and chains of rare estimation. His pages and guard of his person, in blue velvet laid with silver lace for their best suit; and one suit, for to exchange, of other silk; whitish coloured hats, with bands embroidered; most of them either white or blue stockings; his trumpeters in white satin doublets, blue velvet hose, trimmed with silk and silver lace, watchet (blue) cloaks guarded with sundry colours, and white hats with blue silk and gold bands embroidered; his common guard of soldiers with muskets furnished very rich, white fustian doublets, watchet hose with white and blue lace, loose cassocks (horsemen's great coats) large and fair (like footmen's coats), with white and blue lace, hats with bands suited like, and all his common soldiers in cassocks and hose of watchet colour; the master and his mates, gunners and chief officers, being very rich in their apparel; his trunks, and other provision for carriage, covered with red velvet, trimmed with blue silk and gold lace; his sumpter-cloths (horse-cloths), and coverings to cover his lading, of red velvet with blue silk and gold lace, all made after the English fashion. For the government of his followers of all sorts, according to his kingly pleasure, he ordained a marshal, who had under-marshals many, with great charge from his Majesty, that if any man of his company should be drunk, or otherwise to abuse himself in any manner towards Englishmen, or his own followers, to be punished sharply."

Sir John Harrington summed up the main characteristics of the festivities of the royal visit in the following letter, written from London to Secretary Barlow : " In compliance with your asking, now shall you accept my poor account of rich doings. I came here a day or two before the Danish King came, and from the day he did come till this hour, I have been well-nigh overwhelmed with carousal and sports of all kinds. The sports began each day in such manner and such sort, as well-nigh persuaded me of Mahomet's paradise. We had women, and indeed wine too, of such plenty, as would have astonished each beholder. Our feasts were magnificent, and the two royal guests did most lovingly embrace each other at table. I think the Dane hath strangely wrought on our good English nobles ; for those whom I could never get to taste good liquor, now follow the fashion, and wallow in beastly delights. The ladies abandon their sobriety, and are seen to roll about in intoxication. In good sooth, the parliament did kindly to provide his Majestie so seasonably with money, for there have been no lack of good living, shows, sights, and banquetings from morn to eve. One day a great feast was held, and after dinner the representation of Solomon, his temple, and the coming of the Queen of Sheba was made, or (as I may better say) was meant to have been made before their Majesties, by device of the Earl of Salisbury and others. But, alas ! as all earthly things do fail to poor mortals in enjoyment, so did prove our presentment thereof. The lady who did play the Queen's part did carry most precious

gifts to both their Majesties; but, forgetting the
steps arising to the canopy, overset her caskets
into his Danish Majesty's lap, and fell at his feet,
though, I think, it was rather in his face. Much was
the hurry and confusion; cloths and napkins were
at hand to make all clean. His Majesty then got
up, and would dance with the Queen of Sheba; but
he fell down and humbled himself before her, and
was carried to an inner chamber, and laid on a bed
of state, which was not a little defiled with the
presents of the Queen, which had been bestowed on
his garments—such as wine, cream, jelly, beverage,
cakes, spices, and other good matters. The entertainment and show went forward, and most of the
presenters went backward or fell down; wine
did so occupy their upper chambers. Now did
appear, in rich dress, Hope, Faith, and Charity.
Hope did essay to speak, but wine rendered her
endeavours so feeble that she withdrew, and hoped
the King would excuse her brevity. Faith was
then all alone, for I am certain she was not joined
to good works, and left the Court in a staggering
condition. Charity came to the King's feet, and
seemed to cover the multitude of sins her sisters
had committed; in some sort she made obeiance,
and brought gifts, but said she would return home
again, as there was no gift which Heaven had not
already given his Majesty. She then returned to
Hope and Faith, who were both sick . . . in the
lower hall. Next came Victory, in bright armour,
and presented a rich sword to the King, who did not
accept it, but put it by his hand; and by a strange
medley of versification, did endeavour to make suit
to the King. But Victory did not triumph long;
for, after much lamentable utterance, she was led

then Rector of Halstead in Suffolk—and, appointing him one of his chaplains, delighted in hearing him preach. Dr. Birch wrote : " The Prince being known to be extremely curious with regard to ships, Mr. Pett, who was in his service, as well as one of the King's shipwrights, made a model of a ship for his Highness, which being adorned with carving and painting, and placed in a frame, arched, covered, and curtained with crimson taffety, was, on the 10th of November, presented to the Lord Admiral at his lodging at Whitehall. His lordship ordered him to carry it to Richmond, which was done the next day ; and on Wednesday morning, the 12th, Mr. Pett having acquainted Sir David Murray with his business, who informed the Prince of it, order was given to have the model brought and placed in a private room in the long gallery, where his Highness determined to see it. But the Lord Admiral, unknown to Mr. Pett, and with a view to do him service, had already informed the King of this model, and prevailed upon him to take a journey from Whitehall to Richmond, on purpose to view it ; which he did about three of the clock of the afternoon of the same day."

The Court spent the latter part of the year between Hampton Court and Whitehall. On Christmas Day the King heard the customary discourse from Bishop Andrewes, and on the same day the Earl of Pembroke, having in mind the restless movements of his Sovereign, wrote from Whitehall to the Earl of Shrewsbury : " These holidays have brought us some rest, as welcome as to schoolboys, for till Christmas-eve we have been in perpetual motion ; and as soon as Twelve Tide is past, we shall begin our ' voyage ' again, I am afraid."

1608. In the first month of 1608—when the river and outside world were lying bound in the hard grip of an Arctic frost—the Court at Whitehall was absorbed in a course of gay festivities. On the Sunday evening after Twelfth Night, the Queen presented Ben Jonson's "Masque of Beauty." In this Volturnus, the Wind, speaks to the river Thamesis, " that lay along between the shores leaning upon his urn that flow'd with water, and crowned with flowers ; with a blue cloth-of-silver robe about him ; and personated by Master Thomas Giles, who made the dances."

VOLTURNUS—" Rise, aged Thames, and by the hand
　　　　　　Receive these Nymphs within the land.
　　　　　　And in those curious squares and rounds,
　　　　　　Wherewith thou flow'st betwixt the grounds
　　　　　　Of fruitful Kent, and Essex fair,
　　　　　　That lends the garlands for thy hair,
　　　　　　Instruct their silver feet to tread,
　　　　　　Whilst we again to sea are fled."

with which the Wind departs, and the River receives the Nymphs into the land by couples and fours, their Cupids coming before them.

On Shrove Tuesday the marriage was solemnised of Viscount Haddington and Lady Elizabeth Ratcliffe, daughter of the Earl of Sussex ; the festivities concluding at night with a nuptial masque, by Ben Jonson and Inigo Jones, called " The Hue and Cry after Cupid."

The King heard a sermon in the chapel from Bishop Andrewes on Easter-day, and at this season dubbed a batch of knights. Three were made on Whitsunday at Greenwich, when he listened to another of the Bishop's sermons.

On May 6th, Robert, Earl of Salisbury, was made

Lord Treasurer, and the King and Queen deferred their departure for Greenwich, in order to attend, with the Prince and Court, a sumptuous banquet in the city house of the Earl, and witness the passing of the pompous procession of George, Earl of Dunbar, Lord High Treasurer of Scotland, and Philip, Earl of Montgomery, on their way to Windsor for investiture with the Garter. The two Earls were invested at the Castle on the 20th, at the time Dr. George Abbott, Dean of Winchester, was preaching the funeral sermon of Edward Sackville, Earl of Dorset, in Westminster Abbey.

Thomas Overbury was knighted at Greenwich on June 19th, and three weeks afterwards the bells of St. Margaret's were rung when the King came to Whitehall. He set out for Windsor a few days later, leaving the Queen at Somerset House. In July, as large quantities of grain had arrived and relieved the pressing scarcity in the country, it was arranged that they should meet at Theobalds and set out on a progress. On the 30th the Venetian Ambassador wrote in a despatch : " The Court began its progress to-day. Hitherto it has lain at Theobalds, whence the King made a run to Greenwich, for no other reason than to see the silk manufactory which he is trying to introduce into England. He is so charmed with the industry that he has brought over a number of workmen from France. They promise excellent results, and he has set up all the plant, and expects in a short time to manufacture here as much as is at present imported." The progress terminated at Windsor on August 29th, when the King knighted three gentlemen, and afterwards went on to Hampton Court.

George Justinianus, the retiring Venetian Ambassador, was knighted at Whitehall, on November 1st ; and on the anniversary of Gunpowder Plot the King attended a service in the Chapel, when Dr. John King, Dean of Christ Church, Oxford, preached. On the 28th, Marc Antonio Correr, the new Ambassador from Venice, wrote in a despatch, that on the Sunday, after mass, his predecessor and train, returning home, left London in the royal barges for Gravesend.

After other wanderings, the King was greeted by the bells of St. Margaret's, on December 20th, when he returned to Whitehall for the Christmas festivities, which were of so quiet a character that the Court fell back on the mild excitement of the arrival of a ship in the river from Syria, with a cargo largely composed of indigo and silk, said to be worth two hundred thousand crowns.

1609. On February 2nd, 1609, the Queen and her ladies performed the " Masque of Queens," written and devised by Ben Jonson and Inigo Jones. Later the King went to his Kentish palace, and on March 19th, the Venetian Ambassador wrote : " Fine cold weather since the middle of February has diminished deaths from Plague by more than half. All the same two cases have occurred at Greenwich. This has caused the King to go to Hampton Court." Writing again in May he said : " The King has caused a revised edition of his book to be printed. It will appear shortly. His Majesty, freed from this care, set out yesterday for Greenwich. The King began his stag hunts recently. They had been suspended during the winter. He is so keen about it that on the 16th of this month he and the Prince— worn out by the gallop, in which a number of horses died, one under the Prince himself—were forced to sleep at a village cottage. The Queen and the Court were in great anxiety that night, for a gentleman sent by the King to her Majesty, stopped halfway, as he was tired like the others. He is now paying the penalty in prison. Last Monday the King, Prince, and some of the principal members of the Council went to see a ship of 1,500 tons, which is being built in his Highness' name, eight miles away (at Deptford)."

On Easter Sunday Bishop Andrewes preached before the King at Whitehall; and, on May 10th, a Commission was issued under the Great Seal for knighting Prince Henry.

The Venetian Ambassador wrote in a despatch on June 18th: " Last Tuesday, the last feast of Pentecost, the King bade me to dinner at Greenwich. His Majesty has shewn me such honour, both in the invitation, in sending to my house to fetch me, in word, and in every other way that I could not record it without blushing. He summoned to attend him that day all the members of the Council, by whom he was served in high state. The King pledged me to the health of your Serenity and the preservation of the Republic. I invited the Prince to join in the toast and he accepted gladly, and both the King and he stood up till the pledge was drunk. By the Queen, too, with whom I went to see the bear-and-bull baiting, I was highly honoured."

On July 6th, the bells of St. Margaret's welcomed James to Whitehall, where he knighted four gentlemen; and then, after a visit to Theobalds, went to Windsor on the 22nd. The Queen came to the Castle soon after, and early in August the royal couple went on a progress towards Salisbury.

The King was hunting all day at Windsor on September 1st, and killed a stag with his own hand. A few days later we find him with the Queen at Hampton Court, and on the 10th, the Venetian Ambassador wrote : " Yesterday I went to Richmond to visit the Duke of York, and to Kew to kiss the Princess's hand, as I know his Majesty likes such attentions. I found their Highnesses in excellent health, and with increased beauty and stature. The Duke, in particular, who is, in manner, far in advance of his age, replied by saying that he hoped to visit me some day in Venice, when he came to present himself in person to the Doge." Between the intervals of the King's activities in the hunt, he received at Hampton Court the Spanish and Venetian Ambassadors, and the Florentine Envoy ; and towards the end of the month he gave public audience to the Tuscan Ambassador before leaving for Theobalds.

In October the Court scattered to escape the Plague, which had spread to many villages around London. Cases occurred at Hampton Court, and two of the Queen's grooms of the Wardrobe died of it. The royal household at Royston was also affected. By the end of the month, however, the violence of the pestilence had abated in London, and this brought the King and Queen to Whitehall on the 30th.

Bishop Andrewes preached in the chapel on the anniversary of Gunpowder Plot, and about the middle of November the Venetian ambassador wrote : " His Majesty is troubled with pain in a foot. The doctors say it is gout, but do not dare to tell him so, as he does not like to hear of it. This has kept him here longer than he intended. It is said that he means to leave on Monday next for Royston. The Plague has again broken out at Court, and has carried off two pastry-cooks, to the great alarm of everyone. On this account the Queen is thinking of going to Hampton Court. But as the number of deaths has fallen this week, she will not change her plans unless some further misfortune occurs."

The Ambassador was again writing on December 3rd : " The Queen intends to retire to Greenwich on Monday, until the King's return, in order that the palace (Whitehall) may be freshened up. To-day when I went to take leave of the Queen she told me that the gout has again attacked the King, and he is at present more occupied in study than the chase."

The Court gathered at Whitehall for the close of the year, and on Christmas day (Monday) Bishop Andrewes preached in the chapel.

1610. On Saturday, January 6th, 1610, the King, at Whitehall, knighted one gentleman; and in the evening—it being Twelfth Night—Prince Henry met the challenge he had issued, in the character of " Mœliades," to a great feat of arms. The performance was exhibited in the presence of the King and Queen, the Spanish and Venetian Ambassadors, and Peers and Great Ladies, together with a crowd of inferior rank. The words of Dr. Birch well describe the scene : " The assembly was held in the great banqueting-house, at the upper end of which was placed the King's chair, and on the right of it a magnificent pavilion for the Prince and his companions, whence they descended into the middle of the room. There his Highness maintained the barriers against all adventurers, being assisted only by the Duke of Lennox, the Earls of

Arundel and Southampton, the Lord Hay, Sir Thomas Somerset, and Sir Richard Preston, the Prince's instructor in arms, soon after created Lord Dingwall, and at last Earl of Desmond. Against these challengers came six and fifty defendants, consisting of Earls, Barons, Knights, and Esquires, who in the lower end of the room had erected a very commodious apartment, where themselves remained in private with their train, which was so great that it was not imagined that half the number could have been concealed there. Hence they issued in proper order and marched into the middle of the room, where their Majesties sat with the Ambassadors to see the barriers, with the several shows and devices of each combatant. Every challenger fought with eight several defendants, two combats at two different weapons, push of pike and single sword. The Prince himself gave and received thirty-two pushes of pike and about three hundred and sixty strokes of swords, and performed his part very well and gracefully, and to the admiration of all spectators, though not then full sixteen years of age. These feats of arms, with their triumphant shows, began before ten at night, and continued till three the next morning, being Sunday." The rhymical speeches at Prince Henry's barriers were composed by Ben Jonson.

On the 23rd, John Chamberlain, in a letter to his friend, Sir Dudley Carleton, wrote : " There was a quarrel hatching at Greenwich 'twixt Sir Edward Herbert and one Boghnar, a Scot gentleman, Usher to the Queen, about a ribbon or favour taken, as it were, by force from Mrs. Middlemore. But the matter was timely taken up, and compounded by the Council."

On February 1st, the bells of St. Margaret's were ringing for the King's return to Whitehall, and three days later, Francesco Contarini, a Venetian Ambassador-Extraordinary, just arrived in London, wrote in a despatch to the Doge and Senate: "Last Saturday, I, Contarini, arrived at Court, thus closing, by God's grace, this part of a long and troublesome journey, whose details may be imagined without any description by me. The day before I had been met at Deptford by Signor Pietro Loredano and Signor Vincenzo Correr, son of the illustrious ambassador, accompanied by Secretary Surian. There, too, came Sir Lewis Lewkenor, Receiver of Ambassadors, and, as he is styled in these parts, Master of the Ceremonies. He informed me that he was sent on purpose to honour me, and that he had brought with him the royal carriages. In these I made my entry into London."

John Beaulieu, in a letter on the 15th, to William Trumbull, Resident at Brussels, wrote: "Upon Sunday, Monsieur de la Boderie, and the two Ambassadors of Venice, extraordinary and ordinary, were solemnly and magnificently feasted at Whitehall by the King, where there passed good mirth and plenty of healths between his Majesty and them. At the same table the Prince did sit with them. Upon Tuesday those of Saxony had the like entertainment."

The special Venetian Ambassador left England early in March, and a few days later the ordinary Ambassador Correr, wrote: "On Sunday last Contarini left by the Flanders route. He received in a present many goblets of silver gilt, and was escorted by the royal barges, and received other unusual honours. The French Ambassador accompanied him down to the water, and I some way down the Thames."

The Court resided at Whitehall in April, and on the 15th, the Venetian Ambassador wrote in a gossipy despatch : " All this week the King—as bearing the title of King of France—has touched for scrofula. To-day—Maunday Thursday, old style —the King received communion in his chapel. Afterwards he and the Prince, and the Prince of Brunswick, went down to dine at Greenwich, where the Queen is for change of air, as she has not been quite well." The Ambassador was writing again on May 12th : " Her Majesty is in retreat at Greenwich ; she is extremely fond of the air of that place, and will stay there till the King's return, which will be about twenty-five days hence."

On Whitsunday, the 27th, the King, at Whitehall, heard Bishop Andrewes preach ; and on the following Wednesday, Prince Henry, in preparation for his creation as Prince of Wales, started about twelve o'clock noon, from St. James's, attended by various young nobles and a train of servants, and rode to Richmond, where he supped and reposed himself for the night. Next day the Lord Mayor of London, the Aldermen, and fifty-four members of the City Companies, in barges with distinguishing ensigns, banners, and streamers, passed up the river to Chelsea, where, from nine in the morning, they awaited the prince's coming. It was said on this occasion the aquatic procession of the Lord Mayor. literally drummed the speaker out of the House of Commons : " At nine o'clock in the morning he came to wait upon the Prince Henry at Whitehall ; and as he passed up the Thames, the company was so small, and the drums and fifes so loud, as Mr. Speaker thought not fit to proceed in business, but to arise and depart."

Meanwhile, the Prince taking water at Richmond about nine o'clock in the morning, attended by some barges with his followers and such noblemen and others as accompanied him the day before, was presently prevented from proceeding by the low ebb of the tide. A banquet of sweetmeats and other hurriedly obtained delicacies was spread in an arbour by the water-side at Barn Elms, and here, at about eleven o'clock, the Prince was entertained.

After an extended wait another start was made, and passing softly down the stream, he was encountered by divers Lords, who had come to meet him on the way. Boats and barges crowded around, and every point of vantage along the shores was covered with enthusiastic people. Chelsea was reached at about four o'clock in the afternoon, and here speeches were delivered by one representing Neptune upon a dolphin, and by another as a sea-goddess upon a whale. The procession then re-started with the barges of the City Companies first, and that of the Lord Mayor, having on either side the two sea-monsters, immediately preceding the royal barge. When they came within sight of Whitehall, the craft of the City Companies kept along the City side and the Prince's procession on the Lambeth side, and so a direct course was steered, in view of an enormous concourse of people on land and water, for the Stairs at Whitehall.

The Prince, having taken leave of the Lord Mayor and Aldermen, landed amidst a salute of ordnance, and was received by the Officers of the King's household. At the gate were the Knight Marshal and Serjeant Porter ; in the Hall, the Treasurer

and Comptroller of the Household; in the Great
Chamber the Captain of the Guards; and in the
Presence Chamber the Lord Chamberlain, who
finally conducted him to the Privy Chamber, where
he was met and welcomed by the King and Queen.

A Tract was printed on this occasion, entitled:
" London's Love of the Royal Prince Henrie, meeting
him on the River of Thames, at his returne from
Richmonde, with a worthie fleete of her citizens,
on Thursday, the last of May, 1610. With a briefe
reporte of the water-fight and fire-workes." After
recalling previous creations of Princes of Wales,
the treatise continued : " But now our royal Henry
coming to be the twelfth Prince in this great dignity,
and London's Chief Magistrate the Lord Mayor
(Sir Thomas Cambell) with his worthy Brethren
the Aldermen, having very short and sudden intelligence thereof ; after some small consultation,
understanding that the Prince was to come from
Richmond by water, they determined to meet him
in such good manner as the brevity of the time would
then permit them. Wherefore, upon Thursday,
being the last day of May, about eight of the clock
in the morning, all the Worshipful Companies of
the City were ready in the barges upon the water,
with their streamers and ensigns gloriously displayed, drums, trumpets, fifes, and other musics
attending on them, to await the Lord Mayor and
Aldermen's coming. No sooner had his Honour
and the rest taken barge, but on they rowed, with
such a cheerful noise of harmony, and so goodly
a show in order and equipage as made the beholders
and hearers not meanly delighted ; besides a
peal of ordnance that welcomed them as they
entered on the water."

Two persons were richly habited, one to personate Corinea, the genius of Cornwall, the other Amphion, the Father of Harmony or Music, the genius of Wales. " Let if suffice then, that thus was this goodly fleet of citizens accompanied, and ushered the way so far as Chelsea; where, hovering on the water until the Prince came, all pleasures that the time's interim could afford were plentifully inter-coursed, and no disorder, or breach of array in the whole navy. Upon the Prince's near approach way was made for his best and aptest entertainment, which by multitude of boats and barges (of no use but only for desire of sight) was much impeached for a while, till order being taken for the contrary, the Prince's barge accosted the Lord Mayor's, where duty entertaining on the one side, and princely grace most affably accepting on the other; Corinea mounted on her whale presented herself to his Highness." This allegorical figure, with a coronet of pearls and cockle-shells on her head, saluted the Prince, and delivered a complimentary speech; after which they set on towards Whitehall in so soft, mild, and gentle a pace as the very Thames appeared proud of this gallant burden, swelling her breast to bear them with pomp and majesty; and not one wrinkle appeared in her brow, but as plain and even as the smootheth ivory."

The King and Queen, with the young Duke of York, stood in the Privy gallery window to view the approaching pageant.

" Being come near Whitehall, the barges (according to their quality and degree in order and dignity) divided themselves on either side, to make a spacious passage for the Prince and his train between them even until they came near to the Court bridge, the

L

Lord Mayor's barge being then the foremost and nearest." The Prince preparing to land, Amphion, on his dolphin, with a wreath of sea-shells on his head, and his harp hanging before him, made a speech, and at its conclusion " off went the chambers, and such a triumphal noise of drums and trumpets as made the very air to echo ; which done, they returned back to London again, wherewith we conclude this solemn day's triumph."

On Sunday, June 3rd, the King made twenty-five Knights of the Bath ; and, on the following day, at about half-past ten in the morning, the King, Prince, and all the nobility went by water from the Privy Stairs at Whitehall, and landing at the " Queen's bridge " at Westminster, proceeded to the palace for the creation ceremony of the Prince of Wales. Dr. Birch wrote : " The place provided for this solemnity was within the great white chamber in the palace of Westminster, where both the houses of Parliament being for that time assembled, together with the Lord Mayor and Aldermen, and Ambassadors of Spain, Venice, and the States General, the King entertaining in his royal robes, and with his crown upon his head, first took his place of state, his train being supported by the Lord Viscount Cranborne, and the Lord Burghley, son of the Earl of Exeter. After a good space of time, the Prince entered at the lower end of the great chamber, having a fur coat of purple velvet, close girt. The order of his entrance was this : the trumpets sounding, in the first place came the Earls of Worcester and Suffolk, the former Lord Chamberlain, the other Earl Marshal. In the next place followed the twenty-five Knights of the Bath, all in their robes of purple satin. Next these followed Garter King-at-Arms, bearing the letters-patent ; the Earl of Sussex, the Prince's robes of purple velvet ; the Earl of Huntingdon the train ; the Earl of Cumberland the sword ; the Earl of Rutland the ring ; the Earl of Derby, the rod of gold ; and the Earl of Shrewsbury the cap and crown. The Earls of Nottingham and Northampton supported the Prince, who, presenting himself before the King with very submissive reverence, kneeled upon the uppermost step leading to the state, while his patent was read by the Earl of Salisbury, till it came to the putting on of his robes, sword, and the rest, by the Lords who carried them ; but the crown, rod, ring, and patent were delivered to him by the King's own hands. This being done, and the Prince with a low reverence offering to depart, the King stept to him, and took him by the hand, and kissed him. His Highness then took his place on the left hand of his Majesty, sitting there in his royal robes, with the crown upon his head, the rod in one hand, and the patent in the other, while a Public Act was read, testifying his having been declared Prince of Great Britain and Wales. After this they returned down through Westminster Hall, to the palace bridge in this manner ; first the Masters of the Chancery, the King's Council, etc. ; then the Officers-at-Arms ; then the Knights of the Bath ; after them the Judges ; who were followed by the whole Parliament, Barons, Viscounts, Earls, and Marquises, having their coronets on their heads ; Norrey and Clarencieux going next before the Lord Treasurer and the Lord Chamberlain, and Garter-King-at-Arms next before the sword. Thus they proceeded to the King's stairs, where all took water in several barges ; the Heralds and trumpets sounding all the way, going in the row-barge next before the Knights, and landed at Whitehall bridge, where the officers of arms, the Knights of the Bath, and the Lords, being first landed, attended the King; and when his Majesty and the Prince were landed, they went all before him into the hall, and so into the great chamber, whence the Prince came to dinner in the great hall. His Majesty dined privately in his Privy Chamber; but his Highness was served in such state that greater could not have been done to the King himself. The table, being very long, was served with two messes of meat; and he who sat nearest the Prince, was at the full distance of half the board from him. The Earl of Pembroke performed the office of sewer; the Earl of Southampton was carver; the Earl of Montgomery, cupbearer; and the Lord Walden, eldest son of the Earl of Suffolk, brought the glass with water. The noblemen, who sat at this table, all in their robes as well as the Prince, were the Marquis of Winchester, the Earls of Salisbury, Northampton, Nottingham, Shrewsbury, Derby, Cumberland, Huntingdon, and Sussex. At a long side-board dined all the Knights of the Bath, and no other person. During the whole time of dinner, the hall resounded with all kinds of exquisite music."

On Tuesday a magnificent masque, devised and written by Inigo Jones and Samuel Daniel, one of the Queen's grooms of the Privy Chamber, and entitled "Tethys Festival, or The Queen's Wake," was performed. Dr. Birch wrote of this: " In the first act came in first the young Duke of York, between two great sea-slaves, the chiefest of Neptune's servants, attended upon by twelve little ladies, all daughters of Earls or Barons. One of

merchants waxing to be somewhat distressed (by reason that the castle likewise often played upon them), two men-of-war, happening then to be near, made in to help and relieve their hard detriment. And now the fight grew on all sides to be fierce indeed, the castle assisting the pirate very hotly, and the others withstanding bravely and courageously; divers men appearing on either side to be slain and hurled over into the sea, as in such adventures it often comes to pass, where such sharp assaults are used indeed. In conclusion, the merchants and men-of-war, after a long and well-fought skirmish, proved too strong for the pirate, they spoiled both him, and blew up the castle, ending the whole battery with very rare and admirable fireworks, as also a worthy peal of chambers." During all these festivities the Tower ordnance saluted for several hours, and the bells of St. Margaret's, Westminster, and other churches, were kept constantly ringing.

St. Margaret's bells were again ringing, on the 9th, when the King and Queen came back together to Whitehall, an event the Venetian Ambassador said " rarely happens."

On June 23rd, the Ambassador wrote : " Their Majesties have retired to Greenwich. The King will not go far during the whole coming month, as he is occupied with Parliament. The Prince, too, will go to Greenwich in a couple of days. On July 30th they will set out on their progress, which this year is to be in Northamptonshire."

James went to Oatlands on July 4th, and four days later the bells of St. Margaret's were ringing for his arrival at Whitehall.

In the course of the Queen's progress in August,

she visited Bisham Abbey, the seat of Sir Edward
Hoby ; and at the end of the month, the Venetian
Ambassador visited the Princess Elizabeth at Kew,
and the Duke of York at Richmond.

The King and Queen were at Hampton Court in
September; and, on October 7th, the Venetian
Ambassador was writing the following peep into
the way of life of the monarch : " For many days
past his Majesty has been suffering from violent
relaxation of the bowels, brought on by the fruit
he eats (grapes). He did not pay attention to it,
but on Tuesday, at Greenwich, where he had gone
to act as god-father to a son of the Earl of Argyll,
he was sick and had to go to bed, and to send to
London and Cambridge for doctors, a thing he had
never done in the whole course of his life, as he
himself assured me recently at Woodstock. At
the baptism the Prince took the King's place, the
second god-father was the Earl of Salisbury, and
god-mother the Marchioness of Winchester, niece
of the Earl of Salisbury on his brother's side. Everyone tries to win Lord Salisbury's favour, as his
authority and reputation are without parallel in
this kingdom. The moment the Queen heard of
the King's indisposition, she left Hampton Court
for Greenwich, and finding him much better they
returned the same day to Hampton Court, which
the Court loves for its size, and for its excellent air.
The King will soon leave again for his usual chase
at Royston, to which he attributes so much of his
health, apart from the great pleasure he takes
therein."

In the course of November, Prince Christian of
Anhalt was the guest of the King, and it was
said : " He surveyed the City of London with great

pleasure and admiration, and beheld the pleasant triumphs upon the water, and within the city, which at this time were extraordinary in honour of the Lord Mayor and citizens."

On December 2nd, the Venetian Ambassador wrote another of his illuminating glimpses : " All the royal family left London on Saturday last ; but I hear the Queen does not like the air of Greenwich at this season, and will come back (to London) soon. . . . Last week there died at Greenwich a young lady of the Lady Drummond, who is in the highest favour, and alone has free access to the Queen. There was a great suspicion that the cause was the plague. Five days later one of her companions also died. On this account the Queen was much troubled, and as soon as the danger was manifest she left Greenwich for London. The King received the news at Royston from one who had been sent for other reasons and was not well informed, and for some hours he was in deep grief, which he bore very ill until letters arrived from Lord Salisbury, who had to delay their despatch for a while, as he had set out to meet the Queen. Mercifully the rest of the Court is well, and the plague has so decreased that it no longer gives cause for anxiety."

The King returned from Royston to Whitehall on December 19th, and on Christmas day—Tuesday— he heard Bishop Andrewes preach in the chapel.

1611. The night of New Year's day, 1611, saw the Palace of Whitehall brilliant with light and gay company. A masque, entitled " Oberon, or the Fairy Prince," composed by Ben Jonson, and the machinery and dresses devised by Inigo Jones, was performed in the Banqueting House, under the personal direction of the Prince of Wales ; assisted by two Earls, three Barons, five Knights, and two Esquires.

During the next few days the King knighted five gentlemen ; and, on the 10th, he created two more knights at Hampton Court.

The French Ambassador, M. de la Verdyne, Marshal of France and Governor of Maine, and his train came to Lambeth on January 16th, and were lodged in the Archbishop's palace, which, by the King's direction, was royally furnished for the purpose. The Ambassador had his audience on Sunday, the 20th ; and a week later the King swore to the new League made between the two kingdoms.

On the 21st the Venetian Ambassador wrote : " Two days ago the King went to Hampton Court to spend this time in sport ; he will not fail to return to receive and dismiss the Marshal, and will then proceed to Royston."

On February 3rd and 4th the King was at White-hall, and on the latter day the Venetian Ambassador wrote : " The King wishes to have the Marshal with him at Hampton Court, and thither he has gone for a couple of days " ; and, on March 16th : " The Queen left last Tuesday for Greenwich ; she will stay there till the King's return, which will not be till Holy Week. Meantime the Court is quite empty." On Easter day the 24th, the King heard Bishop Andrewes preach at Whitehall, and on the morrow he created Sir Robert Carr, the rising favourite, Viscount Rochester.

The Venetian Ambassador wrote on April 7th : " The King has gone back to Theobalds, and on Monday will be followed by the Prince. The

Queen has gone to Greenwich, and will stay there three weeks." On the 27th the bells of St. Margaret's were ringing when the King and Queen removed from Whitehall to Greenwich.

The King went to Whitehall on May 4th to settle some matter connected with the Mint, and on the occasion Viscount Fenton wrote from Greenwich to Lord Salisbury : " The King will be at Whitehall at eleven o'clock instead of two. The parties are to be there in time, as the King is unpleasant when he must attend the coming of others."

On the first Sunday in May, the Venetian Ambassadors—Antonio Foscarini and Marc Antonio Correr —were received in audience at Greenwich, and in a later despatch from London to their government they wrote : " Last Sunday week on the orders of the King, the Viscount Cranborne, son of the Earl of Salisbury, Thomas Howard, son of the Great Chamberlain, General Cecil, Sir Henry Wotton, and various other gentlemen of quality, visited this house. We entered the royal carriages, which took us down to the river Thames, where we found the royal barges, which took us to Greenwich, five miles off, where the King lay with a numerous court, crowded with the greatest personages in the Kingdom. . . . We also sought audience of the Queen, and when the date was fixed she sent her barges for us and received us at Greenwich surrounded by a number of ladies. We made our compliments and she caused us to be seated and discoursed with us for three-quarters of an hour. We returned to London in the same barges, and went to wait on the Prince at his palace."

Sir Henry Wotton wrote to Sir Arthur Throgmorton on the occasion of the reception of the

Venetian Ambassadors : " On Sunday last the new Venetian Ambassador had his first audience at Greenwich ; at which time the old took his leave, and received from the King three honours, an addition of the English lion to his coat-armour, knighthood, and the sword with the furniture from the King's side, wherewith he had knighted him ; which last, being more than was done to any of his predecessors, and done to him who had deserved less than any, is enough to prove that wise kings know how to do graces and hide affections ; so mystical things are Courts."

The King was at Hampton Court on the 8th, and four days later—Whitsunday—he heard Bishop Andrewes preach at Windsor.   On the 13th, Charles, Duke of York, the Earl of Arundel, and Viscount Rochester were made Knights of the Garter at the castle ; and on the same date Sir Robert Stewart was writing and begging Lord Salisbury to consider his pressing necessities, as his creditors had obliged him to fly to the Court at Greenwich for sanctuary from imprisonment. His debts amounted to a round sum, but he hoped the King would pay them, as he had neither liberty nor means for searching out new suits.

The two Ambassadors of Venice wrote on the 25th, that on the previous Sunday, after visiting the Princess Elizabeth at Kew, they were entertained by the King at Hampton Court.

In another despatch of June 9th, the retiring Ambassador, Correr, made his last remarks on Court life : " After a very long drought, the like of which has never been known before in this kingdom, which threatened a famine and a notable rise in the price of bread, it has pleased God to send a little rain ;

it was welcomed, but as the season is far advanced the benefit to the country is but slight. The King, who had stopped his progress and dismissed M. de Vitry, as he thought that in such a burnt-up land he could not journey with all his Court, save to the great damage of his subjects, has now changed his mind, and will set out towards Salisbury. Both he and the Queen are at Greenwich."

Correr left London late on a Thursday, so that he might embark at Gravesend the next morning with a fair tide. The wind, however, arose, and he was detained two days in the river.

On July 6th, the King granted an audience at Greenwich to the Envoy of the King of Morocco.

The Court moved to Hampton Court later in the month, and on the 25th, the Queen granted an audience to the new Venetian Ambassador.

The next day Prince Henry and Prince Otto of Hesse rode from Richmond to Hampton Court and hunted in the park. Early in August the Venetian Ambassador wrote : " At nine o'clock on Saturday morning I was at Richmond, at the hour appointed by the Prince, of whom I had sought audience the day before. I had sought the same of the Princess, who lives at Kew, and she granted it to me after ten o'clock on the same morning." Towards the end of the month the Court was at Oatlands, and the Earl of Northampton informed Lord Salisbury that search was to be made in the neighbourhood for a suspicious man who was practising to shoot the King.

On September 15th, the Venetian Ambassador wrote : " The Queen is at Oatlands, where the King will join her on Saturday. On Sunday they will go to Hampton Court, where the Prince is, and on Monday they will move to Theobalds, where his Majesty will receive all Ambassadors." At Hampton Court, on Sunday the 29th, William, Earl of Pembroke, was sworn a Privy Councillor.

The Queen was at this time exhibiting symptoms of some internal complaint, and on October 5th, Dr. Theodore de Mayerne wrote in a letter from Hampton Court to Lord Salisbury : " The Queen's general health good, and her local affection improving. Wishes to stay with her till she is well."

The King knighted six gentlemen at Whitehall on November 10th, and later in the month, whilst the Queen was at Greenwich, he was hunting at Newmarket. On the 20th the Venetian Ambassador wrote in a despatch : "The Savoyard Ambassador has delayed a day longer at Gravesend. The royal barges were sent to meet him, and on his arrival, which will be late, he will find the royal carriages waiting to take him to the lodging destined for his use."

The Venetian Ambassador had an audience of the Queen at Greenwich, on a Saturday in December, when she kept him a long time in conversation.

1612. On January 29th, 1612, the Earl of Dunbar, Lord High Treasurer of Scotland, died at Whitehall, just when he was on the point of magnificently solemnizing the marriage of his daughter with Lord Walden.

The bells of St. Margaret's welcomed the King and Queen, on February 15th, coming to Whitehall from Royston on the way to Greenwich. James then went on to Theobalds, and two days later journeyed again to Greenwich, and after dining with his Consort, spent the night at Whitehall. Bishop Andrewes preached in the chapel on Easter Sunday, and, on April 26th, the King

stood there as godfather at the baptism of
James, eldest son of Lord D'Aubigny. The
Venetian Ambassador wrote on May 4th:
" On Sunday the French Ambassador goes down to
Gravesend to meet (the Duc) de Bouillon, who,
they say, will be in London on Monday."

Early in the summer Count Hanau came to
England as Ambassador from the Elector Palatine,
to treat of a match with the Princess Elizabeth.
The Prince of Wales warmly supported the project,
and treated the Count with marked respect. Dr.
Birch wrote : " After the departure of the Count,
as well as of the Duke of Bouillon, from England,
which was in the beginning of June, the Prince went
to Richmond, where he continued till the progress.
Here the river of Thames, which ran close by his
house, invited him now and then in an evening to
learn to swim. This practice was indeed objected
to by several, who thought it dangerous after
supper with a full stomach ; and Dr. Theodore
Mayerne declared himself afterwards of the same
opinion ; and that this custom of the Prince stopped
the bleeding at his nose, and occasioned the fever
that proved so fatal to him. But he could not be
prevailed on to discontinue the practice, while he
stayed at Richmond ; where he took likewise great
delight in walking by the side of the Thames in
moonlight, to hear the sound and echo of the
trumpets ; both the situation and season exposing
him too much to the evening dews."

When the French Ambassador came to take his
leave, he found the Prince exercising with a lance,
and to his question if he had any commands for
France, answered, " Tell your master how you left
me engaged."

John Chamberlain wrote to Sir Dudley Carleton, on July 9th : " Zuniga, the Spanish Ambassador, has had his first audience, and the King is coming from Windsor to Whitehall to give him a second. His chief errand is to acquit himself of accusations about the Gunpowder treason laid against him by the late Lord Treasurer (Lord Salisbury), whom he would have accused of ' some unwarrantable practices ' had he been living."

Four days later the Venetian Ambassador wrote in a despatch : " The Marquis de Flores Davila, Ambassador Extraordinary of Spain, arrived on Tuesday. He was met at Dover in the King's name by the Master of the Ceremonies and two royal carriages. Twenty miles out of London the Earl of Dorset met him with the royal barges. . . . On Sunday he will have his first audience at Hampton Court, where the King arrives on Saturday."

Early in August the Dutch Ambassadors left London, but were detained for several days at Gravesend by head winds.

On Thursday, September 3rd, the King, drawing near the end of his progress, arrived at Bisham Abbey and passed the night with Sir Edward Hoby, thence returning to Windsor and Whitehall.

James was at Hampton Court in October, and the remains of his mother, Mary, Queen of Scots, were removed in great state from Peterborough Cathedral, and interred on the 8th, in Westminster Abbey.

On Tuesday, the 13th, the Prince of Wales was seized with a violent attack of diarrhœa, but slightly recovering, he was removed on Thursday from Richmond to St. James's, in readiness to receive the Elector Palatine, who was expected in a day or two.

The Elector embarked at the Hague on Thursday, the 15th, and after a prosperous passage entered the Thames, escorted by three Dutch warships and eight smaller vessels. Landing at Gravesend about ten o'clock on Friday evening, he was at the moment welcomed by Lord Hay, attended by Sir Lewis Lewkenor, Master of the Ceremonies. Later the Elector received a second reception from the Duke of Lennox and a large company of courtiers, who had gone in the royal barges to meet him.

After a day's rest at Gravesend, the Duke conducted the young Prince, on Sunday morning, to his barge, and, accompanied by about one hundred and fifty boats of various kinds, was rowed towards London. As the procession approached the capital, the throng on the river became very dense; two hundred guns thundered from the Tower, and the shipping joined in the salute with their smaller artillery. This, added to the noise of trumpets, drums, and other warlike music, and the cheers of the huge multitude, made up a scene of vast hubbub and confusion.

Arrived at the Water Gate, Whitehall, at about five o'clock, the Elector was met by the Duke of York, attended by the Earls of Shrewsbury, Sussex, Southampton, Worcester, and others, and conducted through the Hall, and along the Terrace to the great new Banqueting House, where the King—who had come up from Theobalds—and the rest of the royal family were waiting to receive him. The Elector, at some disadvantage from the fatigues of his journey and the coldness of the weather, yet bore himself with gracefulness and charm, and speedily won the regard of the Princess and her family. The Venetian Ambassador thus described his reception by the

M

Court : " The Queen was with him (the King) on
a dais raised up ten steps, which is unusual, and
under a baldachino of gold brocade. The Prince,
Princess, and Duke of York stood by. The guard
were all in rich dresses of velvet and gold ; the Hall
was thronged with lords and ladies in the richest
robes and laden with jewels ; a display that this
kingdom could not excel, nor was its like seen even
at the coming of the King of Denmark. The
Palatine was preceded by a number of gentlemen
who had gone to meet him ; then came his gentlemen all in gala dress ; then came thirty-six Barons
and gentlemen who hold fiefs, who were in his
train ; finally eight Counts, among them three of
the House of Nassau, and one brother of Prince
Maurice, Prince Henry, who has in his own private
suite above sixty persons, between gentlemen and
servants. The Duke of Lennox walked with Prince
Henry, and all preceded the Palatine. When he
had made his reverences at the due distances he
mounted the steps and was embraced by the King,
whereupon he made a profound reverence with great
humility and grace, and offered himself in the very
terms I have reported. The King was extremely
pleased, all the more so as he had been in some
doubt, and tenderly embracing him he said he took
him for his son, as such he desired and as such he
would treat him. The Palatine then paid his
respects to the Queen, who looked favourably on
him, and then after two bows he approached the
Princess, and boldly kissed her ; the King looked on
approvingly at the spirit and grace with which this
was done, and at the blush which suffused the
Princess' face and enhanced her beauty. Then, after
fulfilling his devoirs to the Princes and having stayed

as long as he thought suitable, he withdrew to the lodging prepared for him, leaving a most excellent impression behind him in all the Court, on their Majesties, and above all on the Princess." Bearing a ring of the value of £1,800, presented to him by the gratified King in his bedchamber, the Elector was conveyed through the Privy lodgings and galleries to the water, and then in a barge to Essex House, where he was lodged.

The illness of the Prince of Wales now gave cause for the gravest apprehensions, as he rapidly grew worse in spite of all the doctors could prescribe. About three o'clock in the morning of Friday, November 6th, Dr. Birch says : " His backbone, shoulders, arms and tongue, by reason of the violence of the convulsions, disjointing and dividing themselves, he fainted, and seemed now twice or thrice to be absolutely dead. This raised prodigious exclamations of grief in the chamber, court, and adjoining streets ; the noise of which, with some other means used, awakened him from his swoon. The cry was so great that all who were in the streets thought him to be actually dead ; and the rumour of it immediately spread into the city and country, and occasioned an universal lamentation."

At a quarter to eight in the evening the unfortunate Prince expired, to the great grief of all the nation.

On the 10th, Sir Thomas Lake, in a letter from Charing Cross to Sir Dudley Carleton, wrote : " The King, apprehending the worst, and not enduring to be so near the place, removed to Theobalds, and kept his bed. The Queen is at Somerset House. They have not seen each other for fear to refresh the sense of the wound."

On Monday, December 7th, the remains of the

lamented Prince were interred in Westminster Abbey.

Dean Stanley wrote : " His funeral was attended by two thousand mourners. Nine banners went before, each preceded by ' two trumpeters that sounded wofully.' His effigy was clothed with the richest garments he had, which ' did so lively represent his person, as that it did not only draw tears from the several beholders, but caused a fearful outcry among the people, as if they felt their own ruin in that loss.' "

On the 18th, Sir William Fleetwood, in a letter to Sir Dudley Carleton, wrote : " The King has returned from Royston to Whitehall : his grief moderated."

Bishop Andrewes preached before James at Whitehall, on Christmas Day—a Friday ; and on the 27th, in the Banqueting House, the Elector Palatine was affianced and contracted to Princess Elizabeth, in the presence of the King, sitting in state. At the end of the month James went to Hampton Court.

1613. The year 1613 opened with rather cheerless prospects, and the dismal feeling prevailing at the mourning Court at Whitehall was voiced in a letter of January 6th, from Sir Thomas Lake to Sir Dudley Carleton, in which he wrote : " The black is wearing out, and the marriage pomps preparing. The winter has been stormy and rainy. The physicians hope for much sickness in the spring, and the countrymen fear a murrain of cattle."

In some directions, however, the gloom was dispelled by the preparations for the approaching marriage of the Princess Elizabeth. On January 30th, an Order was issued for paying £1,000 imprest to Sir Roger Dallison, Lieutenant of the Ordnance, " towards the defraying of the wages of the gunners, carpenters, and other artificers employed about the provision of fireworks and other shows upon the water against the solemnizing of the marriage of the Lady Elizabeth to the Prince Elector Palatine."

John Chamberlain, writing on February 4th to Mrs. Alice Carleton, said, in reference to the near date of the royal marriage : " There is extra-ordinary preparations for fireworks and fights upon the water, with three castles, built upon eight western barges, and one great castle upon the land, over against the Court. One or two of the pinnaces are come already from Rochester ; and divers other vessels, to the number of six-and-thirty, are provided, some like galleys, some galleasses, and some like carracks, and other ships of war ; and above five hundred watermen, already pressed, and a thousand musqueteers of the Trained Bands, in the shires hereabout, made ready for this service, which, in all computation, cannot stand the King in so little as £5,000."

On the 10th an Order was made for paying £2,000 imprest to Sir Robert Mansell, Treasurer of the Navy, to be employed in providing a naval fight on the Thames, " for the more magnificent and royal solemnizing of the marriage of the Lady Elizabeth." Five days later another sum of £800 was provided for the same purpose.

John Chamberlain, in a letter of this date to Sir Ralph Winwood, wrote : " The marriage draws near, and all things are ready. On Sunday was their last time of asking openly in the chapel. The Queen grows every day more favourable, and there is hope she will grace it with her presence. Here

is a troop of three or five hundred muskets, made
ready by the City, to guard the Court, during these
triumphs; and we have extraordinary watches
of substantial householders every night, and
an alderman in person to oversee them." The
same correspondent wrote to Sir Dudley Carleton:
" The preparations for Fireworks and Fights upon
the water are very great, and have already consumed
above £6,000, which a man would easily believe
who sees the provision of six-and-thirty sail
of great pinnaces, galleys, galleasses, carricks,
with great store of other smaller vessels, so trimmed,
furnished and painted that I believe there was never
such a fleet seen above the Bridge, besides four
floating castles with fireworks, and the representation of the town, fort, and haven of Algiers upon
the land. This day they are to begin their prizes,
and so to continue and hold on to-morrow and
Saturday. The tides fall out very fit, it being both
spring tides and the water at the best height from
three to six; so that if the weather serve as well,
they can wish no more, for they will have the whole
river at liberty, being shut up both above and
beneath with a large number of lighters, that no
boats can come to trouble them. Sir Robert Mansell
is chief commander, who takes great pains, and no
doubt will do his best to shew his ability."

The Firework display was given on the night of
Thursday, the 11th. " At the which Fireworks,"
wrote John Taylor, " the master-gunner of England
on the shore did perform many skilful and ingenious
exploits with great bombards, shooting up many
artificial balls of fire into the air, which flew up in
one whole fiery ball, and in their falling dispersed
into divers streams like rainbows in many innumer-

able fires. After all which was discharged a great peal of chambers, to the contentment of the royal spectators, and the great credit of the performers."

The King and Queen, Prince Charles, Princess Elizabeth, the Elector Palatine, and the principal nobility witnessed the show from the galleries and windows of Whitehall, "where, in the sight of thousands of people, many artificial conclusions in fireworks were upon the Thames performed, and that the pleasureable sights on the water might equal the sumptuous shows on the land thus they proceeded : First, for a welcome to the beholders, a peal of ordnance, like unto a terrible thunder, rattled in the air, and seemed as it were to shake the earth, and mounted so high into the element, that it dazzled the beholder's eyes to look after it. Secondly, followed a number more of the same fashion, spreading so strangely with sparkling blazes, that the sky seemed to be filled with fire, or that there had been a combat of darting stars fighting in the air, and all the time these continued certain cannons planted in the fields adjoining, made thundering music, to the great pleasure of the beholders. After this, in a most curious manner, an artificial firework, with great wonder, was seen flying in the air, like unto a dragon, against which another fiery vision appeared, flaming like to St. George on horseback, brought in by a burning enchanter, between which was then fought a most strange battle, continuing a quarter of an hour or more ; the dragon being vanquished, seemed to roar like thunder, and withal burst in pieces and so vanished ; but the champion, with his flaming horse, for a little time, made a show of a triumphant conquest, and so ceased.

" After this, was heard another rattling sound
of cannons almost covering the air with fire and
smoke, and forthwith appeared out of a hill of
earth made upon the water, a very strange fire,
flaming upright like unto a blazing star. After
which, flew forth a number of rockets so high in the
air, that we could not choose but approve by all
reasons, that art had exceeded nature, so artificially
were they performed ; and still, as the chambers
and culverins played upon the earth, the fireworks
danced in the air, to the great delight of his highness
and the princes. Out of the same mount or hill of
earth flew another strange piece of artificial firework, which was in the likeness of a hunted hart,
running upon the waters so swiftly, as it had been
chased by many huntsmen. After the same, issued
out of the mount, a number of hunting hounds,
made of fire burning, pursuing the aforesaid hart
up and down the waters, making many rebounds
and turns with much strangeness, skipping in the
air as it had been a usual hunting upon land. . . .

" When this fiery hunting extinguished, and that the
elements a little cleared from fire and smoke, there
came sailing up, as it were upon the seas, certain
ships and galleys, bravely rigged with top and top-
gallant, with their flags and streamers waving
like men-of-war, which represented a Christian navy
opposed against the Turks, where, after they had a
while hovered, preparing as it were to make an
incursion into the Turkish country, they were
discovered by two towers or castles of defence,
strongly furnished to intercept all such invading
purposes ; so sending forth the reports of a cannon,
they were bravely answered with the like from the
galleys, banding fire and powder one from another,

as if the god of battles had been there present.
Here was the manner of a sea-fight rightly performed ; first by assailing one another, all striving
for victory, and pursuing each other with fire and
sword, the culverins merrily played betwixt them,
and made the air resound with thundering echoes,
and at last, to represent the joys of a victory, the
castles were sacked, burned and ruinated, and the
defenders of the same forced to escape with great
danger.

" During the time of all these triumphant
exercises there was not a man unbusied ; but every
one laboured, some on land, some on water, some
one way, some another, to move his highness, and
the rest of his princely friends, a pleasing content,
which he and the other princes, with a gracious
acceptance, applauded, to the great comfort of the
performers and no little joy to the beholders. The
next morning, being Friday, his highness, not
intending to grace the following sports with his
presence, gave cause of forbearance, with some
rest to the engineers for their great toil the night
before. Moreover, it was thought convenient, that
a whole day's preparation should be made, in
providing against the Saturday's pastimes, which
moved a more longing desire in the hearts of his
subjects to see the same, which, at the time appointed,
was in this manner accomplished.

" Between the hours of two and three of the clock,
the same day in the afternoon, being Shrove-
Saturday, the King's majesty, accompanied with
the Queen, and the rest of the princes and peers of
estate, to add the more glory to these pretended
shows, placed themselves in great royalty upon the
Privy Stairs of Whitehall, where, after a while

expecting the beginning of the desired fireworks, the Lord Admiral sent forth two or three
gentlemen in a wherry, with a flag or banner to
signify the King and the nobilitys' tarriance for the
representations, which was answered with an intelligence by the report, from a great cannon, whereupon
a certain Venetian man-of-war, and a ship called a
Carvell, came proudly with their flags and colours
sailing up, in the sight of seventeen Turkish galleys,
which lay hovering upon Lambeth side, betwixt
whom was a most royal and praiseworthy imitation
of a sea-fight, in such sort performed, as if the danger
of such an enterprise had been by true action
attempted; all which explains the honours of
martialists, and made his Majesty, with many
thousands of people of all sorts, and of many nations,
eye-witnesses of the true manner of such like encounters. . . .

" But not to be troublesome in my discourses, I
will briefly explain the encounters as they passed.
There was a bar, or kind of artificial fence, made
upon the river Thames, with barges and lighters
chained together, to keep passengers, which otherwise, with much unruliness, would have hindered
the pastimes, and much troubled the performers;
but being thus hemmed in, as it were, upon the main
seas, the two Venetian ships, as I said before, falling
within danger of the Turkish galleys, endured a
fresh encounter, and long most worthily defended
themselves; but by reason of the number of the
galleys, they were at last boarded, taken, and
carried as boot and prize under the command of a
Turkish castle, which represented and bear the
name of the castle Argeir, furnished with twenty-
two well approved great pieces of ordnance, which

was contrived and built up Lambeth side, at a place
named Stand Gates, environed with craggie rocks,
as the said castle is now situate in Turkey. After
the galleys had taken those Venetian ships, and
delivered them into the Turkish Admiral's command,
they had sight of another argosy or ' galliaza,' which
seemed to be of Spain, which, likewise, after a fierce
conflict, they made prize of, and with much triumph
rendered the same up also to the Turkish Admiral.

" After this, upon a sudden, there was a thundering
of ordnance or chambers placed in Lambeth Marsh,
whereupon the scouts and watches of the castle discovered an English navy, to the number of fifteen
sail, of the King's pinnaces, making up towards the
point, with their red crossed streamers most gallantly
waving in the air, to the great delight of all the
beholders, which as then seemed to cover over the
Thames in boats and barges. Near upon this place
stood a high built watch-tower, or beacon of the
Turks, which at the first sight of the English navy
was set on fire, as the manner is at all such incursions,
with blazing light, as it seemed, gave notice to the
castle, and caused a readiness in some for defence.
In the meantime, the King's pinnaces and the
Turkish galleys joined, betwixt whom were shewn
many strange attempts, even as they had ventured
their very lives for their countries' safeties ; they
spared neither powder nor policy, to sack one another,
but on both sides bestirred themselves so bravely,
that his highness, with all the rest of his attendants,
were therewith much delighted. At last the galleys
being overcharged with long and forward encounters
of the English navy, for refuge and shelter made
now unto the castle, which began likewise to play
bravely upon the English, and with their thundering

ordnance, made as it were the ground to shake. The King's navy to answer them was not backward in a performance, but made the air gloomy with fire and smoke roaring from their loud-mouthed cannons.

" The fight for a time continued fiercely, the victory leaning to neither side, either of them attempting to assault and board each other, but at last the galleys being sore bruised-beaten began to yield, whereupon the English Admiral fell down, and cast anchor before the castle, and then spared not in the best manner to thunder off their ordnance, whereat the Turks yielded both castle and galleys, and sub-mitted to the conquest of the English admiral, who fired many of the said galleys, sacked the castle, and took prisoner the Turks' admiral, with divers bashaws and other great Turks, and also recovered the Venetian and Spanish ships, before taken by the galleys.

" After the performance of all these afore-said, the English admiral in a most triumphant manner, carried as a prisoner the admiral of the galleys, attired in a red jacket with blue sleeves according to the Turkish fashion, with the bashaws and the other Turks guarded, to his highness Privy Stairs of Whitehall, where his grace, Prince Pals-grave and his lady remained ; which prisoners were led by Sir Robert Mansfield (Mansel) to the Lord Admiral, and by him they were conveyed to the King's majesty, as a representation of pleasure, which to his highness moved delight, and highly pleased all there present.

" All these aforesaid pastimes were most nobly performed between the hours of three and six in the afternoon, to the great content as well of foreign nations as of our own country people, whereof in one place, and at one time, hath been seldom seen a greater number. Also, for a farewell to this day's pleasure, a train of chambers were discharged in St. George's Field, of a long continuance, and of such an echoing thunder, that they even amazed the hearers. Thus ended Saturday's shows upon the waters, being the eve of this great marriage day."

The foregoing description of the water festivities is from a Tract printed by T. C. for W. Basley.

John Taylor, the water poet, witnessed and wrote thus of the Fights and Fireworks : " In this representation of a sea-fight there were sixteen ships, sixteen galleys, and six friggots ; of which Navy the ships were Christians and the galleys were supposed Turks, all being artificially rigged and trimmed, well manned and furnished with great ordnance and musquettiers. One of the Christian fleet was a great vessel or a supposed Venetian argosy, and another was a tall ship, as it were appointed for the safe convoy of the argosy. And, for the avoiding of the troublesomeness of boats and wherries, and other perturbatious multitudes, there was a lists or bounds made with lighters, hoys, and other great boats to the number of two hundred and fifty or thereabouts ; the one end of the lists was as high almost as Lambeth-bridge (stairs), and the other end as low as the Temple-stairs, and so fastened to the south shore, or the upper end of the Bank or Southwark side, in the form of a half-moon or semi-circle, so that boats might pass up and down the river betwixt London side and the lighters any way. The aforesaid Turkish galleys lying all at an anchor over against Westminster, in a haven or harbour made artificially with masts and other provisions, sixty yards into the river (which harbour

or haven was belonging to a supposed Turkish or
Barbarian Castle of Tunis, Algiers, or some other
Mohametan fortification, where the galleys might
scout out for purchase and retire in again at their
pleasure), about two of the clock on Saturday, the
13th of February, the aforesaid argosy and the other
Venetian ship her convoy, set forward from the
Temple, and driving up with the wind and tide till
they came as high as York House; where four
galleys met and encountered with them; where,
upon a sudden, there was friendly exchanging of
small shot and great ordnance on both sides, to the
great delectation of all the beholders, the drums,
trumpets, fires, weights, guns, shouts and acclamations of the mariners, soldiers and spectators, with
such reverberating echoes of joy to and fro, that
there wanted nothing in this Fight, but that which
was fit to be wanting, which was ships sunk and torn
in pieces, men groaning rent and dismembered;
some slain, some drowned, some maimed, all expecting confusion. . . .

" But in the end, in this friendly fight, the
ship and argosy were encompassed round by
the galleys, and surprised and taken; whereupon, the whole fleet made towards them to
rescue them, and revenge their received injuries.
Then there was a beacon fired by the Turks, which
gave warning to the Castle and galleys of the coming
of the Christian fleet. Then all the ships and
galleys met in friendly opposition and imaginary
hurley-burley battalions; then the lofty instruments
of war's clamorous encouragements sounded;
the thundering artillery roared, the musquetiers
in numberless volleys discharged on all sides, the
smoke, as it were, eclipsing Titan's refulgent beams.

filling all the air with a confused cloudy mist, the
castle and the land adjacent continually discharging
great shot in abundance at the ships, and the ships
at them again ; so that after this delightful battle
had doubtfully lasted three hours, to the great
contentment of all beholders, the victory inclining
to the neither side, all being opposed foes and
combined friends ; all victors, all triumphers, none
to be vanquished, and therefore no conquerors ;
the drums, trumpets, flutes and guns filling the air
with repurcussive acclamations ; upon which, for a
catastrophe or period to these delightful royalties,
command was given that the retreat should be
sounded on both sides. And thus these Princely
recreations were accomplished and finished."

The marriage was celebrated on Sunday, the
14th, with splendid ceremonial, and the masque
performed at night in the Banqueting House was
written by Dr. Campion, and named " The Lords'
Maske." The nuptials of the Princess inspired
John Donne to compose his poem " Epithalmium."

On the following day there was running at the
ring in the tilt-yard adjoining Whitehall, and at
night the gentlemen of the Inns of Court presented
masques and revels before the King and the royal
company. The invention was designed by Inigo
Jones, and the matter written by George Chapman.

The two other Inns of Court, on the Tuesday
evening, went by water to Whitehall prepared to
present their masque, but on account of the King's
fatigue it was, much to their chagrin, put off for a
few days. Phineas Pett was employed for the
water show on this occasion, and he wrote : " After
the sea-fight was performed, I was entreated by
divers gentlemen of the Inns of Court, whereof

Sir Francis Bacon was chief, to attend the bringing of a masque by water to Whitehall, in some of the galleys. But, the tide falling out very contrary, and the company attending the masquers very unruly, it could not be performed so exactly as purposed and expected; but yet they were safely landed at the Privy Stairs at Whitehall, for which my pains the gentlemen gave me a fair recompence."

The disappointed Inns of Court gentlemen were permitted to perform their masque, written by Francis Beaumont, on the following Saturday, the 20th, in the Banqueting House at Whitehall; but the presentment suffered from the damped enthusiasm of the performers.

John Chamberlain sat down after the conclusion of the royal wedding rejoicings, and wrote, on the 18th, his impressions of the displays to Mrs. Alice Carleton, thus: " On Thursday night the fireworks were reasonably well performed, all save the last castle of fire, which bred most expectation, and had most devices, but when it came to execution had worst success. On Saturday, likewise, the fight upon the water came short of that show and brags had been made of it; but they pretend the best to be behind, and left for another day, which was the winning of the castle on land. But the King and all the company took so little delight to see no other activity but shooting and putting of guns, that it is quite given over, and the navy unrigged, and the castle pulled down, the rather for that there were divers hurt in the former fight, as one lost both his eyes, another both his hands, another one hand, with divers others maimed and hurt, so to avoid further harm it was thought best to let it alone; and this is the conclusion of all the preparation with so much expense of powder and money, which amounted to no less than £9,000."

Later in the same letter he described the two masques performed by the Inns of Court gentlemen. The first, prepared by the Middle Temple and Lincoln's Inn, went on the Monday night " in gallant and glorious show," with a great blaze of torches, to Whitehall, where the King viewed the scene from the gallery, and made them ride about the tilt-yard. " On Tuesday, it came to Gray's Inn, and the Inner Temple's turn to come with their masque, whereof Sir Francis Bacon was the chief contriver ; and, because the former came on horse-back and in open chariots, they made choice to come by water from Winchester Place in Southwark, which suited well with their device, which was the marriage of the river Thames to the Rhine ; and their show by water was very gallant, by reason of infinite store of lights, very curiously set and placed, and many boats and barges, with devices of light and lamps, with three peals of ordnance, one at their taking water, another in the Temple Garden, and the last at their landing ; which passage by water cost them better than three hundred pounds. They were received at the Privy Stairs." For some reason, probably from the weariness of the King, they returned in great disappointment, without having been given the chance of exhibiting their device, their dainty apparel, and the grace of their dancing.

Among the charges afterwards recorded for the Princess Elizabeth's wedding, were the two items : " For the naval fight of fireworks on the Thames at her marriage, Four thousand eight hundred pounds," and " More Fireworks on the Thames at her marriage, Two thousand eight hundred and eighty pounds."

On Saturday, April 10th, the King and Queen, together with Prince Charles, Princess Elizabeth, and the Elector Palatine, in presence of a great cheering crowd, went by barge from Whitehall to Greenwich ; and on Tuesday they all proceeded to Rochester, where the bride and bridegroom bade their family farewell and journeying by Canterbury to Margate embarked there for home.

Soon after this the Queen started on a progress to Bath, and on the 27th was entertained till the next day by Lord Knollys at Caversham House, near Reading, when revels and a masque, written by Dr. Thomas Campion, were performed.

On Whitsunday, May 23rd, the King heard Bishop Andrewes preach at Whitehall ; and on the 11th of the following month, he gave audience at Greenwich to Antonio Foscarini, the Venetian Ambassador.

Prince Charles started housekeeping at Richmond Palace on July 1st.

In a day or two the King came to Hampton Court, and between the 3rd and 7th the Court and Council were at Oatlands. On Sunday, the 4th, James knighted Lionel Cranfield, and on the 8th he was at Whitehall and the Queen at Somerset House ; both preparing for the annual progress. On his return the King called at Windsor on August 29th, and, after a visit to Whitehall, was again at the Castle on September 8th. Towards the end of this month the King and his Consort were at Hampton Court.

On November 4th the favourite, Robert Carr, was created Earl of Somerset at Whitehall. The next day the King heard Bishop Andrewes preach in the chapel, and three days later he knighted Henry Yelverton, the Solicitor-General. On the 30th the bells of St. Margaret's were ringing for the royal return to Whitehall, and early in December the King was at Hampton Court. As customary James took up his residence at Whitehall for the close of the year, and on Christmas Day—Saturday— he listened to a sermon from Bishop Andrewes.

The Court was given up to gay festivity on St. Stephen's Day, when, in the presence of the King, Queen, and Prince Charles, the marriage of the Earl of Somerset and the divorced Countess of Essex was performed in the chapel by the Bishop of Bath and Wells. A masque was presented at night, and the next day the Prince and the bridegroom ran at the ring. Arthur Wilson wrote of this wedding: " The City of London and the Court at Whitehall, like two great stars in conjunction, had one and the same influence and operation ; they must do something for the man whom the King loves ; therefore a great feast is prepared by them in Merchant Taylors' Hall (and all the grandees and ladies are invited) with so much magnificence, as if it had been competitor and vied with Whitehall for glory. They all rode on horseback into the City in the evening, following their two leaders, the men attending the bridegroom and the women the bride ; so mounted, furnished and adorned with trappings, and so bespangled with jewels that the torches and flambeaux (which were numerous) were but little light to the beholders."

On the 29th the gentlemen of the retinue of Prince Charles performed an Irish masque, written by Ben Jonson.

1614. On Twelfth Night, 1614, the gentlemen of

Gray's Inn, under the patronage of Sir Francis Bacon, performed the " Masque of Flowers," in the Banqueting House at Whitehall ; and, on January 10th, Ben Jonson's Irish masque was presented at Court for the second time. A Pastoral Tragi-comedy, named " Hymen's Triumph," written by Samuel Daniel, was performed on February 3rd, before the Queen's Court at Somerset House, on the occasion of the marriage of Lord Roxburgh.

The King witnessed a Tilt at Whitehall on March 24th, and a month later, on Easter Day, he heard Bishop Andrewes preach in the chapel. The Rev. Norwich Spackman delivered a sermon there on Sunday, May 1st.

After angrily dissolving the " Addled " Parliament on June 7th, the King knighted Randolph Crew, the Speaker, and left for Greenwich, where, on Whitsunday, he heard a sermon from Bishop Andrewes, and later gave audience to the Spanish Ambassador, removing to Richmond on the 29th. James returned to Whitehall on July 10th, and after making the Earl of Suffolk Treasurer, and the Earl of Somerset Lord Chamberlain, went away again on Sunday, the next day, after dinner. At Greenwich he gave audience to the French Ambassador, and puzzled his Excellency of Venice, who wrote in a despatch : " I have not yet been able to discover what they discussed."

The Rev. Thomas Lorkin hastened, on the 22nd, to inform Sir Thomas Puckering that, " Scarce had I despatched away my former letters, when lo ! news was brought me of the King of Denmark's arrival, who came this day to Somerset House ; which was so sudden, strange, and unexpected, as a long time I believed it to be a fable, till, by a diligent inquiry, I resolved myself of the contrary. He comes very slenderly attended, accompanied only with some half a dozen persons. What the occasion of this so strange accident may be, I cannot attain unto, otherwise than by blind guess ; and therefore leave you to your own divination."

On Sunday, the 24th, the two Kings and the Queen and Prince heard Dr. King, Bishop of London, preach at Somerset House. On the following Sunday, after a week of hunting, bear-baiting, running at the ring, and fencing, the monarchs listened to a sermon from Dr. Mountaine, Dean of Westminster, at Whitehall. Afterwards a great feast was given in the Banqueting House, and the night finished up with fireworks in the gardens of Somerset House.

Early on Monday morning, August 1st, the King and the Danish monarch, accompanied by the Prince, and attended by the Lord Admiral and many of the nobility, took barge and were rowed down the river to Woolwich, where they visited the dry dock, and went on board the almost finished ship " Mer Honeur," which pleased them much. The royal party then proceeded to Gravesend, and after dining at the " Shippe," boarded the King of Denmark's ship. Here two hours were spent in partaking of collation and in kindly courtesies and compliments, and then the English King re-entered his barge, and returning to Blackwall, took coach and rode that night to Theobalds ; afterwards going forward on a progress. On Tuesday, the King of Denmark and Prince Charles visited Rochester, and retracing their steps to dine at Gravesend, the Prince returned with his uncle to his ship, and having bidden him an affectionate farewell, was taken in the evening to London. The Danish King immediately after sailed from the Thames, with his three vessels, for his own country. On Monday, the 29th, James, coming from Woodstock, spent some time at Oxford, and the next day ended his progress by passing the night at Bisham Abbey.

The Venetian Ambassador wrote on September 19th : " On Sunday, after dinner, the Ambassador of France had audience of the King at Windsor. . . . The Count of Scarnafes (Ambassador of Savoy) had audience of the King at Windsor, on Monday morning."

On October 3rd the Count of Scarnafes visited the Queen at Oatlands.

A Russian Ambassador came up the river on the 26th, and was received on landing at Tower Wharf by Lord Danvers, attended by Sir John Finett and other servants of the King.

The King knighted Lawrence Hyde, the Queen's Attorney, at Whitehall, on November 7th, and after a short visit to Hampton Court in the latter part of December, he returned to Whitehall, and on Christmas Day heard the usual sermon from Bishop Andrewes in the chapel.

1615. On Twelfth Night, 1615, Ben Jonson's masque, " Mercury Vindicated from the Alchemists," was performed before the Court at Whitehall. The King, after hearing prayers and preaching, and witnessing a Tilt at Whitehall, on March 24th, journeyed to Hampton Court. On Easter Sunday, April 9th, he heard a sermon from Bishop Andrewes in the Chapel at Whitehall, and a few days later the Venetian Ambassador wrote : " On Wednesday, the Ambassador of Brandenburg had an audience of the King at Hampton Court." On the 24th, George Villiers, the rising favourite, was knighted at Somerset House. The Whitsunday sermon was delivered by Bishop Andrewes at Greenwich.

On June 27th the Venetian Ambassador wrote : " On Monday the Ambassador (of Savoy) had audience of his Majesty at Gravesend. The King sent one of the royal barges for him."

July found the King at Oatlands, but on the 21st he dubbed three knights at Whitehall, and set out the next day on his summer progress.

On September 2nd he met the Queen and Prince Charles at Windsor, where he knighted Robert Naunton, the author of " Fragmenta Regalia." Later in the month James went to Greenwich, and on October 9th, Antonio Foscarini, the retiring Venetian Ambassador, wrote in a despatch : " To-morrow, please God, the illustrious Barbarigo (his successor) will arrive in London. To-day the Master of the Ceremonies has dined with me. He has since gone in the King's barge to Gravesend to fetch him in the King's name. . . . Three large ships are being put in readiness here to sail to the East Indies." And, " The Queen, in accordance with the advice of the physicians and the wishes of the King, has gone to the baths at Greenwich, where I had an audience on Sunday."

Gregorio Barbarigo, the new Venetian Ambassador, wrote, on October 13th, that the Master of the Ceremonies took the royal barges down the river to bring him from Gravesend. " He stayed with me, and on the following day we proceeded together in the same barges towards London, meeting on the way, some miles out, my illustrious predecessor with a distinguished company.

When we reached the coaches we mounted the royal one, and I was taken to my predecessor's house."

On November 5th, the Archduke's Ambassador dined with the King at Whitehall, and Bishop Andrewes preached in the chapel. On the last Sunday of the month the Venetian Ambassador had an audience of the Queen.

The Court moved to Whitehall for the close of the year, and, on December 23rd, the King delivered the staff of Lord Chamberlain, taken from the disgraced Earl of Somerset, to the Earl of Pembroke. Christmas Day saw James suffering from an attack of gout, and he heard the customary sermon from Bishop Andrewes in private.

1616. On the evening of New Year's Day, 1616, Ben Jonson's masque, " The Golden Age Restored," was given before the Court, and the performance was repeated on January 9th.

The King knighted John Finett, the Annalist, on March 21st, and four days later he, in company with the Queen, witnessed a Tilting. Bishop Andrewes preached in the chapel on Easter Sunday, the 31st. Late in April, James, after making Francis, Earl of Rutland, and Sir George Villiers, Knights of the Garter, left for Greenwich, where, on Whitsunday, May 19th, he heard Bishop Andrewes preach. Edward Sherburn wrote, on the 31st, in a letter to Sir Dudley Carleton : " The King boxed the Prince's ears, for turning a water-spout on Sir George Villiers in jest, in the garden at Greenwich."

On June 3rd, the Venetian Ambassador wrote : " The Count of Schomberg, who came here for the Elector Palatine, has stayed on at Greenwich since Sunday with their Majesties, and has had various conversations with the King." The Ambassador, Gregorio Barbarigo, died soon after this, and his Secretary wrote, on the 16th, in a despatch to the Venetian government : " Last Monday the Ambassador Barbarigo's funeral ceremony was celebrated by his sons in their house. The Ambassadors and a large gathering of English and foreign Catholics were present. This is the more remarkable as there is no memory of any other ambassador of a foreign prince who has died in this kingdom. They have not yet gone to kiss the King's hands, as he has been spending some days at Theobalds hunting. He is returning to Greenwich to-day, when we will see him."

The King, at the end of the month, was at Oatlands, where he knighted several gentlemen, and then proceeding to Windsor, was, on Sunday, July 7th, present at the installation of the Earl of Rutland, Sir George Villiers, and Robert Sidney, Viscount Lisle, as Knights of the Garter.

In August the Queen left Oatlands to join the King in his progress, and on their return arrived at Woodstock on a Saturday, when James hunted and dined with Lord Danvers at Thornton Park. On the morrow, the Vice-Chancellor and Doctors of Oxford welcomed the royal party with an oration, and presented a petition ; and on Monday the King killed two or three stags in the forest, in presence of the Queen, the Prince, and the whole Court. The next day Dr. Laud preached with much applause, deducing from the story of Miriam's leprosy a warning to detractors against government ; and the ceremony of making Villiers a Viscount was performed by the doting King with much alacrity.

The French Ambassador had an audience; and

then, on the 28th, while Prince Charles was visiting Oxford and dining at Christchurch, James went from Rycott to Bisham, and spent the night at the Abbey, arriving at Windsor the next day.

The Court spent September at Hampton Court, where the King held meetings of the Privy Council, and dubbed several knights.

October 4th found the Queen at Oatlands, whilst three days before the King had acted as godfather at the baptism of James, the son of Sir John Egerton, in the chapel at Whitehall, and directly after left for Royston. On the 14th, the Venetian Ambassador wrote that the Ambassador of Savoy had, on the previous Friday, been received in audience at Hampton Court. Later in the month the Queen journeyed from Oatlands for her usual autumn residence at Greenwich.

On Thursday, the 31st, Prince Charles, Duke of Cornwall, surrounded by a noble company of lords and gentlemen, and attended by a numerous train, came by barge in royal state from Barn Elms to Whitehall, to be created Prince of Wales. At Chelsea a great crowd met him, headed by the Lord Mayor, Aldermen, and citizens of London, together with the City Companies, all in their several barges, flying stately banners and rich streamers.

Trumpets, drums, and a variety of music added to the tumult of the welcome from the infinite number of people on shore and in boats and barges. There were also, at the City's charge, trophies and ingenious devices on the water, and the rhyming speeches, delivered by persons in the characters of London, Thamesis, Neptune, Hope, and Peace, were composed by Thomas Middleton, and were printed in a Tract with the title : " Civitatis Amor,

The Citie's Love ; an entertainment by water, at Chelsea and Whitehall, at the joyfull receiving of that illustrious hope of Great Britain, The most High and Mighty Charles, to bee created Prince of Wales, Duke of Cornwall, Earle of Chester, etc."

The Prince landed at the Common Stairs at Whitehall, and preceded by the nobility and his officers, moved to the Hall, where he was received by the Great Officers of the Household.

John Chamberlain wrote on this occasion : " The King came to town on Allhallows Eve, and stood on the gallery stairs at Whitehall to see the Prince come along from Richmond, attended by the Lord Mayor, and all the Companies of London in their barges, in very good order, and made a goodly show. The Queen would not be present at the creation, lest she should renew her grief, by the memory of the last prince, for whom the Bishop of Ely prayed by mistake at a Court sermon."

The actual ceremony of creation took place on November 4th, within closed doors, owing to the sharp weather, and the Prince's delicate health. Twenty-four sons of the noblest houses were made Knights of the Bath. On the following day, Bishop Andrewes preached before the King at Whitehall ; and on the 11th, James, after knighting one gentleman, left for Theobalds, whilst the Queen remained at Somerset House.

In connection with the attendance of the City fathers on Prince Charles, a curious entry was made in the accounts of the Carpenters' Company of refreshments, partaken of on the occasion, headed " Chargyde thirty-first October when the Companye went to meete the Prince, before the Companye tooke bardge, and in the bardge." There were items for carrying the wine-sellers to and fro, bread, sugar and cakes, beer, one gallon of claret wine, one quart of canary, and a bottle and a half of sack.

As customary, the King returned to Whitehall for the close of the year, and on Christmas Day Bishop Andrewes delivered the usual sermon.

1617. On January 4th, 1617, John Chamberlain wrote : " The Queen removed yesterday to Whitehall from Somerset House, where she had lain this fortnight sick of the gout, or something else, it being suspected she dreams and aims at a Regency during the King's absence in Scotland." In another part of the letter the writer said : " The Earl of Arundel received the communion on Christmas Day. His house at Greenwich, left him by the Earl of Northampton, is burned, which the Papists will think just retribution." The house contained household stuff of great value.

On the 5th, Viscount Villiers, the rapidly advancing favourite, was created Earl of Buckingham, at Whitehall ; and the next evening, being Twelfth Night, Ben Jonson's " Masque of Christmas " was presented to the Court.

After a visit to Theobalds, the King dubbed a knight at Hampton Court on the 16th, and returned to Whitehall in February. On the 22nd John Chamberlain wrote : " The French Ambassador and his company were feasted at Whitehall on Sunday," and " The Queen's musicians (whereof she hath more than a good many) made her a kind of masque or antic at Somerset House, on Wednesday night last."

When serious riots were taking place in London on March 4th, the King was dining with his Consort at Somerset House, on which occasion the mansion was renamed Denmark House.

The Lord Mayor, John Leman, was knighted at Whitehall on the 9th, and within the week seven other knights were created. On Sunday, the 11th, the King and the Earl of Sussex stood as godfathers, in the chapel, at the baptism of the infant James, son of Viscount Harrington ; and on the following Tuesday, at the baptism service conducted by Bishop Andrewes over James, son of Sir William Fielding, the King and the Earl of Buckingham stood as godfathers, and the Countess of Bedford as godmother. John Chamberlain wrote on the 15th : " On Tuesday, Sir Robert Mansell married his old mistress Roper, one of the Queen's ancient maids-of-honour. The wedding was kept at Denmark House at the Queen's charge, who gave them a fair cupboard of plate, besides many good and rich presents from other friends."

On April 5th the Queen was at Greenwich, where she held her Court during the King's absence in Scotland. Ralph Winwood wrote about the middle of the month : " The Lords will attend her Majesty this Easter at Greenwich, but on Easter Monday will go to the Spital Sermon, and dine with the Lord Mayor." George Gerrard said at this time the Queen never missed one Lenten sermon. An entertainment was given to the Queen at Deptford, on May 4th, by the girl students of " Ladies' Hall," then probably one of the principal boarding schools of the period. The masque performed on the occasion, named " Cupid's Banishment," was written by Robert White, and the part of Diana was acted by the twelve years old Master Richard Browne of Sayes Court. On the 24th, John Chamberlain wrote : " The Queen would not let Mr. Comptroller (Sir Thomas Edmonds) depart for France till she had feasted him. Most of the Council keep at Greenwich about her, saving such as have necessary attendance at the Term ; and these come still on Saturday night, and tarry Sunday."

In June the Queen moved for the summer to Oatlands, and the Prince of Wales took up his residence at Richmond, where, on the last day of the month, he gave audience to the Venetian Secretary.

On September 12th, the King, returning from a long progress through England and Scotland, passed the night at Bisham Abbey, the seat of the Hoby family. As he approached the mansion the bells of Great Marlow, and other neighbouring parishes, were rung in welcome. Continuing his journey on the morrow, he arrived at Windsor, and rested there till the 15th, when he moved on to Whitehall. At Hyde Park he was met by the Lord Mayor, Aldermen, and a large body of the chief citizens of London, well mounted and wearing chains of gold ; whilst the bells of St. Margaret's and other churches rang joyous peals. Giovanni Battista Lionello, the Venetian Secretary, wrote : "On Monday the King entered London. He was met by five hundred of the leading burgesses on horseback, and a countless multitude of people, who shouted for joy of his return. On Tuesday his Majesty proceeded to Theobalds."

Immediately after his return the King published his "Book of Sports," and ordered a more cheerful observance of the Sunday, after evening service.

Later in the month James went to Hampton Court, where, on Monday the 29th, he knighted six gentlemen, and Sir John Villiers, eldest brother of the favourite Buckingham, was married in the chapel, by the Bishop of Winchester, to Frances, youngest daughter of Sir Edward Coke and Lady Hatton, the King giving the bride away.

The next day Adam Newton, in a letter from Deptford to Sir Thomas Puckering, wrote : " I was at Hampton Court on Sunday last, where the Court was indeed very full ; King, Queen, and Prince all residing there for the time. The King and Prince, after their coming from Theobalds this day se'nnight, went to Windsor to the hunting of the wild boar, and came back on Saturday. Yesterday, which was Michaelmas Day, the marriage betwixt Sir John Villiers and the lady was celebrated in the presence of their Majesties. Of the particulars I cannot inform you, because I came from thence on Sunday in the afternoon, when I met, near unto Kingston Bridge, the parties to be married going towards the Court ; Sir Edward Coke bringing them from his son's house at Kingston town's end, with eight or nine coaches."

On October 9th, Horatio Busino, Chaplain of Pietro Contarini, the new Venetian Ambassador, wrote in his diary of their arrival : " His Excellency having given orders for the hire of a vessel, one was procured immediately at a cost of twenty-two crowns for our conveyance to England, this identical ship having taken ambassadors across on previous occasions. The skipper chose to delay our departure until Wednesday, the 16th, so as to avoid making the coast of England by night. Meanwhile the steward laid in stores for the voyage consisting of good beer, yet better Rhenish, excellent French claret, with capital Mayence ham and a flask of Spanish ' aromatico.' On the twenty-third hour the skipper came to fetch his Excellency, and invoking God's blessing, we all went merrily on board. We had expected to be alone, but found the whole ship crowded with passengers of every description, musicians, women, merchants, bearded Jews, tatterdemalions and gentlemen, crowded together as they are on the boats to Padua. We were rather annoyed at this, but berths were assigned to each of us, his Excellency being taken into the State cabin, which was so low and narrow that it could not even contain four persons. After a very tempestuous passage, about the thirteenth hour we saw the land, or rather one continued mass of cliff, which forms the bulwark of this kingdom seaward, and after coasting the island, we entered the Thames at the seventeenth hour precisely. As both wind and tide were against us, we dropped anchor. At the twenty-third hour we raised anchor, and at the fifth hour of the night we were carried by the tide to Gravesend, the usual halting-place for all ambassadors and grandees, preparatory to their introduction at the Court in London. . . . His Excellency went to the ' Post ' Inn, which is accustomed to receive such guests."

A few days later Busino continued his narrative as follows : " On the morning of Thursday the 12th, three hours before daybreak, we sent the courier to London, and at the twelfth hour he was followed by the House Steward, they being charged to acquaint Giovanni Battista Lionello, the Venetian Resident Secretary, with our arrival, and to request his presence at Gravesend forthwith. He consequently arrived in haste at the first hour of the night. It was at once settled that his Excellency should go to London *incognito*, to choose a house and superintend the furnishing of it, expecially as the charges at the inn were exorbitant—namely, two golden crowns per meal for each person. So on the evening of the

12th, we wrote to Venice, and on the morrow of the 13th, after dinner, his Excellency set out for the metropolis. At the sixth hour of the night he reached the Tower, the usual landing-place, where the coach of Sig. Lionello was waiting to take him to his dwelling. The House Steward and courier had engaged a very commodious mansion in Bishopsgate Street Without, which had heretofore served as the residence of several former ambassadors. His Excellency took possession on the evening of Saturday, the 14th, assigning the gallery of the palace for the chapel, as it was long and very handsome, and a decent altar was erected there immediately. The first mass was celebrated there on Sunday, the 15th. We next occupied ourselves with furnishing the house, obtaining servants and other things. On Thursday, the 19th, his Majesty's Master of the Ceremonies, a man of experience and piety, was informed that his Excellency wished to make his public entry into London. It was therefore arranged that this ceremony should take place on the afternoon of Saturday, the 20th. His Excellency returned to Gravesend on Friday, and the same evening the Master of the Ceremonies arrived with the King's barges, in very gallant trim, having left orders for the royal coaches to be in waiting at the Tower."

The bells of St. Margaret's welcomed the King and Queen back to Whitehall on the 31st.

On November 5th, a Russian Embassy landed at Tower Wharf, and was received by Lord Compton, " having been first met at Gravesend by Sir Richard Smith and others, sent in the name of the City, and brought up in their barges. The King's coach and five or six others took them in at Tower Wharf,

o

but with such disorder of gentlemen come from Court (more than were appointed) that too soon pressed into them, as, without my care and boldness to displace, some of the better sort of Musses must have walked on foot to their lodgings. They were welcomed at their landing with a volley of great ordnance from the Tower and ships, and were encountered on Tower Hill by the Aldermen of the City in their scarlet gowns and other citizens in their velvet coats and chains of gold, all on horse-back, and thence conducted to their house in Bishops-gate Street, where they were lodged and defrayed at the charge of the Muscovy Company." So wrote Sir John Finett.

On the 29th an Ambassador-Extraordinary from the King of Sweden was fetched from Gravesend by the Master of the Ceremonies, and lodged in Crutched Friars.

The King returned to Whitehall on December 20th for the Christmas festivities.

1618. On January 1st, 1618, George Villiers was created Marquis of Buckingham and on Twelfth Night the Court was entertained with Ben Jonson's masque, "The Vision of Delight," in which the Prince of Wales took the principal part. In February, the King being "troubled with a defluxion upon his knees, could not be present at sermon." On Shrove Tuesday, the 17th, the Twelfth Night masque was again performed, and three days later Dr. John Donne preached the sermon in the chapel. Nathaniel Brent, in a letter to Sir Dudley Carleton, wrote on the 28th : " The King came from Theobalds to Whitehall, and will spend his Sundays in Town, for the convenience of Buckingham, who practices running at the Tilt against St. George's Feast."

On March 7th, John Chamberlain wrote to Carleton :
" The King hath not looked abroad since his last
coming to town, being detained by a defluxion, as we
call it, in his knees." And a few days later he said :
" The Queen lies still at Denmark (Somerset) House,
whence she hath made two or three journeys to Whitehall to visit the King, while he kept within doors."

All through April the King resided at Whitehall, making several knights, and hearing Bishop
Andrewes preach on Easter Sunday, the 5th.

On the 29th John Chamberlain wrote to Sir
Dudley Carleton : " On Monday was se'nnight, the
Queen went from Denmark House to Whitehall,
with somewhat more than usual state, being accompanied with most of the nobility about the Court,
and seven or eight-and-twenty coaches. Yesterday
she removed to Greenwich, and the King, the day
before, to Theobalds, whence he comes back at the
end of the week, and after some little stay here
(London) means to settle at Greenwich for some
time." On Whitsunday, May 24th, Bishop Andrewes
preached at Greenwich ; and on the last day of the
month, George Bowles, Lord Mayor of London, was
knighted there.

At the end of June the King was at Oatlands,
where he gave audience to the Venetian Ambassador
on July 3rd, and returned to Whitehall a few days
later, only to leave at once for Wanstead. On the
14th the Rev. Thomas Lorkin wrote in a letter to
Sir Thomas Puckering : " The next week the
Prince removes to Richmond, and after some four
or five days there, begins a little progress by himself
to Chertsey, Bagshot, Windsor, and then after meets
the King." James returned to London on the 18th
from Theobalds, and the Queen removed from

Greenwich. Two days later the King dubbed three knights at Whitehall, and then started on a Western progress.

On August 15th Sir Robert Naunton wrote : " The King has had the colic, but is better, and has been on horseback these two mornings by sunrise." A petition was presented on the 25th to the Council by Passwater Saxbey, a prisoner in Bridewell, " that his whipping and imprisonment for ten weeks may be considered sufficient punishment for having thrown his hat in the King's face, in a drunken fit ; deserves much more, but throws himself on his Majesty's mercy for release."

The King arrived at Windsor from his progress on September 3rd, and went from thence by way of Westminster to Wanstead. At this time the Queen was indisposed at Oatlands.

The Court was at Hampton Court in October, and on the 13th Sir John Finett wrote : " A Chiaus, or messenger from Turkey, being arrived at Gravesend, was received there by the Lord (late Sir Robert) Rich, accompanied with his brother, Sir Henry Rich, the Master of the Ceremonies (Sir Lewis Lewkenor), myself, and half a score other gentlemen. That Lord entertained nobly, at his own charge, all the company ; went the next morning from his own inn to the Chiauses, and thence conducting him to the King's barge and two others come down for his service, and landing him at Tower Wharf, we there entered the Lord's coach and others of his friends and of the City, and brought him to his lodgings, defrayed, as was also his diet during his stay here, by the Turkey merchants."

On November 3rd the King, at Whitehall, made one knight, and gave public audience to the Turkish

Ambassador in the Banqueting House. Bishop Andrewes preached in the chapel on the 5th, and the next day the King went to visit the Queen lying sick of a dropsy at Hampton Court, returning to Whitehall in the evening. On the 9th, another knight was dubbed, and on the morrow James left for Theobalds. Abraham Williams, in a letter from Westminster to Sir Dudley Carleton, wrote on December 3rd : " The King going to Theobalds to give audience to the States Commissioners. The physicians advise the Queen not to remove from Hampton Court."

The King again visited his sick Consort on the 22nd, and returned to Whitehall in the evening. Bishop Andrewes delivered a sermon in the Chapel on Christmas Day, and John Tonstall wrote from Hampton Court : " The Queen's health improves ; she heard the Bishop of London on Christmas Day. The Prince and Buckingham have been to see her, and the King comes twice a week. The Countess of Derby is the only lady constantly with her."

At this time Buckingham was both Master of the Horse and Lord High Admiral, and the following lines were circulated about the town :—

> " O joyful newse, for Buckingham is nowe
> Both maister of the horse and frothie mayne."

1619. On New Year's Day, 1619, the King made three knights at Whitehall. The next day John Chamberlain wrote in a letter to Sir Dudley Carleton : " The King came hither on Thomas's Day, and the Wednesday following went to visit the Queen at Hampton Court, whither he went again on Monday, the last of our Christmas holidays. We begin now to apprehend the Queen's danger, when the physicians begin to speak doubtfully ; but I cannot think the case desperate as long as she was able to attend a whole sermon on Christmas Day preached by the Bishop of London in her inner chamber. Yet I hear the courtiers lay about them already, and plot for leases of her land, for the keeping of Somerset House and the rest, for implements and movables, as if they were to divide a spoil."

On Twelfth Night, the 6th, Ben Jonson's masque, " Pleasure Reconciled to Virtue," was performed, and two days later the King left Whitehall for Theobalds.

Six Commissioners from the States of the United Provinces, and the Secretary of their Commission, arrived at Gravesend in January, and were brought up the river and lodged in Lombard Street. Some days later Lord Clifford and several other gentlemen of the Privy Chamber conveyed them in a procession of over twenty coaches to Whitehall, where they had their first audience in the Privy Gallery.

The King returned to Whitehall on February 1st, and on the morrow dubbed five knights. On the 6th, accompanied by the Marquis of Buckingham, he visited the Queen at Hampton Court, and returning to Whitehall there witnessed in the Hall, on Shrove Tuesday, the 9th, a repetition of Ben Jonson's New Year's masque, with the addition of an anti-masque, " For the Honour of Wales."

Queen Anne, who was forty-three years old, died of dropsy on March 1st, at Hampton Court. The Venetian Ambassador wrote of the sad event : " She breathed her last amid a few attendants in a country place, without the help of those remedies which might have lengthened her days, even if they did not cure her. However, before dying, she had time to embrace the prince, her son, and had this satisfaction as mother of the succeeding king."

The King at the time was at Newmarket, and five days afterwards, at night, the late Queen's servants conveyed the royal remains by water to Denmark (Somerset) House.

On the 12th, Ranier Zen, Venetian Ambassador in Savoy, in a despatch to the Doge and Senate, wrote of the reception in England of Antonio Donato, the new Venetian Ambassador : " The Ambassador first speaks of the honour accorded to him at his reception, greater than had been shown to any other Ambassador, by sending the royal barges to Gravesend, by salvoes of artillery and by receiving him in the great hall, and then more privately at his request. To his thanks for what had been done for his Highness the King replied graciously, saying he had done little by comparison with what he desired, and with what he would have done if peace had not ensued."

On May 1st the King removed from Theobalds to Greenwich, and on the same day the Marquis de Tremouille, French Ambassador-Extraordinary, was entertained at Gravesend, and conducted to London. On Thursday, the 13th, the body of the late Queen-Consort, in a chariot, containing her effigy, drawn by six horses, was taken to Westminster and buried in Henry VII.'s chapel.

John Chamberlain, describing the funeral to Sir Dudley Carleton, wrote : " The procession was very dull ; the Prince rode before the corpse ; the hearse was very stately ; there were 280 poor women ; the Countess of Arundel was chief mourner. . . . It was full six o'clock at night before all the solemnity was done at church, where the hearse is to continue till the next term, the fairest and stateliest that I think was ever seen there. This business passed not without some disaster, as is commonly seen in such assemblies ; a young man (a scholar named Appleyard of Lynn), being killed outright (as he stood on a scaffold underneath) by the falling of a stone from Northampton House (Northumberland House, Charing Cross), which was one of the letters S that serve for the battlements, and thrust out by mischance and carelessness by those above " (by some on the leads leaning over to see).

The Rev. Thomas Lorkin wrote : " He was presently removed thence to St. Martin's Churchyard, where divers flocking to see him, amongst the rest a scrivener's wife beheld the sad spectacle, and was so deeply affected by it, that, returning home to her house, she immediately died."

John Chamberlain's letter continued : " The King came to Greenwich on Tuesday, and the next morning the Queen's trunks and cabinets with jewels were brought thither from Denmark House, in four carts, and delivered by inventory by Sir Edward Coke and Auditor Geston. . . . A portion of them given to Buckingham, with the keeping of Denmark House and £1,200 a year in land, for his attention to the King in his last sickness."

On Whitsunday, the 16th, the King heard Bishop Andrewes preach at Greenwich. Four days later, a banquet was given to the French Special Ambassador at Whitehall, by the Duke of Lennox ; and on Tuesday, the 25th, the King held the feast of St. George at Greenwich. Of this latter occasion the Venetian Secretary wrote : " Owing to the Queen's death they postponed the annual celebration of the feast of St. George. It took place the day before yesterday at Greenwich, being performed by the Knights of the Garter, of whom his Majesty is the chief. He took part in all the ceremonies, both in the chapel and in the procession through the streets, as well as at the public dinner at which all the knights assisted. He is now in the best of health as appears by the cheerful, glad, and hearty way in which he eats. While he was drinking his eighth glass the Dutch Commissioners entered the hall, and came one by one to kiss his Majesty's hand. He did not move or say anything, but simply raised his hat from time to time, putting it on again at once. The Commissioners stood awhile, and then proceeded to the other table of the cavaliers, giving and receiving salutations with everyone. They went out to another room, where by the King's orders they found a meal prepared for them."

The following day saw the States Ambassadors feasted and entertained in the Council Chamber, and the Rev. Thomas Lorkin, writing the next day to Sir Thomas Puckering, of an event in connection with the visit of the embassy, said : " This day se'nnight, the States Commissioners and our East India Company's met before the King in the gallery at Greenwich, the one standing at one end of the gallery and the other at the other, his Majesty interposing himself between them for the accommodating of the difference, not without probability of accord, his Majesty being inclined to overrule his own people, to cause them to accept of such conditions as otherwise they would refuse, and the States yielding in some particulars likewise."

Before leaving Greenwich for Theobalds on the 28th, James received the French Ambassador Extraordinary, and took leave of him. Pier Antonio Marioni, the Venetian Secretary in England, writing of this, said : " The King is exceedingly pleased with him, and after causing many honours to be showered upon him by his ministers and magnates in London, presented him with his portrait framed in a beautifully designed frame containing two large diamonds, attached to a chain, also covered with diamonds, to wear round his neck. There must be quite 500 diamonds in all. . . . On Monday, the Dutch Commissioners (to settle disputes with England) had audience of his Majesty to take leave, as they could not arrange the point about the division of fortresses in the Indies."

On June 1st, the King on his arrival at Whitehall was met by the Recorder of London and the citizens in state. John Chamberlain wrote : " He was gaily dressed and attended, which will seem strange to the Ambassadors in mourning, come to condole (on the Queen's death) ; he stays at Greenwich and the neighbourhood till July 18th, and then goes on his progress."

On the 8th, James, at Greenwich, knighted one gentleman, and feasted an Ambassador from the Duke of Lorraine ; and during the next few days he dubbed several knights.

On Sunday, the 13th, by a special royal command, the Privy Councillors partook of the Sacrament at Greenwich, " in order to shew mutual charity one to another."

A week later the King left Whitehall for Theobalds, but on the 24th was back at Greenwich knighting a gentleman, and he dubbed several more before the 30th, on which day he left for Oatlands, after first causing a Proclamation to be issued, " for all tent keepers, artificers, and idle persons to depart from the Court within twenty-four hours, under a penalty of imprisonment."

At this time John Chamberlain wrote : " The King going to Oatlands, Oking, and Windsor ; his legs are recovered ; he bathes them in every stag and buck's belly on the place where he kills them."

On July 1st the King dubbed two knights at Oatlands, and then at Windsor, on the 7th, three more were produced before the Court returned to Whitehall. Three days later Nathaniel Brent wrote to Carleton : " The King has sat in Council about altering the price of gold 2s. a jacobus. He has gone from Whitehall to Greenwich." At the end of August the King, returning from his progress, called at Bisham Abbey and Windsor ; and on September 9th he dined at Greenwich, " being in haste to go to Wanstead."

On October 2nd, John Chamberlain wrote : " The King was here yesterday at Whitehall, but is now gone to Theobalds. He came from Hampton Court, where Sir Thomas Rowe presented him with two antelopes, a strange and beautiful kind of red deer ; a rich tent, rare carpets, certain umbrellas, and such like trinkets, from the Great Mogul."

In the opening days of November, the King dubbed one or two knights at Whitehall, and on the 7th he dined at Greenwich and named some ships launched that day at Deptford. Two more knights were turned out on the 8th, then James returned to Whitehall, and on the morrow made five knights. On December 23rd the King arrived at Whitehall for the season, and having given the Venetian Ambassador an audience, he, on Christmas Day— Saturday—heard a sermon from Bishop Andrewes.

1620. The year 1620 opened with great quietude in the nation. The King, now quite averse to all public gaiety, was content with the society of the Prince, Buckingham, and a few favourites, who kept his conceit alive by rather gross flattery. After a short excursion from Whitehall he returned, and on Ash Wednesday, February 10th, heard Bishop Andrewes preach.

George Shirley, Chief Justice of Ireland, was knighted by the King at Whitehall, on March 2nd; and two days later the Prince of Wales invited the Peers to a banquet and a play at Somerset House.

At this time the Conde de Gondemar, Spanish Ambassador, arrived at Dover and was conducted by the Master of the Ceremonies to Gravesend, where the Earl of Dorset and a train of the King's servants met him, and escorting him up the river in the royal barges, landed at Tower Wharf, where nearly thirty coaches were waiting to take him and his retinue in procession to Ely House in Holborn. On the 12th, he had his first public audience of the King at Whitehall, and on the occasion the floor of the Terrace sank down as the Ambassador passed, causing a superstitious panic among the courtiers, but the King refused to see anything ominous in the accident.

The Spanish Ambassador, on the 21st, had an audience of the King, lasting two hours, in the Private Gallery at Whitehall.

On Friday, the 24th, the Prince of Wales, the Marquis of Buckingham, and other nobles, performed tilting at the ring and other exercises in honour of the monarch's accession day.

Two days later—Mid-Lent Sunday—the King

rode on horseback, in royal pomp, to St. Paul's Cathedral, and attended a service for commencing a subscription for the repair of the edifice, especially the restoration of the spire, which was struck by lightning and destroyed by fire in 1561. After the rendering of an anthem in the church, a sermon was preached at the Cross by Dr. King, Bishop of London, from a text given by the King—Psalm cii. 13, 14 : " Thou shalt arise, and have mercy upon Zion : for the time to favour her, yea, the set time, is come. For Thy servants take pleasure in her stones, and favour the dust thereof."

At the conclusion of the sermon, James and his suite proceeded to the Bishop's house and dined there, when it was resolved to issue a royal commission for raising the necessary funds.

The following ballad was composed for this event :—

" God bless our noble King,
  Was there ever such a thing !
In March, when the weather waxed cold,
  He wen. from Whitehall
  To the Church of St. Paull,
Which ofttime hath been bought and sold.

When he came to Temple Bar,
  Which you know it is not far,
The streets were rail'd on every side ;
  There were many gay babies,
  And fair brave painted ladies,
' God bless our noble King ! ' they all cried.

The Mayor of the town
  Came in a velvet gown
And with him never catchpole or varlet,
  But jobbernolls there were plenty,
  Aldermen almost twenty,
And most of them were clad all in scarlet.

The Mayor laid down his mace
And cry'd ' God save your Grace,
And keep our King from all evil !
With all my heart, I then wist
The good mace had been in my fist,
To ha' pawn'd it for supper at the 'Devil.'

The master Recorder,
In very seemly order
Made unto the King such a speech,
In such mild and loving sort,
As most men do report,
It made their hearts to fall into their breech.

It would have done your hearts good
To ha' seen how the company stood,
With their flags and their banners so gay ;
Their wives they were not there,
Might a man not safely swear
There was many a cuckold made that day ?

Archie came in gold
Most glorious to behold,
Which made the people fall into a laughter ;
Some men that stood by,
When the fool they did spy
Expected many lords to follow after.

When they miss'd the King's cloak
It sore amaz'd the folk
To see him in his doublet and his hose ;
His horse had, before and behind,
To feathers to keep off the wind,
Which was as good as you may well suppose.

But when he came to Paul's
God bless all Christian souls !
Open flew the great west door
And in the King did enter,
Was he not bold to venture,
That never was in Paul's in life before.

The priests in their copes,
Like to so many popes,
Sung all to rejoicing of the people ;

And as they all sung,
The bells they should have rung,
But i' faith there was but one in the steeple.

God bless our noble King,
In winter and in spring,
The prince and the lady so gay !
God bless our lords and many more,
The bishops, earls and judges,
Would ever rejoice to see this day."

On April 2nd, Dr. John Donne preached at
Whitehall, and early in the month the King went to
Hampton Court, where he made two knights, and
on Easter Sunday, the 16th, was back again at
Whitehall hearing a sermon from Bishop Andrewes.
The Prince of Wales and the Marquises of Bucking-
ham and Hamilton were running at the ring in the
Tiltyard on the 18th, while the King made a knight
in the palace.

John Chamberlain wrote to Carleton on the 29th :
" The King is now at Greenwich, where the solemnity
of St. George's Day was kept on Thursday last."
On Sunday, the next day, Dr. Donne again delivered
a sermon at Whitehall. After entertaining Prince
Charles and the other Tilters to a splendid banquet
on May day, the King shortly after went to Greenwich for the rest of the month. On Whitsunday,
June 4th, he took the Sacrament from Bishop
Andrewes, and heard Dr. Mountaine, Bishop of
Lincoln, preach. Sir Henry Wotton was at Court
at this time, writing a sonnet on the Queen of
Bohemia. On the following Sunday, the monarch,
after evening prayers, went from Greenwich to
Whitehall, and on the 19th he celebrated his birth-
day at Windsor. Oatlands was visited in July, and
on August 4th John Chamberlain wrote to Carleton :

"The Spanish Ambassador went yesterday to Hampton Court, where he hath obtained leave to lie and lodge this summer."

In another letter of September 9th, Chamberlain said : "Sir Robt. Mansell and his companions gone to Windsor to take leave of the King ; their equipage is so rich that it is thought they cannot be going merely against Algiers pirates. Some Aldermen of London have gone to Windsor to surrender their new Charter, for which Mr. Attorney suffers so much. . . . Lord Doncaster made a feast at Syon (House) to Buckingham and others." The King came to Whitehall on the last day of this month, and on the morrow, after touching for the evil, left for Theobalds. Thomas Locke wrote to Carleton on November 11th : "The King gave an audience to the Spanish Ambassador in the gallery at Whitehall ; he caused several pieces to be cut out of pictures in the gallery which reflected on the Spaniards."

Towards the latter part of December, the King suffered from an attack of the gout, and could not go to chapel. Bishop Andrewes preached before him on Christmas Day, when he dubbed two knights.

On December 28th a French Ambassador Extraordinary, the Marquis de Cadenet, arrived at Gravesend from Dover. The Earl of Arundel, accompanied by Lord Hunsdon and various gentlemen of the King's Privy Chamber, in about twenty royal barges, went down the river, and that night welcomed, in the King's name, the Ambassador in his lodgings at Gravesend. The next day he was brought up the river, and landing at the Garden Stairs, was conducted to Somerset House. On Sunday afternoon, the 31st, the Ambassador had his first audience at Whitehall—"which was the occasion that many thousands profaned the day to behold that fading spectacle, neglecting the service of God in the meantime in their several parish churches."

1621. On Monday, New Year's Day, 1621, the Marquis was conducted from Somerset House to Westminster, where the King, who had come from Whitehall in his barge, met him before entering the House of Lords, and gave him, together with the accredited Ambassador, a gracious audience. Next day the Duke of Lennox entertained him at Hampton Court with hawking and hunting. On Wednesday the King went by water to Westminster, and in the Upper House of Parliament gave the Ambassador a splendid banquet. Sir Symonds D'Ewes wrote of the Marquis : " Before his departure in the morning from Somerset House, I went thither and had three several sights of him, and found him to be a proper tall man and a gallant courtier, notwithstanding his original was very mean and base. His hatband, scarf, and clothes were so richly set out with diamonds, as they were valued to amount unto between £30,000 or £40,000 ; but most of them were conceived to be the jewels of the Crown of France, and only made use of for this occasion." On Twelfth Day, January 6th, the King attended service in the chapel at Whitehall, " but they had much ado to support him." He offered gold, frankincense and myrrh, and touched eighty persons for the evil. In the evening the French Ambassador and the Court were present at the performance of Ben Jonson's masque, " News from the New World, Discovered in the Moon." No person below the rank of a Baron was allowed to be present.

John Chamberlain wrote that at this masque

P

there were disputes for precedency, and " a puritan was flouted and abused, which was thought unseemly, considering the state of the French Protestants."

On this same day an Order was issued for paying to John de Crites, the King's Serjeant Painter, Clement Chapman, joiner, Maximilian Colt, carver, and William Bourdman, the royal locksmith, £200, in part payment of £400, for building and finishing a privy barge for the King's service during the coming Parliament.

On Monday, the 8th, the French Ambassador enjoyed the spectacle of the Prince of Wales, the Marquis of Buckingham and others running at the ring in the Tiltyard at Whitehall.

Thomas Locke wrote the same day to Sir Dudley Carleton : " Cap. North, who returned from the Amazon River well fraught, is committed to the Tower."

On the 13th an Order was given in Council for joining in the operations for the recovery of the Palatinate, and the next day the King left Whitehall for Theobalds.

John Chamberlain wrote to Carleton on the 20th : " The French Ambassador went hence on Sunday morning, having sent away the most part of his train two days before, being himself such a fresh-water sailor, that he rather chose to go by coach through all the foul ways than take the benefit of the river to Gravesend."

At this time six Commissioners from the States of the United Provinces arrived at Gravesend, and were conducted to London and lodged in Lombard Street.

James was back at Whitehall, making one or

two knights, in the latter part of the month, and in the evening of Shrove Sunday, February 11th, Ben Jonson's masque, " News from the New World," was repeated before the Court. On Shrove Tuesday evening, the King, after dubbing a knight, witnessed in the Hall a masque presented by the gentlemen of the Middle Temple.

On March 10th, the King, after conducting business with the House of Commons, enjoyed the recreation of hawking.

A Polish Ambassador landed at Gravesend on the 16th, and was welcomed by Sir Lewis Lewkenor, Master of the Ceremonies (who resided at Chiswick), Sir Robert Stewart, and other gentlemen. The next morning a royal and three other barges brought them all up the river, and landing at Tower Wharf, the Ambassador was received by the Earl of Warwick, Lord Cromwell, and others. Seven or eight coaches then conducted the Embassy to Crutched Friars, where a lodging had been taken at a certain agreed daily rate, " without attendance of any of the King's servants."

On Sunday, the 18th, the Polish Ambassador had his public audience at Whitehall, when he delivered a Latin oration before the King.

On the 24th—the anniversary of the King's accession—a great Tilting took place at Whitehall ; and the next day James knighted Thomas Richardson, the Speaker. He heard Bishop Andrewes preach on Easter Sunday, April 1st, and later in the month celebrated the feast of St. George, at which the Polish Ambassador was one of the guests.

About the middle of May, the King made one or two knights at Greenwich ; and on Whitsunday, the 20th, again listened to Bishop Andrewes.

On July 9th, the King was at Windsor making one knight ; and the next day the Great Seal was bestowed on John Williams, Dean of Salisbury and Westminster.

The King arrived at Windsor from his progress on September 9th. During the monarch's short stay at the Castle, Ben Jonson's masque, " The Metamorphosed Gipsies," was performed ; and, on the 11th, James dubbed a knight at Whitehall, where he resided over Christmas, holding a Council on December 30th, and making a knight on the last day of the year.

1622. On January 5th, 1622, the King dubbed two knights, and on Twelfth Night, the 6th, Ben Jonson's " Masque of Augurs " was performed by the Prince of Wales and other lords and gentlemen. It was said that later : " The Gentlemen of Gray's Inn, to make an end of Christmas, on Twelfth Night, in the dead time of the night, shot off all the chambers they had borrowed from the Tower, being as many as filled four carts. The King, awakened with the noise, started out of his bed, and cried, ' Treason, Treason,' etc., and that the city was in an uproar, in such sort (as it is told) that the whole Court was raised and almost in arms, the Earl of Arundel running to the bedchamber with his sword drawn as to rescue the King's person."

On April 3rd, Sir John Finett wrote : " I had order from my Lord Chamberlain that the Master of the Ceremonies being imployed to Dover with the King's coach and fourteen other at his Majesty's charge, to bring up the Emperor's Ambassador Swartzenberg, and that the said Ambassador was in the interim landed at Gravesend, I should take one of his Majesty's barges, and hasten thither to

receive him, and excuse that cross encounter, letting
him know that the Marquess of Hamilton was to
come down to receive him that evening. With
which order I took barge when the tide was far
spent, and rowed down till we met a flowing water
and a strong contrary wind at Woolwich, so was
forced to land there, and, finding no horses, to go
on foot five miles to Dartford ; where, taking post
to Gravesend, I found there Sir Lewis Lewkner
returned from Canterbury, and delivered my message
from his Majesty to the Ambassador. That evening
my Lord Marquess Hamilton, accompanied with the
Lord Wentworth, Lord Bruse, and about twenty
gentlemen, came to his lodging, and was met by
him in the entry, almost at the street-door of the
Inn, conducted by him to his chamber, the Ambassador, after some little refusal, preceding (though in
his own house), and after brought back by them to
the street door. The next morning my Lord
Marquess again repaired to him with the company
of the Lord Viscount Doncaster, then on his way
Ambassador-Extraordinary for France, and a while
after the Ambassador repaid their visits at the
Marquess's Inn ; when, the tide serving, we all
came to London in ten barges—the Ambassadoi,
the Marquess, the two English lords, three Dutch
lords, and the Master of the Ceremonies, in the first
barge ; two Dutch barons, myself, and four or five
English in the second ; and the rest in the rest as
they encountered. Landing at Denmark House
garden stairs, the Marquess accompanied him to his
chamber there, and was by the Ambassador re-
accompanied to his coach. The Sunday following,
April seven, the same Lord Marquess, accompanied
with the Earl of Montgomery, the Lords Candish,

Bruse, two other Lords, and about twenty gentlemen listed with divers voluntaries, in near forty coaches, besides others hired at the King's charge to attend daily, fetched him from Denmark House to his audience in the Higher House of Parliament, where he made his oration in High Dutch, interpreted by Sir Robert Anstroder, to whom it had been the day before imparted in writing. He was conducted by the Marquess and the rest to the Prince at St. James's, with whom he passed his compliment in Italian, whereto the Prince called me for interpreter, and thence returned with the same attendance to his lodging in Denmark House."

The King, before leaving Hampton Court on the 6th, knighted Matthew Brand, and the next day Marmaduke Lloyd at Whitehall.

On the 11th the Imperial Ambassador had his second audience. He was fetched from Denmark (Somerset) House " by the service of six or seven barges, by the Earl of Aubigney and other Lords and gentlemen ; landing at the Privy-stairs at Whitehall, and passing through the shield-gallery and the late Queen's lodgings into the King's privy-gallery and his Withdrawing-room there, where the King held discourse with him an hour together ' remotis arbitris.' "

On Sunday, the 14th, the Earl of Rutland conducted the Imperial Ambassador by water from Somerset House to the Upper House of Parliament, where, seated on the King's left hand, he was publicly feasted. The Ambassador went on the following Wednesday, with all his followers, in six of the royal barges to Gravesend, where all embarked in two ships—" appointed by the King, but paid by himself "—and sailed for Dunkirk. Sir John Finett

wrote : " At his parting he left his Majesty's officers
and servants little satisfied with the gratuities."

The next day James made one knight at Whitehall, and on Easter Sunday, the 21st, heard Bishop
Andrewes preach.

The King listened to a sermon from Dr. Walter
Curll, Dean of Lichfield, on Sunday, the 28th ; and
on May day he supped with the Lord Treasurer
Middlesex at Chelsea.

A new Spanish Ambassador, Don Carlos de Colona,
arrived in May, and had his first audience at Whitehall. Sir John Finett wrote : " Three or four days
after the Conde de Gondemar took his leave of the
King at Greenwich, and with an extraordinary
honour dined that day privately with his Majesty."

Dr. Laud wrote in his diary on the 10th : " I
went to the Court to Greenwich and came back in
the coach with the Lord Marquess of Buckingham."

On June 12th, the King made one knight at
Whitehall ; and the next day the Russian Ambassador departed. Sir John Finett wrote on this
occasion : " We went together in the King's coach
to the Ambassador's house, and thence with five
other to the Tower Wharf, where the Lord Stanhope
leaving the Ambassador, he entered the King's
barge, and his followers in another, and, with the
company of Sir John Merrick (formerly English
Ambassador to Russia), Alderman Hammersley, and
other merchants, we came to Gravesend, lodged at
the ' Christopher,' were there feasted that night by
the Muscovy Company, and the next morning making
use of the King's barge to carry us to their ships
riding four miles off at Tilbury, he there embarked,
and we returned that night to London."

Dr. Laud wrote in his diary on the 15th : " I

became C (chaplain or confessor) to my Lord of Buckingham. And June 16th, being Trinity Sunday, he received the Sacrament at Greenwich."

On Friday, the 17th, Signor Valeresso, the new Venetian Ambassador, was brought by the Master of the Ceremonies from Gravesend to London.

The King crossed the river on Sunday from Greenwich, and proceeded to Wanstead House, where he knighted one gentleman ; and returned to the Kentish palace the next day in time to give the Venetian Ambassador his first audience.

John Chamberlain wrote to Carleton on the 22nd : " On Sunday, the Lord Mayor (Edward Barkham) went to Greenwich to be knighted, where the Recorder made a good speech, which was graciously accepted, and the suit granted, after some few memorandums to the Lord Mayor and his brethren, about Middleton's water (the New River), the swarming of beggars, the cleansing and removing the shelves of sand out of the Thames, the building (repair) of Paul's, and the like."

On the 28th, a letter to the Rev. John Mead ran : " His Majesty, the Prince, etc., were feasted on Tuesday night at Cobham Hall, by the lord Duke (of Lennox). On Wednesday early, he went to Chatham, viewed the navy, and came back to Greenwich that night."

At the end of June the King left Greenwich, and after a brief visit to Norwich, he proceeded to Oatlands, where a knight was dubbed on July 3rd.

On the 6th, the young Prince-Landgrave of Hesse, after a three months' sojourn in England, embarked at Gravesend for his own country. Sir John Finett wrote that he accompanied the Prince to Gravesend, " though without order, or without use of the King's barge, or other respect of extraordinary honour by present, or the like, only I moving the Lord Admiral (the Marquis of Buckingham) for a ship of his Majesty to transport him, he had assigned him a lesser of two ships then riding in the Downs."

The King made two knights at Windsor on the 10th, and one at Whitehall a fortnight later.

On August 5th, the anniversary of the Gowrie conspiracy, Bishop Andrewes preached before the King at Windsor. On the same day the Spanish Ambassador was feasted at the Castle, " where there passed only three healths, to the King of Spain, the Infanta of Brussels, and the Infanta Maria, which the Prince pledged with much ceremony. He and the Marquess of Buckingham went every evening into the Thames near to Eton, where the best swimming was, but so attended with choice company and a boat or two, that there could be no danger."

A Scotchman was knighted at Windsor on the 6th, and an Italian a month later. On October 5th the King moved from Hampton Court to Theobalds ; and on Christmas Day he heard the usual sermon from Bishop Andrewes at Whitehall.

1623. With the early days of 1623 came an attack of gout to the King, and held him prisoner for a time at Whitehall. On Twelfth Night, Ben Jonson's and Inigo Jones's masque, " Time Vindicated to Himself and to his Honours," was performed at the Court ; and it was repeated on Sunday, January 19th.

On February 1st, Sir John Finett wrote that the States Ambassadors, " after they had spent here the full time of fourteen months in negotiating, and had had of the King and Council above sixty audiences, they went in coaches of their own without the

King's to Tower Wharf, and there embarked in hired and borrowed barges to their ships which laid not far off, and were purposely sent to transport them."

In connection with the secret romantic journey of the Prince of Wales in search of a Spanish bride, John Chamberlain wrote to Carleton, on the 22nd : " On Monday the Prince with the Lord of Buckingham, going from Theobalds, and giving out they were going to New Hall, turned down towards the Thames, and coming to Tilbury, ferried over to Gravesend, so to Rochester, Canterbury, and Dover, where taking ship, on Wednesday morning, it is thought they had a fair passage to Dieppe, and so mean to post into Spain. Their fair riding coats and false beards, of which one fell off at Gravesend, caused suspicion, and messengers were sent after them, who overtook them near Sittingbourne." Sir Henry Wotton said : " When they passed the river against Gravesend, for lack of silver they were fain to give the ferryman a piece or two of twenty shillings, which struck the poor fellow into such a melting tenderness that so good gentlemen should be going (for so he suspected) about some quarrel beyond sea, as he could not forbear to acquaint the officers of the town with what had befallen him, who sent presently post for their stay at Rochester, through which they were passed before any intelligence could arrive."

On Ash Wednesday, March 5th, Bishop Andrewes preached before the King at Whitehall ; and on the 23rd, Dr. Laud, now Bishop of St. David's, recorded in his diary that he preached in the chapel.

The Earl of Leicester wrote to Sir Dudley Carleton on April 4th : " The King has a swelling in his knee, but returns to town to-morrow, and will go to Windsor for St. George's Day, when Marquis Hamilton is to be made Knight of the Garter."

On Palm Sunday, the Archbishop of Canterbury delivered a sermon to the Court ; and, on Easter Sunday, the 13th, Bishop Andrewes preached before the King at Whitehall. A move was then made to Hampton Court, where four days later three knights were dubbed. James was at Windsor on the 24th, returning in the following week to Hampton Court, and finally on the 30th to Whitehall.

On May 3rd, John Chamberlain wrote from London to Carleton : " The King kept St. George's Feast at Windsor, where there was no great show, nor the knights and procession went not out their ordinary circuit, by reason of the King was fain to be carried in a chair, not for any grief or infirmity more than the weakness of his legs. . . . Secretary Conway was there, gallantly attired in white hat and feather. . . . On Monday the King moved to Hampton Court ; on Thursday hither ; and on Thursday, the first of this month, went a-maying to Theobalds. He passed through a muster of 6,000 men with little applause, but the firing terrified Secretary Conway's horses. This day the Court removes to Greenwich, and where it is like to continue till towards the progress, which will be westward."

On the 17th, Chamberlain wrote : " On Sunday was sevennight, Captain Burroughs, coming from Gravesend, landed at Greenwich before coming to this town (London). Secretary Conway carried him presently to the King, who used him very graciously, and made him knight."

Secretary Conway wrote to the Earl of Rutland

on the 30th : " The King dines at Whitehall, and sleeps at Greenwich."

On June 8th, Peter Proby, the Lord Mayor of London, was knighted at Greenwich.

John Chamberlain wrote to Carleton on the 14th : " The Council are going about to eat at ordinaries, in order to choose which is fittest and cheapest to furnish diet for the expected Spanish Ambassador, whom Lord Kelly has gone to meet at Gravesend, with the King's barges."

On Sunday, the 15th, the King made a knight, and next day, the Marquis Inojosa, Spanish Ambassador-Extraordinary, went from Gravesend, by way of Dartford, to Greenwich, and, after a banquet in the Presence Chamber, had an audience and delivered his letters. He was then brought to London, and, through a street full of coaches and people, conducted to Exeter House, in the Strand.

Early in July the King was at Oatlands and Windsor ; and on Sunday, the 20th, a splendid entertainment was given at Whitehall to the two Spanish Ambassadors.

The King returned to Windsor from a Western progress on September 7th, and after a few days stay left the Castle, and was welcomed to Whitehall by the ringers of St. Margaret's. On the 25th he was at Hampton Court.

On October 6th, great public rejoicings on the river marked the return of Prince Charles from Spain. The Prince came to Lambeth Stairs, where Archbishop Abbot received him and kissed his hand. He then, accompanied by Buckingham, the Archbishop, and a brilliant train of nobles, embarked in the archiepiscopal barge, and after being rowed some little time on the water, landed at York House.

John Taylor described the scene in a book entitled, " Prince Charles, his welcome from Spain, with the triumphs of London for the same, his happie arrivall, etc." An attached note remarked : " This is to be remembered, that two watermen at the Tower burnt their boats in a bonfire, most merrily."

Dr. Francis Ryves, in a letter to Bishop Usher, of Meath, wrote : " All London rang with bells and flared with bonfires, and resounded all over with such shouts as is not well possible to express."

Robert Tanfielde wrote from the Temple to Edward, Lord Mountague, at Boughton : " If we may believe bonfires, bells, or the reports of the Tower ordnance, I may then confidently report the Prince is safely landed. This morning the streets were so stuffed with fires as that betwixt Whitehall and Temple Barr my man told three hundred and odd, and at Whitehall, Northampton House, York House, and Somerset House there is hogsheads of wine set forth into the street."

The bells of St. Margaret's, Westminster, Lambeth, Kingston, and elsewhere also pealed out a joyous welcome, and much relief was felt at the safe conclusion of the Prince's foolishly romantic escapade.

On November 5th, Don Diego de Mexia (Mendoza), Spanish Ambassador - Extraordinary, arrived in the Thames, and, received at Gravesend by Lord Chichester of Belfast, was conducted to the lodgings of the three other Spanish special Ambassadors, " whither he came on foot after his landing at the Savoy, whilst the King's and noblemen's coaches, sent from Court to receive him at Denmark House had a countermand to take him in at the Tower, but the tide falling fair otherwise than was supposed to give him safe passage under the Bridge, they missed him." On Saturday, the 15th, the Earl of Kelly brought Don Diego from Exeter House to an audience of the King at Whitehall. After a visit to Theobalds, the bells of St. Margaret's welcomed the King's return to Whitehall for the Christmas season, and on December 25th, the faithful old Bishop Andrewes preached his customary sermon.

1624. On Twelfth Night, January 6th, 1624, the masque—alluding to the return of Prince Charles —named "Neptune's Triumph for the Return of Albion," the joint invention of Ben Jonson and Inigo Jones, was performed at Court. A Welshman was knighted on the 10th, and, after a visit to Hampton Court, the King, on Ash Wednesday, February 26th, heard Bishop Andrewes preach at Whitehall. On the morning of the 16th, Ludovick Stuart, Duke of Richmond and Lennox, died suddenly in bed in his lodging at Whitehall. His corpse was conveyed " with all magnificence from Ely House in the Holborn to interment in Westminster Abbey." Calderwood wrote of this prince : " His death was dolorous both to English and Scottish. He was well liked of for his courtesy, meekness, liberality to his servants and followers."

On the 25th, the Master of the Ceremonies, Sir Lewis Lewkenor, welcomed at Gravesend two Ambassadors from the States of the United Provinces, and the next day they were brought up the river in the King's barge, and received on landing at Tower Wharf by Lord Wentworth, who conducted the whole embassy in six coaches to lodgings in Lombard Street.

Dr. Laud wrote in his diary on Sunday the 29th :

" In the evening the Duke of Buckingham's coach was overthrown between Exeter House and the Savoy. The Spanish Ambassador lay there. No omen I hope more than they thought to soil him. Secretary Conway was in the coach with him. Mr. Bond came in to the help, and told it me." On the same day the King gave audience at Whitehall to the two Ambassadors of the United Provinces.

Dr. Laud preached at Whitehall on Sunday, March 7th.

The two ambassadors of the United Provinces had another audience on the 25th.

On Friday, April 23rd, Ernest, Count Mansfeldt, General of the Protestant army in Germany, who a few days before had landed at Gravesend, was made a Knight of the Garter at Whitehall. The King kept St. George's Day at Windsor, where the new Duke of Lennox was installed a garter knight.

The Court was at Greenwich in May, and here Martin Lumley, Lord Mayor of London, was knighted. At this time the favourite Buckingham, recovering from an indisposition, was taken to Greenwich by the King, who helped him into the coach with his own hands. The Court spent all June at Greenwich, and various knights were made.

At the beginning of July, the King, although suffering from a touch of the gout, journeyed to Oatlands, and from thence to Windsor. On Thursday, the 1st, Sir Lewis Lewkenor wrote to Secretary Conway : " The Marquis d'Effiat has arrived, will be at Gravesend to-morrow, and will go for London on Saturday at 7 A.M., as the tide will then serve him to shoot the Bridge, and go by water to Suffolk House. This will be more convenient than landing at Tower Wharf, since the

noblemen who usually send carriages on such
occasions are out of Town." This French Ambassador-Extraordinary, brought to Suffolk House by
the Earl of Warwick, was allowed £40 per day for
provisions. On Sunday, the 4th, James gave
audience at Windsor to the French Marquis, and
made one knight. The next day the King reminded
the Privy Council of the violation of the proclama-
tions for the reformation of buildings in and
about London.

On September 4th, John Chamberlain wrote in a
letter to Sir Dudley Carleton : " The King comes
this night to Windsor (from his progress). The
Lord of Buckingham and his Lady meet him there
from New-hall, where he feasted the French Ambassador this day se'nnight, when he came to town
to christen his brother the Earl of Anglesey's young
daughter at Fulham. Art. Brett is released from
the Tower, but forbidden Court." The King left
Windsor for Whitehall, where, on the 9th, he knighted
John Cook, the Master of Bequests. On the 26th,
James dubbed two knights at Hampton Court,
where the Prince of Wales was laid up, after suffering
a bad fall from his horse. Dudley Carleton wrote
on the 30th to his uncle, Sir Dudley : " The King
arrived in town last night, but before going to
Whitehall conferred two hours with Buckingham
at Wallingford House."

In October, the Prince, recovered from his fall,
was living quietly at Hampton Court and Richmond.

On the 9th, John Chamberlain wrote to Carleton :
" The Earl of Somerset is pardoned, and has taken
a house at Chiswick, but promises not to go near
the Court."

At the end of November another French Ambas-

sador—M. de Villiauler, Secretary of State—arrived
at Gravesend from Dover, where, Sir John Finett
wrote, he was received by the Earl of Dorset and
twenty-five gentlemen, " and others come down
thither with two-and-twenty barges. These (with
regard of the tide's unfitness) were commanded to
attend at Tower Wharf about noon, and his lordship hastening thither by land in coach, we rowed
two hours against the tide, and coming to our Inn
in the evening, waited on his lordship to the Ambassador's lodging, where in the midst of the entry
towards the stair foot, my Lord was met by the
Marquis de Rothelin, brother-in-law to Monsieur
de Villiauler, and Monsieur de Massy, his other
brother-in-law, and received by him and his colleague
on the top of the Stairs (no sooner). Thence, after
a long contention, the Earl of Dorset entered first
the chamber, after him Mon. de Villiauler, next
him (with the like strife) Sir Edward Herbert (not
long before Ambassador ordinary in France), and
then M. de Fiat. At his lordship's return the
Ambassadors (enforcing likewise upon him the
precedence) brought him to the street door. In
the time of my lord's supper the Ambassador sent
a gentleman to know of him his commodity
of embarking the next morning, and had the
like compliment returned from my lord by a
gentleman, with the good-night, and the liberty
of his time to embark (howsoever the tide
would invite him to be ready against eleven of
the clock the next day), and after some question
from his lordship, whether he were again to repair
to the Ambassador's, if he did not personally return
his visit the next morning, and a resolution here-
upon from the Master of the Ceremonies, Sir Edward

Q

Herbert, myself, and others there, that though they
should fail of their compliment, he must not of his
to fetch them from their Inn to their embarking,
he performed it, and with the two Ambassadors,
the Marquis de Rothelin, Sir Edward Herbert,
M. de Massy, and the Master of the Ceremonies in
the first barge, some other principal persons and
myself in the second, we came to our landing at
Suffolk House."

On December 23rd, the King, whose health was
now very infirm, made a knight at Whitehall ;
and on Christmas Day—Saturday—he heard Bishop
Andrewes preach, and knighted two Scotch captains.
Several other knights were created before the end
of the month. John Chamberlain said the King
" kept his chamber all that Christmas, not coming
once to the chapel, nor to any of the plays ; only,
in fair weather, he looked abroad in his litter to see
some flights at the brook."

1625. The King knighted several gentlemen early
in January, 1625, and on Sunday, the 9th, Ben
Jonson's Twelfth Night masque, " The Fortunate
Isles and their Union," was performed before the
Court. Another masque presented there early in
the year was " Pan's Anniversary, or the Shepherd's
Holiday," the joint work of Ben Jonson and Inigo
Jones.

The King died on March 27th, of an ague, at
Theobalds, aged fifty-nine. The same day—which
was Mid-Lent Sunday, Dr. Laud wrote in his diary :
" I preached at Whitehall. I ascended the pulpit
much troubled, and in a very melancholy moment,
the report then spreading that his Majesty King
James, of most sacred memory to me, was dead.
Being interrupted with the dolours of the Duke

of Buckingham, I broke off my sermon in the middle. The King died at Theobalds about three-quarters of an hour past eleven in the forenoon. He breathed forth his blessed soul most religiously, and with great constancy of faith and courage." William Neve, in a letter to Sir Thomas Hollonde, wrote that the body was embalmed, " and remained there until the 4th of April; it came from there in a black velvet coach, and by torchlight, thereto being allowed three hundred dozen. Yesternight, between nine and ten of the clock, it was conveyed through Smithfield, Holbourne, Chancery Lane, so to Denmark (Somerset) House in this manner: First the guards; secondly, gentlemen, esquires, knights, etc.; then pensioners, then trumpets, then heralds, then the body, then the lords in coaches—the prince first, most of them meeting the body at Wood's-close; then of others in coaches, about 120, which would have been more had not the weather been extreme. The body was, by the gentlemen of the bedchamber, carried into the withdrawing chamber to the privy-chamber, wherein is an effigy to be laid on a bed of honour, and there reposed. The privy-chamber is also fringed with velvet, the presence-chamber with cloth, and the guard's chamber with bays. All state observed there by the servants, as if the King were living."

The interment took place in Westminster Abbey.

RELIGIOUS LIFE ALONG THE RIVER.

1603. At the death of Elizabeth, Archbishop Whitgift, a man of most estimable private virtues, feared that his strenuous and lifelong labours in resisting both the Catholics and Puritans, and since his accession to the Primacy in 1583, in obtaining an absolute uniformity in the religion of the country, would be rendered abortive by the reported indifference of the new monarch to the Church of England.

During the closing days of the late Queen, the Archbishop had, on the last Sunday in February, consecrated in the chapel at Lambeth, Dr. Bennet to the bishopric of Hereford, and Dr. Griggons to that of Norwich.

On May 4th, William Laud—the Churchman whose fortunes rose to almost limitless power and sunk in disastrous eclipse with the Stuarts—was chosen Proctor of the University of Oxford.

In August, David English was presented to the Vicarage of St. Dunstan's, Stepney. This church was the favourite one for the marriages of the riverside population, and the contracting parties came not only from Stepney, but Limehouse, Ratcliffe, Shadwell, Poplar, Wapping, and other parishes; and many of the bridegrooms were watermen, mariners, and shipwwrights.

1604. On Saturday, January 14th, 1604, the

much-talked-of Conference on Conformity in Religious Worship and " for the determining of things held to be amiss in the Church," was opened at Hampton Court Palace, under the presidency of the King ; and the discussions, continued into the following week, were maintained on the one side by the Archbishop of Canterbury, eight bishops, five deans, and two doctors ; and on the other by Dr. Reynolds and four other Puritan divines. No permanent result was obtained from this religious disputation beyond some slight alterations in the Book of Common Prayer.

Sir George Paule, Comptroller of the Archbishop's household at Lambeth, wrote that Dr. Whitgift, in connection with the Conference, appointed a meeting at the Bishop of London's house at Fulham, " to confer with some of the Bishops and Judges of his court, concerning the affairs of the Church, which were there to be treated upon. As he was thus going in his barge upon an extraordinary cold day, and having his barge-cloth tied up (as his custom was) to the top of the bale, the wind blew very sharply ; so that the young gentlemen (shaking with cold) desired to have the cloth down, which he would by no means permit, because the water was rough and he would therefore see his way. By reason whereof the slashing of the water and sharpness of the air did so pierce the Archbishop (being above three score and thirteen years of age) that he complained the same night of a great cold, which he had then taken in the mould of his head." Notwithstanding his indisposition, the Archbishop went to the Court at Whitehall on the following Sunday—the first in Lent—and with Bishop Bancroft of London had a long speech of the King, both before and after service in the chapel. Presently going to the Council Chamber for dinner, he was seized with a paralysis and carried to the Lord Treasurer's chamber, afterwards being conveyed in his barge to Lambeth.

The King visited the sick Primate on the following Tuesday, and on Wednesday, the 29th of February, he died in great peace.

Meanwhile James and his Privy Council issued from Whitehall a proclamation for banishing from the kingdom all Jesuits and Seminary priests; and, on July 16th, a proclamation, issued from Oatlands, enjoined " Conformity to the form of the service of God established."

After an interval of more than nine months Dr. Richard Bancroft, Bishop of London, was appointed Archbishop of Canterbury on December 10th. This staunch Anglican prelate, who had taken a principal part in the Hampton Court Conference, and disputed with Dr. Reynolds on predestination, came to the Primacy with feelings of stern severity against the steadily increasing power of the Puritans; and it is probable that to this he owed his advancement. Camden called him " a person of singular courage and prudence in all matters relating to the discipline and establishment of the Church." His estimation of Puritanism was set forth in a sermon preached some years before in St. Paul's, in these words : " A very strange matter if it were true that Christ should erect a form of government for the ruling of His Church to continue from His departure out of the world until His coming again, and that the same should never be once thought of or put in practice for the space of fifteen hundred years."

One of the Primate's first acts was the consecration in Lambeth Chapel, on December 30th, of Dr. Richard Parry as Bishop of St. Asaph's.

Early in 1604, David Lindsay was presented by the King to the Rectory of St. Olave's, Southwark, where the new incumbent found his parishioners lamentably decimated by the Plague.

A few weeks later Thomas Harvey became Rector of Woolwich, on the presentation of the Bishop of Rochester ; and in November Francis Burley was appointed Rector of St. Benet's, Paul's Wharf.

1605. On January 30th, 1605, Edward Elton was presented to the Rectory of Bermondsey by Rowland Trappes. A few months before the advent of the new Rector, the singular ceremony took place in Bermondsey Church of the re-union of a man and his wife, after a long separation, during which the woman had married another husband and now forsook him for her rightful partner. The entry in the register concluded : " Ralphe Good-child, of the parish of Barkinge in Thames Street, and Elizabeth his wife, were agreed to live together, and thereupon gave their hands one to another, making either of them a solemne vow soe to doe."

Early in 1605, Archbishop Bancroft exhibited to the King and Council " certain articles of abuses which are desired to be reformed in granting of prohibitions " ; and on March 30th, " sitting in his library within his Manor of Lambeth," he issued a process against the clergy of the diocese of Exeter. At this moment the Venetian Ambassador was writing in a despatch : " The persecution of the Catholics is vigorously conducted, all suspect houses are searched and if crosses or anything indicat-

ing the Catholic religion are found, the owner is
imprisoned. The search for priests is also keen,
and all that are found are imprisoned and threatened
with execution ; as happened recently at Oxford,
when a priest was actually taken up to the gallows
to terrify him and the others, and to induce them
to leave the country."

On June 30th, the Archbishop consecrated Dr.
William Barlow as Bishop of Rochester in Lambeth
chapel.   Other bishops consecrated there were Dr.
Henry Parry to Gloucester in 1607, and Dr. James
Montague to Bath and Wells the following year.
The King presented Samuel Hodges to the Vicarage
of Chertsey in 1606, and the next year Owen Hughes
to that of Kingston, on the resignation of Dr. James
Fytch.

1608. At the end of August, 1608, two Scotch
priests, named Hamilton and Paterson, were sent
south by the Earl of Dunbar, and lodged in the
Tower.

1609. On April 28th, 1609, Dr. William Laud
wrote in his diary : " I changed my advowson of
North Kilworth (Leicestershire) for West Tilbury
in Essex ; to which I was inducted October 28th
to be near my Lord of Rochester, Dr. Neile." Dr.
Laud only stayed here till 1610 (although he held
the parsonage till 1616), when a living in Kent was
presented to him.

The Venetian Ambassador wrote on September
26th : " In London, a few days ago, a Scottish
Capuchin has been arrested. He was at one time
much sought after and flattered by the Scotch
ministers of the Crown. He had gone to the house
of a certain knight, his countryman, whom he
examined and confessed in France. In friendship

he revealed himself to this man, who, however, either because he had changed his religion, or mastered by a desire to ingratiate himself with the King, caused him to be arrested. He has been taken to the Tower, which is a bad sign for him."

Two consecrations took place at Lambeth on December 3rd—Dr. George Abbot to the see of Lichfield and Coventry, and Dr. Samuel Harsnet to that of Chichester.

In the course of 1609, Chelsea College, for dealing with theological subjects, was founded by the King, who appointed the first Provost and Fellows ; and in the early part of the next year a Declaration was made " of the King's determination to revive the ancient tribute of ' King's silver,' a poll-tax to be paid on taking the oath of allegiance and supremacy, which shall yearly be enforced as a safeguard against popery ; the profits to be devoted to the erection of a College at Chelsea, for the better handling of religious controversies."

1610. On February 12th, 1610, Dr. George Abbot, translated from Coventry and Lichfield, was installed in St. Paul's Cathedral as Bishop of London.

A certified extract was made from the register of the Archdeacon of Essex, on August 1st, setting forth the opinion of the Churchwardens of Barking, that Thomas Adams, of the parish, was suspected of living incontinently with the widow Allen.

Archbishop Bancroft, in pursuance of the King's letters-patent, issued on October 9th, a prescript from his manor of Lambeth, for consecrating three Bishops of Scotland, who were then resident in England. The ceremony took place in the chapel on the 21st, and the three prelates were John Spottiswood of Glasgow, Gawin Hamilton of Galloway, and Andrew Lambe of Brechin.

The Archbishop died of the stone, after protracted suffering, at Lambeth, on November 2nd, and was buried the next day in the chancel of the church. He left £40 to the poor of Lambeth.

In November Alexander Haythwaite, on the presentation of the King, was instituted Rector of Weybridge, on the resignation of Richard Massey.

On December 2nd the Venetian Ambassador wrote : " They are proceeding against Catholics with unusual rigour. The oath is being administered everywhere, expecially to recusants. They are trying to lay their hands on priests. Six were arrested last Sunday in London, and another has been hung and quartered in Oxfordshire. The protection of many great men and all his many friends failed to save his life."

1611. In April, 1611, Dr. George Abbot, Bishop of London, was translated to the Archbishopric of Canterbury, and on the 9th was " very honourably installed " at Lambeth. The new Primate was sworn of the Privy Council at Greenwich on June 23rd ; and, by the King's advice, maintained a lavish hospitality at Lambeth, which secured him the favour of many " lords spiritual and temporal, divers councillors, and men of highest rank." On June 9th, Dr. Giles Thompson was consecrated Bishop of Gloucester in Lambeth Chapel ; and on the following September 8th, the consecration of Dr. John King to the Bishopric of London was performed.

Among the ecclesiastical appointments this year were those of Francis Taylor to the Rectory of Lambeth, and Thomas Gataker, a strict Calvinist, to the Rectory of Rotherhithe. On May 10th, Dr.

William Laud was chosen President of St. John's College, Oxford.

1612. In the course of 1612, John Rider became Rector of Bermondsey. He had published an English and Latin Dictionary—the first in which the English was printed before the Latin—and was afterwards Bishop of Killaloe.

1613. Early in 1613, William Becket, following the death of the Rev. Owen Hughes, was presented to the Vicarage of Kingston by the King.

1614. On April 3rd, 1614, Dr. John Overal was consecrated Bishop of Lichfield and Coventry, in Lambeth Chapel. Other Church appointments were Robert Wilkinson to the Rectory of St. Olave's, Southwark, and Thomas Jones to the Rectory of Barnes.

1615. On June 10th, 1615, Archbishop Abbot summoned a prebendary of Christ Church, Oxford, " to appear before the King on a charge of coquetting with Popery, because he had complained of the prevalence of Puritanism, and had failed to denounce its antithesis with fitting severity or frequency." Dr. Richard Milbourne was consecrated Bishop of St. David's, on July 9th, in Lambeth Chapel ; and on December 3rd, the Primate's brother, Dr. Robert Abbot, was consecrated there as Bishop of Salisbury.

George Gunter was this year presented by the King to the Rectory of St. George's, Southwark.

1616. On January 18th, 1616, John Chamberlain wrote in a letter to Sir Dudley Carleton : " The Archbishop of Spalato is still at Lambeth, very well used and esteemed. He hath been at our service in St. Paul's, at the Bishop's—of London—at Westminster, at the printing house, at Sutton's Hospital, at the Exchange once or twice, both above and beneath, and all about where anything is to be seen." The same correspondent wrote on December 21st: "The Archbishop of Spalato is lodged at Lambeth, but the Archbishop of Canterbury desires to remove him to the Dean of Westminster's." Anthony de Dominis, Archbishop of Spalato, had been kindly received on his arrival in England, as having renounced all communion with the Church of Rome.

The following Bishops were consecrated in Lambeth Chapel: Dr. Thomas Morton of Chester, on Sunday, July 7th; and Dr. Lewis Bayly, of Bangor, and Dr. Arthur Lake, of Bath and Wells, on December 8th. John Cotton was presented by the Crown to the Rectory of Greenwich.

1617. On February 23rd, 1617, Sir Henry Savile wrote from Eton to Sir Dudley Carleton that he had dined with the Archbishop of Spalato at Lambeth, and liked him well. In October the Archbishop was received by the King at Windsor, and was taken by the Archbishop of Canterbury to Eton, where Sir Henry and Lady Savile "loaded him with caresses." The foreign prelate was brought back to Lambeth, where, he wrote, he was well treated, but had no power over his own movements.

On Sunday, December 14th, Dr. Richard Felton was consecrated Bishop of Bristol, and Dr. George Mountaine Bishop of Lincoln, in Lambeth Chapel.

1618. In 1618 the consecrations in Lambeth Chapel were: Dr. Martin Fotherby as Bishop of Salisbury on April 19th, and Dr. George Carleton as Bishop of Llandaff, on July 12th. In the course of April Dr. John Bridges, Bishop of Oxford, died. In February Dr. Daniel Featlye, or Featley or Fairclough, succeeded Francis Taylor in the Rectory of Lambeth.

1619. On May 9th, 1619, three consecrations took place in Lambeth Chapel : Dr. John Howson as Bishop of Oxford, Dr. John Bridgman as Bishop of Chester, and Dr. Rowland Serchfield as Bishop of Bristol. Later in the year Dr. Theophilus Field was consecrated to Llandaff. Dr. John Boys, who was installed on May 3rd as Dean of Canterbury, when preaching once on November 5th in St. Paul's Cathedral, turned the Lord's Prayer into the following execration : " Our pope, which art in Rome, cursed be thy name ; perish may thy kingdom ; hindered may thy will be, as it is in heaven, so in earth. Give us this day our cup in the Lord's Supper ; and remit our monies which we have given for thy indulgences, as we send them back unto thee ; and lead us not into heresy, but free us from misery ; for thine is the infernal pitch and sulphur, for ever and ever, Amen."

Thomas Adams was appointed Rector of St. Benet's, Paul's Wharf, on June 15th.

1620. On July 9th, 1620, Dr. Robert Tounson was consecrated Bishop of Salisbury at Lambeth ; and Dr. Williams admitted Dean of Westminster.

1622. Dr. Robert Wright was consecrated Bishop of Bristol in Lambeth Chapel, on March 22nd, 1622 ; and on the 30th a Commission was issued to Archbishop Abbot, the Bishops of London, Durham, Winchester, and several other Privy Councillors to inquire into the offences imputed to Anthony de Dominis, Archbishop of Spalato, who, on his coming to England, had met with a very honourable reception, both in the Universities and at Court, upon the presumption of his having renounced all communication with the Church of Rome. The King had recommended him as a guest to Dr.

Abbot, and the foreign prelate was said to have attempted to control, with imperious and dominating temper, the Archbishop in his own house. " In the chapel of Lambeth he assisted at the consecration of some English bishops. He was also preferred by his Majesty to the Mastership of the Savoy and the Deanery of Windsor. He appeared personally before the Commissioners at Lambeth, when the Archbishop, by the King's special command, recapitulated in a long Latin speech the many misdemeanours of Spalato, principally insisting on his changing of religion, as appeared by his purpose of returning to Rome ; and that, contrary to the laws of the realm, he had held correspondence, by letters, with the Pope, without the privity of his Majesty. To which charges when Spalato had made rather an evasive answer than a just defence, the Archbishop, in his Majesty's name, commanded him to leave the Kingdom within twenty days, and, at his peril, never to return again."

Dr. John Donne was presented in August to the prebend of Chiswick.

1623. On February 15th, 1623, Dr. John Hanmer was consecrated Bishop of St. Asaph's, in Lambeth Chapel ; and a year later, on Saturday, March 6th, 1624, Dr. Godfrey Goodman was consecrated Bishop of Gloucester. On March 12th, the Privy Council was advised by the Vice-Chancellor and Mayor of Oxford and others that proceedings by the Mayor of Evesham against John Brent, charged with uttering scandalous speeches against the late Queen Elizabeth and the Church of England, had been taken at Oxford, and it was found that the man was an obstinate papist, and the carrier of letters between recusants.

In response to the petition of Parliament, a Proclamation was issued from Greenwich, on May 6th, charging all Jesuits, seminary priests, and others holding orders under the see of Rome, to depart the land before June 14th, on penalty of the utmost severity of the law.

LIFE OF THE PEOPLE ALONG THE RIVER.

1603. While the wealthier of the merchants and burgesses in London and the towns enjoyed many solid social comforts, the life of the mass of the people was hard, and devoid of much that even the most poverty-stricken now consider as necessaries. Their shelters were mean, cheerless, and very insanitary. The choice of food was restricted, and in winter fuel was hard to obtain. The wretched and roofless condition of the lowest ranks of the poor can hardly be realized in these later days. Nameless beggars and "masterless vagabonds" swarmed in town and country. The destitute had no refuge from the stress of want and weather, but in the chance charity of the kind-hearted. The parishes had overseers of the poor, but these were mostly dependent for funds on the uncertain contributions of private individuals. Hundreds knew no other sleeping or dying place than the hedgerow, the stack, or the barn. The desperate found a vile covering for their heads in some den of a prison, where, with curses and blasphemies on their swollen lips, they died like flies of the horrible fevers engendered by the reeking filth of these neglected sinks of iniquity.

We obtain from the old Register of the Parish Church of Wandsworth many glimpses of the end of the poor. In various years such burials as these were recorded : " A poore woman wch dyed in a rust, so that they precisely resemble those ancient weapons with which the executioners guarded the holy sepulchre. Hence comes it that one can really go about by night unarmed and purse in hand. The slightest theft is punished with death ; even a youth of fifteen for his first crime, or theft, is hanged, unless he chances to know how to read and write, in which case, in consideration of his acquirements, they spare his life and brand one of his hands with a hot iron. If found stealing a second time he is hanged inexorably. A few months ago a lad was seen on his way to the gallows merely for having stolen a bag of currants. They have a gaol delivery every month, and pass sentence in an extravagant manner according to the law enacted of yore, and which is applicable to every crime. The Court, which consists of certain judges, summonses twelve men of various professions, styled ' jury,' who examine the prisoner's case, and after discussing among themselves the reality of the fact, they agree together and on returning into Court utter one of these two words, ' Guilty ' or ' Not Guilty,' according to which sentence is passed without mercy. As there is no mitigation, such as banishment or the galleys, this invariably involves life or death. They take them five-and-twenty at a time, every month, besides sudden and extraordinary executions in course of the week, on a large cart like a high scaffold. They go along quite jollily, holding their sprigs of rosemary and singing songs, accompanied by their friends, and a multitude of people. On reaching the gallows one of the party acts as spokesman, saying fifty words or so. Then the music, which they had learned at their leisure in prison, being repeated, the executioner

hastens the business, and beginning at one end, fastens each man's halter to the gibbet. They are so closely packed that they touch each other, with their hands tied in front of them, wrist to wrist, so as to leave them the option of taking off their hats and saluting the bystanders. One careless fellow availed himself of this facility to shade his face from the sun. Finally, the executioner, having come down from the scaffold, has the whip applied to the cart horses, and thus the culprits remain dangling in the air precisely like a bunch of fat thrushes. They are hard to die of themselves, and unless their own relations or friends pulled their feet or pelted them with brickbats in the breast as they do, it would fare badly with them. The proceeding is really barbarous and strikes those who witness it with horror. Here one never hears the noise of broils, and consequently no murders are committed, from fear of the law. Rather from despair or difficulties than on any other account the people occasionally hang and drown themselves."

In normal times hard drinking and rough horseplay filled the leisure hours of the people at large. Many of their coarse jests denoted a keen sense of humour, and the jest-books and ballads of the time are full of merry pranks, although most of them are now unprintable.

The following selections will give the reader a glimpse into the most readable of these :

" There was three young men going to Lambeth along by the water side, and the one plaid with the other, and they cast each other's cap into the water, in such sort as they could not get their caps again ; but over the place where their caps were, did grow a great old tree, which did cover a great deale of the water. One of them said to the rest, ' Sirs, I have found out a notable way to come by them. First I will make myself fast by the middle, with one of your girdles unto the tree, and he that is with you shall hang fast upon my girdle, and he that is last shall take hold on him that holds fast on my girdle, and so with one of his hands he may take up all our caps and cast them on the sand.' And so they did ; but when they thought that they had been most secure and fast, he that was alone felt his girdle slack, and said, 'Soft, sirs, my girdle slacketh.' ' Make it fast quickly,' said they; but as he was untying it to make it faster they fell all three into the water, and were well washed for their pains."

" Maister Hobson, and another of his neighbours, on a time walking to Southwarke faire, by chance drunke in a house which had the signe of Sa. Christopher, of the which signe the good man of the house gave this commendation. ' Saint Christopher,' quoth he, ' when hee lived upon the earth bore the greatest burden that ever was, which was this, he bore Christ over a river.' ' Nay, there was one,' quoth Maister Hobson, ' that bore a greater burden. ' Who was that ? ' quoth the in Keeper. ' Mary,' quoth Maister Hobson, ' the asse that bore both Him and His mother.' So was the Inne keeper called asse by craft. After this, talking merely together, the aforesaid Inne keeper being a little whitled (intoxicated) with drinke, and his head so giddy that he fell into the fire, people standing by, ran sodainely and tooke him up. ' Oh, let him alone,' quoth Maist. Hobson, ' a man may doe what he will in his owne house, and lie where so ever he listeth.' The man, having little hurt, with this sight grew immediately sober, and, after, foxed

Maister Hobson and his neighbour so mightely, that comming over London Bridge, being very late, ranne against one of the posts, which Maister Hobson, thinking it to bee some man that had justled him, drew out his dodgion dagger, and thrust it up into the very hilt into the hollow post ; whereupon verely hee had thought hee had kil'd some man ; so, running away, was taken by the Watch, and so all the jest was discovered."

" There was a man that had been drinking so hard that he could scarse stand upon his feet, yet at night he would go home, and as he went through a green meadow, neer a hedge side the Bryers held him by the cloaths and the legs, and he had thought that one had holden him, and would have had him to drink more, and he said, ' Good fellow, let me go ; by my troth I can drink no more. I have drank so much already, that I cannot go home ' ; and there he abode all the same night, and on the morrow went his ways."

" A witty Rogue coming into a lace shop, said he had occasion for some lace. Choice whereof being shewed him, he at last pitched upon one pattern, and asked them how much they would have for so much as would reach from ear to ear, for so much he had occasion for, and they told him for so much ; so, some few words passing between them, he at last agreed, and told down his money for it, and began to measure on his own head, thus saying, 'One ear is here and the other is nailed to the Pillory in Bristoll, and I fear you have not so much of this lace by you at present as will perfect my bargain ; therefore this piece of lace shall suffice at present in part of payment, and provide the rest with all expedition.' "

" There was a faire ship of two hundred tuns lying at the Tower Wharfe at London, where a countryman passing by, most earnestly looked on the said ship, and demanded how old shee was. One made answer that she was a yeare old. ' God bless me,' said the countryman, ' is shee so big growne in one yeere; what a greatness will shee bee by the time she comes to my age ? "

" Myselfe carried an old fellow by water, that had wealth enough to be Deputy of the Ward, and wit sufficient for Scavenger. The water being some-what rough, hee was much afraid, and (instead of saying his prayers) he threatened me, that if I did drowne him, hee would spend a hundred pound, but hee would see me hanged for it ; I desired him to be quiet and feare nothing, and so in little space I landed him at the Beare's Colledge on the Bankside. (Paris Garden, Southwark). ' Well,' said he 'I am glad I am off the water, for if the boat had mis-carried, I could have swum no more than a goose."

" A country fellow going down Ludgate Hill, his heels by chance slipping from him, fell upon his Breech. One standing by told him that London streets were stout and scornful. ' It may be so,' quoth he, 'yet I made them to kisse my Breech, so stout as they were."

" A notable fellow, that, as 'tis said would not be drunk above seven days in the week ; and when he was drunk was so besotted that he knew not what he did. Once his Prentice was sent by his wife to fetch him home, and when he found him out, he found him reeling ripe also. And as they came down Ludgate Hill, in a moon-shiny night, saw the reflection of the Bell-Savage sign post upon the ground, and it seems took it for a Block, and went to lift his leg over it, his Prentice having him by the arm for his supporter, askt what he meant by that ? 'Why,' says he, ' to go over this Block.' He told him 'twas not a Block. ' What is it, then ? ' says he. ' 'Tis a sign,' says the boy. ' What sign, I prithee ? ' ' Why, master,' ' 'tis a sign you are ' drunk.' ' "

Finally, here are two verses of a favourite ballad called " The Great Boobee," describing the London adventures of a witless countryman :

> " To Paris Garden then I went,
>   Where there is great resort,
> My pleasure was my punishment,
>   I did not like the sport :
> The Garden Bull with his stout horns
>   On high then tossed me,
> I did bewray myself with fear,
>   Like a great Boobee."

> Then o'er the Water did I pass,
>   As you shall understand,
> I dropt into the Thames alas
>   Before I came to Land :
> The Water-man did help me out,
>   And thus did say to me,
> 'Tis not thy fortune to be drown'd
>   Like a great Boobee."

Henry Gosson, who dwelt on London Bridge, " neare the Gate," between 1607 and 1641, published many of these ballads and jests.

A print of this period exhibited a fantastic and humorous chimney-sweeper, called " Mulled Sack." He was attired in a cap and feather and laced band ; a cloak tucked up and a ragged coat ; a scarf on his arm ; a fashionable boot with a spur on his left leg, and a shoe with a rose on his right foot ; a sword by his side, and a holly bush and pole on his shoulder.

In his left hand was another pole with a horn on it, and in his right a pipe with smoke issuing from it. At the bottom of the print were these lines :

" I walke the Strand and Westminster, and scorne
To march i' the Citie, though I bear the horne.
My feather and my *yellow*-band accord
To prove me Courtier ; my boote, spur and sword,
My smokinge pipe, scarf, garter, rose on shoe,
Shew my brave mind t' affect what gallants doe.
I sing, dance, drink, and merrily passe the day,
And like a chimney sweepe all care away."

Horatio Busino, the Venetian Secretary, set down in his diary on January 10th, 1618 : " One of the most notable things I see in this kingdom, and which strikes me as really marvellous, is the use of the Queen's weed, properly called tobacco, whose dried leaves come from the Indies, packed like so much rope. It is cut and pounded and subsequently placed in a hollow instrument a span long, called a pipe. The powder is lighted at the largest part of the bowl, and they absorb the smoke with great enjoyment. They say it clears the head, dries up humours, and greatly sharpens the appetite. It is in such frequent use that not only at every hour of the day but even at night they keep the pipe and steel at their pillows and gratify their longings. Amongst themselves they are in the habit of circu-lating toasts, passing the pipe from one to the other with much grace, just as they here do with good wine, but more often with beer. Gentlewomen, moreover, and virtuous women accustom themselves to take it as medicine, but in secret. The others do it at pleasure. So much money is expended daily in this nastiness that at the present moment the trade in tobacco amounts to half a million in gold, and the duty on it alone yields the King 40,000 golden crowns yearly. Throughout the city pipes and tobacco are sold in most of the shops, so that these with the others, where they merely sell ruffs and wristbands, would of themselves form a large city. This is in truth an affair of vanity and smoke, and his Majesty therefore abhors it. It is prohibited throughout the Court, though not by a decree. In my opinion no other country ought to introduce tobacco, for it enters cities with vapouring ostentation, and then, after being well pounded, departs loaded with gold, leaving the purses of its purchasers empty and their wits addled."

Later in the year, on September 21st, Busino wrote : " I observe a bad habit prevalent in this nation. They eat very little bread at table, placing it near the salt-cellar in the trenchers, and each one takes a bit by way of condiment, but meat they devour. They do not generally put fruit on the table, but between meals one sees men, women, and children always munching through the streets, like so many goats, and yet more in the places of public amusement."

Emerging from the rough and rude manners prevailing among all classes, a new spirit of progress was, however, growing up not only in the urban but in the rural districts ; and as the people made steady advance in knowledge and political power, so came stirrings in the corporate life of the towns and cities, accompanied by the stern Puritan conduct that was preparing the way for near and vital changes in the whole life of the nation.

1603. The streets of London were narrow, dark from the overhanging houses, and indescribably noisome from the stinking offal and filth that festered undisturbed and contaminated the air with the seeds of loathsome diseases. The most horrible of these the Plague, or black-death, was never entirely absent, and the dread of it clouded all men's minds. Its dark shadow began to loom large with the early days of 1603, and in the first week of March alarming rumours spread of many stricken mortals in the city and suburbs of London, especially in Southwark, where the lowest dregs of the populace were herded. The Privy Council made an effort to get rid of the numerous crowd of vagrant and useless by issuing a Warrant to the Justices of the four metropolitan counties ordering them to apprehend able-bodied men, who were " masterless and vagabonds," and send them to Winchester House in Southwark, from whence they were to be shipped to the Low Countries for the military service of the States. As a result of this order, eight hundred vagrants were seized in London alone.

On May 29th, King James, through his Council, issued a proclamation commanding gentlemen to depart the Court and the City of London on account of the rapidly increasing virulence of the pestilence.

A person venturing to approach the Court when his house was infected was whipped through the town.

Special regulations were made for the Tower during the sickness, and part of Trinity Term was adjourned.

In June Dr. Launcelot Andrewes preached to an affrighted congregation at Chiswick on the terrible wrath of God that had descended on a sinful people.

In the week preceding the Coronation on July 25th, about eight hundred and fifty persons were carried off, and August saw London a city of nightmare horrors. Terrible scenes of agony were witnessed in every street ; the smell of death pervaded nearly all dwellings, and the groans and cries of the living were frightful to hear.

Thomas Decker, an eccentric but vivid chronicler, in a black-letter tract entitled " The Wonderful Yeare, 1603, wherein is shewed the Picture of London lying sicke of ye Plague," gave a lurid description of the fearful effects of the pestilence. He compared the city to a vast charnel-house, with " lamps dimly and slowly burning," and where the pavement, instead of green rushes, " is strewed with blasted rosemary, withered hyacinths, fatal cypress and yew thickly mingled with heaps of dead men's bodies ; the bare ribs of a father that begat him lying there ; here the chaplesse hollow sculle of a mother that bore him, round about him a thousand corses. . . . For he that durst in the dread hour of gloomy midnight have been so valiant as to have walkt through the still and melantholy streets, what think you should have been his musicke? Surely the loud groanes of raving sicke men : the struggling panges of soules departing. In every house griefe striking up an alarum : servants crying out for masters ; wives for husbands, parents for children, children for their mothers ; here he should have met some frantickly running to knock up sextons ; there others fearfully sweating with coffins, to steale forth dead bodies, least the fatal hand-writing of death should seale up their doores. . . . How often hath the amazed husband waking found the comfort of his bedde lying breathlesse by his side ; his children at the same instant gasping for life ; and his servants mortally wounded at the heart by sickness, the distracted creature beats at death doores, exclaims at windows, his cries are sharp enough to pierce heaven ; but on earth no eare is open to receive them ! And in this manner do the tedious minutes of the night stretch out the sorrowes of ten thousand. . . . It is now day, let us looke forth and try what consolation rises with the sun ; not any, for before the jewel of the morning be fully set in silver, a hundred angry graves stand gaping, and everyone of them (as at a breakfast) hath swallowed down ten or eleven lifeless carcasses ; before dinner in the same gulfe are twice so many more devoured ; and before the sun takes his rest, those numbers are doubled. Threescore that not many houres before had every one severall lodgings here very delicately furnisht, are now thrust altogether into one close roome—a little noisome roome not full ten feet square."

In October the fury of the pestilence shewed little signs of abatement. St. Bartholomew's and all other fairs within fifty miles of the metropolis were suspended. In the Tower, Lord Cobham was in bad health and the Lieutenant feared the plague would attack his prisoners.

The Courts of Law were removed from Westminster—the Court of Exchequer to Richmond and the Michaelmas Term to Winchester.

The ravages of the disease lessened perceptibly with the closing days of this dismal year, but the gloomiest apprehensions still filled the minds of the people at large. The Plague had gathered a terrible harvest in London and the home counties, and was still reaping its victims when the year died. The capital alone lost thirty thousand persons, and the environs added more thousands to the staggering total. In Southwark the register of St. Mary

Overy's Church recorded fourteen burials in March, twenty in April, twenty-eight in May, sixty-three in June, one hundred and eighty-three in July, six hundred and twenty in August, seven hundred and thirty-five in September, two hundred and forty-one in October, seventy-six in November, and twenty-nine in December. Among the last was Alice Pinke, aged 112. While the register of St. Olave's Church gave five hundred and seven burials in July, twelve hundred and seventeen in August, seven hundred and forty-one in September, and one hundred and forty-five in October.

During August, September, and October four hundred and forty-one burials took place in Lambeth Churchyard, against twenty-nine in the corresponding period of the previous year. Altogether there were five hundred and sixty-six burials in the course of the year at Lambeth, of which five hundred and twenty-two were in the last six months. Chelsea and Battersea suffered less than Putney and Mortlake; there were only thirteen burials in the year at Chelsea. Wandsworth buried ninety-six, among these being " a childe found on the back side of the towne "; " Drowned at the upper Mill by chance, Peter, the son of Peeter Wraxall of London "; " A Vagrant man, whose name wee know not, he died in the cage "; and " A vagrant Dutchman, whose name wee know not, was buried in the fields."

The pestilence was very fatal at Isleworth, for although the average annual interments did not exceed ten, yet this year there were sixty-seven persons buried from the beginning of August to the beginning of December.

At Kingston, from September 1st to December 31st, fifty-four persons died; and one hundred and twenty-one were buried in the parish of Hampton, ninety-nine of whom were said to have been carried off by the scourge. Only three burials were entered in the register of Staines Church.

Below London Bridge the infection spread like wildfire. At Bermondsey eight burials took place in April, nine in May, twenty-one in June, one hundred and forty-one in July, two hundred and seventy-eight in August, one hundred and forty in September, forty-two in October, fifteen in November, and eleven in December.

Deptford suffered severely, and the register of St. Nicholas' Church, which had been shewing an annual average of thirty-eight interments, jumped up this year to two hundred and thirty-five ; among whom, in September, was Richard Byrde, a farrier and churchwarden of the parish. Greenwich was visited quite as heavily, and the tale of suffering and sorrow could only be completed by the inclusion of every hamlet, village, and township for miles around the capital.

1604. Although mild compared with the past ravages, the scourge in 1604 still claimed many victims. Twenty-five persons were carried off from the small population of Wandsworth ; and at Deptford Sir Richard Browne, whose family had for many years held Sayes Court, died in May. In London, when large numbers were succumbing in March, the authorities levied a rate for the support of the infected, who, under a penalty of death, were forbidden to leave the shelter of their houses while bearing "any infectious sore uncured." At the same time an attempt was made to remedy the evil of the inflammable nature of the buildings in London, which for ages had been framed entirely of wood

with mantlings of straw thatch. A royal command was issued that in future " the fronts, at least, of all edifices should be of brick or stone, which would promote the farther views of decoration and embellishment, as well as be an additional security against fire." This Order took effect, and from now the inveterate partiality for wood rapidly gave way to a growing sense of the fragile and dangerous nature of the material, and more substantial buildings were erected.

In August the Plague raged with increasing violence at Oxford, and on the 10th carried off, among others, John Eveleigh, who had been Principal of Hart Hall since 1599.

1605. Many cases in London continued to keep alive the fear of the pestilence, and in October, 1605, there was a question of instantly proroguing the session of Parliament that was to reassemble in the next month, on account of an increase in the victims of a loathsome disease which proved to be the small-pox.

The wretched condition of the poor quickened the benevolence of those safe from want, and it now became common for merchants and burgesses of substance, who had in their younger days felt the pinch of poverty, or who in the course of business and the daily round had come into contact with the aggravated misery caused by the pestilence, and been touched to the heart, to found hospitals or almshouses in their lifetimes, or leave money or property in their wills for charitable purposes. The considerable relief the destitute could always obtain from the bounty of the Monasteries and other religious houses now dissolved, was lost, and these private benefactors were at this time the principal means of easing a huge load of undeserved distress.

1606. In 1606, when the plague was still very prevalent in London and its neighbourhood, George Swain left two rent-charges in St. Olave's, Southwark, for the general relief of the poor ; and Henry Browker left the money (£10) obtained from a messuage in Red Lion Street, Southwark, one moiety to the Grammar School, the other to the general poor of the borough.

In Bermondsey, Stephen Skidmore bequeathed money to buy firing for the poor of the parish of St. Mary. At Deptford, Mr. Ady, Master Shipwright of the King's Yard, who was buried in the churchyard of St. Nicholas, willed to the poor of the parish a piece of land called the " Gravel-pit." And Sir George Wright founded an Almshouse for eight poor women, on the lower road beneath the Hill at Richmond.

1608. The first half of 1608, following a terribly severe winter, was a time of great scarcity in the country, and it was not till July that a large quantity of grain arrived from abroad, and relieved the pressing want of the people.

In a letter to the Earl of Suffolk, Lord Chamberlain, the Lord Mayor, dealing with the stoppage of a quill of water formerly granted for the use of Essex House, wrote : " The water in the conduits becoming very low, and the poor very clamorous in this time of dearth, it became necessary to cut off several of the quills. Moreover, complaints had been made of the extraordinary waste of water in Essex House, it being taken not only for dressing meat, but for the laundry, the stable, and other offices, which might be otherwise served."

s

1610. About October, 1610, the magistrates of the City of London, being apprehensive that the great increase of its inhabitants might produce a famine, prepared against the evil by erecting twelve public granaries at Bridewell, large enough to contain six thousand quarters of corn, which in case of a scarcity, or a combination among the dealers in that commodity, was to be sold to the poor at prime cost.

1611. A very long and unprecedented drought in the early hot summer of 1611 threatened a general famine, and the price of bread and other provisions rose rapidly. Rain in June, although it came too late to revive the burnt-up crops, eased matters a little, but not enough to prevent much suffering and distress among the indigent poor.

On August 5th, a letter was directed to Sir Julius Cæsar and other Commissioners, instructing them to assemble and devise means for remedying the shortage of the London water supply; and on the 10th of the following month a proclamation was issued from Hampton Court for restraining building in and about the Metropolis.

1612. In 1612, John Selman was hanged near Charing Cross for picking the pocket, during divine service, of Leonard Barry, servant to Lord Harrington.

1613. The winter of 1612-13 was very stormy and wet. Physicians openly anticipated much employment from the inevitable sickness in the spring, and fears were entertained by the yeomen in the country of a murrain among the cattle.

1617. On Shrove Tuesday, March 4th, 1617, riots broke out in London, and Drury Lane playhouse was attacked, Finsbury prison broken open, and houses at Wapping pulled down and wrecked.

John Chamberlain, writing a day or two afterwards to Sir Dudley Carleton, said : " There is a new Lieutenant of the Tower, Sir Allen Apsley, whose wife is sister to Sir Edward Villier's lady, having compounded with Sir George More for £2,500. On the 4th of this month, being our Shrove Tuesday, the 'prentices, or rather the unruly people of the suburbs, played their parts in divers places, as Finsbury Fields, about Wapping by St. Katherine's, and in Lincoln's Inn Fields, in which places, being assembled in great numbers, they fell to great disorders, in pulling down of houses, and beating of guards that were set to keep rule, specially at a new playhouse, sometime a cock-pit, in Drury Lane, where the Queen's players used to play. Though the fellows defended themselves as well as they could, and slew three of them with shot, and hurt divers, yet they entered the house and defaced it, cutting the players' apparel into pieces, and all their furniture, and burnt their play-books, and did what other mischief they could. In Finsbury, they broke the prison, and let out all the prisoners, and spoiled the house by untiling and breaking down the roof and all the windows. And at Wapping they pulled down seven or eight houses, and defaced five times as many, besides many other outrages, as beating the sheriff from his horse with stones, and doing much other hurt too long to write. There be divers of them taken since and clapped up, and I make no question but we shall see some of them hanged next week, as it is more than time they were."

1620. William Lilly, the astrologer, in the "History of his Life," said that as a young man of eighteen he took leave of his father—in Leicester

Gaol for debt—on April 4th, 1620, and, travelling by a carrier, arrived at Smithfield on Palm Sunday afternoon, the 9th, with only a few shillings in his possession, and " one suit of clothes upon my back, two shirts, three bands, one pair of shoes, and as many stockings." He entered the service of a Gilbert White, and " my work was to go before my master to church ; to attend my master when he went abroad ; to make clean his shoes ; sweep the street ; help to drive Bucks when we washed ; fetch water in a tub from the Thames. I have helped to carry eighteen tubs of water in one morning —weed the garden ; all manner of drudgeries I willingly performed ; scrape trenchers, etc."

1623. On May 15th, 1623, Secretary Conway wrote to the High Sheriff and Justices of Kent : " The King is much displeased with a highway robbery near Dartford, on a (Spanish) post, sent by his Majesty with express letters, who was wounded and had 100*l.* taken from him ; the offence is aggravated by being committed on the person of a post, who is a sort of Ambassador. The surety of the highways being necessary for commerce, they are diligently to enforce the laws thereon, discover and punish the offenders if possible, and order restitution of the money stolen by the county or hundred in which the robbery occurred."

STATE AFFAIRS ALONG THE RIVER.

1603. While the remains of Queen Elizabeth were awaiting interment in Whitehall Palace, a Warrant of the coming King released her prisoners, the Earl of Southampton and Sir Henry Neville, from the Tower of London.

At the same time the Privy Council transacted business at Whitehall, and one of their Orders directed that Lord Chief Justice Popham should further examine a prisoner in the fortress, named Philip May, and put him to the rack if he proved recalcitrant.

The pacific policy of the new King rendered him proof against any foreign insults, but at home he soon became offensive to the main body of his people by a blind assertion of the doctrine of divine right, which was fated to bring irretrievable disaster on his family. A strong republican spirit, fostered by this strange doctrine, speedily manifested itself in the country, and the fearless Puritan members returned to Westminster coming into collision with the royal will, the testy monarch frequently summoned the refractory Parliament to Whitehall, and told them, in his slobbering speech, amidst an ominous silence, that they held their privileges only during his pleasure, and they could as lawfully question the acts of God as his. The imposition of taxes by royal authority was highly resented.

Henry Montague, Member for Higham Ferrers, was on the popular side against arbitrary taxation, but notwithstanding this he was elected Recorder of London on the King's recommendation, and was one of the numerous Coronation knights.

In August, while the King was on a progress in the west, and the Plague was doing its dismal worst in London, a conspiracy was hatched to place the Lady Arabella Stuart on the throne ; and its discovery resulted in the seizing and throwing into the Tower of Sir Walter Raleigh, Lords Cobham and Grey of Wilton, Sir Edmund Parham, Sir Griffen Markham, George Brooke, Anthony Copley the Spy, two secular priests, William Watson and William Clarke, and others. One afternoon, when some of these prisoners were being examined, it seems that Raleigh, in his lonely chamber, was overcome with a temporary fit of despair, and gave himself a slight wound in the breast. He was found in agony of mind lamenting his misfortunes, and protesting innocence and carelessness of life. The black humour, however, soon passed, and he regained his natural courage and dignity. The unfortunate hero's fortunes were now sunk in total eclipse ; his possessions were taken from him, and Toby Matthew, Bishop of Durham, had little difficulty in recovering Durham House in the Strand for his see. The ruined man remonstrated with the Lord Keeper Egerton that in the course of his twenty years' occupation of the house he had expended on it £2,000 out of his own purse. The house was never again occupied, and soon after the stables came down to make way for a new Exchange.

The Michaelmas Term having been removed to

Winchester to escape the Plague, Raleigh, Lord Cobham, and others, conveyed there, under a strong guard, from the Tower, were tried and condemned on very unsound evidence. Some of the minor men were executed, but Grey, Cobham, and Raleigh were returned to their miserable confinement in the Tower, with the threat of death hanging over them. Raleigh's one consolation was the company of his amiable and affectionate wife. The years that were to follow were filled with study and the practice of chemistry; and he composed his " History of the World," and several political discourses. It has been said : " Great ladies from Court cast wistful glances at his room. Men from the streets and ships came crowding to the Wharf, whence they could see him walking on the wall. . . . Raleigh's lodge under the Tower wall became a Court to which a crowd of men who stood highest among the learned and the great repaired for profit and delight. Raleigh was still a centre. Bacon sought in him a patron of the new learning. Percy dined with him in the Lieutenant's house. Hariot brought him books and maps. Pett came over with his models ; Jonson with his epigrams and underwoods. The ' magi,' Hariot, Hues, and Warner, made a part of Raleigh's court. Selden was often there ; Mayerne sometimes, Bilson now and then. Nor were these all. Queen Anne sent messages to the prisoner. Prince Henry rode down from Whitehall to hear him talk. . . . Princess Elizabeth looked on her brother's friend as her own best guide. . . . The talk of the old sailor and the young prince ran much on the sea, on ships, and on naval war, for which the lad was already quickening with heroic fire. . . . Riding away from the Tower after one of the mornings thus spent, the Prince cried aloud to his attendants, ' No man but my father would keep such a bird in a cage.' "

1604. On March 15th, 1604—the day of the royal progress through London—Sir Robert Shirley, a Member of Parliament in attendance, was arrested for debt at the suit of a goldsmith named Sympson, and sent to the Fleet. Four days later, the first Parliament of the reign assembled at Westminster, and the indignant Commons seized on the occurrence to assert their own privileges, and the liberties of the people. They then proceeded to recognise James's right to the crown, and voted him tonnage and poundage for the " defence of the realm and keeping and safeguard of the seas." The sitting of Parliament was concluded on July 7th.

General information now spread rapidly, and a public opinion in political matters was growing with a strength that refused to be ignored. On August 3rd, the Privy Council, sitting at White-hall, ordered the Lieutenant of the Tower not to permit free access to the condemned Lords in his charge.

At this time the Constable of Castile, Governor of the Netherlands, bent on a peaceful mission from the Spanish government, was brought up the river to Gravesend and lodged at Somerset House—decorated with gorgeous hangings for the occasion—and magnificently entertained till he left on the 25th, with a signed Treaty of Peace. The Earl of Northampton described in a letter to the King, the Spanish grandee's journey to London, how the Queen met him " masked in a boat on the Thames," and flattered the vain monarch with the conclusion that the Constable was delighted with his reception,

" and praises his Majesty's learning, sweetness, frankness, and faithfulness." The Venetian Ambassador, in a despatch to the Doge and Senate, asserted that the Constable, when passing Gravesend on his way to Dover, saw a number of ships in the river, full of men for the service of Count Maurice. " He thought this monstrous, that while the ink of the treaty was hardly dry it should be thus quickly and openly violated. For the terms are that the King shall neither send aid, nor permit aid to be sent. The Constable sent to the justices of the district calling on them, upon pain of his Majesty's displeasure, to arrest the troops. The justices seemed to be convinced, and the troops were forbidden to sail ; but no sooner had the Constable crossed the sea than the ships continued their voyage." Soon after the King despatched a return mission to Spain, and in a Tract published in Pope's Head Alley, entitled, " The Royal Entertainment of the Right Honourable the Earl of Nottingham, sent Ambassador from his Majestie to the King of Spain," it was written that on Thursday, March 28th, 1605, the Lord High Admiral Nottingham went from Arundel House to Greenwich, in company with the Earl of Perth, Lords Effingham, Norris, and Willoughby and a large number of knights and gentlemen in barges and boats. The next day the Ambassador and his train boarded the royal ship, " Beare," the Admiral of the Fleet, and sailed with the other King's ships " Repulse " and " Warspite," and the " George " hoy. Queenborough was left on Saturday, and Dover reached on April 4th, where anchor was cast till the next day, when a course was shaped for Spain.

The contemplated Union with Scotland now

engaged the general attention, and on September 15th, a proclamation was posted from Windsor Castle, appointing the day and place for the meeting of the Commissioners of England and Scotland to treat of the Union between the two kingdoms.

On October 6th, the Venetian Ambassador wrote in a despatch : " The King and Queen are come to Hampton Court, and most of the Scottish Commissioners have arrived. The King cares for nothing else save this question of the Union, and so, in spite of its difficulties, it is thought it will be carried through." Although the opposition was strong among the influential, both in the North and South, the proposal was successfully accomplished, and following a meeting of the Privy Council at Whitehall on the 21st, Viscount Cranborne wrote two days later from the palace to Ralph Winwood : " I do send you here a proclamation published this day of his Majesty's changing his title, and taking upon him the name and style of King of Great Britain, France, Ireland, etc."

While this important question was being settled, a Scot, named Thomas Douglas, a close prisoner in the Tower, who in his character of envoy from the Count Palatine of the Rhine had counterfeited the King's privy seal to some German princes, was drawn upon a hurdle to Smithfield, and there hanged and quartered.

And now a small body of fanatic Papists, thinking they saw in the popular discontents their opportunity for upsetting the Protestant monarchy and government, and possibly restoring the Pope's authority, plotted the destruction of the King, Lords and Commons while assembled in Parliament ;

and towards the end of the year the conspirators finally met and commenced active operations. Late one night all of them, with the exception of Keyes, who remained at the abode they had hired at Lambeth, entered, with great secrecy, the house Thomas Percy had taken at Westminster. " They had provided themselves with the tools requisite for making an excavation, and had also brought with them supplies of hard eggs, baked meats and pasties, wine and beer, sufficient to last them twenty days, that they might not create suspicion by going abroad for food. By way of resource in the last extremity, they had likewise provided arms and ammunition, that they might be enabled to defend themselves against hostile attacks should the plot be discovered. In the garden attached to Percy's dwelling was an old building raised against the wall of the Parliament House, and within that building the conspirators began to open the mine. They divided each day into two portions, devoting sixteen hours to labour, and the remainder to repose ; and arranging their several tasks in such a manner that while one rested the other three continued to work, in the day-time at the mine, and in the night removing rubbish, and concealing it under the soil of the garden. Fawkes meanwhile kept watch round the house, in which he alone was seen giving notice, by some private signals, to his accomplices to abstain from working when any one approached the spot, lest the noise should betray them. They had continued their labour for a fortnight, when Fawkes informed them that the Parliament had been prorogued from the 7th of February to the 3rd of October following. They then separated to spend the Christmas holidays at their own homes, warily engaging to suspend all intercourse with each other, either by letter or message."

1605. When the conspirators re-met they were obstructed in their operations by the influx of water from the Thames, and the enormously thick foundation wall of the Parliament House. At this moment a coal cellar under the House of Lords was hired by Fawkes, and the excavations were abandoned. Fawkes having purchased the remaining coals in this vault, about twenty barrels of gunpowder were transferred from the house at Lambeth, and hidden among them. This powder, obtained in Holland and landed at Lambeth, was gradually conveyed across the river by night. All the large stones, iron bars, and other working tools they had used in the mine excavation were thrown in, and the whole covered with faggots and billets of wood. Then to complete the deception a quantity of old lumber and empty bottles were placed in the cellar.

The preparations of the conspirators were completed in May, and they then quitted London, purposing to return when the time was ripe for carrying out the terrible completion of their desperate project.

During the progress of October dark rumours accumulated forboding a violent interruption of the public calm. At last, on the 26th, Lord Monteagle imparted to Lord Salisbury at Whitehall an anonymous letter he had received urging him to absent himself from the near meeting of Parliament. This was submitted to the Privy Council, and after a short period of secret and anxious inquiry it was determined to inform the King ; and on November 1st, the alarming letter was laid before him, on his return from a hunting excursion. Instant and silent measures were taken to foil the plot, and early in the morning of the 5th, Guy Fawkes was seized in the vault at Westminster, where the barrels of gunpowder were stored for blowing up King and Parliament. His fellow-conspirators escaped by flight for the moment, and this chief culprit was briefly examined in the King's bedchamber at Whitehall, and then committed to the Tower.

The news of the plot spread like wildfire, and created a tremendous impression on the populace, consternation sitting on all men's faces. Later in the day, Lord Chief Justice Popham sent from his chambers in Serjeant's Inn a messenger to Lord Salisbury to advise him of Thomas Percy's escape towards Gravesend, and assuring him that measures had been taken for his apprehension. Archbishop Bancroft also sent information from Lambeth that Percy had been seen that morning riding towards Croydon, and adding that " all London is up in arms." It was ascertained that Percy had dined on Monday, the 4th, with his relative, the Earl of Northumberland, at Sion House ; and on the 6th the Chief Justice supposed Percy to be now in London, and assured Salisbury that escape by the Thames would be guarded against. The 8th brought news from Richard Ferrers, Messenger of the King's Chamber, at Gravesend, that as Percy had been seen riding towards Rochester the Constable of Gravesend had gone to Dover in pursuit.

In the midst of intense excitement, the King, accompanied by the Queen and Prince Henry, opened the second session of the Parliament, only to prorogue them after a speech giving an account of as much as was known of the plot.

The investigation into the desperate conspiracy went on apace ; on the 30th, it was elicited from Thomas Keyes, in the course of an examination, that he had charge of the house at Lambeth where the powder was kept. The Earl of Northumberland —who this year had been adding to or re-building Northumberland House at Charing Cross—having sheltered his relative, Thomas Percy, was committed to the custody of the Archbishop at Lambeth, and afterwards fined £30,000 and sent to the Tower. This nobleman, disproving of the politics of the Court, had, early in the autumn, retired to Sion House at Isleworth, with the apparent intention of devoting his time to the more congenial study of science and literature.

1606. On January 21st, 1606, the King opened the third session of the Parliament with a speech in which he declared that he did not impute the guilt of the Gunpowder Plot to any but the actual perpetrators. At Whitehall, two days later, James knighted Nicholas de Molin, the Venetian Ambassador. In the meantime the conspirators had been hunted down, and in the following week, those taken alive were conveyed in a boat from the Tower, and tried and convicted in Westminster Hall, by a Commission under the presidency of Charles Howard, Earl of Nottingham. Sir Everard Digby pleaded guilty, and Guy Fawkes, Bates, Grant, Keyes, Rookwood, and the two Winters not guilty, " to the admiration of all hearers," wrote Stow. Tresham had died in the Tower, and Percy and Catesby had both been killed when the rest were taken at Holbeach.

After an interval of only three days for preparing to meet their awful fate, Digby, Grant, Bates, and

Robert Winter were hanged, drawn, and quartered at the west end of St. Paul's Cathedral ; and on the morrow Fawkes, Rookwood, Keyes, and Thomas Winter were executed in a similar manner in Palace Yard, Westminster.

Still the tragedy was not ended. On February 13th, James Stanley, a scrivener, of Cornhill, stated in an examination that Catesby hired a house in Mr. Churchill's name at Erith, and there the conspirators had frequent secret meetings. In the beginning of March, a priest named Owen, a native of Oxford and servant of the Jesuit Garnet, and who had been seized in Worcestershire, and thrown into the Tower, killed himself by ripping up his belly with a blunt knife, given him for cutting his meat. About the same time several players were arrested in Blackfriars, and committed to Bridewell for certain speeches in a comedy, called the " Isle of Gulls," written by John Day, of Caius College, Cambridge.

On the 28th, the short trial of Garnet the Jesuit, for complicity in the plot, ended in a sentence of death. One of the witnesses was Anne Vaux, who stated that her cousin Francis Tresham and Garnet often visited her at White Webbs, Erith, Wandsworth, and elsewhere, when the Jesuit would counsel Tresham to be patient and quiet.

Father Garnet was dragged on a hurdle from the Tower, and executed in St. Paul's Churchyard on May 3rd. Bishop Challoner wrote of him : " His head was fixed on London Bridge, and it was much remarked that his countenance, which was always venerable, retained for above twenty days, the same lively colour which it had during life, which drew all London to the spectacle, and was interpreted as a testimony of his innocence."

In August, Lord Montague was freed from the Tower, on the payment of a fine of £200.

The fourth session of the Parliament opened at Westminster on November 18th, and ten days later the bells of St. Margaret's were rung when the King came to the House.

1607. Early in 1607, the royal recommendation to both Houses of a Union between England and Scotland being coldly received, the proposition was dropped for the present. On March 31st, the King made a speech to both Houses in the great chamber at Whitehall.

1608. On April 10th, 1608, a brother-in-law of the rebel Irish Earl of Tyrone, venturing to this country from Flanders, was seized and thrown into the Tower. Parliament was prorogued by a proclamation issued from Windsor Castle, on September 4th ; and on the 18th the Venetian Ambassador wrote : " The Council is meeting at Hampton Court, where the King has arrived to-day from progress. In two days he intends to go further off, and has summoned the Council to meet him for the discussion of current business, and especially the alliance proposed by the French Ambassador, who is pressing Lord Salisbury for a reply."

1609. Towards the end of March, 1609, the Ambassador wrote again : " The Queen herself yesterday sent to Hampton Court, where the King is, to intercede for the President of Scotland (Lord Balmerinoch). There is news that he has been condemned to death for ' læsa majestas.' The King replied that he had already written to Scotland to carry out the sentence. The Queen was very ill-pleased, as the President had always professed to be of her party."

1610. On February 9th, 1610, the fifth session of the Parliament was opened at Westminster, and on a Wednesday towards the end of March both Houses assembled in the Banqueting House, at Whitehall, and listened to a two-hours' speech from the King, wherein, it was flatteringly said, " he shewed great learning, admirable memory, and exceeding piety, to the great contentment of all parties."

Parliament was adjourned on July 23rd, when men were talking of the Lady Arabella Stuart, who, having contracted an unauthorized marriage with William Seymour, second son of the Earl of Hertford, was, with her husband, summoned, before the Council. The Lady was given into the custody of Sir Thomas Parry, to be kept a close prisoner in his house at Lambeth ; and Seymour was committed to the Tower for life.

The Parliament re-assembled at Westminster on October 16th, to be adjourned on December 6th, and dissolved by proclamation on the last day of the month. The Venetian Ambassador remarked that the business in Parliament had gone from bad to worse.

1611. The Venetian Ambassador wrote on February 4th, 1611 : " Lady Arabella is in bed so afflicted and so ill that the King has been obliged to postpone her departure for Durham (where she was to be the charge of the Bishop) for another twenty days. She is relegated to Durham, and her husband is a closer prisoner than ever."

On March 16th, the Bishop of Durham intimated to the Council that he had received the Lady Arabella at Lambeth Ferry, in a weak and ailing condition, and conveyed her to Highgate.

T

Through the influence of the favourite Rochester, Sir William Waad was removed from the Lieutenancy of the Tower, on May 6th, to make way for his creature, Sir Gervase Elwes ; and on the 18th, a proclamation was issued from Greenwich against melting or conveying out of the King's dominions gold or silver coins.

On June 4th, the King caused a proclamation to be issued from Greenwich, forbidding any person to harbour or assist the Lady Arabella Stuart and William Seymour, who had made their escape from confinement. The former had broken from the custody of the Bishop of Durham, and disguised in man's attire, reached Blackwall, where she entered a boat, with several attendants, and gained a French vessel below Leigh. Seymour eluded his guards at the Tower, and joined another small unarmed vessel, but the wind detained them for some time at the mouth of the river, and when at last they sailed in company for Calais, a King's ship intercepted them at sea, and brought the disappointed lovers back to the Tower, where they were shut up apart. The Countess of Shrewsbury was also committed to the grim prison as an accomplice of the unhappy pair.

On the 8th, John More, in a letter to Sir Ralph Winwood, thus described the attempted escape : " On Monday last in the afternoon my Lady Arabella lying at Mr. Conier's house near Highgate, having induced her keepers and attendants into security by the fair shew of conformity and willingness to go on her journey towards Durham (which the next day she must have done) and in the meantime disguising herself by drawing a pair of great French-fashion'd hose over her petticoats, putting on a man's doublet, a man-like perruque with long locks over her hair, a black hat, black cloak, russet boots with red tops, and a rapier by her side, walked forth between three and four of the clock with Mr. Markham. After they had gone a-foot a mile and half to a sorry inn, where Crompton attended with their horses, she grew very sick and faint, so as the hostler that held the stirrup said that gentleman would hardly hold out to London. Yet being set on a good gelding astride in an unwonted fashion, the stirring of the horse brought blood enough into her face, and so she rid on towards Blackwall ; where arriving about six o'clock, finding there in a readiness two men, a gentlewoman, and a chambermaid, with one boat full of Mr. Seymour's and her trunks, and another boat for their persons, they hasted from thence towards Woolwich. Being come so far they bade the watermen row on to Gravesend. There the watermen were desirous to land, but for a double freight were contented to go on to Leigh ; yet being almost tired by the way, they were fain to lie still at Tilbury whilst the oars went a land to refresh themselves. Then they proceeded to Leigh, and by that time the day appeared, they discovered a ship at anchor a mile beyond them, which was the French barque that waited for them : here the lady would have lain at anchor, expecting Mr. Seymour, but through the importunity of her followers they forthwith hoisted sail to seaward. In the meanwhile Mr. Seymour with a perruque and beard of black hair, and in a tawny cloth suit, walked alone without suspicion from his lodging, out of the great west door of the Tower, following a cart that had brought him billets. From thence he walked along by the Tower Wharf, by the warders of the south gate, and so to the iron-gate, where Rodney was ready with oars to receive him. When they came to Leigh, and found that the French ship was gone, the billows rising high, they hired a fisherman for twenty shillings to set them aboard a certain ship that they saw under sail. That ship they found not to be it they looked for, so they made forwards to the next under sail, which was a ship of Newcastle. This with much ado they hired for forty pounds, to carry them to Calais; but whether the collier did perform his bargain or no, is not as yet here known. On Tuesday, in the afternoon, my Lord Treasurer, being advertised that the Lady Arabella had made an escape, sent forthwith to the Lieutenant of the Tower to set straight guard over Mr. Seymour; which he after his ' Yare manner,' would ' thoroughly do, that he would.' But coming to the prisoner's lodgings, he found (to his great amazement) that he was gone from thence one whole day before. I may not omit in this relation to insert the simple part of two silly persons; the one called Tom Barber, servant to Mr. Seymour (who believing his master spake bonâ fide) did according to his instructions tell every one that came to inquire for his master, ' that he was newly betaken to his rest, being much troubled with the tooth-ache.' And when the matter was discovered, did seriously persist to persuade Mr. Lieutenant ' that he was gone but to lie a night with his wife, and would surely return thither of himself again.' The other, a minister's wife attending the lady; who seeing her mistress disguise herself and slip away, was truly persuaded that she intended but to make ' a private visit to her husband,' and did duly attend her return at the time appointed.

Now the King and the Lords being much disturbed with this unexpected accident, my Lord Treasurer sent orders to a pinnace that lay at the Downs to put presently to sea, first to Calais Road, and then to scour up the coast towards Dunkirk. This pinnace, spying the aforesaid French barque which lay lingering for Mr. Seymour, made to her, which thereupon offered to fly towards Calais, and endured thirteen shot of the pinnace before she would strike. In this barque is the Lady taken with her followers, and brought back towards the Tower. Not so sorry for her own restraint, as she should be glad if Mr. Seymour might escape, whose welfare she protesteth to affect much more than her own."

The King came up [to Whitehall from Greenwich, on the 15th, and held a long consultation with his Council concerning the charges against the unfortunate Lady Arabella. In October several Council meetings were held at Hampton Court for the discussion of home and foreign affairs. On the 9th, the Earl of Shrewsbury requested Lord Salisbury to order shutters for the windows, boards before the doors, and the repair of a hole in the roof of the rooms in the Tower, where his wife was lodged for complicity in the Arabella Stuart marriage.

1612. On February 12th, 1612, John Chamberlain wrote in a letter to Sir Dudley Carleton : " The Lady of Shrewsbury is still in the Tower, rather upon wilfulness than upon any great matter she is charged withal, only the King is resolute that she shall answer to certain interrogatories (relative to the marriage of Lady Arabella with Lord William Seymour), and she is obstinate to make none, nor to be examined."

Robert Cecil, Earl of Salisbury, the deformed

statesman, died on May 24th, in a blaze of public success, but in private a miserable man. All his ambitions had been gratified, and his wealth had enabled him to build a palace at Hatfield, an Exchange in the Strand, and to make of Salisbury House on the river an abode of luxurious splendour.

1613. In March, 1613, some information having been pressed from the imprisoned Lady Arabella, the Countess of Shrewsbury, who had been allowed the liberty of the Tower, was committed to much closer confinement. Lord Keeper Ellesmere, in May, took a prominent part in sending Whitelocke to the Tower, for indirectly questioning the royal prerogative by denying the powers of the Earl Marshal's Court.

The Privy Council met at Greenwich on June 1st ; and a little later the Earl of Essex divorce case was heard at Lambeth, when, after many shameful disclosures, the Countess obtained her desired freedom. Sir Thomas Overbury, a courtier of questionable character, had attached himself to the fortunes of the arrogant favourite Rochester, but he gave mortal offence by endeavouring to dissuade him from marrying the Countess, and at the instigation of the vengeful pair, was committed to the Tower, ostensibly for refusing to proceed on a foreign embassy.

In the examination, on June 14th, at Lambeth Palace before the Archbishop, and the Bishops of London and Coventry and Lichfield, of John Cotton, a Hampshire Catholic, who was charged with high treason, he said he was in London during Easter term for three or four days, " and lay in Fleet street, first for one night at the sign of the ' Eagle and Child,' at the house of one that selleth stockings, and then at the house of one Lovelesse, at the sign of the ' Lute.' '' After a visit to Stoke he returned to London, and '' on Saturday last came to the sign of the ' Dog and the Bear,' in Southwark, having heard that he was sought after for some matter of State, which he chanced (in the time of his examination) to name to be a libel or book, as he thought.'' At Southwark, '' having not slept one wink all the night before,'' he rested himself on a bed for an hour or so, and in the afternoon went to the Earl of Southampton's house. '' Being in a boat upon the water he heard of the waterman that carried him that there was a proclamation out against one Cotton, which made his heart very heavy, and yet he went on to the Earl of Southampton's house, whither he came about four o' clock, but by the way he went very warily, as fearing that he should be taken by some pursuivants, whereof some of them know him well.'' He landed at the Temple Stairs, and went to Mr. Watson's house in Chancery Lane, where his brother, Richard Cotton, and Mr. Wakeman were. Mr. Wakeman and others went with him to Southampton House, where a gentleman had the proclamation, and he saw his name and description.

After a six months' rigorous confinement in the Tower, Sir Thomas Overbury died from foul play on September 15th. Weston, a warder, and other agents were afterwards executed for poisoning him; but the Earl and Countess of Somerset, the instigators, escaped condign punishment.

1614. On April 5th, 1614, the King, with Prince Charles and the Lords, all in their robes, rode in procession to Westminster for the opening of the second Parliament of the reign. This, after refusing to vote supplies, and making an effort to curb the power of the Crown, was, on June 7th, arbitrarily dissolved by the angry King, without having passed a single Act, for which it was nicknamed the "Addled Parliament." Christopher Neville, Sir Walter Chute, John Hoskins, and Thomas Wentworth were sent to the Tower for the part they had taken in the discussions. Dr. Lionel Sharpe, Archdeacon of Berkshire, was also committed to the Tower (and confined there a year), on a charge of suggesting to John Hoskins—afterwards Serjeant-at-Law and one of the Judges of Wales—an allusion to the Sicilian Vespers, which Hoskins introduced into a very free speech in the Commons.

Sir Charles Cornwallis, late Ambassador to Spain, was accused of complicity with Dr. Sharpe in prompting Hoskins, and sent to join his friend in prison.

On July 7th, John Chamberlain wrote in a letter to Sir Dudley Carleton : " Dr. Palmer and Crompton, a gentleman usher, committed to the Tower, for some business concerning the Lady Arabella." And in another letter, a week later, he mentioned the death of Lord Grey in the Tower. In the autumn the most famous prisoner there, Sir Walter Raleigh, published his "History of the World," to the equal amazement of friend and foe.

Early in October, the Privy Council, in various sittings at Hampton Court, was engaged in a deep consideration of foreign affairs.

1615. On January 18th, 1615, the Council, sitting at Whitehall, required Secretary Winwood, the Master of the Rolls, the Lieutenant of the Tower, and others to examine Edmund Peacham, a prisoner in the Tower, respecting his authorship of a treasonable book, and if he should obstinately refuse to give needful information to use the manacles upon him.

In June, Sir Charles Cornwallis, Dr. Sharpe, and John Hoskins were released from the Tower.

On September 27th, the unhappy Lady Arabella Stuart, her reason shattered by the severity of her confinement, died in the Tower. The body was brought " at midnight by the dark river," and laid, " with no solemnity," upon the coffin of Mary, Queen of Scots, in Westminster Abbey.

The Commissioners on the late Sir Thomas Overbury's murder, sitting at York House, on October 17th, required the Countess of Somerset " to keep her chamber at the Blackfriars, or at Lady Knolly's house near the Tilt Yard, seeing none but her own servants." Ten days later Sir William Smithe, who was charged with the custody of the Countess, reported to the Commissioners from the Cockpit that he had taken the lady in charge, and continued : " The cockpit is unfit for her, there being so many doors and few keys. She intends to go to Lord Aubigny's house in Blackfriars. Desires he may first inspect the place, and appoint her apartment. She wishes to diet his family. She will have six women servants and several men to attend her. Has refused Hen. Howard, who wished to see her. . . . Thinks Lady Somerset's list of attendants too large ; she has no means to maintain them."

Edward Norman, in the course of an examination on November 2nd, stated that he was told " by Jeffry Platt, waterman, that a gentleman came to him at Blackfriars ferry, and bade him tap at a certain window at the Countess of Somerset's house, and deliver letters to her man, saying they were from the King and Council, which he did."

On the 18th, Sir Gervas Elwes, late Lieutenant of the Tower, was condemned for his share in the Overbury murder, and two days later he was hanged by the neck on Tower Hill.

The Lord Chancellor, the Duke of Lennox, and the Lord Chief Justice held a conference on December 14th, with the disgraced Earl of Somerset in the Tower.

1616. On March 20th, 1616, Sir Walter Raleigh, was liberated from the Tower. At the age of sixty-four, and after thirteen years' confinement, the distinguished knight, a tall, gaunt figure with a commanding face, was free again to walk the streets of London. Two days later the Countess of Somerset was committed from Blackfriars to the Tower, " upon so short warning that she had scant leisure to shed a few tears over her little daughter (Anne) at the parting. Otherwise she carried herself very constantly enough, saving that she did passionately deprecate and entreat the Lieutenant that she might not be lodged in Sir Thomas Overbury's lodging ; so that he was fain to remove himself out of his own chamber for two or three nights, till Sir Walter Raleigh's lodging might be furnished and made fit for her."

The Countess was tried on May 24th, in Westminster Hall, for complicity in the murder of Sir Thomas Overbury, and, confessing herself guilty, was condemned to be taken back to the Tower, " and from thence to the place of execution, to be hanged by the neck till she were stark dead." On the following day the Earl was tried and similarly sentenced.

Early in June Sir Robert Cotton and the servants of the Earl and Countess were released from the Tower.

On July 24th, Patrick Ruthven, a Scotch prisoner in the Tower, was granted the sum of £200 per annum, to enable him to purchase apparel, books, physic, and other things.

Sir Henry Montague succeeded Coke as Chief Justice of the King's Bench, on November 16th, and two days later, he rode in great state, attended by " earls, lords, and others of great quality, to the number of fifty horse," to Westminster Hall, where he was installed by Lord Chancellor Ellesmere.

1617. On March 15th, 1617, the Lord Chancellor died at York House. Sir Francis Bacon succeeded him, and on May 10th, John Chamberlain, in telling his friend Carleton that he had returned to London from a visit to Ware Park, wrote : " We came to town after the old manner, the day before term ; and the rather to see the new Lord Keeper (Bacon) ride in pomp to Westminster, as he did the next day, accompanied by most of the Council and nobility, with other gallants to the number of more than two hundred horse, besides the Judges and Inns of Court."

The King left early this year for a journey to Scotland, and during his absence the Council met frequently at Greenwich, where the Queen held her Court.

During August the Earl of Somerset occupied Sir Walter Raleigh's old lodgings in the Bloody Tower, and the Countess was put in rooms adjoining, with the doors open between.

Sir Ralph Winwood, the Secretary of State, died on October 27th, at Mordant House, in the parish of St. Bartholomew the Less, and was buried in the church.

The Privy Council met at Whitehall on December

4th, and nine days later Gervase, Lord Clifton, was committed to the Tower for threatening to kill the Lord Keeper. In the latter part of the following year this violent nobleman put an end to his own existence.

On March 28th of this year a long and curious relation of divers criminal articles against an Irishman named Florence M'Carty, was sworn to by one Tieg Hurly, sometime the said M'Carty's servant. He alleged that twenty-seven years before he went with M'Carty as his footboy into England, and afterwards wandered with him in France, Spain, and Germany. Leaving this service, he had become a soldier and other things, and at last coming back to London, found his old master in the Marshalsea prison. Entering the service of Lord Courcy, Tieg became involved in intrigues, and after a visit to Ireland found on his return to London M'Carty at liberty and inclined to accuse him of bad faith. The relation then went on : " But frequenting the said Florence's house, and lying in one bed with one of his men called Thomas O'Hanloane for the space of three weeks, for some two or three days in that time the said Tieg, as his former custom was, came to Florence's chamber to visit him, and still found him and his men absent, which he wondered at, but conceived not the cause until one day coming thither early he found one John O'Voleghane, Cnogher O'Voleghane, and Tieg M'Cormock, all three Desmond men born, and one of them brother to the Franciscan friar, Tieg O'Voleghane, all being new comers out of Ireland. The said Tieg Hurly bade them welcome, and was inquisitive of news out of Ireland, and asked them when they came into London, to which they answered some two days since. That very night coming into his lodging where the aforesaid Thomas came late to his lodging about eleven o'clock at night, where Tieg Hurly asked him where he had been so late, and he answered with his master, and after other discourse he made relation to him of some friends of his that were two or three days in town, and were bound for beyond sea. 'What friends of mine,' said Tieg, 'that have been poor so long, and would not acquaint me with their being in town ? What ! dare they not walk the streets, or are they friars or men ashamed of any their actions ? ' ' John Entlea one of them,' quoth Thomas. 'Then,' quoth Tieg, 'what a devil should John here ? ' 'He is here, and Tieg O'Voleghane, the Franciscan friar, with him,' said Thomas. 'Oh ! is it so ? I know,' said Tieg, 'it was to keep them company Florence was missing this two or three days out of his chamber.' 'It is true,' said Thomas, 'although I was not with them ; they did all five that come over dine at the Boar's Head within Ludgate, and Florence with them there, and they think no man can better procure them a pass from the four ministers of the Custom-house than yourself, in regard you are acquainted there.' 'I assure you there is nothing I can do for them but I will do it,' said Tieg ; 'but yet, believe me, it is hard for me to undergo such danger, and how may I effect it ? ' 'Nothing,' said Thomas, 'but instead of Tieg O'Voleghane, let your name serve for the friar, and it will prejudice you nothing.' And then after many persuasions to that purpose, the said Tieg, Thomas and John Entlea went to the Custom-house, where there was got one pass in the name of Tieg Hurly and John Entlea. This Franciscan friar the said Tieg saw in Ireland before this time, and knew

him to have been collecting of moneys within the
counties of Cork and Kerry under pretence of
mending an abbey within the county of Kerry,
called the Abbey of Ireelagh, under colour of which
work the said Tieg saw him going up and down the
country and levying of monies, having some masons
working of a few stones only to colour his intent
and blind the people with a seeming zeal of mending
a work so charitable, and thereupon through the
devotion of many well-minded men he obtained a
good purse of money, wherewith he took his journey
into England and from thence beyond seas.   After
the receipt of the pass out of the Custom-house,
they went to the friar's lodgings in Thames Street
as he takes it, being the sign of the Sugar-loaf,
where he saw the friar with Donell and Cormock,
Florence's two sons, the friar's brother called John
O'Voleghane, and Cnogher O'Voleghane, his kinsman, with whom the said Tieg there broke his fast
and warned the friar to make as much haste as he
could away, and being so far engaged for him
hastened him still.   And after that, the very self-
same day, the said Tieg and John Entlea went to
Billingsgate to provide a tilt-boat to go down to
Gravesend, and the said Tieg procured the boat, but
the tide serving not till nigh in the evening, went
the friar, Tieg Hurly, and John Entlea into the boat,
till at last landing at Gravesend they took a chamber.
The next morning the said Tieg and John Entlea
went to enquire what ships were going for the Low
Countries, and hearing certainly that there were in
the harbour two barks ready to go, the one bound
for Dunkirk, the other for Flushing, the said Tieg
and John came back to the friar and told him of
those two ships that were immediately departing

and wished him pack away, the friar answering, 'I will go in the ship to Dunkirk'; but Tieg told him it was unlikely he should have an allowance to go in that ship, having in his pass but to arrive in Damme in Flanders, and that it were convenient for him to go into Flushing. But the friar's inclination being towards the Spanish shore, still resolved to go in the ship of Dunkirk, and with that resolution they went to the water's side. A boat then being ready with passengers to go to the Dunkirk bark, the friar stept into it; the searcher standing on shore asked him whither he was going or where his passport was, he answering, 'Here it is,' delivered him the same, which the searcher reading, 'This bark,' quoth he, 'goeth to Dunkirk, and your pass is to Damme in Flanders'; with that they cried, 'Come ashore, you shall not go there; whereupon the searcher grew very angry, and told that the State was much abused by such dealing, and presently carried him to a justice of the peace, and was there examined what the reason was that he intended to go contrary to the effect intended in his pass. He made answer that he was unacquainted either with Damme or Dunkirk, but his business being in the Low Countries, he desired to arrive there in any place, and that he was desirous not to lose his passage. 'You shall not then go into Dunkirk,' said the justice of the peace, and with that cold comfort they parted and came to their chamber, whereupon they consulted what was best to be done, and then the friar more dismayedly than he had any cause given, bewrayed his guiltiness by his outward changing of colour, began to suspect the searcher would follow and search what he had about him, which Tieg perceiving, advised him, if he had anything that might endanger

him, he should do well to hide it in the chamber, who told him he had his book and two letters that were folded like wrapt sheets of paper, without sealing or superscription, which they put between the hanging and the wall, being formerly sewed up in John Entlea's doublet; which being done, the said Tieg went upon the quay, where he met with the former justice of the peace, who demanded of him where his company was, and he answered they were in their chamber taking a pipe of tobacco, for getting no leave to go, it behoved them not to walk on the quay. One of the standers-by said that there was another bark going for Flushing, whereupon the said Tieg came back and told the friar thereof, advising him to look boldly and to entreat the justice to let him have his pass back again to London if he would not let him go ; upon which admonition he went out and met the justice, whom he entreated with a great deal of fear (his heart failing him to look aright on the justice), whereupon he, looking on him, said, ' I know not what to think of you, but I have nothing to say to you,' after which words he took boat and went to the ship, and this about mid-August 1616."

1618. Early in August, 1618, Sir Walter Raleigh returned from his disastrous expedition to Guiana— having lost his son Walter, been betrayed by his King, and drawn upon himself the deadly enmity of Gondomar, the Spanish Ambassador, whose brother had been killed in resisting the adventurers—was brought from Plymouth to London in charge of his relative, Sir Lewis Stukeley. Filled with gloomy forebodings of the fate awaiting him, he determined to make an effort to get over to France out of the grasp of his enemies. The French agent in London had contrived to gain his ear at Brentford, and from his suggestions a plan of escape was concerted with one of his old captains, Samuel King. Hart, a boatswain who had served under King, and Cottrell, one of Raleigh's old Tower servants, were brought in to help, and it was arranged that a ketch, belonging to the former, should be in readiness off Tilbury. These two knaves, however, secretly betrayed the project to Mr. William Herbert, who imparted the matter to Sir William St. John, and preparations were made to prevent the attempt. Stukeley was warned, but he exhibited such seeming anxiety for his relative's safety, that both Raleigh and King were deluded into trusting to his goodwill, and imparted all their plans to him. On the dark Sunday evening of the 9th, the fugitives embarked in two wherries, hired at Tower Dock. The knight, wearing a false beard and a hat with a green band, was attended by one of his pages, Stukeley and his son, King and Hart. Sir William St. John and Herbert quietly followed in another boat, which was discovered by Raleigh, and when he saw it first making as if it would go through the Bridge and then returning down the river, he became alarmed. Clinging to the hope that with the assistance of the ebb-tide and the loyalty of the boatmen he might force his way to Tilbury in spite of an attempt to capture him, he offered the now frightened rowers ten gold pieces to hold on in face of all demands to stop. Stukeley and King encouraged the men to proceed, and they had passed Deptford and were drawing near to Greenwich when another wherry crossed their course and checked the rowers. Urged on again by King, the men pulled in a half-hearted manner, till the tide was found to be spent, and then the idea of landing and pursuing the rest of the way to Tilbury on horseback was discussed and abandoned as impracticable. When a mile beyond Woolwich, at the Gallions Reach near Plumstead—Raleigh, feeling certain he was betrayed, ordered the men to row back, and almost immediately after a wherry hailed them in the King's name, but was disregarded. Raleigh, however, perceiving that the accomplishment of his object was no longer possible, declared to Stukeley that he would remain his prisoner. They landed at Greenwich, and then Stukeley, throwing off all pretence of friendship, bluntly declared they could not go back to his house, and arrested the unfortunate knight and the faithful King, giving them in charge to two of St. John's men. The remainder of the night was passed at a tavern, and in the morning a gloomy party passed up the river, and King, after a last farewell, saw the gate of the Tower close upon his master.

An order was sent from Westminster to Lord Chancellor Bacon to issue warrants to the Lieutenant of the Tower and the Sheriff of Middlesex for the beheading of Sir Walter Raleigh ; and the next day, October 29th, the sentence was carried out on the distinguished victim of misfortune, in Old Palace Yard, Westminster ; the day being selected, it has been said, because the Lord Mayor's Show would draw away the people from the sacrifice of a popular hero. His head was delivered to Lady Raleigh, and his body buried privately near the high altar in St. Margaret's Church.

1619. On January 9th, 1619, G. Gerard, in a letter from Salisbury House to Sir Dudley Carleton, wrote : " Sir Lewis Stukeley is close prisoner ;

all his instruments etc., for clipping gold are found in his chamber, in the King's house at Whitehall."

At this time Sir Thomas and Lady Lake and their son and daughter, Lady Roos, were charged with casting injurious imputations on the character of the Countess of Exeter. Sir William Smithe, in a letter to Carleton, wrote on February 13th : " The King has fined Sir Thomas Lake and his wife 5,000*l.* each, Lady Roos 10,000 marks, Sir Thomas Lake, jun., 1,000*l.*, with imprisonment in the Tower for life." G. Gerard related that when the culprits were on their way to the Tower, " Lady Roos was cursed horribly by the people as she went." On April 24th, John Chamberlain wrote : " Sir Thomas Lake has more liberty in the Tower, through the mediation of his brother, the Bishop of Bath and Wells." He was, however, not permitted to enjoy the company of his wife and daughter. In May, Sir Art. Lake was committed to the Tower for perjury.

On August 20th, Nathaniel Brent wrote to Carleton : " Earl Gowrie's son, whose release from the Tower was procured by Lord Haddington, has followed him into France."

In November the Earl and Countess of Suffolk were sent to the Tower for bribery and corruption. Shortly after Sir Thomas Edmondes wrote : " After eleven days' hearing of the cause the Earl of Suffolk and his Lady are fined 30,000*l.*, and sentenced to restore all money wrongfully extorted, and to be imprisoned apart in the Tower during pleasure." Their confinement only lasted till December, when the King released them.

Towards the end of the year, Lord Chancellor Bacon frequently consulted Sir Giles Mompesson—

who had gained an unsavoury reputation as an unscrupulous and audacious Commissioner for Licencing Inns—on matters affecting the public revenue, and, on December 12th, invited him to Kew in order to confer with him the more quietly.

1620. On February 26th, 1620, John Chamberlain wrote to Sir Dudley Carleton : " Peacock, a schoolmaster, committed to the Tower, and tortured for practising sorcery upon the King to infatuate him in Sir Thomas Lake's business." Thomas Locke wrote to Carleton on November 18th : " Lady Lake is sent again to the Tower for writing to the King to complain against the Countess of Exeter, and for blaming the proceedings against herself." John Chamberlain said, on December 22nd : " Lady Lake is released from the Tower on making submission to Lady Exeter, and giving bond for her appearance in the Star Chamber."

On November 27th, an order was issued for paying £100 to Patrick Ruthven, a prisoner in the Tower, as half of his yearly allowance of £200 for apparel, books, and other necessaries over and above such allowances as were to be paid to the Lieutenant for his diet.

Sir Robert Naunton wrote to Carleton on December 2nd : " The Attorney-General is displaced, fined, and sent to the Tower."

1621. On Tuesday, January 30th, 1621, after an interval of nearly seven years, a new Parliament met at Westminster, and heard a speech from the King. John Chamberlain wrote on the occasion : " The Parliament began on Tuesday, with the greatest concourse and throng of people that hath been seen ; so that there was some hurt done by the breaking of two scaffolds and otherwise. The

King went on horseback, and was very cheerful all the way; and from the Church was carried in a chair to the Parliament House, being so weak in his legs and feet, that it is doubtful he will find little use in them hereafter." A Harleian MS. said: " In the King's short progress from Whitehall to Westminster, these passages following were accounted somewhat remarkable : " First, that he spake often and lovingly to the people standing thick and threefold on all sides to behold him : ' God bless ye! God bless ye!' contrary to his former hasty and passionate custom, which often, in his sudden distemper, would bid a pox or plague on such as flocked to see him. Secondly, that though the windows were filled with many great ladies as he rode along, yet he spake to none of them but to the Marquis of Buckingham's mother and wife. Thirdly, that he spake particularly and bowed to the Count of Gondemar, the Spanish Ambassador ; and fourthly, that, looking up to one window as he passed, full of gentlemen and ladies, all in yellow bands, he cried aloud, ' A pox take ye, are ye there!' at which, being much alarmed, they all withdrew themselves suddenly from the window."

This Parliament proceeded to reform abuses in monopolies, patents, and licences. Lord Chancellor Bacon was forced by the action of members to confess to the acceptance of presents or bribes, and deprived of his office. Villiers, brother of Buckingham, Yelverton the Attorney-General, and many others were convicted of malversations.

On February 17th, John Chamberlain wrote to Carleton : " Parliament sits closely ; two subsidies granted, but no fifteenths as they press more heavily on the meaner sort. The King has summoned the

Houses to Whitehall, to thank them and promise redress of grievances."

A week later Thomas Locke wrote : " Sir Giles Mompesson's patent for inns is dashed, and was found full of abuses. Sir Fras. Michell was sent on foot and bareheaded to the Tower, on account of his patent for alehouses ; he is a justice of Middlesex." Michell had made disgraceful exactions upon the public innkeepers and the sellers of beer and ale. Some months later he was degraded from knighthood, fined £1,000, and imprisoned during the King's pleasure.

After a short prorogation the two Houses, on April 23rd, were summoned to Whitehall, where the King made a speech to them. On Tuesday, May 1st, Sir Symonds D'Ewes wrote : " The Count of Gondomar, fearing some mischief from the apprentices of London, there were divers companies of soldiers appointed to guard and watch in several quarters of the City, which still did more and more argue the potency this Spanish Ambassador had in the English Court."

On May 5th, John Chamberlain wrote to Carleton : " The Lord Chancellor (Bacon) sentenced to 40,000*l.* fine, imprisonment in the Tower during pleasure, and disability ever to bear office, etc. ; he escaped degradation by only two votes. Sir Fras. Michell sentenced to a fine of 1,000*l.*, imprisonment, and degradation."

Chamberlain again wrote to Carleton on the 19th : " The Earl of Arundel urging warmly (in the Lords) that Yelverton (Sir Henry—the Attorney-General) should be condemned without further hearing, Lord Spencer reminded him of sentences similarly passed on his ancestry, on which he retorted that

Lord Spencer's ancestry were shepherds then.
Arundel was called to the bar of the House, but
only consented to apologise in his place where he
sat, wherewith Lord Spencer not being satisfied,
he was sent to the Tower, where he was welcomed
by the Earl of Northumberland, and is visited by
Buckingham and others."

Six days later Thomas Locke wrote : " The Earl
of Arundel prefers enduring restraint in the Tower
to acknowledging his error to Lord Spencer."

Parliament again adjourned on June 4th, on
which day Bacon was liberated from the Tower,
and went to Sir John Vaughan's house at Fulham.

On the 15th, the King, from Greenwich,
commanded the Council to commit the Earl of
Southampton to close custody with the Dean of
Westminster, under the Keepership of Sir Richard
Weston, who was to allow him no intercourse with
any other person.

On Monday, the 24th, certain agents or commissioners sent from Rochelle to desire the King's
aid, had their audience at Whitehall ; " but received
small comfort from him, and less assistance."

The Earl of Northumberland was released from
the Tower on July 18th.

Parliament re-assembled at Westminster on
November 20th, when the King, being indisposed,
commanded a message to be delivered to both
Houses by the Lord Keeper Digby and the Lord
Treasurer. The Commons proceeded to quarrel
with the Sovereign, who tore a protest from their
Journal with his own hand.

At this time Edward Floyde, or Lloyde, was impeached by the House, and committed to the Fleet
prison, for saying, " I have heard that Prague is

taken and Goodman Palsgrave and Goodwife Palsgrave have taken to their heels and run away, and as I have heard Goodwife Palsgrave is taken prisoner "—meaning the Elector Frederic and his wife Elizabeth, daughter of the King. After several barbarous suggestions for his punishment, he was sentenced to stand in the pillory two hours before Westminster Hall with a paper on his hat inscribed : " For false, malicious, and despiteful speeches against the King's daughter and her husband." and to ride thence on a bare-backed horse, with his face to the tail, to the Exchange, there again to be pilloried for two hours, and then taken to the Fleet prison, only to stand and ride the next day, and finally to pay a fine of £1,000.

1622. On January 17th, 1622, Sir Allen Apsley, Lieutenant of the Tower, was ordered from Westminster to set at liberty the Earl and Countess of Somerset.

The King, in high displeasure, dissolved the Parliament on February 8th. He called some members of the Commons, " ill-tempered spirits " and Sir Edward Coke and Sir Robert Philips were committed to the Tower, whilst Selden, Pym, and Mallory were imprisoned elsewhere. On the 19th, the King commanded the Council to give order for Mrs. Sadler to visit her father, Sir Edward Coke, in the Tower, " she being a discreet woman, and likely to endeavour to bring him to more conformity."

On April 13th, Thomas Locke wrote to Sir Dudley Carleton : " Dr. Winniffe committed to the Tower for a remark in a sermon at Whitehall, comparing the Palatinate to a soul in hell, and Spinola to the devil, from whom it was impossible to get back the soul." Locke again wrote on Easter Eve : " The

Earl of Oxford committed to the Tower, for saying, in reference to suing out the livery for the Earl of Berkshire's daughter, that he hoped the time would come when justice would be free, and not pass only through Buckingham's hands."

On the last day of July the King, from Windsor, commanded Secretary Calvert that Patrick Ruthven, brother of Earl Gowrie (who had been a prisoner since the beginning of the reign) should be delivered from the Tower, and confined to Cambridge, or within six miles thereof.

Abraham Williams, in a letter from Westminster to Carleton, wrote on August 13th : " Mr. Ruthven, Sir Edward Coke, Sir Robt. Phelips, and Mr. Mallory are released from the Tower, and it is hoped that Earl of Oxford will be though he is still a close prisoner."

1623. On October 9th, 1623, Sir Allen Apsley, Lieutenant of the Tower, in a communication to the Council, wrote : " The prisoners remaining in his charge are, the Earl of Oxford, committed seventeen months ago, for causes best known to their Lordships ; Countess of Shrewsbury, five years ago, for Star Chamber offences ; Sir Cormack O'Neale, the Earl of Tyrone's brother, seventeen years ago, for offences best known to Lords Grandison, Carew, and Chichester ; Sir Neale O'Donnell, alias Garry, fourteen years ago, a good subject during the late reign ; Neal O'Donnell, his son, at the same time ; Con O'Neale, Tyrone's son, taken from school, and sent thither in August, 1622 ; and Bryan O'Rourke, transferred from the Gatehouse, February, 1623, offence not known."

On November 12th, an order was issued for paying to Michael Chambers and John Goulsborough,

" messengers sent by command from the Right Honourable the Earl of Middlesex, Lord High Treasurer of England, from Pissaberry, with warrant of the 13th of September, 1623, to Stantonberry, in the county of Bucks, to bring up five men, and hired five horses, and bore all their charges to London, and from London to Chelsea, by water, three several times, and back again, and from London, by horse, brought them to Hampton Court, by his Lordship's command, where his Lordship discharged them, but with command to bring them to London, in which time they attended the said five men the space of sixteen days, and were at all charges for horse-hire, boat-hire, meat, drink, and lodgings and all other charges 25*l.* in reward—to wit, 20*l.* for charges and 5*l.* for pains."

1624. On January 1st, 1624, the Earl of Oxford, who was just released from the Tower, after twenty months' imprisonment, married Lady Diana Cecil, daughter of the Earl of Exeter, and received with her a portion of £30,000.

The fourth Parliament of the reign was ready to meet at Westminster on Monday, February 16th, and the King with the Lords in their robes were already mounted on horseback in the presence of thousands of spectators, when the unexpected announcement of the sudden death of the Duke of Richmond and Lennox at Whitehall, caused a postponement to the following Thursday, when the opening ceremony was performed by the King with much pomp and show.

War was declared with Spain on March 10th.

On April 3rd, Sir Francis Nethersole wrote in a letter to Sir Dudley Carleton : " Mr. Lovell is sent to the Tower by the Lower House, for returning himself a second time as a member, without being elected afresh." The Council met at Whitehall on the 15th, and about the same time Lionel Cranfield, Earl of Middlesex, the Lord Treasurer, was, at the instigation of Buckingham, impeached by the Commons for corruption.

On May 5th, the King summoned the Upper House to Whitehall, and told them to sing a psalm of mercy and justice for the Lord Treasurer. Dr. Laud wrote on the same date in his diary: "Wednesday, being Ascension Eve, the King's speech in the Banqueting House at Whitehall to the Upper House of Parliament concerning the hearing of the Lord Treasurer's cause, which was to begin the Friday following."

The Earl was convicted by his Peers, on the 13th, of bribery and neglect of duty, fined £50,000, and declared incapable of sitting in Parliament. The next day he was sent to the Tower, and put into the late Sir Thomas Overbury's lodgings.

On the 28th Parliament was prorogued by the King.

John Chamberlain wrote to Carleton on June 5th: "The Earl of Middlesex is liberated from the Tower by paying 60,000l. in bribes, and is at his house at Chelsea."

Sir Allen Apsley, in a letter from the Tower to Secretary Conway, on the 14th, said: "A Scotch unbeneficed minister or schoolmaster was apprehended by the bystanders, for making notes of the weight, number, etc., of the ordnance on the Tower Wharf. Thinks he meant no harm, and asks whether he shall be liberated."

On November 12th, a Treaty of Marriage was concluded between Charles, Prince of Wales, and the Princess Henrietta Maria, sister of Louis XIII. of France.

THE GOVERNMENT OF THE RIVER.

1603. A Water Bailiff had charge of the river Thames from its head or source to Staines House ; and on July 4th, 1604, Richard Copiter was appointed to this office, on the surrender of William Bareward.

From Staines to its mouth, the river was under the jurisdiction of the Lord Mayor of London for the time being.

1605. In the first Charter of James granted to the City of London, at Westminster, on August 20th, 1605, the text, so far as concerned the government of the river, ran : " Whereas our beloved, the Mayor and Commonalty and citizens of our City of London, time out of mind, have had, exercised, and ought, and have accustomed themselves to have and exercise the office of bailiff, and conservation of the water of Thames, to be exercised and occupied by the Mayor of the same city for the time being during the time of his mayoralty, or by his sufficient deputies, in, upon, and about the water of Thames, that is to say, from the bridge of the town of Staines in the County of Middlesex, and towards the east, unto London Bridge, and from thence to a certain place called Kendall, otherwise Yenland, otherwise Yenleet (Yantlet Creek), towards the sea, and east, and in Medway, and in the Port of London aforesaid, and upon whatsoever bank, and upon every shore, and upon every Wharf of the same water

of Thames, within the limits and bounds aforesaid, and in, upon, and about all and every of
them. . . .

" And, further, of our special grace and certain
knowlege, and mere motion, we have granted, and by
these presents, for us, our heirs and successors, do
grant to the said Mayor and Commonalty and citizens
and their successors, that they may exercise and
execute the said office of bailiff and conservation
of the water of Thames, by the Mayor of the same city
for the time being, during the time of his mayoralty,
or his sufficient deputies, from time to time, for ever,
in, upon, or about the same water of Thames;
(that is to say) from the bridge of Staines to the
bridge of London, and from hence to a certain place
called Yenland, otherwise Yenleet, towards the sea,
and towards the east, and Medway, and in the port
of the City of London aforesaid, and upon whatsoever bank, shore and wharf of the same water of
Thames, within the limits and bounds aforesaid, in,
upon, and about everyone of the same, and to have,
exercise, and collect and enjoy all and singular
wages, rewards, fees and profits, to the same office
of bailiff pertaining, to the proper use of the said
Mayor and Commonalty and citizens, by the Mayor
of the same city, for the time being, during the time
of his mayoralty, or by his sufficient deputies."

The Charter also effectually secured to the citizens
their right of metage of coals, grain, and salt ; also
of apples, pears, and other fruits, which had been,
previous to this, frequently a matter in dispute
between the Lieutenant of the Tower of London
and the citizens.

This portion of the grant ran : " And whereas
the said Mayor and Commonalty and citizens, for

all the time aforesaid, have had and exercised the office of measurer, and measuring of all coals, and grain of whatsoever kind ; and also of all kind of salt, and all kinds of apples, pears, plums, and other fruit whatsoever, and also all kinds of roots, eatable of what kind soever, and of onions, and all other merchandises, wares, and things whatsoever measurable, and the measuring of every of them, in or unto the said port of London, coming, carried or brought upon the said water, in whatsoever ship, boat, barge, or vessel, floating, laden, and being on whatsoever part of the said water of Thames, or upon whatsoever bank, shore, or wharf of the same water of Thames, which shall come to, arrive, abide, be delivered or laid down, from the said bridge of the said town of Staines westward, to the said bridge of London, and from thence to the said place called Yendall, otherwise Yenleet, towards the sea, and east, and in Medway, and in the said port of the City of London aforesaid ; to exercise and occupy the same office, by the mayor of the said city for the time, during the time of his mayoralty, or by his sufficient deputies ; and also, for all the said time they have had and taken, and ought to have and take to their proper use, by the mayor of the said city for the time being, during his mayoralty, or by his sufficient deputies, all wages, rewards, fees and profits to the same office belonging. And, notwithstanding they, the Mayor and Commonalty and citizens, of late time thereof have been disquieted, and in some measuring aforesaid unjustly hindered, etc." The Charter then grants this office of measuring " without the hindrance of us, our heirs or successors, or any of our officers, bailiffs, or ministers, or of our Admiral of England, or of our successors, or any others of our subjects, or of our heirs or successors to be made to the contrary."

The Lord Mayor, now acting on his authority, issued orders for the preservation of fish in the river. Two of these ran : " That no fisherman or other shall rug for flounders either by ebb or by flood, at any time of the year, between London Bridge and Westminster, but only two casts at low water, and two casts at high water ; and no flounder shall be taken under the assize of six inches ; and that no fisherman or other shall float with any bloy net upon the benches from Whitehall to the Temple Stairs, upon high water, from Whitsuntide to Bartholomewtide " ; and " That no fisherman or other shall fish with any kind of net or use any angle rod with more than two hooks upon a line, or saw or scratch for barbel, within the limits of London Bridge, or shall use any other engine nearer unto the bridge than St. Botolph Wharf and the Bridge House Wharf, on the east side, nor nearer on the west side than St. Mary Overy's Stairs and the Old Swan."

For some long period a dispute regarding the rights of fishing at Chelsea had remained unsettled between the Lord Mayor and the Lord High Admiral.

1607. A correspondence passed between them in June, 1607, regarding the restoration of certain goods forfeited by Bennett Jay, " and the trial by law of the unlawful fishing at Chelsea." And during this or the previous year the Lord Mayor sent a letter to the Lord Admiral, " upon a complaint made by the fishermen of the river Thames, of certain persons that of late had by warrant from his Lordship, fished for salmon before Chelsea, which place had never before been allowed for fishing, and that in consequence divers other fishermen had taken the liberty to fish disorderly in other parts, to the great discontent of many poor men, and the prejudice of the government of fishing in the river, the Conservancy being in the Mayor of this City, and requesting his Lordship to withdraw his said Warrant." On March 9th the King granted a right of Ferry from Richmond for forty years.

1608. In the latter part of May, 1608, a correspondence took place between the Lord Mayor and the Lord High Admiral, regarding a complaint of the latter that the Water-bailiff had driven stakes in the bed of the river, before his house at Chelsea, for marking the fishing bounds. The matter was deferred till the Water-bailiff's return from Yorkshire.

On September 20th, the Second Charter of James to the City of London was granted at Hampton Court. It confirmed all the ancient rights, privileges, and immunities of the citizens in the fullest manner ; and the precincts of the Duke's Place, St. Bartholomew the Great and the Less in West Smithfield, Blackfriars, Whitefriars, and Cold Harbour or Herberge, in Thames Street, were added to the city's jurisdiction. The clause in the Charter touching the Port of London ran : " And whereas, with the said City of London, the liberties and suburbs, and port of the same, we are informed the search and surveying of oil, hops, soap, salt, butter, cheese, and such other like things, coming or brought to the port of the same city, to the intent to be sold or exposed to sale by way of merchandise, and also the measuring of all corn whatsoever, of any kind, onions, salt, sea-coals, and fruit of all kinds, fish called shell-fish, measurable, and used to be measured, which are coming, or brought to the said City of London, to the intent to be sold by way of merchandise, hitherto have pertained to the Mayor and Commonalty and citizens of the City of London, and their predecessors, to be exercised and executed by the Mayor of the same city for the time being, according to the laws, ordinances, and statutes made concerning the same, and the custom of the same city; we, of our certain knowledge and mere motion, for us and our successors, do ratify the same search, surveying and measuring abovesaid, in and by all things as the said Mayor and Commonalty and citizens of the said City, or their successors, lawfully had or enjoyed before this time, and to the said now Mayor and Commonalty and citizens of the said City of London, and their successors, confirm by these presents."

1611. On January 12th, 1611, the Lords of the Council sent a letter to the Lord Mayor of London, and to Sir Daniel Dunn, Judge of the Admiralty, and other officers of the Admiralty, reading: "On account of grievous complaints made to the Council of the great spoil and destruction of fry and small-fish in the river Thames by the Trinckermen and others, through their unlawful manner of fishing, it had been lately ordered, on the motion of the Lord High Admiral, that he should appoint two sufficient and discreet persons, to join with two others to be appointed by the Lord Mayor, to go down the river and take notice of the abuses complained of, and define some cause for prevention thereof. The Council had been informed that some special persons had been appointed by the City and the Admiralty, yet, by whose default they knew not, the course directed had not succeeded, and the

x

abuses still continued. They therefore required the Lord Mayor and the Judge of the Admiralty to appoint, each of them, two sufficient and discreet persons, without delay, to go down the river and examine particularly the abuses complained of, as well concerning the Trinckermen as the Heyberne-men, and to consider some means for prevention thereof, and submit the same to the Council."

On June 13th, the Lord Mayor sent a letter to the Lord High Admiral, "enclosing a paper of matters complained of as wrongs offered to the City by some of his officers, concerning the Conservancy of the River Thames, and appoint-ing next for the hearing of the matter." In reply the Lord Admiral objected to the short warning, but agreed to attend a meeting in the Council Chamber, Whitehall, on the following Thursday.

1612. On January 12th, 1612, the Council issued from Whitehall an order to Sir James Pemberton, Lord Mayor of London, and Sir Daniel Dunn, Judge of the Admiralty, reading : " On complaint of destruction by the trinckermen of fry and small fish in the Thames, the Lord Admiral is ordered to appoint two persons who, with two others to be appointed by the Lord Mayor, shall go down the river, take notice of the said abuses, and prescribe some course to rectify them ; by some default, the persons before sent down by the city, and by the Admiralty officers, did not succeed in preventing their unlawful fishing. You are therefore to appoint two discreet persons who shall examine the nets, standings, and manner of fishing of trinckermen, hebbermen, etc., and give in a certificate of their proceedings." The officers appointed to examine into the unlawful fishing reported to the Council :

" The destruction of the fry and brood of fish is occasioned by the Trinck nets."

Articles were submitted at the same time for the regulation of the size of nets, and times and manner of fishing of the trinckermen and hebbermen. Later in the year, an order was issued by the Lord Mayor, Sir John Swinnerton, for the preservation of the fish, especially salmon, in the river.

1613. Howe, the Continuator of Stow, wrote : " Concerning the controversial question about the rivers Thames and Medway, all variance and difference was absolutely concluded in the year 1613 on the 20th of May. Sir John Swinnerton, Knt., being then Lord Mayor."

The same chronicler said : " At eight several times yearly within the four counties of Middlesex, Surrey, Kent, and Essex, the Lord Mayor of London, for the time then being, with his brethren the Aldermen, for the better maintaining of the River's right and privileges do sit in person judicially, and charge four juries by oath to make inquisition after all offences committed upon the said River."

The Lords of the Council sent a letter, on June 19th, to the Lord Mayor, " concerning complaints, made by the farmers of the imposition on sea-coals, of abuses by coastmen of Newcastle in the lading of coal ships by bulk, and not measuring the coals, whereby his Majesty was defrauded of the imposition due upon them. These abuses could only be found out by inspection of the coal-meters' books, to which the farmers had hitherto had access, but had lately been refused. The Council therefore required the Lord Mayor to enjoin the coal meters to make out books of all coal ships, and the number of coals unladen from them in the Port of London from the

1st of January till the last of May last past, and deliver the same to the Clerk of the Cockets, in order that the farmers or their deputies might inspect them as they had formerly done, and further to direct them to deliver such books in future monthly to the Clerk of the Cockets for their inspection."

1614. On July 14th, 1614, the Lord High Admiral Nottingham, in a letter from Hampton Court to the Lord Mayor, "understood the water-bailiff had molested the fishermen of Chelsea, whom the writer had allowed to fish there, as had been usual time out of mind, but who had lately been complained of to the Lord Mayor for fishing out of their bounds. He requested the Lord Mayor to give directions that they should not be further troubled in the matter."

A week later the Lord Admiral ordered the Master, Wardens, and Assistants of the Trinity House, to commit to the Marshalsea, without bail, until further orders, all masters and owners of ships unlawfully taking up ballast from the river.

The third Charter of James to the City of London was granted at Westminster, on September 15th. It confirmed to the citizens the right of measuring and weighing of coals on the river from Yenland to Staines Bridge, comprehending the whole Port of London, allowing them eightpence per ton for such service for the use of the City, and forbidding the unloading of coal vessels until notice was given to the Lord Mayor. The text of the Charter continued : " And whereas it is notoriously known, that the river of Thames is so necessary, commodious and profitable to the said City of London, and without the said river our said City would not long subsist, flourish and continue ; and for that by forestalling, ingrossing and regrating of coals in and at the port of the said City, brought from the water of Thames aforesaid, such coals are made more dear, to the great loss and prejudice as well of us as of our subjects. And whereas divers ill-disposed persons, more affecting their own private gain and profit than the general and public good and benefit of our said City, little weighing the conservation of the said river, of late, and at the present do daily and usually sell coals and other things by retail, in less quantity, in boats commonly called lighters, and other vessels, floating and being on the water of Thames aforesaid, after such coals have been unladen from the ships and other vessels which first brought them within the limits aforesaid, which persons make the same boats or lighters as their common shops and warehouses, and in them do daily hold upon the said water of Thames a common market for selling such coals, and other things, having one, two, three, and sometimes more boats or lighters lying together, and fastened one to the other in the river of Thames aforesaid, to the great cozenage, damage and oppression, as well of the poor as the rich, ily increases and augments, and the price of coals and other things is made dearer. And for that by the frequent importation, unlading, and measuring of such coals, and such like things, in and from the said boats or lighters, very many of the same coals and other dirt often fall and are cast into the river of Thames, to the great harm and choking up the stream of the same river, and the said boats so placed do greatly hinder the stream of the said river, and the passage of the passengers upon the water of the said river. We, therefore, thinking it fit that such an evil ought not to be permitted to continue, do command, and for us, our heirs and successors, prohibit all persons whatsoever, that they, nor any of them, from henceforth sell or presume to sell any coals, of what kind soever, upon the water of Thames, in any boat, lighter or other vessel whatsoever, except only in such ships or other vessels which at first brought the same coals within the port of the said city, and the limits abovesaid, unless upon some port, quay or wharf, near the said river ; upon pain of contempt of our royal mandate, and incurring such pains and punishments, which may be inflicted by the laws and statutes of this our Kingdom upon such contemners and neglecters."

1615. Soon after the new Lord Mayor of London, Sir John Jolles, had assumed office in 1615, he issued an order regarding the preservation of fish in the Thames.

1616. On April 4th, 1616, Lord Zouch ordered the Mayor of Rye to commit to custody certain fishermen of Barking for using nets unlawfully small.

After a lapse of many years a session of Conservancy was held at Gravesend on July 3rd. The Lord Mayor, Sir John Jolles, accompanied by the Aldermen and Sheriffs and the Common Serjeant, and attended by the sub-Conservator of the river, and fifty officers and servants, took barge at Billingsgate, and all were rowed down the river to Gravesend, where a Session of the Conservancy was held. A jury of freeholders was sworn in, and, in the absence of the Recorder, the Common Serjeant claimed, in his charge, "the jurisdiction of the City of London in the River Thames from Staines Bridge westwards, unto the points of the river next the sea eastwards."

A letter of November 22nd, sent by the Lords of the Council to the Lord Mayor and Aldermen of London, ran : " Having before written to them on behalf of Mr. Digby, and recommended him for a redress of a wrong received from one, Robert Elliott, by an encroachment made by him upon the Thames below the bridge, to the prejudice of the waterworks there, the Council did not anticipate (considering the benefit derived by the City from that engine) that a second letter would have been necessary. Elliott still continued his unlawful courses of throwing in rubbish and encroaching upon the river, thereby diverting the stream from the engine. The reason for his protraction they could not conjecture, the wrong being apparent enough, and twice found by a jury before the Commissioners of Sewers, who ordered the piles set up by Elliott to be removed. Although Elliott had proceeded against the officers appointed by the Commissioners of Sewers to execute the order, the Court of the Exchequer had, as the Council were informed, left the cause to the Court of Aldermen to proceed therein as they should think fit. The Council had, therefore, written this second letter to the Court of Aldermen, requiring them, for the public good, and for Mr. Digby's, who demanded nothing but justice, to give directions for the suppression of the encroachments." Soon after the Council committed Elliott to the Tower for stubbornly persisting in his offence.

On December 29th, the Lords of the Council sent a letter from Whitehall to the Lord Mayor, " reminding him that the King had previously directed his attention to the necessity for the removal of shelves and banks in the river, which it was thought would speedily choke up, and so hinder the passage of shipping as to prejudice very greatly the trade of the City. His Majesty now commanded him, without further excuse or delay, to call a Common Council, and by authority thereof take effectual steps for the removal of such sands, shelves and banks, within the City's jurisdiction, as were offensive, or meet to be taken away for the conservancy of the river, or impeded the passage of boats, vessels, or ships, and to put in execution such statutes as had been formerly made for the due conservancy of the river."

1618. On February 16th, 1618, the Council sent a letter to the Lord Mayor, and Court of Aldermen, "concerning the removal of shoals from the river Thames, and recommending to their notice a new engine for that purpose, invented by John Gilbert, Gentleman, one of his Majesty's servants, and Anthony Gibson, Citizen of London, and recommending its employment if found useful and advantageous." This advice was adopted, and on July 18th, the King granted a Licence for John Gilbert to make, for twenty-one years, an engine called a Water-plough.

The Lord Admiral, in a letter from Whitehall on April 24th to the Lord Mayor, "had been informed by Sir Henry Marten, Knight, Judge of the Admiralty, of daily encroachments on the jurisdiction of the Admiralty on the river Thames. He had thought fit, before taking any other course, to inform the Lord Mayor of the matter."

In May a Petition of Innocent Lanier, Alfonso Ferabosio, and Hugh Lidiard was presented to the King reciting that : " in consequence of the number of shelves daily increasing in the river Thames,

prejudicial to the navigation, and dangerous to the
shipping, the City had, so far as in them laid, made
an agreement with the Petitioners for cleansing the
river, as appeared by the Certificate annexed ; yet
the Petitioners could not undertake the work unless
his Majesty allowed them some recompense from all
strangers' ships and vessels, as well as they had from
the City, and also means to vent the gravel, soil
and sand, which the City had no power to make
provision of. The Petitioners therefore prayed that
the City might be in some part eased, and themselves in some part recompensed, by his Majesty
allowing a charge to be made on all strangers' ships
and vessels coming into the river, of twopence per
ton per voyage, and granting that all who took
ballast upon the river should take the same for
thirty-one years next ensuing of the Petitioners
only, at the usual rates then paid for land ballast,
and that all builders, brickmakers, and others using
river sand, might do the same, and that it might
be lawful for any of his Majesty's subjects to
take the same for ballast if they should think
good."

A royal order was directed on the 28th to the Lord
Mayor and Recorder commanding the City to consider the Petition, and the Court of Aldermen having
discussed the matter and arrived at an opinion the
following certificate was submitted :—

" As to the charge of twopence per ton on
strangers' ships—

" 1. It would be grievously taken by the
merchant stranger ;

" 2. It might lead to a similar imposition on
English ships abroad ;

" 3. It would enhance the price of merchandize,

to the detriment of trade and prejudice of the Customs ;

" 4. It would discourage the importation of victuals from abroad.

" As to the taking of ballast for ships, it would be fit and convenient if the strangers would willingly ballast their ships with river ballast and sand ; but they should not be compelled to do so.

" The suit of the Petitioners was unexpected, seeing the City had long before agreed to pay them for the cleansing of the river, twopence for every ton taken thereout, and to find them lighters to carry it and wharves to cast it upon.

" But it appeared that they desired a further benefit by this suit, which they had concealed from the City for six weeks after his Majesty's reference, by which means the summer had been lost."

1619. Early in 1619 a petition was presented by Anthony Gibson and John Gilbert to the Lord Mayor and Court of Aldermen " stating that their engine for the cleansing of the banks and shelves in the river had been idle for six months past, that Mr. Lanere (Lanier) and his partners had promised, more than three months ago, to set it on work, but had neglected to do so to hinder the Petitioners from seeking other employment for the same, and praying the Court to give directions for its use, and for the payment of a competent allowance in respect thereof."

On October 14th a Licence was granted to Alphonso Ferabosco, Innocent Lanier, and Hugh Lydiard to cleanse the Thames of flats and shelves, with grant of the fines, etc., incurred under Statutes 27 and 34 Henry VIII., for annoyances in the river ; also permission to sell the sand and gravel dug out, and an allowance of 1d. per ton on strangers' goods imported and exported.

A letter, dated December 12th, sent from Secretary Calvert to the Lord Mayor, ran : " The King had been informed that the Court of Aldermen had cited divers shipwrights and ships' carpenters to appear at a Court, to be holden at Westminster on the 13th of December, for some supposed misdemeanours on the River Thames, which his Majesty thought strange, considering the persons were merely depending on the Admiralty, His Majesty therefore desired that the men should be discharged of their appearance until he had heard the cause himself, or by such as he might appoint."

The long-continued disputes between the Corn and Salt porters of Billingsgate, and the tackle and ticket house porters and others, culminated in the matters of dispute being considered by a Special Committee of the City Corporation, and acting on their report an Act of Common Council was, on December 13th, passed, whereby, after reciting that the moving and porterage of corn, coals, grain, salt, fruit, etc., between Staines and Yantlet, time out of mind, belonged to the Mayor and Corporation and Commonalty of London, and had been exercised by porters free of the city, called Corn and Salt porters, who had been much interfered with of late. Therefore it was enacted : " That the company and fellowship of Billingsgate porters, called by the name of corn and salt porters, should remain and be one company or brotherhood, and be called by the name of porters of Billingsgate : That the number should be increased from one hundred and twenty to four hundred : That they should elect twenty-four of the saddest, discreetist, and meetist of them

to be assistants :   And at Midsummer in each year
they should select thereout six persons as rulers and
governors." It was further enacted : " That no
bargeman, hoyman, waterman, etc., not being of the
said fellowship, should intermeddle with the landing
or carrying out of any ship, barge, boat, lighter, or
other vessel, upon pain of forfeiting twenty shillings,
or if they should convey away any goods by water,
without payment of the proper charges, they should
incur the same penalty ; one half to go to the poor
children harboured in Christ's Hospital, and the
other half to the Company."

At this time, by order of an Act of Common
Council, a sermon was preached, on the next Sunday
after every Midsummer day, to the Company of
Porters, in the parish church of St. Mary-at-Hill.
On the eve of this Sunday the Porters " furnished
the merchants and their families about Billingsgate
with nosegays over night, and in the morning went
from their common hall in good order, each having
a nosegay in his hand ; they walked through the
middle aisle to the communion table, where were
two basins, and everyone offered something to the
relief of the poor, and towards the charges of the
day ; after they had all passed, the deputy, the
merchants, their wives, children, and servants all
went in order from their seats, and bestowed their
offerings also ; which was a ceremony of much
variety."

1620. In 1620 a complaint was made to the
Lord Mayor's Court regarding the injury done to
the houses and garden walls in Blackfriars by the
barges and other large vessels moored at Bridewell
Wharf.

1622. On July 21st, 1622, a warrant was issued

from Westminster to the Lord Treasurer and others, " to grant Commissions for finding out encroachments made upon the Thames within sixty years past, and for granting the same in fee-farm to the Lord High Admiral Buckingham, by whose means, in discharge of his place as High Admiral, their existence has been discovered."

1623. On April 9th, 1623, the Earl of Nottingham, Lord Lieutenant of Middlesex, requested the Lord Mayor to cause two mills on the river, built by Thomas Lake near Sunbury, to be suppressed as they prevented many poor men from getting a living along the river thereabouts.

The Lords of the Council issued an order to the Lord Mayor, on May 30th, requiring him to take speedy measures for the clearing and well keeping of the river. On the following October 3rd, Lord President Mandeville wrote in a letter from Whitehall to Secretary Conway : " The City has given an account of proceedings in clearing the Thames."

1624. In October, 1624, John Gilbert, " His Majesty's ancient servant," and William Burrell applied to the King, " beseeching that orders might be given to the Lord Mayor and Aldermen that the first inventor, and Mr. Burrell, now owner of the engine to cleanse the river, might be employed, and that those who neither were at charge for engine nor invention (but by a colourable undertaking to do the service) should not reap the benefit of others' invention and labours."

The disputes among the Thames fishermen, and the abuses arising from the irregularity of the occupation, had resulted at last in a Petition for the Incorporation of the body of lawful fishermen on the river. On October 12th, Sir Martin Lumley, the Lord Mayor, and the Court of Aldermen, in answer to this petition, certified " that the liberty and privileges of fishing in the River Thames and the Conservancy thereof between Staines Bridge and the Waters of Medway, of right belonged to the City of London. For their better information as to the Fishermen's suit, they had caused a book to be drawn in the form of a charter, upon which both parties might advise, wherein it was provided that if the proposed Corporation should be found inconvenient, and so declared by the Court of Aldermen, the same should be void ; that the ordinances to be made should be approved by the Court of Aldermen before they should be put in execution, with other necessary provisions, and a saving of the City's rights and privileges and conservancy of the river. They thought it meet (if it pleased his Majesty) to incorporate the fishermen under the aforesaid reservations, etc., and such others as were contained in the said draft, so prepared in the form of a charter, which they prayed might be perused by the Recorder before it was passed. It would be a means the better to discover and reform the abuses practised by fishermen and others, with unlawful nets and engines, and at unseasonable times."

NAVAL AND MILITARY AFFAIRS ALONG THE RIVER.

1603. King James, with a weakling's horror of physical conflict, and his dreadful fear of a naked sword, hastily ended the long-drawn war with Spain, and throughout his reign little of soldiers or military doings were seen along the shores of the river. Regular troops were not required, and the militia musters were considered sufficient for all purposes of defence. Naval matters received some attention, and the young Prince Henry early exhibited a lively interest in ships of war.

When the Stuart King appeared on the scene, six men-of-war and two armed pinnaces were fully equipped in the river, and ready to sail on a cruise for harassing the Spaniards, but these were quickly put out of commission. In connection with the dismantling of these ships, an intimation was sent, on June 4th, to the Custom House officers that former orders for detaining all outgoing vessels in the Thames failing to buy part of their provisions at the King's Storehouse on Tower Hill, having been generally disobeyed, they were forbidden to discharge any vessel without a certificate declaring that such purchase had been made, and the duty upon it paid. On the same date the Deputy Serjeant of the Admiralty received a warrant from the Lord Treasurer Buckhurst and the Lord Admiral Nottingham giving a similar order, and adding that the surplus of provisions at the Storehouse, now to be dispersed, was made for victualling a fleet, under Sir Richard Leveson, ordered South against the Spaniards, but now dissolved.

On August 31st, Captain Edward Fenton, who had spent the latter part of his life at Deptford, was buried in the Church of St. Nicholas there. This old veteran had fought against the Armada, and sailed on two voyages with Martin Frobisher.

1604. In January, 1604, Walter Gore was made Captain of the Fort, or Blockhouse, at West Tilbury, in reversion after Gregory Riggs ; and on December 7th, of the following year, Edward Roberts was appointed Captain of the same Fort.

Early in the year it was decided to build a small vessel, not only for the amusement of Prince Henry but for his instruction in navigation, an art for which he shewed a very apparent inclination.

The Earl of Nottingham, Lord High Admiral, instructed Phineas Pett, the King's shipwright, to construct the vessel at Chatham, with a keel of twenty-eight feet, and a breadth of twelve feet; and when completed to adorn it with painting and carving, both outside and in. The rapidly built craft was launched on Tuesday, March 6th, and brought up the river to Limehouse to complete her outfit. On the 14th—the day before the royal progress through London—the vessel, gay with ensigns and pennants, was riding before the King's lodgings in the Tower for his inspection, when the Prince expressed unbounded delight with his gift. She was then moored against the Privy Stairs at Whitehall, and on Thursday afternoon, the 22nd, after dinner, Prince Henry, attended by the Lord Admiral Nottingham, the Earl of Worcester, and a brilliant train, proceeded on board. The anchor was immediately weighed, and under top-sails and foresail, they dropped down the river to Paul's Wharf. Here again coming to anchor, Henry, using the customary forms, baptised the ship with a bowl of wine, naming her the " Disdain." Phineas Pett, the builder, was then presented, and so commended himself to the boy's favour as to be at once received into his service, and was sworn-in the next day at St. James's House, the prince's residence. At this time Pett was chief of the King's shipwrights, and various members of his family were long known on the river for their skill as shipbuilders.

During this spring the Dunkirkers took by violence seven ships of Holland and Zealand in the Thames and other English waters. This prompted the Privy Council to issue a warrant, on April 7th, for paying Sir Robert Mansell the charges of ships appointed to guard the Narrow Seas, the Thames and the Medway.

1605. We also find the Council, on June 2nd, 1605, writing from the Court at Greenwich to Secretary Winwood : " Are sorry to find so many petitions and complaints from divers of his Majesty's subjects, hardly intreated by the Hollanders. Have sent some of them before. Now Matthew Brownerigg, a merchant of Ipswich, having laden grain in a Hollander's ship for England, the ship was assailed at sea by a Dunkirker, and the master taken out of her, and set at a ransom of 5,500 guilders ; and the rest that were in the ship have carried off the ship and grain, with purpose that the poor merchant's goods shall serve for redemption of their master. Deal with the States for restitution."

Y

Deptford and Woolwich were the two naval dockyards on the Thames, where not only ships of war were built, but where the storehouses contained all that was required for fitting-out and provisioning them for sea. There was also a storehouse for provisions on Tower Hill. On June 22nd, 1604, Hugh Lydyard was appointed Clerk of the Prick and Cheque of the Navy and Works, and clerk of the storehouse at Woolwich.

1606. In August, 1606, John Jackson received in reversion the office of Clerk of the Cheque of the Navy at Woolwich.

1607. A list of officers and men garrisoning the " Townes of Warre, Castles, Bullwarks, and Fortresses " of the Kingdom, was compiled in 1607, and in this the East and West Tilbury Bulwarks or Forts were given as having each a Captain with a pay of 12d. per day. The former had a porter, four gunners and two soldiers; and the latter a porter, five gunners, and two soldiers, all receiving 6d. per day, except the porters, who had 8d.

1608. In April, 1608, Edward Altham, on the surrender of Edward Roberts, was appointed to the Captaincy of the Blockhouse and new Fortifications at West Tilbury.

Prince Henry was now shewing a growing affection for the Navy, and this led him early in August to pay a visit to Woolwich.

Dr. Birch, in his life of the Prince, wrote : " In the beginning of that month, he sent word to Mr. Pett of his intention to come thither at his return out of Essex from the Lord Petre's house, whither he was going in progress ; and on the Saturday following, the 13th of August, he took his barge at Blackwall, and came to Woolwich about noon,

accompanied only with his train. He was received
by Mr. Pett on shore at the Yard Stairs. On the
poop of the ' Royal Anne ' were placed trumpets,
and an ensign, and on the heads of both the mizens
two ensigns. Mr. Pett having paid his compliments
to the Prince, and represented how great a satisfaction it would be to all the seamen to perceive
his Highness so well affected to the Navy, he
conducted the Prince round about the Dock, and
so directly aboard the ' Royal Anne,' to the very
top of her poop, where he gave a signal to Mr.
William Bull, then Master Gunner of England,
who stood ready prepared upon a mount, with
thirty-one great brass chambers, orderly and
distinctly placed, which had been procured from
the Tower for that purpose by Mr. Pett, with the
assistance of the Master Gunner ; who upon the
signal made gave fire to the train, and discharged
the whole volley with such good order, as was highly
satisfactory to the Prince, and the more so because
it was unexpected. When the ordnance ceased
firing, Mr. Pett kneeled to his Highness, and
requested him to accept this poor sea-entertainment
as an unfeigned earnest of duty to him. The
Prince returned a most gracious answer, and then
ordered Mr. Pett to lead him into all the parts of
the ship ; which having viewed with a singular
pleasure, he was conducted to the Dockyard, where
the keel, stem and stern of his own ship, which was
to be built, lay ready framed. Having examined
these with great attention, his Highness caused the
length of the keel to be measured ; and being then
desired to walk into the house to rest himself, he
readily consented, and found in the parlour a set
banquet of sweetmeats, and all other fruits, which

the season yielded, with plenty of wine, Rhenish, white, sack, Greek, and claret. After he had refreshed himself, and given his hand to kiss to divers gentlewomen of the town, who were in the room with Mr. Pett's wife, he desired to be conducted to the mount, where the chambers were placed, which were again charged and ranged in their former order, with the train made ready. This sight delighted him so much, that he was desirous to have the train fired while he stood by; but at Mr. Pett's entreaty and representation of the danger, he ordered that at the holding up of his handkerchief in his barge, they should be discharged; which was accordingly done, after his Highness had expressed his satisfaction in the whole entertainment."

On December 9th, a warrant issued from Westminster ordered the payment of £500 to Sir Alexander Hay, " for masts and scantlings of Scotch fir, to be delivered within the Thames for the Navy."

1609. A Commission, composed of Lord Admiral Nottingham and the Earls of Suffolk and Worcester, met at Woolwich, on April 28th, 1609, to investigate a complaint lodged against Phineas Pett, the King's shipwright, of the imperfections, as set forth in a certificate of Captain Wentworth, and other shipwrights, of a ship now in course of construction in the Dockyard there. On Monday, May 8th, the King, resolving to hear Pett's case himself, went to Woolwich, accompanied by Prince Henry, and in the words of Dr. Birch " appointed Sir Thomas Chaloner, his Highness's governor, and Mr. Henry Briggs, then Professor of Geometry in Gresham College, to decide the controversy about the proportion of the ships. The measurers having declared in favour of Mr. Pett, the Prince out of zeal for his injured servant, and resentment against the accusers, could not forbear calling out with a loud voice, ' Where be now these perjured fellows, that dare thus to abuse his Majesty with these false informations ? Do they not worthily deserve hanging ? ' And during the whole examination his Highness stood near Mr. Pett, to encourage and support him under his anxiety and fatigue ; and when the King declared himself convinced of his innocence, the Prince took him up from his knees, and expressed his own joy for the satisfaction which his father had that day received, protesting that he would not only countenance Mr. Pett for the future, but likewise take care to provide for him and his family while he lived."

Early in June the King and his son went to Deptford, and were present at the launching of the " Red Lion " warship, built by Mr. Baker. Phineas Pett said : " I attending then near the place, at the great storehouse end, where his Majesty had his standing, he was pleased very graciously to confer with me, and to use me with extraordinary expressions of his princely favour." The next day, Pett continued, " being the Thursday in Whitsun week (the 8th) his Majesty began to hear the great and general cause of the Navy, in his Presence Chamber at Greenwich, wherein three whole days were spent in several examinations of the truth and circumstances of the informations delivered by the Lord Northampton and his agents, against Sir Robert Mansel, Sir John Trevor and Captain Button, Sir Thomas Bluther, Mr. Leggatt, and many others, together with myself."

On July 25th, an order was issued for paying to Sir Robert Mansell, Treasurer of the Navy, the sum of £4,071 9s. 6d., to be expended by him in finishing the reconstructed "Victory" warship, in the dry dock at Woolwich.

1610. Another warrant of January 9th, 1610, ordered the payment of necessary money for victualling and relieving the soldiers—levied in Ireland for service with the King of Sweden—driven by a storm into the Thames, Harwich, and other ports.

On January 31st, Prince Henry visited Woolwich to inspect the progress of a very large warship building there, under the direction of Phineas Pett, who wrote : " I gave him and his followers entertainment." Pett was in London on May 2nd when Princess Elizabeth came to see the great ship, and was entertained, with her train, by the shipwright's wife.

The Prince made a further inspection of the progress on April 25th, when Pett feasted him in his dining-room.

Preparations for fitting up the new warship made the navy departments busy. On May 15th, an order was issued from Westminster, for paying £8,476 9s. 8d. to Sir Robert Mansell " to be disbursed to Benjamin Decrowe, Agent for the Merchants trading into Muscovy, and to William Russell, Merchant, for cordage delivered into the Storehouse at Deptford." A month later the Officers of King's Langley, Hertfordshire, were ordered to deliver to the Officers of the Navy, twenty loads of timber from their Manor, for the finishing of the great ship now nearing completion. On June 18th Prince Henry visited Woolwich Dockyard, and came again the next day in company with the King and a numerous attendant train. Of this latter occasion

Phineas Pett wrote : " In the afternoon his Majesty spent almost two hours in great content, in surveying the ship both within and without, protesting it did not repent him to have taken such pains in examination of the business of the work, since the fruit thereof yielded him such content. His Majesty then did me the honour to come into the house, where my wife had prepared a banquet of sweetmeats and such fruits as were then to be had, whereof he was pleased to taste plentifully, and did very graciously accept of his homely entertainment, giving me special command not to launch the ship till his progress was ended."

In the beginning of September, this, the largest warship hitherto built in England—a present from the King to Prince Henry—was ready for the launching ceremony, and its builder, Phineas Pett, was making anxious preparations for its success. The keel of this fine vessel was 114 feet long, and the cross beam 44 feet. It was to carry sixty-four pieces of great ordnance, and the burden was 1,400 tons. The carving, gilding, painting, and other ornamentations were on a splendid scale. The important circumstances connected with the finishing stages of the construction and the launching can best be told in Pett's own words : " Between Easter and Michaelmas that the ship began to be garnished, it is incredible what numbers of people continually resorted to Woolwich, of all sorts, both nobles, gentry, and citizens, and from all parts of the country round about, which was no small charge to me, in giving daily entertainments to all comers, which could not possibly be avoided in that place at such a time. The 9th of September, being Sunday, about six o'clock in the morning, divers

London maids coming to see the ship, brought in their company a little boy of twelve years old, the only child of his mother, a widow woman dwelling in Tower-street, who carelessly going up and down upon the main orlop, fell down into the hold of the ship, and was thereby so bruised and broken, that he died before midnight, being the first mischance that had happened in the whole time of the ship's building. About the middle of the month, being ready to have the ship strucken down upon her ways, I caused twelve of the choice master-carpenters of his Majesty's Navy to be sent for from Chatham, to be assisting in her striking and launching ; and upon the 18th day, being Tuesday, she was safely set upon her ways ; and this day Sir Robert Mansell, dined with me at my lodgings. The 20th of this month, the French Ambassador came to Woolwich to see the ship, whom I entertained in the best manner I could ; and in the time of his being with me, the Prince, my royal master, sent me a wonderful fat buck, which he killed with his own hand. Now began we on all sides for the preparation to launch the ship, and for that purpose there was provided a rich standard of taffety very fairly gilded with gold, with his Majesty's arms, to be placed on the poop, and a very large ensign of crimson rich taffety, with a canton of the Prince's crest, to be placed upon the quarter-deck ; and all other ornaments were carefully provided befitting that purpose. There was a standing set up in the most convenient place of the yard for his Majesty, the Queen and the royal children, and places fitted for the Ladies and Council (all railed in and boarded). All the rooms, both in my own lodgings and at Mr. Lydiard's, were prepared and very handsomely hanged and furnished with a cloth of state, chairs, stools, and other necessaries. Nothing was omitted that could be imagined any ways necessary both for ease and entertainment. Upon Sunday in the afternoon, being the 23rd, Sir Robert Mansell, Sir John Trevor, and Sir Henry Palmer came to Woolwich to see how every thing was ordered ; and finding all things prepared and fitted to their liking, about three o'clock they returned all to Deptford, where they lodged that night with Sir Robert Mansell. This evening, very late, there came a messenger to me from Court at Theobalds, to give me orders to be very careful to search the ship's hold, for fear some persons disaffected might have bored some holes privily in the ship to sink her, after she should be launched ; but my care had prevented their fears beforehand, so far as could be searched or discovered.

" On Monday morning, assisted by the help of my brother Simonson, and sundry others of my friends, we opened the dock-gates, and made all things ready against the tide ; but the wind blowing very hard at south-west kept out the flood, so that it proved a very bad tide, little better than a neap, which put us afterwards to great trouble and hazard.

" The King's Majesty came from Theobalds, though he had been very little at ease with a scouring, taken with surfeiting by eating grapes, and landed here about eleven o'clock, Prince Henry attending him, and most of the Lords of the Council. The Lord Admiral, attended by the principal officers of the navy, together with myself, received him on land out of his barge, and conducted him to the place provided for him in Mr. Lydiard's house. His dinner was dressed in our great kitchen. After

dinner came the Queen's Majesty, accompanied
with the Duke of York, Lady Elizabeth, and divers
great Lords and Ladies in her train, the drums and
trumpets placed on the poop and forecastle, and the
wind instruments by them, so that nothing was
wanting to so great a royalty that could be desired.
When it grew towards high-water, and all things
ready, and a great close lighter made fast to the
ship's stern, and the Queen's Majesty, with her
train, placed; the Lord Admiral gave me com-
mandment to heave taut the crabs and screws,
though I had little hope to launch by reason the
wind over-blew the tide; yet the ship started,
and had launched, but the dock-gates pent her in
so straight that she stuck fast between them, by
reason the ship was nothing lifted by the tide, as
we expected she would; and the great lighter, by
unadvised counsel, being cut off the stern, the ship
settled so hard upon the ground that there was no
possibility of launching that tide; besides which,
there was such a multitude of people got into the
ship, that one could scarce stir by another. The
noble Prince himself, accompanied with the Lord
Admiral and other great lords, were on the poop,
where the great standing gilt cup was ready filled
with wine, to name the ship so soon as she had been
afloat, according to ancient custom and ceremony
performed at such times, by drinking part of the
wine, giving the ship her name, and heaving the
standing cup overboard. The King's Majesty was
much grieved at the frustrate of his expectation,
coming on purpose, though very ill at ease, to have
done me honour. But God saw it not so good for
me, and therefore sent this cross upon me, both to
humble me, and to make me know, that, howsoever

we proposed, He would dispose all things as He pleased ; so that about five o'clock his Majesty, with the Queen and all her train, departed away to Greenwich, where the household were removed. Prince Henry stayed a good while after his Majesty was gone, conferring with the Lord Admiral, principal officers and myself, what was to be done, and leaving the Lord Admiral to stay here to see that all things were performed that were resolved on. He took horse, and rode after them to Greenwich, with promise to return presently after midnight. So soon as the multitude were gone, and all things quiet, we went presently in hand to make way with the sides of the gates ; and having great store of scavel men and other labourers, we had made all things ready before any flood came ; which performed, every man applied himself to get victuals, and to take rest. The Lord Admiral sat up all night in a chair in his chamber till the tide was come about the ship ; and Sir Robert Mansell, Sir John Trevor, and Sir Henry Palmer, and the rest, made a shift in my lodging to rest themselves. The beginning of the night was very fair, and bright moonshine, the moon being a little past full ; but after midnight the weather was sore overcast ; and a very sore gust of rain, thunder and lightning, which made me doubt that there were some indirect working among our enemies to dash our launching. These gusts lasted about half an hour with great extremity, the wind being at south-west. In the midst of this great gust Prince Henry, and all his (train) were taken upon the top of Blackheath, in their coming to Woolwich ; but his invincible spirit, daunted with nothing, made little account of it, but came through, and was no sooner alighted in

the yard, but, calling for the Lord Admiral and
myself, and Sir Robert Mansell, went all presently
on board the ship, being about two o'clock, almost
an hour before high water, and was no sooner entered
but the word being given to set all taut, the ship
went away without any straining of screws or
tackles till she came clear afloat, in the middle of
the channel, to the great joy and comfort of the
Prince's Highness, the Lord Admiral, and all the
rest of my noble friends; which mercy of God
to me I pray I may never forget.   His Highness
then standing upon the poop with a selected company
only, besides the trumpeters, with a great deal of
expression of princely joy, and with the ceremony
of drinking in the standing cup, threw all the wine
forwards towards the half deck; and solemnly
calling her by the name of the " Prince Royal,"
the trumpets sounding all the while, with many
gracious words to me, gave the standing cup into
my own hands, and would not go from the ship
till he saw her fast at her moorings.   In heaving
down to her moorings, we found that all the hawsers
that were laid ashore for landfasts were treacherously
cut to put the ship to hazards of running ashore, if
God had not blessed us better.   In the interim of
warping to her moorings, his Highness went down to
the platform of the cock-room, where the ship's
beer stood for the ordinary company; and there
finding an old can without a lid, went and drew it
full of beer himself, and drank it off to the Lord
Admiral, and caused him, with the rest of his
attendants, to do the like.   At nine the same
morning, being very rainy, he took his barge,
accompanied with the Lord Admiral and the rest
of his train, and giving us a princely gracious fare-

well, rode against the tide to Greenwich, where he made relation of all the business and the circumstances thereof to the King his father. We then came ashore to refresh ourselves with victuals, and take some rest, having toiled all the night before; and amongst the rest, Sir Henry Palmer was pleased to stay dinner, where we drank Prince Henry's health round, to handsel the standing cup given me at the launching."

On Thursday, December 6th, Prince Henry went to Woolwich, and boarded the " Prince Royal," now fully rigged and ready to sail for Chatham. He stayed aboard three hours, and Phineas Pett said he was " wonderful desirous to have had us set sail, if we could possibly have done it without damage."

On July 9th of this year a warrant was issued from Westminster for paying £13 13s. 8d. to Sir Gamaliel Capell, for cleansing the entrenchment of West Tilbury Fort.

1611. At five o'clock in the morning of Monday, May 6th, 1611, the Prince of Wales, accompanied by the Earls of Shrewsbury, Arundel, and Mar, Sir Thomas Chaloner, Sir Oliver Cromwell, Sir Robert Mansell, and some others of his household servants, embarked on his barge at Whitehall, and was taken down the river till about nine o'clock, when he boarded a small merchant ship provided for his refreshment at Tilbury Hope. Re-embarking after a rest, sail was set for Queenborough, which place was passed, and a course steered up the Medway till Chatham was reached, about six o'clock in the evening. Landing here, the Prince walked to the house of Mr. Lediard, Clerk of the Cheque, where supper was prepared for him and his train.

On Tuesday morning he boarded his own great warship, the " Prince Royal," and afterwards went from ship to ship in the lower reach, accompanied only by Sir Robert Mansell and Phineas Pett, who, whilst the Prince wrote the particulars down in his table-book, gave him private information concerning the state and condition of the several vessels. Returning to shore in a very cheerful humour, dinner was served to the Prince, and when healths were drunk, fifteen great brass chambers in the garden were fired off, under the careful direction of John Reynolds, gunner of the Prince's ship. After dining, the Prince went on board and viewed all the ships and pinnaces in the upper reach, again noting down observations regarding them. The next morning, after breakfast, the barges were brought out, and as they moved off for Stroud, the ships in both reaches fired a royal salute, which the Prince insisted, in spite of earnest persuasions to the contrary, should be shot over his own barge. From Stroud coaches took the party to Gravesend, where the magistrates received the Prince, and the small shot and the ordnance of the Blockhouses gave him welcome.

About the middle of June, Phineas Pett, by order of the Prince of Wales, commenced the framework of a pinnace for the great ship " Prince Royal," which, as the Prince proposed using her at times for short trips to sea, was to be fitted with a roomy cabin and all other suitable accommodation. The keel of this vessel, laid at Chatham on the 30th, was 72 feet in length, and 24 feet in breadth. She drew 11 feet of water, and her burden was about 250 tons.

Before starting from Richmond on a progress, the Prince of Wales summoned to his presence the shipwright Phineas Pett, who came on Saturday, August 1st, accompanied by Captain Thomas King, and John Reynolds, the Prince's master gunner. The next day Pett attended the Prince at chapel and dinner, and had a long private conference with him on matters of importance. Dr. Birch wrote : " After his Highness was risen from dinner, and had talked with him for a while at the bay-window in the presence-chamber, he gave Mr. Pett leave to go to his dinner, which was prepared for him and his company by Mr. Alexander, the principal Gentleman Usher, at the house of Mr. Wilson, his Highness's tailor. During the dinner Mr. Pett was sent for three several times by the Prince, who wanted satisfaction in some points, and ordered him at attend again, after he had finished his dinner, between two and three of the clock. At that time his Highness delivered his pleasure fully to him, with protestation of the trust which he reposed in him, and the good opinion which he had of Mr. Pett's performance of what was committed to his charge, and with many expressions of his favour and intentions to provide for him, concluding with these words, ' Go on cheerfully in that which I intrust you with, and let not the care for your posterity incumber you any ways. For you shall leave the care both of yourself and them to me, who have a purpose carefully to provide for you.' These gracious speeches made such an impression on Mr. Pett, that when he came to kiss the Prince's hand at parting, he could not avoid shedding some tears ; though he then little thought that this would be the last time he should see his Highness alive, or these the last words that he should ever hear from his mouth."

On September 19th, Edward Faulkner was granted the Office of Clerk of the Prick and Cheque at Deptford Strond.

About the middle of December, Prince Henry was at Woolwich, superintending the arrangements for building ships in Ireland.

1613. In 1613 there was a difficulty in properly manning the King's ships in the river, and on March 25th, John Chamberlain wrote on the subject to Sir Dudley Carleton : " Here is a general stay of all shipping, that none may go forth till the Lady Elizabeth be gone (after her marriage), which shows a great penury and decay of navigation, that they cannot provide 2,500 mariners to furnish eight or nine of the King's ships, without all this ado and noise."

1614. On July 2nd, 1614, John Acworth was granted for life the office of Keeper of all Storehouses at Woolwich.

1615. The warships " Mer Honeur " and " Defiance " were launched at Woolwich on March 6th, 1615.

In connection with military defence, the Commissioners of Musters for Middlesex reported to the Council, on October 26th, that on assembling the musters and finding the arms very bad, they had ordered the men, with the ability, to provide and wear new ones. " 1,000 foot are thus supplied, but the horse are backward. The Mint men, Trinity House men, ship carpenters, and Thames watermen pretend exemption from the service."

On January 17th, John Wells was granted for life the office of Clerk and Keeper of the Stores and Storehouses at Deptford ; and John Smith was similarly appointed on December 24th, to the office of keeping the Blockhouse near Gravesend.

1617. On March 28th, 1617, Sir Walter Raleigh, on the way to attempt the formation of a settlement in Guiana, dropped down the river on the " Destiny," and joining his consorts impatiently awaiting the appearance of his flag, sailed on his last disastrous voyage.

The " Destiny " was built at Raleigh's own charge, and his son Walter accompanied him as Captain. Of the two hundred men on board, eighty were gentlemen-volunteers and adventurers, many of them Sir Walter's relations. The ships composing the fleet, and their Commanders were :

" Destiny," 440 tons burden, with 36 pieces of ordnance, Sir Walter Raleigh ; " Jason," 240 tons, 25 pieces, John Pennington ; " Thunder," 180 tons, 20 pieces, Sir Warham Saint Leger ; " Encounter," 160 tons, 17 pieces, Edward Hastings ; " Flying Joan," 120 tons, 14 pieces, John Chidley ; " Southampton," 80 tons, 6 pieces, John Bayly ; " Page," 250 tons, 3 pieces, James Barker.

A Grant was made on October 19th, by the Lord Admiral Nottingham to Henry Mervin, of Fountell, Wilts, of the office of Admiral and Captain-General of the Narrow Seas, from the Thames to the Scilly Islands, with a fee of twenty shillings a day, and wages for sixteen men at ten shillings a month, " without check or muster."

1618. In 1618, Piero Contarini, the Venetian Ambassador, having chartered a squadron of seven English ships to reinforce the fleet of his Republic, gave the command to Captain Daniel Bannister, with the " Royal Exchange " as flag-ship. Contrary winds prevented the ships sailing from the Thames, and the Ambassador wrote in a despatch on April 4th : " Since the last week an easterly wind has been blowing incessantly, preventing the departure of these vessels, the force of the tides alone not being sufficient to take them out of the Thames, although if once at sea this same wind would be fair for them as far as the strait."

He wrote further on the 19th : " So soon as the wind changed, and became fair the ships weighed anchor, and were yesterday to reach Gravesend, and perhaps even leave it, without making any port until they reach the Gulf." And on the 26th : " The ships left Gravesend on the 20th, with a very fair northerly wind, which is yet blowing most prosperously for the voyage. It having come to my knowledge that one of them had remained behind, and choosing to know the reason, I discovered that the vessel had been seized by certain creditors for provisions and repairs. I sent immediately for the owner and his security, to compel him to perform his contract, but being aware that it would prove a tedious business and prejudicial to the interests of your serenity, as part of a company of soldiers must have remained on shore whilst the other vessels would have advanced too far for this one to overtake them, I determined, as the least detrimental course, to give him on account of hire, as much money as would entirely free his vessel, and this, I believe, to be now thoroughly effected so that I am expecting news to this effect, as also of the departure of the vessel, which being a very good sailer, will assuredly catch the others."

The Venetian Secretary, Horatio Busino, wrote in his diary on July 10th : " The military training especially of this warlike nation is of the most regular and careful description. Near our house is a certain spot appointed for the purpose, they flock for the musket and artillery exercise, making such a crash and noise that sometimes they make me drop my mouthful when I am seated at table. They handle the pike wonderfully and perform various evolutions, marching very boldly to the attack of a platform made like a fortress, to accustom themselves to an assault. In like manner they have very frequent general musters all over the city. Well nigh throughout the year they have archery meetings in the fields near London, doing the like throughout the Kingdom, a pastime in which their sovereigns themselves indulged of yore. Some take aim at earthen mounds raised like a butt ; others shoot at oaken marks, carved and painted, and surmounted by gilt pommels, precisely like so many human heads. These for the most part are placed in the ditches of the fields, at equal distances. Others with the bent bow strive to make their arrows' flight surpass that of their comrades. They frequently wrestle before a concourse of two or three thousand curious spectators. They propel the ball to a great distance dexterously and well, both with their feet and arms. The lads throw the ball in the streets, aiming at a mark, according to certain rules, females also taking part with them, as they also like to have a little capering on feast days. Others lads, more spirited, contend with wooden swords and daggers, exchanging rough blows, and when they have had enough, youths and grown-up men assemble and form a ring in sight of our windows, placing on the ground two bucklers and sham daggers and two thick staves instead of swords. Then the champions rush in from either side, throwing off their hats, and seizing the weapons they give each other awful blows, nor do they separate until one or the other is quite weary and yet better supplied with bruises. Were it not forbidden to play with unabated swords, they would push each others' eyes out grievously."

On November 4th, the Commissioners of the Navy sent a request to the Council, " that the £1900 per month formerly paid for cordage, and also the arrears of Sir Robt. Mansell's last account, may be applied to pay discharged workmen, to further the two new ships now in the dock at Deptford, to lay in provisions for the next year, and to begin preparations for the new docks at Chatham, etc."

1619. In November, 1619, John Chamberlain wrote to Sir Dudley Carleton : " The King went to Deptford to see the two ships built by the Commissioners of the Navy, and congratulated the new Admiral on his choice of officers, who reduce the Navy expenses from 60,000*l.* to 30,000*l.* a year ; and yet build two new ships and repair the old ; he called the ships in memory thereof ' Buckingham's Entrance,' and ' Reformation.' " The favourite, the Marquis of Buckingham, had displaced the Earl of Nottingham as Lord High Admiral.

1620. On March 1st, 1620, Richard Chester and others certified to the Commissioners of the Navy that the cordage in the King's rope-yards at Woolwich and Deptford was strong and well-made, and the hemp in store as good as any that usually came from Poland.

Phineas Pett, from Ratcliffe, on July 3rd, recommended to Mr. Aylesbury his kinsman Peter Pett,

" as royal shipwright in the place of the late Mr. Brighte."

1621. On March 19th, 1621, a Grant was made at Westminster to Thomas Lord of the office of keeping the fort at Gravesend, in reversion after the present keeper, John Smith. John King and others certified to the Commissioners of the Navy on April 11th, regarding the good qualities of the cordage, and materials for the same, at Woolwich. Another certificate of October 6th stated that Joshua Downing and others had viewed the cordage at Woolwich and Deptford made by Christopher Arnold, and found it good and well made.

On September 5th, the Commissioners of the Navy requested the Warden and Company of Shipwrights to choose six or more competent persons to survey and report on the tonnage and quality of construction of two ships of war, the " Swiftsure " and " Inheritance," lately built at Deptford.

1622. On January 28th, 1622, a petition was presented to Lord Zouch by William Tatam and three other mariners of Dover, complaining that as they were sailing from London their vessels were stayed at Tilbury Hope, and a sailor impressed out of each ship, contrary to their privileges. They prayed for the release of these men, who had families dependent on them.

The Navy Commissioners dated an Estimate on February 14th, " of the charge of wages, etc., for 80 men for the ship ' Garland,' appointed to transport Lord Digby into Spain, who are to be pressed in the Thames, at 2s. 6d. per man : total, 433*l*. 5s."

In April, John Chamberlain wrote : " Cap. Walsingham, who had been a pirate, but since employed in the Algiers expedition, is sent to the

Tower for threatening to surprise the ' Dreadnought,' one of the King's ships, and return to his old trade."

John Clerke was granted on June 4th, in reversion after Francis Ingolsby, the office of Keeper of the Armoury at Greenwich.

On July 29th an Order of Council was sent from Whitehall to the Officers of the Port of London, and other ports of the Kingdom, running : " Many troops and companies having lately gone over to France, the King requires them, on their allegiance, not to permit any other person to pass from that port, except on necessary occasions, and to take into custody any captain who shall attempt to transport troops."

A list was made in December of the crew of the ship " George," appointed to carry provisions from Deptford to Chatham, and timber from Ireland and Rye to these dockyards, with the days of their discharge or death.

1623. On January 9th, 1623, an Indenture was dated, between the King and Sir Allen Apsley, Lieutenant of the Tower, and Sir Sampson Darrell, Surveyor-General of Victuals for the Navy, for the supply of provisions to the King's ships at sea and in harbour.

In July an Estimate was addressed by Thomas Argoll to Mr. Newman, of the cost of making a certain quantity of cordage at Woolwich.

Two Dunkirk ships, one of them laden with masts, having been captured in the Downs by an English ship, under the command of Captain Best, the Council ordered them to be brought into the Thames, and on their arrival at Gravesend, Best was to appear before them. Best wrote to their lordships, on August 15th, that his prizes were very unwilling to be brought into the river, and although the one laden with masts had promised compliance, it had sailed away in the night. A week later Best again wrote that he had brought the Dunkirker to Gravesend, and having dismissed the "Bona-venture" and "Adventure," was now ready to attend the Council.

Accounts were dated on September 24th, at Woolwich, by Thomas Argoll, of wages paid to rope-makers, spinners, labourers, and others in Woolwich Dockyard, from April 14th, of this year.

1624. On January 30th, 1624, Sir Thomas Smithe and other Navy Commissioners were engaged in considering means for the employment of shipping, and the obtaining of men for the increase of mariners. It was decided that Thames watermen were not to be admitted freemen till they had served two years in the Navy ; and every merchant ship going to sea was to have on board one man in a hundred who was a waterman.

An order was made on May 7th for paying £32 4s. 5d., to Sir Richard Morrison, Lieutenant of the Ordnance, " for emptions to be presently bought and provided for the furnishing of his Majesty's pinnace, the ' Seven Stars,' she being commanded to lie forth in the mouth of the river, as a watch for the guarding of the navy at Chatham."

War being declared with Spain on March 10th, an English force was soon after despatched for the Palatinate to serve under Count Mansfeldt. In connection with the start of this unfortunate expedition, the Earl of Southampton wrote on July 28th to Secretary Conway : " Will observe the King's order as to the precedency between himself and the Earl of Oxford. The soldiers and baggage are on shipboard in the Thames, but the shippers fear to proceed, on account of the Dunkirk vessels which infest the mouth of the river, and have lately rifled many passengers. Some course is now taken to secure the passage."

1625. On January 15th, 1625, a warrant was issued to Sir Thomas Smithe, Sir John Coke, and other Navy Commissioners, " to sell certain decayed brass shivers and old cordage in the Storehouses at Deptford and Chatham."

The Council, sitting at Whitehall, instructed Sir Richard Bingley, on February 11th, regarding a petition for the release of forty-one Hamburg ships detained in the Downs : " Thirty-nine of them, laden with copper and free merchandise, may depart, but the two laden with powder, masts, etc., are to be brought into the Thames, till further orders."

ON THE RIVER.

1603. The Thames of the early seventeenth century was the great highway of traffic for all the population on its banks. The King and his family passed up and down, from palace to palace, in state barges glowing in paint and gold and rich awnings bearing the royal arms, with pennons and the royal standard floating in the breeze, and attended by guard boats filled with yeomen in their quaint Tudor dress, sitting solemnly holding upright halberts. The nobles had their hardly less splendid barges, with servants in gay liveries bearing their masters' distinctive badges. The Lord Mayor of London and the City Companies rivalled royalty in the beauty of their many-oared barges, proudly flying flags and banners brilliantly displaying the signs of their authority and crafts. The merchants and wealthy burgesses owned fine if soberer appointed boats, and the people gave the numerous body of watermen constant employment for their wherries, taking them up and down, from one side to the other, on business and pleasure.

The craft of the rivermen were barges, wherries, lighters, and the more recently introduced tilt-boats.

The public and private stairs or landings were numerous along the river, and the oldest and chief of the water-gates or landing places for materials and goods conveyed to London were: Blackfriars

Wharf and Stairs, Puddle Wharf, Queenhithe, Downgate, Wolfesgate, Ebgate (Old Swan), Oystergate, Buttolphgate, Billingsgate, Watergate (Water lane), and Watergate (Tower).

" An Act concerning wherrymen and watermen," passed by the Parliament in the first year of the reign, ran as follows :

" Forasmuch as it hath often happened, that divers and sundry people passing by water upon the river of Thames, between Windsor and Gravesend, have been put in great hazard and danger of the loss of their lives and goods, and many times have perished and been drowned in the said river, through the unskilfulness, or want of knowledge or experience, in the wherrymen or watermen that did transport and carry them and their said goods, from place to place upon the said river in wherries, tilt-boats and barges, and for that hitherto there hath not been any sufficient provision had or made for remedy herein. . . . Be it now enacted and established, by the King's most excellent Majesty, the Lords spiritual and temporal, and the Commons in this present Parliament assembled, and by authority of the same, that from henceforth no wherryman or waterman that now is, or that hereafter shall be, and shall row upon the said river of Thames, and shall transport or carry any passengers or goods, in any wherries, tilt-boats, or barges (other than western barges, mill boats, and all other vessels ordinarily serving for other uses than the carrying of passengers), shall retain or take any servant or apprentice to serve him as a waterman upon the said river, unless the said wherryman or waterman that shall so retain, take, or have any such servant, shall have been an apprentice to a wherryman or waterman by the space of five years before such retaining. And further, that no wherryman or waterman that now is, or that hereafter shall be upon the said river of Thames shall retain, have, keep, or take any person or persons to serve him to row upon the said river, as his apprentice unless the said person so to be retained, or to become an apprentice, shall then be of the age of eighteen years at the least, and shall be retained and bound to his master to serve upon the said river for and during the term of seven years at the least, upon pain that every person or persons doing the

contrary shall from time to time for every such offence forfeit
the sum of ten pounds of lawful English money ; the one-half
whereof shall be unto our said sovereign lord the King, his heirs
and successors, and the other half unto any person or persons
that will sue for the same, in any of the Courts of Record of our
said sovereign lord the King, his heirs or successors, by action
of debt, suit, bill, plaint, or information, in which no wage of
law, essoign, protection, or other delay shall be admitted or
allowed. Provided always, That this Act, nor anything therein
contained, shall extend to the son or sons which now are, or
hereafter shall be, of any wherryman or waterman abovesaid
(being of the age of sixteen years at the least, and of convenient
growth and strength), that formerly hath been, or that hereafter
shall be, trained and brought up in rowing, or have or hath
accustomed to row upon the said river, and there have used, or
shall use, to transport or carry passengers from place to place.
But that all and every such son or sons, shall and may from time
to time from henceforth be admitted and allowed to serve, and
may serve upon the said river, and there transport or carry
passengers from place to place as an apprentice as heretofore
they have done, anything in this Act contained to the contrary
in anywise notwithstanding. And be it further enacted, and
established, by the authority aforesaid :—That the eight overseers, or rulers of the Society or Company of Wherrymen or
Watermen, that now are, and that from time to time hereafter
shall be, from henceforth twice in every year, that is to say,
upon the first day of September, and upon the first day of
March, shall openly read and publish, or cause openly to be read
and published, in the hall, or place of their common assembly,
where they usually either have, or hereafter, shall appoint, to
assemble and meet together, all and every the constitutions
and orders already made by them, or that at any time hereafter
shall be made, by the overseers and rulers, for the good or better
ordering or government of the said wherrymen or watermen,
upon pain that every of them shall from time to time, for every
such offence, forfeit to our said sovereign lord the King, his
heirs and successors, the sum of six pounds thirteen shillings
and four pence, of lawful English money, the one half whereof
shall be to our sovereign lord the King, his heirs and successors,
and the other half thereof unto any person or persons that will
sue for the same, in any of the King's Courts of Record, by

action of debt, suit, bill, plaint or information, wherein no wager of law, essoign, or other delay, shall be admitted or allowed."

1604. Early in 1604, Sir James Marvin was made Master of the Swans on the Thames, and other waters. In July the Earl of Suffolk wrote from Court to Sir Thomas Lake : " Pray order the drawing of a bill of £20 yearly to Richard Warner, Senior, and another bill for £30 to Richard Warner, junior, appointed Masters of his Majesty's Barges." The elder Warner was also Master of the Queen's barges, with an annual salary of £20.

In the course of this year a dispute arose between the fishermen of Hammersmith and Chiswick regarding the limits of their fishings, and this was adjusted by the Lord Admiral Nottingham and the Lord Mayor.

At this time a boatbuilder named Thomas Wildgoose importuned Viscount Cranborne about a new river craft he had devised, and asked that the first pleasure-boat of the kind should be " for his Majesty and his fair Queen to sport up and down the Thames. . . and no man perceives how it goeth." He also requested a patent for building " ships and boats after the like sort."

1605. In January, 1605, a seal was caught in the river ; and during the next month the Ferry over the Thames at Kew was leased to Walter Hickman.

A petition was submitted to the Privy Council, in July, by the Masters and Rulers of the Company of Thames Watermen (incorporated in 1556), setting forth that in the time of Queen Elizabeth half their number were generally employed on maritime service, but the late peace had, by destroying their

made to Sir William Andrews, in reversion after Sir James Marven and Thomas Knowles, of the office of Master of the Swans on the Thames, etc.

A very hard frost set in on December 8th, and lasted a week, when it thawed. On the 22nd the frost returned with intense severity, and soon people were attempting to cross the river on the ice. At ebb-tide, on the 30th, many of the boldest ran over in several places from bank to bank; and the birth of 1608 saw land and water in the grip of arctic weather. Blocks of ice clustered together in the river at low water, affording a seeming passage across. Several divers scrambled over, but others not so fortunate or bold fell through the gaps into the water. At the return of the tide these islands of ice were scattered, and boats found a perilous way up and down. A thaw set in on Sunday, January 3rd, but a week later the frost returned, and lasted with extreme intensity till the 15th, killing all the artichokes in the gardens about London. All the posts were delayed, and the city cut off as in a time of seige. A ship called the " Husband," which, at the instigation of the Venetian Ambassador, had been arrested in the Thames, with contraband goods aboard on the way to Flanders, was blocked up with thick ice, and her cargo could not be discharged. People were soon passing between the City and Bankside, but the floods of recurring tides moving the ice, new pathways had to be made each day. The river was completely frozen over between Lambeth and the ferry at Westminster. On Twelfth Day the Archbishop passed over from Lambeth to the Court at Whitehall; and Andrew Fuller, liberated at the moment from the Tower, in a joyful spirit of liberty, and vowing he would not lose time by going round by the Bridge, walked straight from his prison over the ice to reach his home.

The ice at last became everywhere very firm and immovable, and crowds of men, women, and children flocked confidently on to the slippery surface. Maitland wrote : " The river not only became as a public fair, for sale of all sorts of commodities, but also a theatre for all sorts of diversions." A variety of booths and standings were erected, and a regular fair was quickly in full swing. There were victuallers selling beer and wine ; fruitsellers, shoemakers, barbers, and other traders, all with roaring fires. Certain youths burnt a gallon of wine, and made all passers partake of it. Some shot at pricks, while others danced, played at bowls, or disported themselves in variable and fantastic pastimes. A tract was printed, containing an account of the frost, and a woodcut representation of the river with London Bridge in the distance, and was entitled : " Cold doings in London, except it be at the Lottery : with newes out of the country. A familiar Talk between a Countryman and a Citizen, touching this terrible Frost, and the Great Lottery, and the effect of them." The Lottery in progress was being drawn at St. Paul's, and, with tickets at one shilling each, the prizes were all of plate, the highest valued at £150.

This Tract—printed for Henry Gosson and sold at his shop on London Bridge—was made up of a talk between a Citizen and a Countryman, and the part of it concerning the frozen river was as follows :

COUNTRYMAN.—But I beseech you tell me. Is that goodly river of yours—I call it yours because you are a citizen and that river is the nurse that gives milk and honey to your city—but is that lady of fresh waters all covered over with ice ?

CITIZEN.—All over, I assure you, father. The frost hath made a floor upon it, which shews like grey marble roughly hewn out. It is a very pavement of glass, but that it is more strong. The Thames now lies in ; or rather is turned, as some think, bankrupt : and dares not shew her head ; for all the water of it floats up and down like a spring in a cellar.

COUN.—God help the poor fishes ! It is a hard world with them, when their houses are taken over their heads. They use not (are not accustomed) to lie under such thick roofs. But I pray, sir, are all the arches of your famous London Bridge so dammed up with ice that the flakes show like so many frozen gates shut up close ; and that nothing passes through them ; nay, that a man cannot look through them as he had wont ?

CIT.—No such matter. The Thames with her ebbing and flowing hath at sundry times brought down, aye winter castles of ice ; which, jostling against the arches of the Bridge, and striving—like an unruly drunkard at the gates of the city in the night time—to pass through, have there been stayed and lodged so long till they have lain in heaps, and got one upon another ; but not so ambitiously as you speak of them.

COUN.—And do not the Western barges come down upon certain artificial pulleys and engines, sliding on the ice ; to serve your city with fuel ?

CIT.—That were a wonder worth the seeing, and more strange than the rowing over steeples by land in a wherry. I assure you these stories shall never stand in our chronicles. There is no such motion.

COUN.—But I hope, sir, you and I may drink a pint of sack in the tavern that runs upon wheels on the river, as well as a thousand have done besides, may we not ? The motion of that wine cellar, I am sure, is to be seen. Is it not ?

CIT.—The water cellar is, but the wine cellars have too good doings on the land to leave that, and to set up taverns on the river. You know more in the country, I perceive, than we do in the city of these matters.

COUN.—Nay, sir, we hear more but know less. We hear the lies, and you know the truth. Why law you now, had not I made this journey to London, I had died in misbelief. Mine ears might thus have made me to have been called an old doting

2 A

fool. For I, giving credit to report, should have uttered these fables for truths : and I, being an old man, should have been believed—for a white head ought not to hold a black tongue— and so my sons and daughters, taking a father's word, might peradventure forty years hence have been called clowns for justifying a lie so monstrous and incredible.

CIT.—Bar all these rumours hereafter out of your ears ; for they are false and deceitful, and fly up and down like lapwings ; their in times being there it is, when it is not.

COUN.—You, sir, are a man, that by your head and beard, as well as myself, should be one of Time's sons, and should therefore love his daughter, Truth. Make me so much beholding to you, as to receive from you the right picture of all these waterworks ; how they began, how they have grown, and in what fashion have continued.

CIT.—Most gladly will I satisfy your request. You shall understand that the Thames began to put on his " freeze-coat," which he yet wears, about the week before Christmas, and hath kept it on till now this latter end of January : how long time soever besides to come none but God knows.

COUN.—Did it never thaw in these many weeks ?

CIT.—Only three days, or four at the most ; and that but weakly, to dissolve so great a hardness. The cakes of ice, great in quantity and in great numbers, were made and baked cold in the mouth of winter, at the least a fortnight or three weeks before they were crusted and cemented together ; but after they had once joined their strengths into one, their backs held out and could not be broken.

COUN.—We may make this good use, even out of this watery and transformed element ; that London upholdeth a State ; and again, that violent factions and combinations albeit of the basest persons in a commonwealth are not easily dissolved ; if once they be suffered to grow up to a head. On, sir, I pray.

CIT.—This cold breakfast being given to the city, and the Thames growing more and more hard-hearted ; wild youths and boys were the first merchant-venturers that set out to discover these cold islands of ice upon the river. And the first path that was beaten forth to pass to the Bank Side, without going over (London) Bridge or by boat, was about Cold Harbour and in those places near the Bridge : for the tides still piling up the flakes of ice one upon another in those parts of the Thames ;

it was held the best and safest travelling into our new-found Freeze-Land by those creeks.

COUN.—But this onset prospering and they coming off well heartened others to come on, sir, did it not ?

CIT.—No soldiers more desperate in a skirmish. Speak it, father, from my mouth for an assured truth, that there was as it were an artificial bridge of ice reaching from one side of the river to the other, upon which infinite numbers of people passed to and fro, jostling one another in crowds : while the current of the water ran in sight, more than half the breadth of the Thames, on either side of that icy bridge ; the bridge itself being not above five yards broad, if so much.

COUN.—It was strange ! But it was said of you Londoners that when you strive to be kind, you turn into prodigals ; when you are cowards, you are arrant cowards ; and when you are bold, you are too desperately venturous.

CIT.—It appears so by this frost ; for no danger could nip their bloods with fear ; but over some went in shoals, when thousands stood gazing on and swore they would not follow their steps in that watery wilderness for many thousands of pounds. Nay, even many of those that were the discoverers and did first venture over, would never undertake the second voyage ; but protested when they were half way they would have lost much to have been again on shore.

COUN.—It is most likely : for perils that are not common make men foolhardy ; but being once tasted, they tremble to come near them.

CIT.—You say true, father : but the fear of this shipwreck and of these rocks grew every day less and less. As the ice increased in hardness, so men's hearts increased in hardiness : so that at length—the frost knitting all his sinews together ; and the inconstant water by that means, being of a floating element, changed into a firm ground as it were—both men, women and children walked over and up and down in such companies ; that, I verily believe and I dare almost swear it, the one half, if not three parts of the people in the city, have been seen going on the Thames. The river showed not now, neither shows it yet, like a river, but like a field ; where archers shoot at pricks (targets), while others play at football. It is a place of mastery, where some wrestle and some run ; and he that does best is aptest to take a fall. It is an alley to walk

upon without dread, albeit under it be most assured danger.
The gentlewomen that tremble to pass over a bridge in the field,
do here walk boldly. The citizen's wife that looks pale when
she sits in a boat for fear of drowning, thinks that here she
treads as safe now as in her parlour. Of all ages, of both sexes,
of all professions, this is the common path. It is the roadway
between London and Westminster, and between Southwark and
London. Would you drink a cup of sack, father ? here stand
some with runlets to fill it out.

COUN.—Ah ha ! that is the tavern then that is talked on.

CIT.—Thirst you for beer, ale, usquebaugh, etc. ; or for
victuals ? There you may buy it, because (in order that) you
may tell another day how you dined upon the Thames. Are
you cold with going over ? You shall ere you come to the midst
of the river, spy some ready with pans of coals to warm your
fingers. If you want fruit after you have dined, there stand
costermongers to serve you at your call. And thus do people
leave their houses and the streets ; turning the goodliest river
in the whole kingdom into the broadest street to walk in.

COUN.—But tell me, I pray, sir, if all the merchants that
undertake this voyage to these your narrow seas ; are none
undone ? Do none of your fresh-water soldiers miscarry, and
drop down in these slippery marshes ?

CIT.—Yes, sir, I have heard of many and have been an eye-
witness of some ; of all which, I will be sparing in report, being
rather willing to be reprehended for telling too little than for
discovering too much.

COUN.—It is a modesty that well becomes any man, albeit
nothing but truth sit upon his tongue. But I pray, sithence
(since) you crack the shell, let us see what kernel there is within
it : sithence you have bestowed the sweet, let me taste the sour.
Let your news be as country folks bring fruit to your markets,
the bad and good together. Say, have none gone, " westward
for smelts," as our proverbial phrase is ?

CIT.—Yes, it hath been a kind of battle for the time. For
some have fallen in up to the knees, others to the middle, others
to the armpits ; yea, and some have been ducked over head
and ears, yet have crawled out like drowned rats : while others
have sunk to the bottom that never rose again to the top. They
had a cold bed to lie in ! Amongst many other misfortunes
that are to be pitied, this is one. A couple of friends shooting

on the Thames with birding pieces, it happened they struck a sea-pie, or some other fowl. They both ran to fetch it. The one stumbled forward, his head slipped into a deep hole, and there he was drowned : the other in his haste slipped backward, and by that means saved his life. A poor fellow likewise having heated his body with drink, thought belike to cool it on the water : but coming to walk on the ice, his head was too heavy for his heels ; so that down he fell, and there presently died.

COUN.—Let his fall give others warning how to stand. Your city cannot choose but to be much damnified (injured) by this strange congealing of the river.

CIT.—Exceeding much, father. Strangers may guess at our harms ; yet none can give the full number of them but we that are the inhabitants. For the city by this means is cut off from all commerce. Shopkeepers may sit and ask, " What do you lack ? " when the passengers (passers by) may very well reply, " What do you lack yourselves ? " They may sit and stare on men, but not sit and sell. It was before called " The dead term," and now we may call this " The dead vacation," " The frozen vacation," " The cold vacation." If it be a gentleman's life to live idly and do nothing, how many poor artificers and trades- men have been made gentlemen then by this frost ? For a number of occupations—like the flakes of ice that lie in the Thames—are by this malice of Winter, trod clean under foot, and will not yet be able to stir. Alas, poor watermen ! You have had cold cheer at this banquet. You that live altogether upon water, can scarce get water to your hands. It is a hard thing now for you to earn your bread with the sweat of your brows.

COUN.—This beating may make them wise. The want that this hard season drives them into, may teach them to play the ants ; and in summer to make a provision against the wrath of winter. There is no mischief born alone, I know. Calamities commonly are, by birth, twins. Methinks therefore, that this drying up of the waters should be a devourer up of wood. This cold ague of the earth must needs have warmth to help it. That warmth must come from fire, and that fire cannot be had without cost : how then, I pray you, in this so general an affliction did poor people shift for fuel to comfort them ?

CIT.—Their care for fire was as great as their care for food. Nay, to want it was a worse torment than to be without meat.

The belly was now pinched to have the body warm : and had not the provident Fathers of this city (the Corporation) carefully, charitably, and out of a good and godly zeal, dispersed a relief to the poor in several parts and places about the outer bounds of the city, where poverty most inhabiteth ; by storing them beforehand with sea coal and other firing at a reasonable rate, I verily persuade myself that the unconscionable and unmerciful raising of the prices of fuel by chandlers, woodmongers, etc., who now meant to lay the poor on the rack— would have been the death of many a wretched creature through want of succour.

Coun.—Not unlikely, sir.

Cit.—For neither could coal be brought up the river, neither could wood be sent down. The western barges might now wrap up their smoky sails ; for albeit they had never so lofty a gale, their voyage was spoiled : the winds were with them, but the tide was clean against them. And not only hath this frost nipped away those comforts that should revive the outward parts of the body ; but those also that should give strength and life to the inward. For you of the country being not able to travel to the city with victuals, the price of victail must of necessity be enhanced ; and victail brought into a scarcity. And thus have I given you, according to your request, a true picture of our Thames frozen over ; and withal have drawn in as lively colours as I can, to my skill, as it were in a little table (picture), all the miseries, mischiefs, and inconveniences, which this hard time hath thrown upon our city.

By February 2nd the ice had quite dissolved and disappeared from the river. Keen distress had been caused to the working classes and the very poor, expecially those depending for daily bread on the river traffic.

On the 5th, the Lord Mayor sent a letter to the Lords of the Council, " concerning a contribution to be given to the watermen for their relief in this extraordinary time of frost, which had closed up the river Thames, and so deprived them of their living. Many other trades were suffering from the severe season, as bricklayers, plasterers, silk-weavers, etc., and if they contributed to one Company, they must do the like for all. He therefore prayed that the watermen might be left to help themselves by their own industry, in the same manner as other manual trades."

A warrant was, however, issued authorizing the delivery to persons nominated by the Council the sum of £200, to be distributed among the poor watermen for their present relief.

On Sunday, the 19th of this same month, a peculiar tide happened in the river. Edmond Howe, in his continuation of Stow's "Annals," wrote : "When it should have been dead low water at London Bridge, quite contrary to course, it was then high water ; and presently it ebbed almost half an hour, the quantity of a foot, and then suddenly it flowed again almost two foot higher than it did before, and then ebbed again until it came near the right course, so as the next flood began, in a manner, as it should, and kept his due course in all respects as if there had been no shifting, nor alteration of tides. All this happened before twelve of the clock in the forenoon, the weather being indifferent calm."

During the course of 1608 a petition of the barge-men of the town of Ware complained that the river Lea had been drawn so low by Sir Robert Wroth and others that their barges could not pass with provisions for the City of London. The Lord Mayor forwarded this petition to the Lords of the Council, praying them to take some action for remedying the evil, and freeing the passage for the barges.

1609. At the end of March, 1609, a warrant

directed that the necessary sums should be paid to James Russell, a bargemaker, and Clement Chapman, for building a barge each for Prince Henry and Princess Elizabeth.

1611. On April 30th, 1611, an order was made for paying £147 to John de Creet, Serjeant-painter to the King, for colouring, painting, and gilding with fine gold, both outside and in, a barge for the Duke of York; and a few days later another order was made for paying £40 to Richard Watford, the King's barge-maker, for building this craft. Of other orders, one was for £46 9s. 8d., paid to Thomas Larkin, Locksmith to the King, for works done on the new barges for the princes and princess; and one for £86 9s. 6d. paid to Clement Chapman, Joiner to the King, for works to the same barges.

An Estimate was dated on May 17th, by Inigo Jones and others, of the charge for piling, planking, and brickwork at the three aits, or islands, at Richmond.

In the course of this year a suit was commenced at Westminster, by information of Sir John Brograve, the Attorney-General, wherein the City of London was called upon to exhibit their claims and proofs of the common or open passages and stairs to the river the freemen had a right to make use of between the Tower of London and the Temple. Several aged witnesses, some upwards of fourscore, were sworn and examined regarding the long-established use of such free passages and stairs.

1612. On May 6th, 1612, the Foreign Shipwrights on the river—so called from being outside the Liberties of the City of London—obtained a Royal Charter of Incorporation, and Phineas Pett, the King's Shipwright, was elected the first Master.

Michael Drayton, in his " Poly-olbion," described the Thames at this time, from Windsor to London, thus :

" But now this mighty flood, upon his voyage prest,
  (That found how with his strength, his beauties still increas'd,
  From where brave Windsor stood on tip-toe to behold
  The fair and goodly Thames, so far as e'er he could,
  With kingly houses crown'd, of more than earthly pride,
  Upon his either banks, as he along doth glide),
  With wonderful delight doth his long course pursue,
  Where Oatlands, Hampton Court, and Richmond he doth view.
  Then Westminster the next great Thames doth entertain ;
  That vaunts her palace large, and her most sumptuous fane :
  The land's tribunal seat that challengeth for her's,
  The crowning of our kings, their famous sepulchres.
  Then goes he on along by that more beauteous strand,
  Expressing both the wealth and bravery of the land.
  (So many sumptuous towers, within so little space,
  The all-beholding Sun scarce sees in all his race.)
  And on by London leads, which like a crescent lies,
  Whose windows seem to mock the star-befreckled skies ;
  Besides her rising spires, so thick themselves that show,
  As do the bristling reeds within his banks that grow.
  There sees his crowded wharfs, and people pest'red shores,
  His bosom overspread with shoals of lab'ring oars ;
  With that most costly Bridge that doth him most renown,
  By which he clearly puts all other rivers down."

In Easter Term, 1612, an action was brought, in the Common Pleas, by the Corporation of Gravesend, against a waterman named Edmunds, to test the question of right regarding the exclusive working of the Long Ferry to London by certain barge-owners. A verdict was given in favour of the exclusive claim, but on an appeal to the judges this verdict was reversed. The question was not, however, definitely settled till 1616, when some stringent bye-laws framed for regulating the Ferry traffic were confirmed by the judges of assize.

During the late Spanish wars quite half the

number of Thames watermen were away fighting on the warships, thus providing abundant labour for the remainder at home, especially in ferrying passengers across the river to the theatres and bear gardens on the Bankside. With the conclusion of peace the absent watermen returned, and this, together with the partial desertion of the players from Bankside for new theatres in London and Middlesex, caused a lack of employment to arise. Violent dissatisfaction was expressed in 1612, and, after numerous meetings, the watermen determined to oppose the migration of the actors to the City. Their further proceedings were described in 1613, by Taylor, the " Water-poet," in a pamphlet headed " The Cause of the Watermen's Suit concerning Players, etc., etc.," and it is here given as supplying interesting particulars of the watermen's occupation at this period, and a vindication of them by one of their own order :

" The occasions that have moved me to write this pamphlet are many and forcible, and the attempt in writing it adventurous and full of danger, for as on the one side I doubt not but with truth to stop the mouths of Ignorance and Malice that have and do daily scandalize me (and withal I know I shall purchase a general thanks from all honest men of my company), so I am assured to gain the hatred of some that love me well, and I affect them no worse, only for my plain truth and discharging my conscience ; but fall back, fall edge, come what can come, I am resolved, and without fear or flattery, thus I begin.

" In the month of January last, 1613, there was a motion made by some of the better sort of the Company of Watermen, that it were necessary for the relief of such a decayed multitude to petition to his Majesty, that the players might not have a play-house in London or in Middlesex, within four miles of the City on that side of the Thames. Now this request may seem harsh and not well to be digested by the players and their appendices. But the reasons that moved us unto it, being charitably considered, makes the suit not only seem reasonable, but past seeming most necessary to be sued for, and tolerable to be granted.

" Our petition being written to purpose aforesaid, I was selected by my Company to deliver it to his Majesty and follow the business, which I did with that care and integrity, that I am assured none can justly tax me with the contrary. I did ride twice to Theobalds, once to Newmarket, and twice to Royston, before I could get a reference upon my petition. I had to bear my charge, of my Company first and last, seven pounds two shillings, which horse hire, horse meat, and man's meat brought to a consumption ; besides I wrote several petitions to most of the Right Honourable Lords of his Majesty's Privy Council, and I found them all compassionately affected to the necessity of our cause.

" First, I did briefly declare part of the services that watermen had done in Queen Elizabeth's reign, of famous memory, in the voyage to Portugal, with the Right Honourable and never to be forgotten Earl of Essex ; then after that, how it pleased God (in that great deliverance in the year 1588) to make watermen good serviceable instruments with their loss of lives and limbs to defend their Prince and country. Moreover, many of them served with Sir Francis Drake, Sir John Hawkins, Sir Martin Frobisher, and others : besides in Cadiz action, the Island Voyage, in Ireland, in the Low Countries, and in the narrow seas they have been (as in duty they are bound), at continual command, so that every summer fifteen hundred or two thousand of them were employed to the places aforesaid, having but nine shillings four pence the month a piece for their pay, and yet they were able then to set themselves out like men, with shift of apparel, linen and woollen, and forbear charging of their Prince for their pay sometimes six months, nine months, twelve months, sometimes more, for then there were so few watermen and the one half of them at sea, those that staid at home had as much work as they would do.

" Afterwards the players began to play on the Bankside and to leave playing in London and Middlesex (for the most part) then there went such great concourse of people by water, that the small number of watermen remaining at home were not able to carry them, by reason of the Court, the terms, the players and other employments, so that we were enforced and encouraged (hoping that this golden stirring world would have lasted ever) to take and entertain men and boys : which boys are grown men, and keepers of houses, many of them being overcharged with families of wife and children, so that the number of watermen, and those that live and are maintained by them, and by the only labour of the oar and scull, betwixt the bridge of Windsor and Gravesend, cannot be fewer than forty thousand : the cause of the greater half of which multitude, hath been the players playing on the Bankside, for I have known three companies besides the bear baiting, at once there ; to wit, the Globe, the Rose, and the Swan. And it is an infallible truth that had they never played there it had been better for watermen by the one half of their living, for the Company is increased more than half by their means of playing there in former times.

" And now it hath pleased God in this peaceful time, that there is no employment at the sea, as it hath been accustomed, so that all those great numbers of men remain at home ; and the players have all (except the Kingsmen) left their usual residency on the Bankside, and do play in Middlesex far remote from the Thames, so that every day in the week they do draw unto them three or four thousand people, that were used to spend their monies by water, to the relief of so many thousands of poor people, which by players former playing on the Bankside are increased, so that ofttimes a poor man that hath five or six children, doth give good attendance to his labour all day, and at night (perhaps) hath not gotten a groat to relieve himself, his wife and family.

" This was the effect and scope of our petition though here I have declared it more at large, to which his Majesty graciously granted me a reference to his Commissioners for suits, who then were the Right Honourable Sir Julius Cæsar, Sir Thomas Parry, Knights, the Right Worshipful Sir Francis Bacon, then the King's Attorney-General, Sir Henry Montague, his Majesty's Serjeant-at-Law, Sir Walter Cope, Master George Calvert, one of the clerks of his Majesty's Privy Council, and Baron Southerton, one of the Barons of the King's Exchequer, these Honourable and Worshipful persons I did oft solicit, by petitions, by friends, and by my own industrious importunity, so that in the end when our cause was heard, we found them generally affected to the suit we prosecuted.

" His Majesty's players did exhibit a petition against us, in

which they said that our suit was unreasonable, and that we
might as justly remove the Exchange, the walks of Pauls, or
Moorfields to the Bankside for our profits, as to confine them ;
but our extremities and cause being judiciously pondered by
the Honourable and Worshipful Commissioners, Sir Francis
Bacon very worthily said that so far forth as the public weal
was to be regarded before pastimes, or a serviceable decaying
multitude before a handful of particular men, or profit before
pleasure, so far was our suit to be preferred before theirs. Whereupon the players did appeal to the Lord Chamberlain, which
was then the Earl of Somerset who stood well affected to us,
having been moved before in the business by Master Samuel
Goldsmith, an especial friend of mine, and a gentleman that
myself and all the rest of my poor Company in general, are
generally beholden, and deeply engaged unto ; for of his own free
will to his cost and charge, we must with thankfulness acknow-
ledge he hath been and is continually our worthy friend. Who
seeing the wants of such numbers of us, he hath often neglected
his own urgent and profitable affairs, spending his time and
coin in any honest occasion that might profit us. Thus much
I thought good to insert in the way of thankfulness, because of
all vices ingratitude is the most hateful.

"The Commissioners did appoint me to come on the next
day that they sat again, and that then the players and we
should know their determinations concerning our businesses :
but before that day came, Sir Walter Cope died, and Sir Julius
Cæsar being Chief Commissioner was made Master of the Rolls,
by which means the commission was dissolved, and we never
yet had further hearing. Thus far did I proceed in this thankless
suit ; and because it was not effected, some of my Company
partly through malice or ignorance, or both, have reported that
I took bribes of the players to let the suit fall, and that to that
purpose I had a supper with them at the Cardinal's Hat on the
Bankside, and that if I had dealt well with my Company, and
done as I might have done, then all had been as they would
have had it."

Taylor goes on to indignantly repudiate this
insinuation, and continues :

" I must confess that there are many rude, uncivil fellows in our Company, and I would some doctor would purge the Thames of them ";

but on the other hand,

" many of the meanest scullers that rows on the Thames was, is, or shall be if occasion serve, at command to do their prince and country more service, than any of the players shall be joined unto."

He asserted that no Company had sharper laws or executed them more severely.

" And banishment from the river Thames for ever, now and then cuts off a bad member. Besides, fines and forfeitures are laid upon the heads of petty offenders, that few or none escapes unpunished if their faults be known."

The watermen were frequently cheated and abused.

" I myself have often met with a roaring boy that hath had nothing about him but a satin outside to cover his knavery, and that none of his own neither, witness his mercer and his tailor ; yet this gallant must be shipped in a pair of oars at least : but his gay slop hath no sooner kissed the cushions, but with a volley of new coined oaths he hath never left roaring, ' Row, row, row,' and when his scurviness is landed where he pleases, he hath told me I must wait on him, and he will return to me presently, and I shall carry him back again, and be paid altogether : then have I attended five or six hours for nothing, for my cheating shark having neither money nor honesty, hath never come at me, but took some other pair of stairs, and in the same fashion cozened another waterman for his boat-hire."

Against this

" We must, and do with thankfulness confess, that the nobility, gentry, and all others of the better sort of this Kingdom, have honest, worthy and charitable considerations of our want of means, and multitude of men ; for they do know that house rent, and victuals, are at four times the rate which it was at when the statute was made in Queen Mary's reign for our fares, and as the price of all things is raised (except poor men's labours) so do they in conscience very liberally raise our fares accordingly."

Taylor ends his pamphlet with :

" As concerning our endeavours to remove the shelves and sands in the Thames (which are a great annoyance to the river, and hurtful to the city) as his Majesty hath commanded, and the Right Honourable the Lord Mayor and the rest of his worshipful brethren, shall direct, we shall with all willingness know our duties we doubt not, both to the King's Majesty's contentment, the good of the city, and the good report of ourselves."

1614. In the early days of 1614 a severe frost covered the river with ice. John Chamberlain, writing the news of the town to Mrs. Alice Carleton on February 1st, said : " Mr. Secretary went on Monday toward the King at Newmarket in a hard and cold weather as hath come this year, for it hath been very sharp these ten days, with much frost and snow, which continuing still, and so is like to do, for aught I see. The Thames hath not been passable, but in a manner closed up almost this sevennight. The flood I wrote you of last week, did a great deal more harm than I could then tell you, for we have certain notice of more than twenty drowned that Saturday within forty miles compass of this town."

The complaints of the watermen against the increasing use of Hackney Coaches were embodied in a Bill entitled, " A Bill against Outrageous Coaches," which was brought before the House of Commons on April 18th. It was, however, rejected on May 7th.

John Taylor, " the Water-poet," now becoming well-known by his writings, and who made William Fennor, " the King's rhymning-poet," call him " the gentlemen-like sculler at the Hope on the Bankside," did a thriving business when his station

on the river was the landing-place of the daily throng
—including the great and gay, foreign ambassadors,
statesmen, gallant courtiers, and even at times
glorious Shakespeare and Ben Jonson—flocking
over the ferry to the Hope, the Rose, the
Globe and Paris Garden, not only to witness
and gloat over the brutalities of the dog and bear
and bull fights, but to listen to and applaud the
immortal tragedies and comedies born from the
incomparable vigour of the Elizabethan age.   Taylor
loved the life and glitter of the river, and the smiles
of the ladies, " whose ancient lodgings were near
St. Katherine's, the Bankside, Lambeth Marsh,
Westminster, Whitefriars, Coleharbor, or any other
place near the Thames."   And in an enthusiastic
moment he wrote :

> " But noble Thames, whilst I can hold a pen,
>   I will divulge thy glory unto men ;
>   Thou, in the morning when my coin is scant,
>   Before the evening doth supply my want."

1616.   On May 13th, 1616, Gregorio Barbarigo,
the Venetian Ambassador, in submitting an account
to the Doge and Senate, of the expenses incurred
by a mission of his Secretary to Holland, included
these items :   " By boat to Gravesend, 8d. ;   by
hostelry at Gravesend, 9s. 6d. ;   by boat to London
(on return), 6d."

John Taylor, " the Water-poet," in a pamphlet
called " Three Weeks, Three Days, and Three Hours
Observations, from London to Hamburgh in
Germany," wrote :   " Upon Saturday, the 17th of
August, 1616 (after I had taken leave of some
friends that would hardly give me leave to leave
them), I was associated with five or six courteous

comrades to the haven of Billingsgate, where I was no sooner come, but I was shipped in the wherry for the port of Gravesend, and having two women and three men in my company thither, we past the way away by telling tales by turns. Where one of the women took upon her very logically to defend the honesty of brokers and she maintained her paradoxical arguments so pithily, as if herself like a desperate pawn had lain seven years in lavender on sweeting in Long Lane, or amongst the dogged inhabitants of Houndsditch. And one of the men replied that he thanked God he never had any need of them, whereupon I began to suspect him to be crafty knave, because the proverb says, ' A crafty knave needs no broker,' and indeed after I had inquired what countryman he was, he told me he was a Welshman, and a Justice's clerk. I left him as I found him, hoping never to be troubled with his binding over, and withdrawing ; and so landing at Gravesend, we all went to the ' Christopher,' where we took a Bacchanalian farewell one of another where I remained till the Monday following, await ing the coming down of the ship that I was to be transported in. About the hour of three in the afternoon, with good hope we weighed anchor, and with a courteous tide and gentle wind we sailed down the river of Thames, as far as the grand oyster haven of Queenborough, where though our ship (the ' Judith ') was not sea-sick, yet she cast (anchor I mean)."

They sailed the next day, and on the Thursday made the coast of Friesland, and after exhausting seventeen days in seeing Hamburgh and other places, Taylor landed at London on the Friday night, after an absence of three weeks and three days.

2 B

At this time Ben Jonson wrote the following song to Celia in " The Forest " :

> " Kiss me, sweet: the wary lover
> Can your favours keep, and cover,
> When the common courting jay
> All your bounties will betray.
> Kiss again ! no creature comes.
> Kiss, and score up wealthy sums
> On my lips, thus hardly sundered,
> While you breathe.   First give a hundred,
> Then a thousand, then another
> Hundred, then unto the other
> Add a thousand, and so more :
> Till you equal with the store,
> All the grass that Rumney yields,
> Or the sands in Chelsea Fields,
> Or the drops in Silver Thames,
> Or the stars, that gild his streams,
> In the silent summer-nights,
> When youth ply their stolen delights ;
> That the curious may not know
> How to tell 'em as they flow,
> And the envious, when they find
> What their number is, be pined."

1617.   In 1617, a sad disaster happened to Lord Abergavenny in the death of three grown-up sons, who were upset from a wherry near Gravesend, and all drowned.

In a letter of August 9th, John Chamberlain wrote that there were " such store of salmons, that the like hath not been seen in the Thames these forty years."

1618.   On October 28th, 1618, the " Ann Speed-well " ship ran down and sank the " Hopewell " in the Thames.

At this time a grant was made to David Ramsay and Thomas Wildgoose, " For the sole use of an invention for raising of water from any low place to

the houses of noblemen and gentlemen, and to cities
and towns, and to make boats for the carriage of
burdens and passengers, to run upon the water as
swift in calms, and more fast in storms, than boats
full sailed in great winds."

Horatio Busino, Secretary to the Venetian
Ambassador, wrote in his diary at various times
his impressions of English life and manners. On
January 10th, of this year, his remarks on the
Thames were : " The river ebbs and flows so rapidly
that under the bridge between the arches any mill
might be kept at work, the tide turning every six
hours with great strength, the difference between
high and low water mark amounting to from ten
to twelve feet. Notwithstanding this the wherries
shoot along so lightly as to surprise everyone.
These wherries look like so many mutilated gondolas,
without prows or ' felzi,' though they have seats
aft with sundry convenient cushions. They row
like galley oarsmen, with extremely long oars, and
are very dexterous at steering clear of each other.
There are also long covered barges like Bucentors,
very handsome, especially those of the King and
other noblemen and gentlemen, pulling six or eight
oars, and which really fly over the water."

And again on June 29th, after recovering from a
long sickness, he wrote : " Verily, I erred in what I
wrote about the real extent of London, as told me
carelessly by others ; when I went down the river
with his Excellency, as I have frequently done for
chartering ships of war for the Republic, I remarked
a series of double suburbs four or six miles in length,
so I was perfectly annihilated with surprise, but
recovered myself on hearing that all those buildings
have been erected within a very short period with

the entrails of the Spaniards as disembowelled by the English pirates, who frequently plundered their fleets. . . . We saw what may be called a new arsenal, begun by the India Company, and on the same day passed alongside of two immense ships called the ' Sun ' and the ' Moon,' which are completely found for the India voyage, with all their hands and munitions. They really looked like two well-appointed castles. This year a score of vessels, but little inferior to these have steered the same course. We likewise passed along the banks of the Thames, in sight of some relics of the ship of the famous Captain Drake, which looked exactly like the bleached ribs and bare skull of a dead horse. In that ship he sailed round the world, passing through the Straits of Magellan, and returned home freighted with much gold and with fragrant spices. Truly such gains and glory sound highly attractive, but when one reflects upon the dangers of the sea the desire vanishes. I merely argue from the trifling inconvenience experienced by me when going with his Excellency to inspect the vessels which have been chartered. It behoved us to go alongside them in very rickety wherries and then mount inconvenient wooden ladders clinging to a rope's end ; descending then into the ship's hold and investigating everything ; the decks, the number of guns, half culverins or sakers, whether well armed in every respect and well found in sails, and whether the captains, gunners, and sailors were able, in such wise that I was quite terrified, whereas his Excellency in the prime of manhood, was indefatigable, going all over the ship quite freely. . . ."

1620. On January 28th, 1620, a Licence was granted to Francis Cotton, empowering him to erect mills on barges, etc., for twenty years, on payment of the yearly rent of £4.

In 1620, John Taylor, "the Water-poet," and Roger Bird, a vintner, engaged in the hazardous venture of going from London to Queenborough at the mouth of the river, in a paper boat, with two stock fish tied to two canes for oars, and eight large and well-blown bladders, secured four on each side. Before they had rowed three miles the paper bottom of their frail craft, soaked and sodden, fell out, and they had only the skeleton framework of the boat and the bladders to trust to. Taylor wrote a poetic account of the desperate voyage, called "The praise of Hempseed, with the voyage of Mr. Roger Bird and the writer hereof, in a boat of brown paper, from London to Queenborough in Kent, etc." In this he said :

> " Thousands of people all the shore did hide,
>   And thousands more did meet us on the tide,
>   With scullers, oars, with ship boats and with barges
>   To gaze on us they put themselves to charges.
>   Thus did we drive, and drive the time away,
>   Till pitchy night had driven away the day.
>   The Sun unto the under world was fled ;
>   The Moon was loth to rise, and kept her bed ;
>   The stars did twinkle, but the ebon clouds
>   Their light our sight obscures and overshrouds ;
>   The tossing billows made our boat to caper,
>   Our paper-form scarce being form of paper.
>   The water four miles broad, no oars to row,
>   Night dark, and where we were we did not know ;
>   And thus 'twixt doubt and fear, hope and despair,
>   I fell to work, Roger Bird to prayer ;
>   And as the surges up and down did eave us
>   He cried most fervently, good Lord receive us ! "

After a long exposure on the water, from Saturday at evening-tide to Monday morning, the exhausted pair reached Queenborough.

> " A land,
> I took my fellow Roger by the hand,
> And both of us ere we two steps did go
> Gave thanks to God, that hath preserved us so;
> Confessing that His mercy us protected,
> When as we least deserved, and less expected."

1621.   On February 3rd, 1621, John Chamberlain
wrote in a letter to Carleton : " The Thames is now
quite frozen over, so that people have passed over,
to and fro, these four or five days ; but not so freely
as in the great frost ; for the winds and high tides
have so driven the ice in heaps in some places that
it lies like rocks and mountains, and hath a strange
and hideous aspect.   It hath been seldom seen
that this river should be twice frozen over in one
winter ; and the watermen are quite undone to
lose the benefit of term and parliament both."

Sir Symonds D'Ewes wrote on Saturday, the
17th : " Walking in our Temple outer garden, I
observed the river Thames to be in a great part
unfrozen and boats to pass up and down freely."

John Chamberlain wrote on July 14th that
much salmon was being caught in the river ; and,
on October 27th, he told Carleton that " A high
tide in the Thames swept through Westminster Hall,
and did much damage."   On December 15th, in
another letter, he wrote : " I do not remember a
more sharp week than this hath been ; and the
extremity at the very first made us think it could
not last, but it holds out still in such sort that the
Thames is not passable."   Maitland wrote : " A
very Great Frost happened, whereby the river
Thames was so strongly frozen that streets of booths
were erected thereon, wherein were sold all sorts of
goods as in a public fair ; as were likewise all sorts

of diversions practised as well as on land." Great distress was caused to watermen and the riverside labouring population.

In 1621 the dissatisfaction of the watermen with the mode of election of their rulers and officers took form in a Bill introduced to Parliament on May 5th. This measure proposed an alteration in the law of Philip and Mary, " which authorizeth the Citie of London to elect the overseers out of the whole number of watermen, which they complain of, and allege, that the Lord Mayor and Aldermen (for affection or some other by respect) do usually choose such watermen to be rulers which are not fit to governe themselves, much lesse to take upon them the charge of so great a company."

Although the Bill was not proceeded with its clauses are given as not only shewing the feeling and aspirations of the watermen, but exhibiting in a fairly accurate manner the condition of the river service at the time :

1. " That they desire to have thirty assistants, to be chosen by themselves, and those assistants to have as absolute a power to rule and governe, in the absence of the overseers, as the overseers themselves.

2. " That the old overseers would choose and present eight persones out of the thirty assistants, of which eight persons the citie should have power to choose four, and four of the ancient rulers should continue another yeare, which eight so chosen should have power to choose four new assistants, to supply the roomes of those four overseers so chosen ; and that if the overseers fayle to present names to the Lord Maior and Aldermen, then the Lord Maior and aldermen shall have authority to choose over-seers of themselves ; yet so as they must be out of the thirty assistants.

3. " Prohibits all persons whatsoever from presuming to use the trade of a waterman or lighterman, unless he have served as

apprentice seven years to a waterman or lighterman, upon paine of imprisonment three months, and to forfeit twenty pounds.

4. " Enjoyneth all the watermen (how remote soever they dwell from the citie of London) to come to their hall once every yeare, to heare their orders read, or else to forfeit twelve pence, to be levied by the overseers for the benefit of the company.

5. " They would have their authority enlarged : and whereas before it was but betwixt Gravesend and Windsor, now they would have it extended from Cliff, in Kent, to Reading, in Barkshire. And that it might be lawfull to and for all free watermen rowing upon the river of Thames to carry and recarry his Majesty's liege people to and from all places betwixt Cliff and Reading, without contradiction of any person or persons whatsoever.

6. " It is enacted that the overseers shall not onely have power to commit offenders to prison, in any of the compters of this city, but also in any other prison in the counties of Kent, Essex, Surrey, Middlesex, and Barkshire, which may be nearest to the place where the offender may dwell.

7. " No person may take upon him the charge and guidance of any barge, tilt-boate or lightersman, unlesse he be approved and allowed by the overseers and six of the assistants, upon paine to forfeit five pounds to the overseers to the use of the company. And if any person so allowed become disordered and unfit, then they shall have power to disallow him, and if he continue his charge, and refuse to be disallowed, then to forfeit forty shillings to the use aforesaid.

8. " It is provided that no waterman using any tide boat, barge, tilt-boat, lightersman, or wherry, shall become partner, or have anything to doe concerning the trade of a waterman with any landman, or with any other but a waterman, unlesse he be allowed so to do by the overseers and assistants, upon paine to forfeit twenty shillings to the use aforesaid.

9. " No person using the trade of a waterman shall take into his service the servant or apprentice of any other waterman, but by the order and allowance of the overseers and assistants, upon paine to forfeit five pounds to the use of the company.

10. " That no master or owner of any ship or vessel belonging to the river of Thames of the burthen of one hundred tunnes or more, may make any voyage to sea, except they take with them for every hundred tuns their ship is of burthen, one waterman's

servant, for which servant or servants they must repaire to the place where the watermen use to assemble, and demand of them ; which servant or servants, together with their conditions and rates, shall be appointed by the overseers ; and every master or owner which shall offend herein, shall forfeit forty shillings to the use of the Company."

The rulers and others of the Company set forth their objections in a Counter-Bill, of which the preamble ran : " Herein is taxed the cities government, which they desire to be alienated from the Citie to themselves, as men more fitter for government, but that the law of second and third Phillip and Marie, for prevention of combination thought fit that the election should be out of the whole company, and not restrained to any certain number." The clauses of this Bill were :

1. " They stated by this branch the cities power of election of assistants is cleere taken away, which the citie had before, because none came to be assistants until they had been overseers.

2. " That altho' the cities power be not excluded, yet it is much weakened by drawing the nomination to themselves, and tying the Court to a necessity to approve their nomination ; and that the overseers will be first served, and they failing, then the Lord Maior and Aldermen.

3. " They stated it would be very prejudiciall to the great ferry by barge betwixt London and Gravesend, which are always steered, and for the most part rowed by mariners and seamen, who are more sufficient for those boats than watermen, and have ever carried passengers with more safety. It would also prejudice all the ferries upon the river of Thames, wherein are few or no watermen employed ; nor in this act is any provision made for them, which would therefore tend to the destruction of all ferries, barges and tide boats.

4. " It is necessary that provision be made that the ordinances of the company receive allowance, according to the statute of nineteenth Henry VII., or otherwise by the Lord Maior and

Court of Aldermen, and Recorder of the Citie of London for the time being, before they be put in execution.

5. " This acte would not only take away the interest and property of the Citie of London and the town of Gravesend in that great ferry, but also all those who have any other ferries upon the river of Thames ; for, if the watermen may freely carry and recarry to and from all places, it would be no benefit but an exceeding great losse to the owners of ferries to maintain boats, sails, oars, and men continually to attend upon the same, and are tyed to entertaine all passengers at small rates, by the statute of sixth Henry VIII., and by prescription before that time, which the owner of the ferry may not exceede ; but by this liberty desired the passenger is likely to be exacted upon, being left to the discretion of the watermen, who are not hereby compellible to attend.

6. " The overseers inhabiting in or neere the citie of London cannot conveniently commit offenders to the next prison from Cliff in Kent, or Reading in Barkshire. It were more necessarie that the Justices of the Peace next adjoyning should continue their power to punish watermen, being offenders, whose judgements are nothing inferior to the watermen.

7. " Hereby the right which owners of ferries have to place maisters in their own boats, and the power which the Lord Maior and other corporations have to displace insufficient maisters is taken away. In which acte is no permission for seamen and mariners, but are restrained unless they be first allowed ; and the watermen are not compellible to allow but whom they please, neither is it provided what shall be given or taken for such allowance, so that by such desired liberty the owners of ferries and mariners to be employed upon the river are like to be subject to the exaction of the watermen.

8. " In the third acte none may presume to use the trade but watermen, and with this no watermen shall have to do with landmen, so that the owners of ferries being altogether landmen, shall be altogether barred both from watermen, mariners and landmen to guide or row their boats ; whereby western barges and boats are included ; whereby allowance and disallowance desired by this acte will draw a great charge upon passengers and provision coming or brought to the citie.

9. " The overseers would have power to take away any man's servants, perhaps against the will both of master and servant,

and the colour of this allowance will be a meanes to draw charge upon the poorer sort of the Company.

10. " This acte is in nature of a presse, which the overseers would have power at all times to execute upon such against whom they shall at any time conceive malice or offence. And it is desired that the masters of the Trinity House may be called to the acte."

In the course of this year the Dutch engineer, Vermuyden, was employed repairing the Longbank, protecting the Dagenham and Barking levels, and the valley of the river Lea.

1622. On the morning of January 3rd, 1622, the Thames shifted four tides in five hours—two floods and two ebbs—and then resumed its normal course.

At the end of January the Court of Aldermen of the City of London, upon receipt of a letter from the Portreeve and Steward of Gravesend regarding the Ferry service between that town and London, directed Thomas Jones of Gray's Inn, the Common Serjeant and Messrs. Stone and Peter Pheasant, to confer with the Council of that town, " touching the orders offered by the Portreeve, Jurats and inhabitants of the towns and parishes of Gravesend and Milton, to be observed concerning the ferry and passage from Gravesend to London, and to report in writing thereon what they conceived fitting for the Court to do for the maintenance of both ferries."

John Stone and Peter Pheasant certified to the Lord Mayor and Court of Aldermen : " In their opinion the Orders proposed would not be prejudicial to the City's ferry, but a means to help them of Gravesend, for the better and more orderly government and maintenance of their ferry."

In July, John Taylor and Job Pennell performed a voyage with a pair of oars from London to York, and Taylor wrote an account in verse, entitled, " A very Merry-Wherry-Ferry Voyage, or York for my Money." After stating that they commenced the voyage down the Thames in a wherry that had been in active service for four years, but which had been repaired and painted, he went on :

> " Thus being furnish'd with good wine and beer,
> And bread and meat (to banish hunger's fear)
> With Sails, with Anchor, Cables, Sculls and Oars,
> With Card and Compass, to know Seas and Shores,
> With Lanthorn, Candle, Tinder-box and Match,
> And with good courage, to work, ward, and watch,
> Well man'd, well shipp'd, well victual'd, well appointed,
> Well in good health, well timbered and well jointed,
> All wholly well, and yet not half fox'd well,
> 'Twixt Kent, and Essex, we to Gravesend fell.
> There I had welcome of my friendly Host,
> (A ' Gravesend ' trencher, and a ' Gravesend ' toast)
> Good meat and lodging at an easy rate,
> And rose betimes, although I lay down late."

Starting next morning with a flowing tide, they

> " . . . left Gravesend, rowing down the stream,
> And near to Lee,* we to an anchor came.
> Because the sand were bare, and water low,
> We rested there, till it two hours did flow ;
> And then to travel went our galley-foist."†

1622. John Chamberlain wrote on October 5th, to his friend Carleton : " On Sunday last, two or three boats were lost in the Thames, both above and beneath the bridge, in one of which ten persons were drowned, some Dutch and some English, who, having been at a marriage at Kingston, and packed thirteen in a wherry, the tempest rising towards

* Leigh.   † A long barge with oars.

eight o'clock at the night, were cast away 'twixt Westminster and the Strand. Only three were saved by strange accidents."

Dissatisfactions still rankling in the minds of the freemen of the Watermen's Company, eight of the Overseers, on November 20th petitioned the Privy Council to suppress the violent proceedings of their leader, David Parry, who, having arrested them all, threatened to overthrow the Company. Two days later an order was issued directing the Lord Mayor and Court of Aldermen to hear and determine certain matters in dispute between them and their rulers.

A more serious trouble pressed upon the watermen in the damage done to their occupation by the increasing use of coaches to the lessening of the river traffic in boats. John Taylor published this year a work entitled :

> " An errant thief,—whom every man may trust
> In work and deed exceeding true and just."

In this he alluded to the merits of watermen, and the injury inflicted on them by the swelling number of coaches :

> " Carroches, coaches, jades and Flanders mares,
> Do rob us of our share, our wares, our fares ;
> Against the ground we stand and knock our heeles,
> Whilst all our profit runns away on wheeles.
> And whosoever but observes and notes
> The great increase of coaches and of boates,
> Shall find their number more than e'er they were
> By halfe and more, within these thirty yeares ;
> The watermen at sea had service still,
> And those that stay'd at home had worke at will :
> Then upstart hel-cart coaches were to seek,
> A man could scarce see twenty in a weeke ;
> But now I thinke a man may dayly see
> More than the Wherrys on the Thames can be."

He vowed it was not fit that :

> " Fulsome madams, and new scurvy squires,
>   Should jolt the streets at pomp, at their desires,
>   Like great triumphant Tamburlaines, each day,
>   Drawn with the pamper'd jades of Belgia,
>   That almost all the streets are chok'd outright,
>   Where men can hardly pass, from morn till night,
>   Whilst watermen want work."

In the course of this year an Abstract was made of the evidence of witnesses, " whose names and references to their depositions are given in the margin in the case of Johnson, owner of the ' Hopewell,' against Hurlock, owner of the ' Ann Speedwell,' which was run down and sunk in the Thames by the ' Ann Speedwell,' 28th Oct., 1618 ; the witnesses being on the side of Hurlock, to prove that the ' Hopewell ' hung out no lights, and that they called aloud to give her warning."

1623. In 1623, Sir Simonds D'Ewes wrote in his diary : " There happened about this time little less than a prodigy in the river Thames, for on Sunday, January 19th, towards the evening, it flowed three several times in five hours ; and during the same time in divers places not far distant from each other, it ebbed one way and flowed another ; and the next day flowed twice and ebbed twice in three hours. I spake with some of the ancient watermen about it, and they affirmed the like had never happened in their memories, but a little before the rising of Robert D'Evereux, Earl of Essex, towards the latter end of Queen Elizabeth's reign." Thomas Locke said, " The Thames of late has had double tides " ; and John Chamberlain's testimony was that, " the tides have ebbed and flowed twice in twenty-four hours."

Since 1606 the fight over the vested interests of the barge-owners in the Long Ferry from Gravesend had raged not only before the Magistrates, but in street battles. The watermen of Gravesend, aided the aggrieved owners, and this year the Corporation appealed for support against their violent practices to the Lord Mayor and Aldermen of London, who submitted the application to the Privy Council. The result was another code of bye-laws, under their sanction, for the regulation and protection of the Long Ferry. Soon after a compromise was effected with the barge-owners by admitting the masters of the tilt boats into the service on payment of an annual rent, and the Corporation assumed the entire management of the Ferry, according to the following entry in their records : " This 18 day of February, the Portreve, Jurats and Inhabitants did take the ferry into their possession, and the masters of the tilt-boats are, from the 18 of the month of March to pay 16d. the tide to the Corporation, according to ancient orders."

John Chamberlain wrote from London to Sir Dudley Carleton, on June 14th : " A tide-boat, with more than thirty passengers, by negligence or want of skill, run upon a hoy that was under sail 'twixt this and Gravesend, so that there were fourteen drowned. The rest very narrowly escaped."

On June 9th, a Petition of Fishermen of the river Thames between Staines and Yantlet, was submitted to the King, " reciting that, with a view to the reformation of abuses in the matter of fishing, they were desirous of being incorporated and entrusted with powers for that purpose. Aiming at no intrusion upon the privileges of the City of London, they had petitioned the Lord Mayor and Court of

Aldermen for their assistance, who had referred the matter to a Committee. The House of Commons, upon consideration of the Petitioners' Bill, had much commended it, but the Lord Mayor and Aldermen, having since been informed by some who wished the interruption of the design, had forborne to put forward their request. The Petitioners therefore prayed his Majesty to recommend their suit to the Court of Aldermen."

In response to this Petition, the King caused an order to be issued from the Court at Greenwich, running : " As he conceived the endeavour of the Petitioners would tend to the preservation of fish, he desired the Lord Mayor and Aldermen, if the liberty and privileges of fishing in the River Thames between Staines Bridge and the waters of Medway of right belonged to the City of London, to consider the said Petition, and certify what they thought meet to be done for furtherance of the suit."

John Taylor undertook, in 1623, yet another voyage in his boat, this time from London to Salisbury, etc. Arthur Bray, a waterman of Lambeth, was " gunner." A book followed, named " A new discovery by Sea, with a wherry, from London to Salisbury, etc." ; and the commencement of the trip was described as follows :

" As some accounts in almanacks agree,
　The yeere called sixteen hundred twenty-three,
　That Juyles twenty-eight : two houres past dinner,
　We with our wherry, and five men within her,
　Along the christall Thames did cut and curry,
　Betwixt the Counties Middlesex and Surrey ;
　Whilst thousands gaz'd, we pas't the bridge with wonder,
　Wheere fools and wize men go above and under.
　We thus our voyage bravely did begin
　Down by St. Katherine's, where the priest fell in ;

By Wapping, where as hang'd, drown'd pirats dye,
Or else such rats I thinke as would eat pie.
And passing further, I at first observed
That cuckolds' haven was but badly served,
For there, old time had such confusion wrought,
That of that ancient place remained nought.
From thence to Debtford we amaine were driven,
Whereat an anker unto me was given;
With parting pints and quarts for our farewell
We took our leaves, and so to Greenwich fell;
There shaking hands, adieus, and drinking store,
We took our ship again, and left the shore,
Thence down to Erith 'gainst the tyde we went,
Next London's greatest maior's town in Kent,
Or Christendome, and I approve it can,
That there the Maior was a Waterman,
Who governs, rules, and reigns sufficiently,
And was the image of authority.
With him we had cheap reck'nings and good cheere,
And nothing but his friendship we thought deere :
But thence we rows'd ourselves, and cast off sleep,
Before the daylight did begin to peep.
The tyde by Gravesend swiftly did us bring,
Before the morning lark did begin to sing."

At this time Taylor wrote a prose tract called
"The World runs on Wheels." In this he said :
"I do not inveigh against any coaches that
belong to persons of worth or quality, but only
against the caterpillar swarm of hirelings. They
have undone my poor trade, whereof I am a member ;
and though I look for no reformation, yet I
expect the benefit of an old proverb, 'Give the
losers leave to speak. . . .' This infernal swarm
of trade-spillers (coaches) have so overrun the
land that we can get no living upon the water ;
for I dare truly affirm that every day in any term,
especially if the Court be at Whitehall, they do rob
us of our livings, and carry five hundred sixty fares
daily from us." This eccentric waterman kept
a public-house in Phœnix Alley (near Long Acre).

2C

On November 21st, John Chamberlain wrote in a letter to Sir Dudley Carleton : " Parker, a Papist, was drowned in crossing the river, with a youth and maiden whom he was carrying over for education in foreign seminaries."

1624. In 1624 an Act of Parliament was passed " For the conveyance of Oxford freestone by water to London, and for coals and other necessaries from London to Oxford, now coming at a dear rate only by land carriage, whereby the roads are becoming exceedingly bad." This Act shews that the river was already navigable from London to Burcot, and for many miles above Oxford ; but hitherto only a few barges proceeded higher up than Marlow or Bisham. There were, as in Elizabeth's time, seventy locks between Abingdon and London, sixteen flood-gates and seven weirs. Eight commissioners were appointed to carry out the authorized works for the further improvement of the river, and licence was given to bargemen and others, in consideration that the passage from Burcot to Oxford was against stream, to hale their barges by winches, ropes, and engines, worked by men and horses from the banks of the river. The deepening of the navigation for a length of about seven miles, under the provisions of this Act, placed London in direct water communication with several inland counties, causing a rapid increase of trade and the employment of greater numbers of watermen and bargemen.

An order was issued on October 14th for paying £9 9s. 8d. to Maximilian Coulte, carver, " due to him amongst many other charges for making a new barge for his Majesty's late dearest wife the Queen." Another order was issued for paying

to the same carver, " the sum of 63*l*. 3s. 4d., due to
him as an arrear for works by him done upon his
Majesty's new privy barge."

1625. On February 2nd, 1625, William Burrell
submitted a petition to the Duke of Buckingham,
"to help him out of a vexatious partnership with
Innocent Lanier, one of the King's Musicians, in
taking up ballast out of the Thames. Has disbursed
1850*l*. in engines, lighters, etc., but receives little
benefit. Lanier caused great inconvenience to shipping by cutting the ropes of his ballast engines, so
that there was no ballast ready. Will sell him the
business at a loss, but will no longer be partner
with him."

On March 4th, a letter from London to the Rev.
Joseph Mead stated : " On Saturday likewise, was
here the highest spring-tide that in thirty or forty
years hath been remembered, whereby very much
hurt is done here in merchandize, and along the
river on both sides in cattle." Of this tide John
Chamberlain wrote to Carleton : " The day I wrote
last, being the 25th of February, here happened a
great disaster, by reason of highest tide that hath
been known in the memory of man, which did great
harm in Thames Street, and all along the river-side,
insomuch that Westminster Hall was full three
feet in water all over."

COMMERCE AND TRADE ALONG THE RIVER.

1603. Sir Robert Cecil, the deformed and clever son of the late Lord Treasurer Burleigh, had attained much authority at the close of Elizabeth's reign, and contrived to retain his office of Secretary at the new Court. He had interests in some commercial enterprises, and at the time a quantity of sugar and pepper belonging to him rested at Ralph's Quay—then known as one of the " fairest " on the river—the merchant who held it, John Plumpton, solicited the Secretary's favour in behalf of his friend John Ramridge, " an honest merchant of London and a languaged and learned man," who desired the appointment of a deputy for farming the silks.

When James ascended the English throne the merchants of London were busy projecting commercial ventures to new and distant lands. One of these, a Muscovy merchant named Francis Cherie, fitted out a vessel called the " Grace," of fifty tons burden, for a trading voyage to Cherry Island in the Russian seas. The vessel, under the command of Stephen Bennet of St. Katherine's, and having on board William Gorden, factor and overseer (who wrote a relation of the trip), sailed from London on April 10th, and, after a successful voyage, arrived back in the Thames on September 10th.

Richard Carmarthen, in June, was promised the reversion of the post of overseer of the Little Customs of London.

At this time the Customers at the Port of London, and their salaries per annum, were as follows : one Collector of the Subsidy on imports, £400 ; One Collector for the Subsidy on exports, £76 13s. 4d.; one Collector of the Petty Custom on exports, £277 6s. 8d. ; one Collector of the Petty Custom on imports, £62 6s. 8d. ; two Collectors of the Ancient Custom, each £50 ; one Surveyor, £300 ; one Comptroller of the Subsidy, £255 ; one Comptroller of the Ancient Custom, £30 ; one Comptroller of the Petty Custom, £20 ; one Searcher, £20 ; one Usher of the Custom House, £4 ; eighteen Waiters, each £44 ; one Pricker of the Steel Yard.

In July a ship at Blackwall, belonging to Alderman Halmeden, was wantonly fired, and the blazing vessel drifted on the tide to Greenwich, where by setting some outbuildings alight the whole town was put in danger, and it was only by energetic action that a general conflagration was prevented.

About the end of September the 50-ton barque, " Elizabeth " of London, commanded by Captain Bartholomew Gilbert, came up the Thames to Ratcliffe, on her return from a voyage to Virginia, which had started from Plymouth the previous May 10th. Gilbert, in his account of the trip, concluded by saying they arrived back, " finding the City most grievously infected with a terrible plague."

The business of life had to be carried on despite the evils of pestilence. At the moment a horrible form of death was in their midst, the Bailiffs and

Freemen of the ancient royal town of Kingston were granted a Charter—dated at Westminster on November 17th, giving them divers privileges and a weekly market on Saturday. The grant recited that during the time of this market " all and singular persons coming and resorting to that market, may and may be able for ever henceforth to sell, buy and expose for sale all and all kinds of animals and live cattle, as well as horses, mares, colts, fat oxen, lean oxen, bullocks, cows, calves, heifers, sheep, lambs, hogs, as other living animals of whatsoever kind, nature or species they may or shall be, at their pleasure." Further, the Bailiff and Freemen " may have and take so much and such like usual toll, tollage, profits, advantages, and customs as and such as, and in as ample a manner and form as is accustomed and used, or as lawfully can or ought to be had or taken in any other market within this our realm of England." A Court of Record was to be held every Saturday before the Bailiffs and the Steward of the Court of the town. One prison or gaol was allowed within the town or the precincts of its liberties, for the safe custody of offenders.

The trade of Henley, Maidenhead, and other towns along the upper river consisted principally of corn, malt, flour, wood, wool, and cattle.

1604. On January 12th, 1604, a warrant directed that Sir Thomas Vavasour should be paid £1,000 in discharge of composition for the butlerage of the Port of London.

Captain Charles Leigh, in the 50-ton barque " Olive Plant," with Captain Martin Pring and a crew of forty-six men and boys, sailed on March 21st from Woolwich, on a voyage to Guiana, for the purpose of starting a settlement and plantation.

Four days later, Captain Henry Middleton sailed from Gravesend on his voyage to the Moluccas for the East India Company, which, since its foundation in 1599 and first venture with four ships to the Far East in 1600, had steadily grown in importance and wealth.

On April 15th, the "God-speed," of 60 tons, commanded by Stephen Bennet, and having on board Thomas Welden, a merchant, and thirteen men and boys, sailed from London on a second trading voyage to Cherry Island. The mate was Jonas Poole, who wrote an account of the expedition. After a successful venture they arrived back in the Thames on October 15th.

The growing trade with the northern parts of Russia prompted the cultivation of friendly relations with the government of that country, and on June 10th, Sir Thomas Smith, a great city merchant, accompanied by Sir T. Challoner, Sir W. Wray, and several other gentlemen and attendants, went to the Court at Greenwich, and kissed hands on his departure on an Embassy to the Czar. The Ambassador and his train sailed on the 13th from Gravesend for Archangel, on board the "John and Francis Admiral."

In August a new Charter of Incorporation was granted to the Fishmongers of London, confirming their Court of Assistants, and giving the Company the power of making bye-laws, together with other privileges.

On October 13th, a Grant was made at Westminster, renewing the former Charters and confirming the ancient privileges of the Corporation of the Masters and Brethren of the Trinity House at Deptford Strond. This Society exercised the powers granted them by Henry VIII. in 1515, for the promotion of commerce and navigation by licensing and regulating pilots, and ordering and erecting beacons, light-houses, buoys, etc. ; and its members at this time consisted nearly, if not wholly, of seamen.

On St. Stephen's Day a letter was sent from Whitehall to the Lord Mayor instructing him to appoint Richard and Robert Wright, joint-packers of woollen cloths, etc., and porters of strangers' goods, in and out of the Port of London.

1605. In February, 1605, the Earl of Cumberland ordered the Farmers of the Customs to licence Peter van Lore to ship from the Port of London certain cloths free of custom.

On April 8th, the Earl of Dorset ordered the Farmers of the Customs to allow certain quantities of beer, wheat, and candles to be shipped for the use of Sir Edward Conway, Lieutenant Governor of the Brill.

Sir Oliph Leigh, of Kent, having fitted out and well-manned a ship named the " Olive-blossom," to reinforce his brother, Captain Charles Leigh—who the previous year went out to form a plantation in Guiana—despatched the vessel from Woolwich on April 14th, under the conduct of Captains Cataline and Nicholas Sainct-John. Many of these new settlers were massacred by the Indians in the following August.

In the middle of April the Levant merchants received a royal order to meet for the purpose of regulating their trade ; and the King, on the expiration of their second Charter, incorporated a perpetual Company with the designation of " The Merchants of England trading to the Levant Seas."

On April 23rd, the Thames Shipwrights were granted Incorporation under letters-patent, by the style of " Masters, Wardens, and Cominaltie of Shipwrights of London."

Captain Stephen Bennet and the Muscovy merchant, Thomas Welden, sailed from London on May 1st, in a ship of 60 tons, with a crew of twenty-two men and boys, on a third voyage to Cherry Island. They returned to the Thames, after a successful trip, on the following August 24th.

1606. In February, 1606, the officers of the Customs in the Port of London petitioned the King for redress against certain merchants, who, since the meeting of Parliament on January 21st, had refused to pay their fees on the ground that the Customs were let to farm. Suggestions were offered for a remedy of the grievance, but it is doubtful if any action was taken.

On April 18th, Captain John Knight, in the " Hopewell " or " Hopefull," of 40 tons, sailed from Gravesend, for the discovery of the North West Passage. The vessel was manned and victualled at the cost of the Muscovy and East India Companies. Later John Knight and three of his crew were killed by savages on a large island in the North American seas.

The East India Company entered into an Agreement, on May 10th, with a Wharfinger as follows :

" This Bill witnesseth, That it is covenanted concluded and agreed between Thomas Watson, Wharfinger of Custom House and Wool Quays, and the Committees for the East India Company, in form following, viz. :—That the said Committees do promise to pay unto the said Thomas Watson, or his assigns, for lighterage, wharfage and craneage, all and other things necessary to this effect, the sum of 3d. for every bag, bale,

canister, hogshead or cask.   In consideration whereof the said
Thomas Watson doth for himself and his assigns covenant promise
and agree to and with the said Committees : That he the said
Thomas Watson at his own proper cost and charges shall find
sufficient staunch and strong lighters and able cranes and men
for carrying and craneing of the said Company's goods now to
be unladen out of their ships lately arrived in the river of Thames.
And further to satisfy the said Company for whatsoever damage
shall happen unto the same goods by the insufficiency of any
of the lighters or cranes, crane-ropes or slings he shall set to work,
or by the default or unfaithfulness of any person whatsoever he
shall employ about the same lighters, cranes or wharfs or any
of them.   And further to carry aboard the said Company's
ships in his said lighters all such bags, empty casks and other
things as shall be needful to be employed for the same goods
without demanding anything for the same.   And to conclude
it is further agreed by and between the said parties, that if at
any time in the performance of the premises the said Thomas
Watson shall be found to deal otherwise than shall be fitting for
the good of the Company : Or if any other will serve the Company
from Blackwall better cheap than is formally agreed upon :
That then and in such case it shall be free for the said Committees
to make choice of others, or to employ the said Thomas Watson
still at their will and pleasures unto the performance whereof
we do bind ourselves by this our present writing."

In May Captain Stephen Bennet and Thomas
Welden sailed from London in a ship of 60
tons, manned with twenty-two men and boys
on a fourth trading voyage to Cherry Island.
A pinnace of 20 tons with Jonas Poole—who wrote
an account of the voyage—as master and eight
men, accompanied the larger vessel. This trip
was fitted out by Master Russell of the Muscovy
Company, and the adventurers arrived back in the
Thames on August 15th.

Merchants were at this time much harassed by
the constant loss of ships and cargoes and the
killing of their crews by pirates, who did not confine

their depredations to the high seas, but with reckless hardihood sailed up rivers, and seizing their prey made off, generally with impunity. The crowd of rich vessels entering the mouth of the Thames offered a tempting bait to these rovers, and considerable damage was inflicted on the commerce of the river. At times when the depredations became more bold and frequent the sufferers directed urgent appeals for protection to the authorities, and, as happened in this June, a proclamation would be issued for the search and apprehension of pirates ; but after the capture and hanging in chains of sundry freebooters at Wapping, vigorous action against them again languished.

On Saturday, December 20th, two ships, going to the planting of the Southern Colony of Virginia, sailed from the Thames, having on board Mr. Percy, · brother of the Earl of Northumberland, four of the Council of the Company, a clergyman, artificers, tools and ammunition. A Charter had been given this year to a Company called the " South Virginia Company, or the London Adventurers " ; and a patent granted to Sir Thomas Gates, Sir George Somers, Edward Wingfield, Mr. Hakluyt (author of the " Voyages,") and others, for all lands in America between the 34th and 41st degrees of north latitude, comprehending what are now called Maryland, Virginia, and Carolina.

1607. Towards the end of January, 1607, the East India Company sent the following resolution to the Lord High Admiral : " Whereas we are informed that there is a press for men to be sent down to Chatham, and we are in doubt that thereby our men appointed for bringing in one of our ships into the dock at Deptford may be pressed thither, the which will prove an exceeding hindrance unto the voyage which we are now in hand to prepare for the East Indies. We humbly pray that your Lordship will be pleased to grant your warrant that our men may not be taken from us in this time of necessity ; and so much the rather as the omitting of this opportunity of bringing the said ship now into the Dock may be the overthrow of our said intended voyage." Notwithstanding the difficulties and discouragements of their commerce with India, some members of the Company courageously persevered in adventuring a third voyage, and with promises of support from the Government, opened a subscription for a new stock, which produced £53,500. Their ships, " Dragon " and " Hector," were fitted out, to which was added the " Consent," of 115 tons. The last-named, commanded by Captain David Middleton, sailed from the Thames in March ; and the two first-named vessels, under Captain Keeling, left the Downs in April. This voyage proved successful, and Capt. Keeling brought the " Hector " back in 1610, without the loss of a single man.

In September the Company hired of a Mr. Greet a Dock and Yard at Deptford, for £30 per annum.

Henry Hudson sailed from Gravesend on May 1st, in the " Hopewell," on his first voyage to find the North-West Passage. Before sailing, Hudson, his son John, a lad of sixteen or eighteen, and his crew, communicated together in the Church of St. Ethelburga, in Bishopsgate.

In October, Anthony Ingram was appointed for life to the office of Comptroller of the Customs in London.

1608. Several members of the East India Company

merchant, notwithstanding his office of Collector of Customs in the Port ; the proposal of the King to the City of London for establishing an English settlement in the much depopulated province of Ulster, which, being accepted, three hundred persons of all sorts of handicrafts and occupations were sent over, and £20,000 raised for the formation of the new plantation ; and the granting in November to Sir James Creichton, Collector of Petty Customs in the Port, of all sums due to the late Queen, or the King therefrom.

1610. Early in 1610 the King granted the East India Company a new Charter, because of the " profit and honour which this trade brought to the nation, wherefore his Majesty was now induced to render the Company perpetual." In the spring the Company raised a capital of £80,163, and sent out a fleet on a sixth voyage, to establish an advantageous trade in the Red Sea. The ships were the " Trades Increase," " Peppercorn," and " Darling," together with a barque as victualler, all under the command of Sir Henry Middleton.

On March 1st, Sir Thomas Smith and other members of the Muscovy Company sailed from Blackwall in the " Amitie," of 70 tons, under the command of Jonas Poole, with a crew of fourteen men and a boy, for Cherry Island, and for further discoveries towards the North Pole with a view to finding a trading passage that way. They dropped down the river to Gravesend, and on the third day were at the Nore, finally getting away to sea on the 9th. The venture was successful commercially, and they returned to London on August 31st.

On April 17th, Henry Hudson sailed from London on a voyage to discover the North-West Passage, in

2D

a vessel fitted out by Sir John Wolstenholm, Sir Dudley Digges, and others. He wrote in his Journal : " We brake ground and went down from St. Katherine's Pool, and fell down to Blackwall ; and so plied down to Leigh, which was the two-and-twentieth day. The two-and-twentieth I caused Master Coleburne to be put into a Pink, bound for London, with my letter to the Adventurers, importing the reason wherefore I so put him out of the ship, and so plied forth." Abacuk Prickett, who wrote an account of the voyage, said of their return later in the year, that after touching at Plymouth they came by the Downs to Gravesend, " where most of our men went ashore, and from thence came on this side Erith, and there stopped ; where our Master Robert Billet came aboard, and so had me up to London with him, and so we came to Sir Thomas Smith's together."

In the autumn some supposed Spanish ships, on their way to Hamburg, were seized and brought into the Thames ; but they were soon after liberated on the demand of Portuguese merchants, who proved that the vessels were entirely their property.

1611. The seventh voyage of the East India Company was undertaken, with a capital of only £15,364, and a single ship, named the " Globe," under the direction of two merchants who had been in India, in the Dutch service. The ship with Captain Anthony Hippon as master, sailed from Blackwall on January 5th, 1611, and at about five o'clock in the afternoon anchored at Gravesend to await the first favourable wind, and finally leaving the Downs on February 5th. This venture ultimately produced 218 per cent. to the proprietors.

The eighth voyage of the Company was subscribed

for with a capital of £55,947, and the ships " Clove,"
" Hector," and " Thomas " sailed in April, under
the command of Captain Saris. All the vessels
ultimately returned to England, loaded with pepper :
that of Captain Saris, having visited Japan, arrived
in September, 1614. The profit of this voyage
was 211 per cent.

On March 31st, Jonas Poole was appointed
by the Muscovy Company master of the barque
"Elizabeth," of 50 tons, with a commission to proceed
on a voyage of discovery to the northward of Greenland. Purchas said that Poole " was, as I have
heard, miserably and basely murdered betwixt
Ratcliffe and London after his return from this
voyage."

On the same date the Muscovy Company gave a
Commission " for Thomas Edge our servant, appointed to go as our factor in the ship called the
' Mary Margaret,' of the burden of 150 tons, for the
killing of the whale and ' morses ' upon the coast
of Greenland, or any other place in the North
Ocean."

A Greenland discovery fleet, fitted out by
the English Company trading with Russia,
sailed from Blackwall on April 11th. The
expedition consisted of four ships, the " Mary
Margaret," of 150 tons, and a crew of forty-nine
men and boys ; the " Elizabeth," of 60 tons, and
a crew of eighteen men and boys ; the "Amitie,"
of 70 tons, and a crew of twenty-four men and boys,
and the " Resolution," with a crew of about sixteen
men and boys. Captain James Vadun, of Rotherhithe, in command of the " Amitie," bound for the
river Pechora, had with him as chief pilot, William
Gourdon, of Hull, who wrote an account of the

voyage. Foul weather soon separated the vessels
after they got to sea.

On October 2nd, Sir Robert Shirley—who in the
previous summer had been on an embassy to the
Persian Court—had an audience at Hampton Court,
when he delivered his letters and submitted a
Commission to the King containing the offer of a
free commerce for his subjects throughout the
Persian dominions.

1612.   Early in January, 1612, a ship bound for
the Straits sank between London and Gravesend.
The capital subscribed for the ninth voyage of
the East India Company was £19,164, and only a
single ship, the "James," was despatched in
February, under Captain Marlow. She arrived
back in 1615, and her cargo realised a profit of 160
per cent. While members of the Company were
fitting out the "James," others subscribed £46,092
for what was accounted the tenth voyage, and the
"Dragon" and "Hosiander," under Captain
Thomas Best, a brave and prudent officer, sailed
from Gravesend and anchored at Tilbury Hope,
on February 1st, as the commencement of the long
trip. Captain Best arrived back in the Thames on
June 15th, 1614, and his cargoes realised a profit
of 148 per cent. A party of the Company also
raised a stock of £10,669, and sent a ship, the
"Salomon," from the Thames, with those above,
for bringing home the remaining property of the
adventurers in the third and fifth voyages; and
after an absence of only twenty months returned with
a cargo, which realised a profit of 340 per cent.

John Chamberlain, in a letter from London, on
the 12th, to his friend Sir Dudley Carleton, wrote :
" The last week, four good ships went hence for the

East Indies, but missed some of their mariners, who, seizing on a Low Country vessel that lay in the river, have carried her away no man knows whither."

On August 22nd, Captain Samuel Castelton, in the " Pearl," departed from Blackwall for Gravesend on the commencement of the eleventh East Indian voyage. Little progress was made at first through contrary winds, and it was November 5th before they arrived at the Land's End.

The Virginia Company obtained, on March 12th, a third Charter from the Crown.

On April 7th, Jonas Poole, with two ships, the " Whale " and " Seahorse," sailed from Blackwall, on a voyage to Cherry Island and Greenland, for the Muscovy Company.

On the 28th, the " Plough," in which were Sir Thomas Gates and Sir George Somers, dropped down the river to Gravesend, and anchored at Tilbury Hope, finally sailing for Bermuda on May 5th. This vessel suffered shipwreck on arrival at its destination.

1613. A stock of £7,142 being raised for the twelfth voyage of the East India Company—chiefly undertaken for the purpose of carrying out Sir Robert Shirley as Ambassador to Persia—the " Expedition," of 260 tons, commanded by Captain Christopher Newport, sailed from Gravesend on January 7th, 1613. The ship carried fifty-six persons, besides the Ambassador and his fifteen followers. This voyage was the last conducted as a separate concern, and the ship returned in July, 1614, with a cargo of pepper, which realised a profit of £133 18s. 4d. on every £100 of capital.

On October 19th, Nicholas Downton, in the " Peppercorn," East Indiaman, of 250 tons, returned from the sixth voyage to the East, after an absence of three years. " The nineteenth in the morning at six o'clock, we set sail (from the Downs), and at night we anchored at Tilbury. The twentieth in the morning, we set sail, and at ten a clock we anchored at Blackwall ; where in the afternoon came down Master Deputy, and divers of the Committees, unto whom I delivered up my charge. And so concluded this our tedious and out-trying journey."

At the same time Mons. J. Luntius wrote from the Hague to Ralph Winwood : " Your London has been more fortunate than our Holland, having received within its port four ships from East India, laden with an unusual quantity of all kinds of spices. But we have lost two out of five, one near the island of St. Helena, the other in the very port of Texel, the loss of which is estimated at eighteen tons of gold, whereof they barely recovered one from the wreck, as the persons in charge of that business have informed me. There was in this ship a very great deal of cotton brought from China, and also porcelain. They came to the Hague to complain of their immense loss, and also to demand assistance against the power of the Portuguese in East India."

On Ascension-day, May 13th, five ships and a pinnace sailed from Queenborough on a Greenland voyage. They were the " Tiger," 260 tons, Admiral ; " Matthew," 250 tons, Vice-Admiral ; " Sea-horse," called the " Gamaliel," 200 tons, Rear-Admiral ; " Desire " ; " Annula," 140 tons, and the pinnace " Richard and Barnard," of 60 tons. The " John and Francis," 180 tons, followed shortly after. The ships on their return entered the Thames, September 6th.

William Baffin, in his account of this second

recorded voyage, wrote : " Being furnished with victuals and other provisions necessary for the killing of the whale, and twenty-four Basks, who are men best experienced in that faculty, at the charge and adventure of the right worshipful Sir Thomas Smith, Knight, and of the rest of the Company of Merchants trading into Muscovy, called the Merchants of New Trades and Discoveries. We came to Gravesend the 30th of April, where we stayed but one tide, and then weighed anchor about six o'clock at the evening, and plied to Tilbury Hope, remaining there all night. The next morning being the first of May we anchored again in Leigh Road, where we continued till the 4th of May, the wind keeping contrary to us, blew betwixt north and north-east. The fourth day about three o'clock afternoon we entered into the ' Swaile,' at Queen-borough, and rid at anchor there till the 13th of May. In which time, namely on the 7th of May, the King's ships came by us on their return out of Holland, from transporting the Count Palatine and the Lady Elizabeth, the King's only daughter. Before they came near us we caused our flags to be furled up, and when they passed by us, our Admiral shot off seven pieces of ordnance, our vice-admiral five, and our rear-admiral three ; and the Admiral of England, called the ' Prince,' gave us three pieces, and the rest of the King's ships each of them one. The 13th of May, about nine o'clock in the morning, we came forth of the ' Swaile,' and passed by the sands called the ' Spitts,' holding our course north-east and north-north-east."

On November 25th, John Chamberlain recorded that on Sunday a ship in the river was fired by mischance and quite consumed.

As shewing the growing wealth of English, and especially London commerce, the Customs of the country this year amounted to £148,075 7s. 8d., of which the City of London alone paid three-fourths, or £100,572 18s. 4d. Howe, in his edition of Stow, enumerated the various countries with which London traded at this period, and the articles imported, adding that it was " one of the best governed, most richest and flourishing cities in Europe, plenteously abounding in free trade and commerce with all nations."

The appointments in the Port were : William Carpenter and Thomas Matthew to the Office of Waiter; Thomas Ivatt and Sam. Jones to the Office of Searcher ; John Holloway, for life, to the Controllership of the Customs and Subsidies ; and John and Daniel Williams, of London, as Keepers of the Books of Entries of Ships coming into the Port with merchandise.

1614. On January 17th, 1614, a Court of the East India Company decided to commence the construction of a new Dock at Deptford ; and a crane was ordered to be fitted for the timber yard. A stone wharf had been built here for the Company, and the foundation of a storehouse laid.

A Committee was appointed on February 17th, to go down to Gravesend with the treasure for the fleet preparing to sail for the East ; and an allowance of £10 was made to the master of the King's barge for towing the Company's ships down to Gravesend. In March a project for making a rope yard and erecting iron works at Deptford was discussed.

The Company, resolving to have no more concern in separate voyages, opened a subscription for conducting the East India trade upon a joint-stock basis, all voyages henceforth being on account of the Company as one united body ; and that they might have the opportunity of regulating their subsequent conduct as circumstances might dictate, they agreed to limit the duration of the joint capital to four years. The stock thus subscribed amounted to £418,691, to be paid in by equal instalments in each of the four years. The first fleet equipped upon this account consisted of four good ships, which sailed in March, under the command of Captain Nicholas Downton. One of these vessels was the " New Yeares Gift," launched at Deptford, on January 1st.

In April a proposition was made to remove the Storehouse from Deptford to Blackwall, and a proposal considered to dig a dock and erect houses for building ships at Blackwall. These works were further discussed in May, and a Committee appointed to deal with the business. Among other matters considered were a request by Conne, the builder of the Deptford Wharf, of the desirability of taking a lease of the ground occupied at Deptford, and the attempt of a Mrs. Mowse to encroach upon the Company's land at Blackwall. On June 15th the ships " Dragon " and " Hosiander," under the command of Captain Thomas Best, arrived in the river from the tenth East Indian voyage, which was commenced on February 1st, 1612.

In the course of July a rate of twenty shillings an acre was laid by the Commissioners of Sewers, upon the Company's land at Blackwall. It was decided in September that a Rope-house at Blackwall was not to be built at present, and certain proceedings of Martyn, the anchor-smith at Deptford, were investigated. One of the Company's barges having been pressed to convey billets for the King to Whitehall, the Governor was requested to write to Lord Knollys, one of the Green-cloth, for its release. On November 9th, a Committee conferred with a Mr. Jones regarding buying his house at Blackwall.

In the middle of April, the Greenland fleet started to sail from the Thames, having on board William Baffin going on his third recorded voyage. Robert Fotherby wrote in his account of the voyage : " The ship ' Thomasine ' went down from Blackwall to Woolwich the sixteenth of April, and from thence to Gravesend the three and twentieth, where she remained until the eighth and twentieth of the same ; and weighing from thence she anchored again in Tilbury Hope, with ten ships more of good burden, and two pinnaces all of the Greenland Fleet, set forth also at the charge of the said Company, under the command of Master Benjamin Joseph, Chief Captain and General of the said Fleet. We set sail out of Tilbury Hope the fourth of May, and came to an anchor the same day in Leigh Road, where we stayed till the morning, then we set sail again, and went forth to sea before night. . . . The fourth of October the ship (' Thomasine ') came to Wapping with the whole number of men that she carried forth (myself excepted that was come before), being six and twenty, all in perfect health."

On September 8th, the Earl of Suffolk, from Northampton House, notified the Officers of Customs in the Port of London that the King having directed observance of the Charter granted to the Company of Merchants trading to France, no entry of goods exported to or imported from France was to be taken except from persons free of the Company.

Later in the month a proclamation was issued from Hampton Court, prohibiting the export of sheep wools, wool-fells, and fuller's earth, as injurious to the manufacture of cloth at home.

The Earl ordered the Officers of the Customs, on October 21st, to desist from charging the duties of Strangers on William Crasse, who had proved himself to be an Englishman; and on November 28th he directed the officers to suffer the Eastland merchants to re-transport their corn to foreign parts without the imposition of export duties, in case of its not finding a sale in England, although by Order of Council dated January, 1613, they were no longer free from import duties.

1615. On January 20th, 1615, a letter was sent from the Lord Mayor to Lord Chief Justice Coke, " reciting that ships laden with sea coals had been wont to ride at a portion of Tower Wharf, holden by grant from the King, for the better receipt of coals, which was also the most convenient place for coal ships to lie at, seeing that they had latterly been built of greater burden than before, and that on account of the shallowness of the water they could not well float at any other place; that carrs which conveyed such coals from the ships to the City had usually passed through the bulwark there, but Sir Jervis Elwes, late Lieutenant of the Tower, had prevented their passage, and the bulwark still remained shut up; the carrs had consequently to go so far round that the cost of carriage was doubled, and the ship-masters not having their wonted utterance by carrs, were forced to sell them to the woodmongers and other engrossers, who had lighters to fetch them, thereby increasing the prices. The dispute between the Lieutenant of the Tower and the Wharfingers having been referred to the Lord Chief Justice, the Lord Mayor had felt it right to acquaint him with these inconveniences."

The second fleet despatched by the East India Company on the joint stock account sailed from Gravesend this month, under the command of Captain Keeling, having on board Sir Thomas Roe, or Rowe, going as Ambassador to the Great Mogul. The fleet consisted of the "Dragon," "Lyon," "Peppercorn," and "Expedition"; the last-named commanded by Captain Walter Payton, who was now making his second voyage to the East Indies.

In consequence of the increased value of the commerce with the East Indies, Sir Thomas Rowe was appointed by the King his and the Company's Ambassador to the Great Mogul, "for treating with him about an intercourse of the commerce of England to and from East India."

The Court of the Company, in January, dealt with the detention of their ships at Gravesend, owing to the unreadiness of the bread-rooms; an offer to take a lease of 100 years, on certain conditions, of houses and a wharf at Deptford, rented from the Bridge-house lands trustees; the sending of Committees to Gravesend to secure the despatch of their ships, detained by the tides and inclement weather; and the ordering of a new ship, of between 500 and 600 tons burden, to be built, and alterations to one now building at Deptford.

A Court of the Company, on February 3rd, discussed a meeting of the Committee at Deptford, concerning shipbuilding, and the alteration of the docks, etc., there. It was ordered that the Committee of Blackwall should join with that of Deptford on matters of great importance. A letter was received from Mr. Baker certifying the misrule of some of the Company's factors at Gravesend; and another letter from the Lord Admiral wished to borrow from the Company timber for the King's ship "Vanguard." On April 13th, Captain Middleton was granted leave of absence to enable him to settle his business, provided he was at Gravesend on the Monday, when the Committees intended seeing the Company's ships despatched away.

A Court, on July 28th, made an allowance to John Lamprey, the Company's officer at Blackwall; and ordered two hogsheads of beer to be provided for the men at the launch of a new ship at Deptford. During this month, Thomas Mun, now a well-known and successful merchant, was elected a Member of the Committee or a Director of the Company, and his life from henceforth was spent in actively promoting its interests. In September the lease of a house and erection of a smith's forge at Blackwall were dealt with; and the suit was refused of Richard Turner, woollen-draper, for employment, " he never having been abroad further than Gravesend."

On March 16th, the "Discovery," of 55 tons burden, commanded by Captain Robert Bileth, weighed anchor at St. Katherine's, and went with the tide to Blackwall, as the start of a voyage for the fourth attempt to discover the North-West Passage. The ship dropped down to Gravesend on the 17th, and the next day to Leigh, where she anchored for the night, and on the morrow put out to sea. William Baffin was on board, and in his account of the ensuing voyage, wrote : " The chief master and commander, under God, was

Robert Bileth, a man well experienced that ways (having been employed the three former voyages), myself being his mate and associate, with fourteen other men and two boys. This ship being in readiness, upon the 15th day of March came aboard Mr. John Wolstenholme, esquire, one of the chief adventurers, and with him Mr. Allwin Carye (husband for the voyage). Who, having delivered our master his commission, and read certain orders to be observed by us in the voyage, giving us good exhortations, and large promises of reward, as treble wages to all, if the action were performed, they departed, charging us to make what speed we could away. So the next day, being Thursday, we weighed anchor at St. Katherine's, and that tide came to Blackwall, and the next day to Gravesend; and the morrow after to Leigh. Sunday, the 19th, it blew hard at south-west, and by south, yet this day we came to anchor near the buoy on the Nore end. The 20th day the wind variable, but by two o'clock this afternoon we came to the North Foreland, where we stayed all the 22nd day, which day we weighed, and that night anchored in the Downs."

Sir Fulk Greville, from Austin Friars, on March 25th, intimated to the Officers of the Customs in the Port of London, that the dispute between Ralph Freeman & Co., late farmers of the pre-emption of tin, and Thomas Dunning & Co., the present farmers, having been decided, the Freeman Company was to be permitted to export tin in bars, according to agreement.

On April 25th a Grant was made at Westminster to Richard Warner, of Greenwich, master of the King's barges, of the sole right for twenty-one years to transport lampreys alive from the Thames to Holland and Zealand, as bait for catching ling and cod, on payment of twenty marks a year, provided he exported as many as might be required.

On Monday, June 8th, the Venetian Ambassador appeared before the Council at Greenwich, and discussed with them a matter connected with the Levant Company.

A Grant was made at Westminster on July 19th, to Richard Giles, of London, of the Office of seizing and burning all logwood and " deceitful " dyeing woods brought into the Port of London, and of keeping a register of all merchandise seized for not paying due customs to avoid its being discharged without due warrant from the Officers of the Customs.

A few days later the Earl of Suffolk ordered the Officers of Customs to permit English merchants to export and import goods in foreign bottoms till August 31st, notwithstanding the late proclamation. The Earl also, on October 16th, directed the officers of Customs to permit Sir Thomas Edmondes, Ambassador in France, to export salt, cheese, fish, candles, and butter for his own use.

1616. On February 3rd, 1616, an East Indian fleet, consisting of six " goodly " ships—" Charles," " Unicorne," " James," " Globe," " Swan," and " Rose "—sailed from Gravesend and fell down to Tilbury Hope. Captain Benjamin Joseph held the command, and accompanying the expedition was Edward Terry, Master of Arts and Student of Christ Church, Oxford, who wrote a relation of the voyage.

On March 26th, the " Discovery," of London, with Robert Bileth as master, and William Baffin as pilot, and having in all seventeen persons on board, sailed from Gravesend in very fair weather, on a fifth voyage for the discovery of the North-West Passage. The ship was fitted out at the charge of Sir Thomas Smith, Sir Dudley Digges, John Wolsten-holme, Alderman Jones, and others.

The next day, the Earl of Suffolk notified the Officers of the Customs at London that the King, having resolved that the operations of the new Company of Merchant Adventurers should proceed, no shipping of imports or exports to or from the places they trade with would be allowed by any not belonging to the Company, and no others were to export white cloth, etc.

A warrant was issued from Westminster on March 9th, for the delivery to Richard Crockford of the bonds, etc., for the recovery of the King's moiety of the fine to be paid by James Browne, brewer of Deptford, for unlawful brewing.

On September 3rd, John Chamberlain wrote, in a letter to Sir Dudley Carleton : " Our Greenland ships are come home, and have made a good voyage, having made more oil than they could bring away, and killed one hundred and thirty whales."

An Order of Council of November 26th to the Lord Treasurer, ran : " On consideration of the controversy between the Thames fishermen and the master of the King's barge, relative to the trans-portation of lampreys, it is ordered that until Christmas, 1617, the Officers of Customs allow the fishermen to tranport their lampreys, paying the customs thereon, and 1s. per 1,000 to Richard Warner, master of his Majesty's barge."

In April, James Maxwell was granted for life the Office of Collector of the Subsidy of Tollage in the Port of London. A similar grant was made on July 1st to Sir Richard Weston and Richard Weston of the Office of Collecting the Little Customs in the Port.

1617. On February 4th, 1617, the East India Company's fleet sailed from Gravesend, under the command of Captain Martin Pring, who was now sailing on his second voyage to the East. " Thursday the sixth, Master Maurice Abbot, Deputy, with divers of the Commissioners were aboard the ships, and mustered all our men and paid their Harborough (Hamburg) wages. The next day they departed, and all our men were entered into whole pay. After much foul weather, the fifth of March, we departed from the Downs." Among the transactions of the Company in September were : A decision to build a tenement on their waste land at Deptford ; discussions as to the alterations and additions to be made in the several departments of their premises at Blackwall, including the repacking and slaughter rooms ; referring the petition of Barrett for satisfaction for building works at Blackwall, and looking into the complaint against the officers at Blackwall of suffering bullocks to be killed during the present hot season. In October the Company gave twenty shillings to the wife of John Nash, shipwright, who was wounded at Blackwall, in a quarrel between the butchers and carpenters ; granted an annuity of £200 to Burrell " for his extraordinary pains at Blackwall in making the docks, overseeing the storehouses, and other works there " ; gave £20 to Nathaniel Salmon for his " extraordinary " services at Blackwall, and appointed John Bonfoye to pay wages at Blackwall, and Richard Hanley at Deptford. On November 18th the Company ordered five dozen leather buckets to be provided for Blackwall and

2E

five dozen for Deptford, to be hung up on their premises for use in case of fire. After four years of prosperous joint-stock trade, the stock of the Company was now currently sold at 203 per cent.

1618. At the end of January, 1618, an important fleet of East Indiamen was gathered at Gravesend, waiting for the order of the Committee to sail for the East. The Committee was instructed on the 27th to deliver commissions and despatches, and get the ships off for Surat as soon as possible. John Chamberlain, writing to Carleton on the last day of the month, said : " Our East Indian fleet is setting out, and some of them gone down to Gravesend. They go stronger and more than ever heretofore, being nine good ships and of great burden, three or four of them new built." On February 3rd the Committee was sent down to Gravesend to hasten the departure of the ships, and again on the 7th, when the allowance of powder and shot to each vessel was increased. The fleet sailed from Tilbury on the 18th, having on board Arnold Browne, who wrote on account of his Indian voyages, ending in August, 1622.

Among the matters discussed and settled by the Courts of the East India Company this year were : An award of forty shillings to Christopher Dive, Constable of Poplar and Blackwall, " owing to losses he sustained by the escape of one of his prisoners." A consideration of the extraordinary expenses incurred by the buildings at Blackwall, and improvements and new buildings here and at Deptford. The report of Burrell on the means of saving the Company £500 in the labourers' charges at their wharves, and on the purchase of timber. The proceedings of the Committees for the Yards of Deptford and Blackwall, and the conclusion of the business with Lord Wentworth for the Yards at the latter place. The lease of a house at Blackwall in the possession of John Lampier, and the report upon Nicholas Sadler's accounts, and building a house at Deptford. The construction of a new ship of 500 tons burden at Blackwall, and the wages of Andrew Burrell its builder. The naming of two new ships building at Blackwall and Deptford, as the "Ruby" and "Diamond." The petition of divers poor men of Blackwall, Ratcliffe, and Limehouse for employment, and their relief from the opposition of the Porters of London. The record of a survey of their workmen, who numbered 232 of Blackwall, and 337 at Deptford. And finally, on December 22nd, the order for the building of a great new ship at Deptford.

In September some of the Company's ships from the East arrived in the river, and a Committee was sent down to Gravesend to welcome the Commander, Lucas Anthemius, on his safe arrival.

Sir William Button was granted for life, in February, the Office of Overseer of the Little Customs, in the Port of London.

On July 22nd, a proclamation granted the Company of Pinmakers the pre-emption of pins imported, which were to be landed only in the Port of London.

In August the first African Company was incorporated by the King, who granted an exclusive Charter to Sir Robert Rich and other Londoners, for raising a joint stock for a trade to Guiana.

Between September 5th and 17th, the depositions were taken of William Heely, John Headland, and Thomas Edge, of London; Robert Salmon, of Deptford; Stephen Smith, of Gravesend; Thomas Wilkinson, of Ipswich; John Johnson, of Limehouse; and others, relative to the wrongs inflicted on the vessels of the Muscovy Company by the Hollanders.

A statement was made this year of the proceeds from the sale of five serviceable ships sold in the Thames for want of employment, and a note added of the loss likely to ensue to navigation if ships could not find employment.

1619. In 1619 the East India Company held frequent Courts for dealing with their rapidly swelling business. In January an order was given for building new ships at Deptford and Blackwall; record was made of a ship of great value lately arrived from Surat; instructions given for dividing the house of John Lempries at Blackwall between the Surgeon and Keeper of the Stores; and consideration given to the suit of " a poor fellow that lost his leg in the ' Hope,' " for some employment, when he was reprimanded, " to his face," for negligence is not attending at the Trinity House by appointment for the purpose of receiving a licence to row upon the Thames; he was therefore " rated," and ordered to wait on Mr. Salmon to be dealt with. In February it was decided to build victualling houses at Blackwall, " to prevent the men going forth to breakfast and afternoon drinkings." In March consideration was given to the business of obtaining a lease of the ground occupied by the Company at Blackwall direct from Lord Wentworth; and the alleged abuses in their affairs at Deptford were examined into. In April improvements at Blackwall were discussed. In May serious attention was devoted to a riot of the Carpenters of the King's Yard at Deptford, and the Company's Yards. Two or three hundred of them came, beating a drum, and violently took and carried away certain apprentices out of the Company's Yards at Deptford and Blackwall. A resolution was carried for punishing the mutinous ringleaders, and this was drastically carried out by summary dismissal from their service.

In July a lease of ground at Deptford was granted to Mr. Salmon for building on ; and Binyon was displaced on certain charges of corruption and William Phillippes appointed Measurer of Timber at Blackwall. In August consideration was given to the petition of James Barker, of Deptford, for Bustian's place of Nailer to the Company. Thomas Goodredge was dismissed from the Company's service at Deptford. Record was made on September 15th of the arrival of their ship " Anne " in the Downs, " and the landing of the Lord Ambassador (Sir Thomas Rowe), whose expenses, with his lady's, are to be defrayed to Gravesend, where a Committee will assemble to-morrow to conduct them to London ; a dozen coaches to be ready at Tower Wharf to carry him to his house." Two days later an order was given for unlading the " Anne " at Woolwich. Names were decided on for various new ships, now nearing completion— the great vessel at Deptford was called the " London," and that at Blackwall the " Exchange." Other smaller ships were called the " Hart," " Eagle," and " Roebuck." With regard to the command of these vessels, " Mr. FitzHerbert, thought to be a very worthy commander, to be conferred with for the chief place. Sir John Hambden referred for further consideration. Petition of a son of Sir John Watts to be employed in some place of command. Letter read from my Lord of Buckingham on behalf of Capt. Pennington, who was in the action with Sir Walter Raleigh, and is suitor for the chief place." On October 1st relief was granted out of the wages of Thomas Jackson and John Sownd to the Churchwardens and Overseers of the poor for the hamlet of Ratcliffe, for the benefit of their motherless children ; and at the same time it was decided to punish John Browne, carpenter in the " Anne," "a very mutinous person, proud, and a ringleader." A week later it was decreed that the principal mutinous members of the crew of the " Anne," especially John Browne and Alexander Eward, the two most notorious offenders, should be severely punished as an example to others. Some hard stones brought from Surat in the " Anne," as ballast, were given to the City of London for paving without Moorgate. Also notice was ordered to be given of the launch at Deptford of the new ship " Exchange."

On December 29th a gratuity was given to George Charles, who died shortly after of a hurt in the Blackwall Yard.

On May 18th, a proclamation was issued from Greenwich, " prohibiting the importation of whale fins by any but the Muscovy Company ; renewed because of neglect of the former proclamation of Sep. 11th, 1614."

A Treaty was concluded at London on July 7th for accommodating the differences and mis-understandings subsisting between the English and Dutch East India Companies, by eighteen commissioners appointed by the King on the one part, and ten deputies from the States General on the other. Immediately after the ratification the King knighted three of the Dutch negotiators.

On July 8th George Tucker, of Milton, and George his son, were granted the place of Searcher in the port of Gravesend. Two days later Sir John Wolstenholme, of London, and John Wolstenholme were granted the Office of Collector of Imposts outwards in the Port of London. On the 30th a Grant of Incorporation was made to the Tobacco Pipe Makers of Westminster.

A Grant of October 21st gave to Hugh and William Bullock, on the surrender of Hugh Bullock, the Keepership of the Books and Registers of the Ship's entries for Imports, and of the making of bills of ships laden in the Port of London.

1620. Early in February, 1620, the Surat fleet of the East India Company was mustering at Gravesend, and their Committees were busy providing for the proper manning and victualling of the ships, and getting them despatched. Complaints concerning the medical care of the fleet produced an order that the Surgeons' chests were to be carefully looked to. A doctor, named Woodall, and an apothecary were appointed to provide the surgery, and the " physical things " were to be sent to and examined by Dr. Atkins, one of the Company, and " a very honest and sufficient gentleman and great adventurer." Finally, all the things provided by Woodall for the Surgeons' chests, were sent to Drs. Torye and Raven, and on their approval were despatched to the respective ships at Gravesend.

The Fleet, consisting of four vessels—the " London " (flagship), 800 tons ; the " Hart," 500 tons ; the " Roe Bucke," 300 tons ; and the " Eagle," 280 tons—all under the command of

Captain Andrew Shilling—sailed for the East on the 26th. The "London," a new Deptford built Indiaman, had William Baffin as master, and left Gravesend on the 4th.

John Chamberlain wrote to Carleton on March 20th : "An East Indian ship, worth £16,000, lost between Gravesend and London, which, with quarrels among themselves, shakes the credit of the Company ; that of the Farmers of Customs is shaken by trade being at such a standstill." The ship was the "Anne," preparing to sail for Bantam under the command of Captain Towerson. The navigation of the river was much endangered by the wreck, which was so complete that nothing in her could be saved.

The East Indiaman, "Exchange," sailed for the East at this time.

On March 29th, the Company awarded a gratuity to Nathaniel Curtis, a labourer in their employ at Blackwall.

In the course of this year the Company sent out ten ships, and exported £62,490 of bullion, and £28,508 of merchandise. All the ships were detained in Indian waters to defend the Company's property against the Dutch, except one, which brought home a cargo of indigo, calicoes, drugs, etc., to the value of £108,887.

On June 23rd, the Brethren of the Trinity House requested leave of the Lord Admiral Buckingham for Edward Wilde, of Limehouse, to arm his ship the "John," of 160 tons, with two "sakers" and eight "mynions." A week or so later similar permission was desired for arming the "Grace" of London, with four "sakers" and eight "mynions." Other mercantile vessels belonging to London and other ports around the coast were similarly armed at this time, not only against pirates, but to enable them to offer defence when molested by their jealous Dutch rivals. An expedition was preparing for despatch against the fierce pirates of Algiers, who not only inflicted incalculable loss on merchant shipping sailing through the Mediterranean, but created terror by killing or selling into chained slavery the Christian crews of all vessels seized. On July 4th, the Marquis of Buckingham instructed Lord Digby, Robert Naunton, and others that three ships were still wanting for the expedition, and laid down that the Trinity House was to levy £1,000 yearly for supplying and furnishing them. Three days later, the Master and Brethren of the Trinity House advised the Council that "The Masters and Owners of ships agree to pay rates varying from 18d. to 3d. per ton, according to the places to which they trade, towards the contribution against pirates; desire a letter to the Custom House, that their Deputy may be allowed to collect the rates." The Council thereupon ordered the Farmers of the Customs in London "to allow no vessel to pass without paying the above rates, and to appoint a place for the Deputy of the Warden and Assistants of the Trinity House, Deptford Strond, to collect them."

On Saturday, October 6th, Captain Richard Jobson sailed from Gravesend on a voyage of discovery to Gambia. This expedition was fitted out by Sir William Saint John and others, and consisted of two ships, the "Sion" of 200 tons, and the "Saint John" of 60 tons. During the voyage the explorers sailed 960 miles up the river into the African continent.

At this time the Ordinances of the Company of

Free Shipwrights were regulated and approved by the Lord Mayor of London and Court of Aldermen, after existing by prescription for at least two hundred years. " The occasion that gave rise to the revision of their ordinances and of their being sealed with the seal of the Mayoralty was a dispute that had arisen between them and the Foreign Shipwrights who carried on their craft on the opposite side of the river at Redrithe or Rotherhithe. This commenced in 1613. The Foreign Shipwrights, so called from being outside the Liberties of the City, had, it appears, recently (1612) obtained a Royal Charter of Incorporation, acting upon which they sought to exact fines and impose duties upon the Free Shipwrights at that time working hard by at Ratcliffe, having previously been compelled to leave the crowded part of the City by reason of the noise occasioned by exercising their trade and from fear of fire. They immediately resented such restrictions being placed upon them, and presented their case before the Court of Aldermen. The commencement of the memorandum relating to their petition throws light upon the origin of their Company, and runs thus : ' Item. Whereas the Company of Shipwrights freemen of this City made their humble petition to this Court shewing thereby that tyme out of mynde they have bin and continued an ancient Guild or Fraternitie within the said City, and have been ever governed and ordered by the Lord Maior and Court of Aldermen as other the Guilds and Fraternities thereof have used to be, as by certain ordynaunces instituted for the good government of the said Guilde in the XXXVth yere of the reigne of King Henry the sixt, may more at lardge appeare, etc.' ; and then goes on to complain

of the Foreign Shipwrights' endeavours to impose
their ordinances upon them. Their case was
eventually referred to Mr. Recorder, Mr. Alderman
Leman, Mr. Alderman Harvey, Mr. Alderman
Cokayne, and Mr. Stone, who on the 28th of October
following presented their Report. In this they gave
a clear account of the rise and progress of the
Company of Free Shipwrights ; how that they
had always preserved their freedoms of the City,
even after they were compelled to leave their yards
adjoining the River Thames, and to cross the
River, without the City's Liberties, to Ratcliffe ;
and how upon examination the trades carried on by
them and the Foreign Shipwrights were very different
and ' may be reputed as two severall distinct
trades ' ; and they finished their Report by recommending the City to support the cause of the Free
Shipwrights, and that any expenses incurred by
them in defending themselves from their neighbours
should be borne by the City, provided they did not
exceed the sum of £30."

In the course of October, Stephen Aynscombe
presented a petition to the Commissioners of the
Treasury, " for a warrant to ship divers pieces of
ordnance of his manufacture from the seaside in
Sussex, in order to bring them to the market at
Tower Hill."

On December 24th the Solicitor-General was
ordered from Whitehall to draw up a patent
to Sackville Crow for the sole manufacture of iron
ordnance for the shipping of the kingdoms, except-
ing that of the King's service, on condition of his
setting unemployed bow-makers to work, keeping
the market on Tower-hill supplied, and not raising
the price above £13 per ton.

1621. In June 1621 propositions were presented to the Council for the better restraint of the unlawful transportation of ordnance—" that none be made but in two authorized foundries, all to be brought to the Tower Wharf and sold at East Smithfield, on certificate and bonds for its employment only in shipping and colonial forts," etc. An Order of Council issued from Whitehall on December 20th, referred to Lord Carew, Master of the Ordnance and the Commissioners of the Navy, " the consideration of a report by the Trinity House of eight or ten Dutch ships lately brought into the Thames, professing to be purchased by Englishmen, and requiring supplies of ordnance, although it is not quite certain whether they will be employed by Englishmen or strangers."

In July, the East India Company ordered the lease of the Stone Wharf at Blackwall, held of the Bridge House, to be let ; and the sale of iron and brass ordnance at Deptford. A Committee was appointed to deal with the building of a new ship at Deptford, and Burrell's contract for the construction was examined and sealed. Another ship was ordered to be built at Blackwall, and in August, after considering the estimates of competitors for its construction, that of Stephens for £400 was accepted, and it was to be launched at Christmas. The offer was referred to a Committee of John Freeman, the Company's carriage maker, to rent the Stone Wharf at Blackwall.

The Court of the Company in September instructed a Committee to order the mast making for the new ship at Blackwall of about 300 tons, to cost £16 ; and for that at Deptford of 600 tons, to cost £30. Acting on the opinion of Stone, " one of the Cities council," that the Company could not take assurance of the Causeway at Blackwall, in fee simple, as a freehold without incurring the danger of the Statute of Mortmain, it was agreed that first a lease of it should be taken for 500 years, and after that, if counsel so advised, the Company might take it at their pleasure, in fee simple.

The Court of the Company, in October, considered the ships to be set forth this year, and weighed the question whether the three ships now building at Woodbridge, Deptford, and Blackwall would not suffice for the Bantam and Surat trade, especially in view of the certainty that the Portuguese would make similar hostile attempts on their Persian fleet next year as they had done this.

Captain Pring, lately arrived at Woolwich from the East, was expostulated with on the unnecessary charges for trimming the " Royal James," and assured that he would have rendered the Company a better service by sinking her. In consequence of this it was decided to write to Captains in the Indies to sink or burn unserviceable ships, the men being distributed among other vessels to fill the places now taken by blacks. The Company had stores in the Indies worth £20,000, sufficient to rig sixteen of the best ships ; but it was estimated that to repair an unserviceable ship in the East cost five times as much as she would be valued at on her return. The " Royal James " was docked at Blackwall, and it was the opinion of some that the King would be willing to exchange a smaller newly-built vessel for her.

The Court of the Company, in November, appointed Committees to deal with the outfit of the several new ships nearing completion at Deptford, Blackwall, and Woodbridge ; and on December 7th

a Court decided that the three new ships, built
for the Surat trade, should be named the " Blessing,"
" Discovery," and   " Reformation." The " Discovery," built at Woodbridge, was now at Blackwall,
and Burrell, the builder of the " Blessing " at
Deptford, was pressed to hasten the completion
of a few finishing strokes. The pursers appointed
were Arthur Sheffield to the " Blessing," Elias
Wood to the " Discovery," and Thomas Read to
the " Reformation."

At this time Thomas Mun, a Director of the
Company, published " A Discourse of Trade from
England unto the East Indies ; answering to diverse
objections which are usually made against the
same."

In this " Discourse " Mun gave the value of the
East India Company's joint property to be £400,000,
and stated that their trade gave employment to
10,000 tons of shipping, 2,500 seamen, 500 ship's-
carpenters, caulkers, joiners, etc., and about 120
factors in India. He defended the Company's
interests as follows : " In trade of merchandize
our ships must go and come, they are not
made to stay at home : yet, nevertheless, the
East India Company are well prepared at all times
to serve his Majesty and his kingdoms, with many
warlike provisions, which they always keep in store ;
such as timber, planks, ironworks, masts, cordage,
anchors, casks, ordnance, powder, shot, victuals
ready packed, wine, cider, and a world of other
things, fitting the present building, repairing and
despatching of ships to sea ; as may be plentifully
seen in their yards and storehouses at Deptford,
and more especially in those at Blackwall ; which
are grown so famous that they are daily visited and

viewed by strangers, as well Ambassadors as others ; to their great admiration of his Majesty's strength and glory, in one only Company of his merchants, able at short warning to set forth a fleet of ships of great force and power. For it is well known to all men who please truly to be informed that the East India Company (besides their fleets of ships, going and coming, and also abiding in the Indies) are constantly building, repairing, rigging, victualling and furnishing to sea, with all provision needful for such a long voyage, some seven or eight great ships yearly ; which are to be seen at anchor in the river of Thames, in a great forwardness some five or six months together, before they commonly depart for the Indies, which is about the month of March ; and they are no sooner got off from the coast of England, but shortly after, is the season of our ships to return from the Indies ; who come not home so weak as some would have them ; for how often hath experience been made of our ships which have performed two or three several voyages to the East Indies ? Yet at their return, they have been indocked, new trimmed, and launched out again, fitted for the like voyages, in less than two months."

During this year the Company sent out four ships and exported £12,900 of bullion, and £6,523 of merchandize. The money sent out to India was wasted in the quarrel with the Dutch, and only one ship returned, with a cargo of pepper, cloves and China raw silk to the value of £94,464.

A custom, over three centuries old, existed of presenting to the Lieutenant of the Tower two black leather bottles or lombards of wine from every ship bringing wine into the river. Lately the merchants, vowing that the bottles had grown much larger, tested their case in a suit at law against the present Lieutenant, Sir Gervase Elwes, who obtained the verdict principally through the witnesses found for him by Taylor the Water-poet, who at the time held the office of collecting this wine. Soon after Taylor was called upon to buy the right to the gathering of the wine, but refused, " because it was never bought or sold before, I would not or durst not venture upon so unhonest a novelty." He was dismissed, and wrote on the occasion a poem called " Farewell to the Tower Bottles," in which were these lines :

> " I was a waterman twice four long year,
> And lived in a contented happy state,
> Then turned the whirling wheel of fickle fate
> From water unto wine : Sir William Wade
> Did freely and for nothing turn my trade.
> Ten years almost the place I did retain,
> And glean'd great Bacchus' blood from France and Spain."

He seems shortly after to have been re-appointed, and wrote of the position as a difficult one :

> " The warders knows, each bottleman (but I)
> Had always a crack'd crown, or a black eye,
> Oft beaten like a dog, with a scratch'd face,
> Turn'd empty, beaten back with vile disgrace.
> And now and then be tumbled overboard
> And tho' these mischiefs I have kept me fro',
> No other bottleman could e'er do so ;
> 'Tis known you have been stabb'd, thrown in the Thames,
> And he that fil'd you, beaten with exclaims."

Finally he lost the thankless office, when he said :

> " But I was slighted with most vile disgrace
> And one that was my 'prentice plac'd in place."

1622. The Court of the East India Company, in February, 1622, allowed Burrell £100 for a lease of the Causeway at Blackwall, for 463 years, to avoid the Statute of Mortmain; orders were given for their outgoing fleet to collect at Gravesend; the petition of John Neale, an anchor-smith, for the use of the Company's forge at Blackwall to make anchors for the King's ships was refused; and Samuel Purchas, who had "undertaken a great volume of all their voyages," was to be allowed to see the Company's journal of voyages into the East, particularly that of Sir Thomas Roe; but he was to take nothing but what was proper to his history and not prejudicial to the Company.

In April the Company ordered a payment on account to Burrell for building the second new ship at Deptford, and considered an assessment on their property there. In June the Company discussed the progress of a new ship at Deptford; and on the 18th a Court minute read:

" Eyre to go down to Blackwall to-day, to break bulk aboard the 'Roebuck.' Style and Browne to go down to-night to the 'Hart,' lying at Erith; to be brought up to Blackwall. . . . Information that on Saturday last, when the King took barge at Blackwall, the 'Roebuck' shot off five pieces, which made so weak a report that it appears the Company is ill served of powder, whilst the 'Rainbow,' though but lately arrived from the bottom of the Straits, made a very good report. The powder not well kept; it ought to be aired in the sun upon fitting days, and skins are provided for that purpose. The Court did not well like that the powder should be so dried ashipboard, because of the many casualties that may happen, but it may

2F

be done ashore. . . . Complaints of the beef ; divers conjectures of the cause ; the Thames water may occasion it ; it may be the fault of the butchers in driving the cattle, and in not bleeding them enough for fear of decreasing the weight."

On August 26th, an East Indian fleet arrived at Erith, having on board Arnold Browne, who wrote an account of his Indian voyages since 1618. In the course of this year the Company sent out five ships to the Indies, and exported £61,600 of bullion, and £6,430 of merchandize. The cargoes brought back in these vessels consisted of pepper, cloves, mace, nutmegs, gum-lack, indigo, calicoes, etc., to the value of £296,500, and of Persian raw silk worth £93,000.

On April 5th a grant was made to Martin Hardaret, in reversion after John Holloway, of the Office of Comptroller of the Customs inwards in the Port of London.

On May 6th, the Master, Wardens and Assistants of the Trinity House of Deptford Strond, petitioned the Lord Admiral Buckingham " that the King's former permission for them to be charged only 1,000l. instead of 2,000l. per annum, for two years, towards the expedition against pirates, may be adhered to, and that they be not compelled by Council to pay the other 2,000l. at suit of the merchants, who by their errors have greatly mismanaged the business."

John Chamberlain wrote from London on July 13th : " A ship arrived from Virginia with news that the savages have by surprise slain about three hundred and fifty of the English through their own supine negligence in living in scattered and straggling houses."

On the 28th, a proclamation was issued from

Oatlands, "prohibiting the export of wools, woollen yarn, fuller's earth, and wood ashes, and inflicting heavy penalties on all Custom House officers conniving at their export."

1623. On July 4th, 1623, the East India Company ordered their ship, the "Charles," to be victualled at Erith, "for the better keeping of the men aboard"; and on the 9th their minutes recorded that the Court was "informed that 150 barrels of powder are to be had, but it must not be known ; ordered that they be bought and laid up at Deptford, and a man appointed to watch them." Soon after this the "Little James," "Eagle," "Star," "Lion," and "Great James" Indiamen arrived at Blackwall from the East, and a committee, after viewing the vessels, reported on those fit for sending again to Surat in the spring. An estimate was obtained for repairing the "Great James," and John Ducy was appointed to be measurer of timber, and over-seer of the workmen about the ships, at a wage of 12s. per week. At this time attention was drawn to the certain fact that the Portuguese, who had lately suffered defeat and loss by the Company's ships, would seek revenge—" Besides it is said there are two French ships bound for the Red Sea, it was thought fit to send a ship of extraordinary 'countenance' for Admiral, and for that service the 'Great James' is ordered to be finished, caulked and tarred ; the 'Lesser James' to go as Vice Admiral if upon report she shall appear fit ; and the 'Star' for a third ship."

On August 9th, Dr. William Garroway made known that certain goods landed at the Custom House Quay, belonging to Weddall, master of the "Jonas," and upon which a watch had been set, had through negligence or corruption been allowed to be conveyed away to the Tower of London. " It appears that some of the officers of the Custom House are over forward in helping our people to take up their goods, and must be restrained by a more commanding hand ; a letter to be gotten from the Lord Treasurer to that effect."

In August estimates were required for repairs, and divers bags of refuse biscuits and seven hogsheads of beef were given to the poor of Stepney, " especially to such widows and fatherless children whose husbands or fathers had died at the Indies in the Company's service." A petition was also considered from the inhabitants of Ratcliffe, Limehouse, and Mile End, for the relief and pension of certain of their poor, as it was alleged that many seafaring men died in the Indian voyages, leaving their widows and orphans a burden on the parish. The Company decided that a chest with a hole in the top should be fixed up in Mr. Hurte's office, and each mariner, factor, and other as he received his wages should be reminded to contribute something. Beyond this it was asserted that the Company helped the poor of those places at Christmas with money, and at other times with relief from the slaughter-house at every killing, and at the return of ships with such victuals as remained, but in no case would the Company be tied to any definite promise of help. Mr. Deputy and some members of Committees were ordered to go aboard the " Palsgrave," a ship newly arrived in the river, welcome the captain and licence the crew to come up, and arrange for the unlading of the vessel.

On September 4th, two of the Company's servants,

Swanley and Stephens, having reported on the insufficiency of the " Little James " ship, it was ordered to be broken up, and the " Jonas " to be brought into dock at her stern. At the same time it was agreed to rent a slip of ground adjoining the south end of the long store-house at Blackwall. On the 19th a Court of the Company received the request of the Master and Wardens of the Watermen's Company that John Taylor, servant to Thomas Bleake, a waterman, and prisoner in the compter for striking the boatswain of the " Palsgrave," might be delivered to them, to ease his master of the charge of his imprisonment, and so that they might " handle him with more severity than a bare restraint." The reply was that the offender must first answer for his " misdemeanour and battery " at the sessions.

An assessment of 5s. per acre upon the Company's lands at Blackwall, for the maintenance of the East Marsh of Poplar, was ordered to be paid. On the 24th, James Browne, lately appointed Engineer in the East Indiaman " Charles," petitioned the Company to pay on account of his wages a debt of £20 for which he had been arrested at Tilbury. " The Court suspected it to be a device between him and his creditors, and entreated Messrs. Stiles and Munnes to take care that the Company be not cozened."

Two days later a letter was caused to be presented to Lady Carleton at Gravesend, " to certify that the Company have given orders to Mr. Barlow to deliver to his Lordship (her husband) 200*l.*, and also a Persian carpet and silk quilt to the value of 20*l.*"

On October 1st, the Company allowed a month's wages of their servant Matthew Spurgeon to his wife

Margaret, whose condition of extreme want was certified to by the Churchwarden, Collector, Constable, Sideman, and Headborough of Limehouse.

In November a Court of the Company dealt with the meeting of Committees at Blackwall in reference to smiths', coopers', and other work done there ; and gave gratuities to the poor of Stepney, " together with the old beef and biscuit and other vails of beef, as have been usually distributed to the poor there."

On December 12th, it was ordered that as great sums of money had been brought to account for fresh victuals consumed on board the Company's outward-bound ships, and the allowance hitherto made had been an inducement to draw large numbers of strangers to board the ships and impose on their hospitality, to the Company's great charge, no fresh provisions should from now be allowed to be shipped after each vessel had passed Tilbury Hope. A week later the Court decided that the distribution of money and food to the poor of Stepney should not be left to the Churchwardens, but they could, if desired, be present on the occasion. At the same time it was resolved that as John Lemprier, their late servant at Blackwall, did not evacuate, in spite of warning, the Company's house there, he should be removed. Violent action, however, was avoided by Lemprier promising to move out at once.

In the course of this year the Company sent out seven ships, and exported £68,720 of bullion, and £17,345 of merchandize. Five of the vessels returned with cargoes of pepper, cloves, mace, nutmegs, indigo, calicoes, etc., to the value of £485,593, and Persian raw silk worth £97,000.

On October 11th, the Master and Brethren of the Trinity House at Ratcliffe advised the Lord Admiral

Buckingham that : " The owners of the ship
' Adventure,' of Ipswich, now in the Thames,
desire his warrant for taking in certain pieces of
ordnance, which are fitting for her defence."

1624. In January, 1624, a Court of the East
India Company ordered that John Ducy was to
have the lodgings at Blackwall lately occupied
by Mr. Fotherby ; that vessels for the spring fleet
should ship their ammunition and fall down to
Gravesend, "for that if the Portugal as he is now
provoked should light upon the Company's ships
without this supply, it might be an occasion of great
mischief." In reply to the request of their servant
Fish, of the salting-house at Blackwall, for some
consideration for work done at nights and on holidays,
the Court refused to allow him anything, " for if
he wrought sometimes at night he was oftentimes
spared by day."

Two new pinnaces built for the spring voyage
were named " Scout " and " Spy." A request of
Thomas Bostock that he might continue the tenancy
of certain lands, held by his family for the last sixty
years, at Deptford, at the rate of 40s. per acre, was
allowed, his tenure to be from year to year at that
rent. A Dr. Page claimed certain tithes from the
Company for lands in Deptford. On the 30th, the
" Great James " Indiaman, deeply laden and drawing much water, was ordered to be taken down
to Tilbury.

In February the Company removed a nailer
named Moore from their house at Deptford, and
requested Thornborough, the late purser of the
" James," to occupy it. Dowles' motion to take
the lease of another house at Deptford was granted,
and Moore's brother-in-law was ordered to be evicted.

On the 27th, the "Great James," drawing twenty feet of water, and the rest of the outward bound East Indian fleet, were ordered to fall down to Tilbury. The fleet having been stayed at Gravesend in consequence of a motion made in Parliament, the Deputy and others of the Committee, on March 5th, presented themselves before the Lord Admiral as humble suitors for the release of their ships. Buckingham protested his innocence of having occasioned the detention, but after hearing the motion with much earnestness in the Upper House, he could do no less than give the order. Finally, he said "he had something in his pocket would do them good, and willed them to set down what reason they could, and he would acquaint the House therewith, and was pleased to give way that their ships might fall down as low as Tilbury to attend further directions."

The fleet was riding at Tilbury Hope on the 10th, and the Despatch Committee went down by the next evening's tide, but it was strictly ordered that the money for the ships, which was to be made up to forty-eight chests of ryals, was not to go down till the fleet was fully released. On the 26th, the Governor and other heads of the Company reported that as commanded they had attended the King, but could not obtain full speech with him concerning the sum of money required to free their ships. Ultimately, however, £10,000 having been extorted from the Company by Buckingham, the King agreed that the fleet might depart on its long voyage. Following this attack in Parliament on the Company an Abstract of the Trade with the East Indies, from March 25th, 1620, to March 25th of this year, was laid before the House of Commons; and during that period the value of exports had been £264,516 and imports £1,255,444. It was added that if the Company had been able to carry on their trade unmolested by the Dutch, the returns in these four years would have been £600,000 more. The anticipated returns for this year were expected to amount to £500,000.

Estimates were prepared in March for repairing all the Company's ships not on service, of which the " Lion " and " London " were already in dock at Blackwall, and the " Palsgrave " was to be brought up from Erith.

A Court of the Company in April decided, having received the report of Mr. Kirby concerning his survey of the Wharf at Deptford, that after the breaking up of the Indiaman, "Lesser James," there would be sufficient stuff for the repairs there, and Messrs. Steevens and Ducy were appointed to view the work and report thereon to the Court.

Offers of £4 per annum for the Nailer's house at Deptford were refused as the Court was informed that £5 would be given, and it therefore resolved " to take their best Chapman," who was their servant Downing.

On the 22nd, the Court ordered Nicholas Girdler, who had been sentenced by Sir Henry Marten for taking imprest of the Company for two voyages and going on neither, to be ducked at the yard-arm, according to the fashion of the sea, by the Serjeant of the Admiralty at Blackwall ; and the Company's servants were to assist in the execution of the sentence.

On May 28th, the Company refused the offer of Simon Bowry to rent part of their yard at Deptford ; and on June 16th, a Court of the Company instructed

Mr. Cappur to put Downing in possession of the Company's house at Deptford, now retained by Thomas Moore, a smith. In July a Court dealt with the unlading of two newly-arrived ships at the Custom House Quay; instructed a Committee to view the ships at Blackwall, see what repairs were required, and how the stores were supplied; referred the complaint of Thomas Moore, late the Company's smith at Deptford, of being put out of their house there; allowed Dr. Page arrears of tithes due for lands in the Company's yard at Deptford; and put off the going down to Blackwall of the Committee "until the Company have some more real comfort in their trade," but ordered them to view the "Elizabeth," and if necessary bring her into dock. On September 1st a Committee was appointed to attend the King at Windsor on Monday, and "to hold one thing for a ground, not to give way to any dispute upon the business of Amboyna, that were the way to make it infinite."

At the same Court it was ordered that the Dock at Blackwall be lengthened and made fit for taking great ships, at a charge of 20 marks.

The King of Denmark having obtained from the government the services of Phineas Pett to build him a ship, a Court of the Company agreed on the 22nd to lend him their Dock at Deptford for the construction of the vessel. On October 22nd, a Court was held, concerning the estate of Thomas Russell, who lately died in the "Hart," and left all he had to the poor of the parish of Stepney, "on whose behalf the charity of the Company is also solicited as in former years." On November 8th, consideration was given to the petition of Gilbert White, over one hundred years old, for the relief of himself and his wife, who were on the point of being turned out of doors, as was testified by the head borough and divers inhabitants of Wapping where they dwelt. On the 10th the assessment made upon the Company's lands at Blackwall was ordered to be paid. And two days later Mr. Fotherby's orders for the government of the yard at Blackwall were read and approved ; he was also required to conceive some order for restraining the workmen from resorting to the tap-house at other than meal times. A complaint was also considered against Morgan the brewer, that the beer of the " Swallow " was very bad, " it was said the Company had been careful to avoid taking beer from Dutchmen, and yet Morgan hath a Dutchman employed in his brewing, and that it is a very easy matter, by casting in some small thing into the copper to the quantity of a nut, to spoil a whole brewing ; he promised careful amendment for the future, and that he would forthwith put away his Dutch brewer for the avoiding of all suspicion."

On December 1st the Company appointed Captain Blythe to be Admiral of their Surat fleet. He was to receive £20 per month—100 marks to prepare himself for sea, and half wages until he was past Gravesend ; and he was bound not to engage in private trade.

In reply to a petition of the Company to the Council of War, a warrant was issued on the 6th for them to draw powder out of the Tower of London at 10d. per pound.

On the 10th, the Indiaman, "Palsgrave," was ordered to be launched, the " Elizabeth " to be brought into dock, and the " London " carried down to Tilbury. Five days later the Company ordered £10 to be given for the relief of the poor of the hamlet of Stepney, " to be distributed especially to women whose husbands have died poor in the Company's service." On the 20th, the " London," having fallen down the river to below Gravesend, a Committee was appointed to view the condition of the ship. A week later it was ordered that the Japan silver and gold brought out of the Indies, to the value of £1,100, should be carried to the Tower to be coined.

On July 11th, Sir Henry Marten wrote to Secretary Conway : " Smith and Long were condemned to die for piracy in the Thames. Thinks it a matter of consequence not to suffer the King's port to be thus infected."

1625. About February, 1625, information was lodged against a Dutch captain, " at Mr. Borough's, Limehouse, in keeping of a man of Sir Henry Palmer's, who is suspected of going out with three ships under a commission from Count Maurice, and having sold one, going with the others to Brazil to bring sugars into the Low Countries."

PLEASURE AND SPORT ALONG THE RIVER.

1603. At the accession of James I. all classes of the population were fond of pleasure and sport, much of it of a rough and brutal nature. The baiting of bulls and bears with fierce dogs of the mastiff breed drew all ranks to the Bear Gardens on the Bankside; and royalty often commanded these formidable dogs to be brought to the Tower to witness them maul a cowed and spiritless lion or other wild beast, or get terribly mangled when the savage natures of these creatures were roused.

In May, 1604, the lion's house at the Tower was enlarged, and John and Alexander Levingston were granted the keeping of these animals and the leopards in reversion after Thomas and Ralph Gill.

Maitland wrote that on the following June 3rd: "King James, taking with him the Duke of Lennox (with divers earls and lords), went to see the lions at the Tower. And here he caused two of them, a he-lion, and a she, to be put forth; and then a live cock was cast to them, which being their natural enemy, they presently killed it, and sucked the blood. Then the King caused a live lamb to be put to them; which the lions, out of their generosity (as having respect to its innocence) never offered to touch, although the lamb was so bold as to go close to them. Then the King caused the lions to be taken away, and another lion to be put forth, and two mastiffs to be turned to him. The mastiffs presently flew upon the lion, and turned him upon his back ; and though the lion was superior to them in strength, yet, it seems, they were his match in courage. There was a spaniel dog, for some offence or other cast into the lion's den ; but the lion did not attempt to hurt him ; and this dog continued in the den, with the lion, several years, and there died." On Sunday, August 5th, a lioness in the Tower, named " Elizabeth," gave birth to a cub, which, however, only lived till the morrow. At the time it was said that this was an event " seldom or never heard of before." This lioness whelped again at the end of February, 1605, but the lion-cub—taken from her to be brought up by hand—lived only sixteen days.

On June 3rd, 1605, the King, attended by a large retinue, went from Greenwich to the Tower, and witnessed the baiting of a lion by three fierce dogs. Notification was dated on the next November 10th of a grant to Thomas and Michael Heneage, of Hogsdon, Middlesex, in reversion after Ralph Gill of the office of Keeper of the Lions and Leopards in the tower, with an increase of 6d. per day for their charge of young lions and leopards recently born there.

On June 23rd, 1609, the King and Queen, with Princes Henry and Charles and Princess Elizabeth, and attended by a large retinue, went to the Tower and witnessed an attempted fight between a lion and a fierce bear, that had recently killed a child negligently left in his den. Maitland wrote of this : " A resolution was taken to make trial of the valour of the lion ; which was by turning him loose to a bear. The bear was brought into an

open yard, and the lion was turned out of his den
to him ; but he would not assault him, but fled
from him. And so it was done with other lions,
one after another. And, lastly, two together were
turned to him ; but none set upon him, but rather
sought to return to their dens. A stone-horse soon
after being put into the yard with the first lion and
the bear, the horse fell to grazing between them.
After he had gazed a little upon them, two mastiff
dogs were let in, who boldly fought with the lion.
Afterwards six more dogs were let in ; who flew
upon the horse, being more in sight at their entrance,
and would soon have worried him to death, had not
three stout bear-herds entered and rescued the
horse, and brought away the dogs, while the lion
and bear stood staring upon them." A fortnight
later the bear was baited to death on a stage, and
out of the money taken for viewing this sight, the
mother of the dead child received twenty pounds.

John Nichols, in his " Progresses," said that on
April 20th, 1610, Prince Henry and his guest and
cousin, Frederick Ulric, son of the Duke of Brunswick,
in company with the Duke of Lennox, the Earl of
Arundel, and others, "came privately to the Tower,
and caused the great lion to be put into the yard,
and four dogs at a course to be set upon him ; and
they all fought with him instantly, saving such as
at their first coming into the yard, in their fury fell
upon one another, because they saw none else with
whom to fight, for the lion kept close to the trap-
door at the further end of the yard. These were
choice dogs, and flew all at the lion's head, whereat
the lion became enraged, and furiously bit divers
dogs by the head and throat, holding their heads
and necks in his mouth, as a cat doth hold a rat, and

with his claws he tore their flesh extremely ; all which, notwithstanding, many of them would not let go their hold, until they were utterly spoiled. After divers courses and spoil of divers dogs, and great likelihood of spoil of more, which yet lay tugging with the lion, for whose rescue there entered in three stout bear-wards, and set a lusty dog upon the mouth of the lion ; and the last dog got full hold of the lion's tongue, pulled it out of his mouth, held it so fast, that the lion neither bit him nor any other ; whereupon it was generally imagined that these dogs would instantly spoil the lion, he being now out of breath, and barred from biting ; and although there were now but three dogs upon him, yet they vexed him sore ; whereupon the above-mentioned young lusty lion and lioness were both put out together, to see if they would rescue the third, but they would not, but fearfully gazed upon the dogs. Then two or three of the worst dogs, which had left the first lion, ran upon them, chased them up and down the yard, seeking by all means to avoid the dogs ; and as soon as their trap door was open they both ran hastily into their den, and a dog that pursued them ran in with them, where they all three, like good friends, stood very peaceably without any manner of violence either to other ; and then the three bear-wards came boldly in again, and took off all the dogs but one from the lion, and carried them away. The lion having fought long, and his tongue torn, lay staring and panting a pretty while, so as all the beholders thought he had been utterly spoiled and spent ; and upon a sudden gazed upon that dog which remained, and as soon as he had spoiled him, espying the trap door open ran hastily into his den, and there never ceased walking up and down, to and fro, until he had brought himself into his former temperature."

In 1607 the keeper of the King's bears at Paris Garden received a fee of £11 8s. 1½d., and the keeper of the mastiffs a fee of £11 10s. 4d.

An order was made on September 11th, 1611, for paying £18 5s. to Philip Henslowe and Edward Allen, masters of the King's Game at Paris Garden, " upon their several allowance of 12d. by the day to each of them, for their charges and pains in keeping of a young lion and two white bears."

Horatio Busino, the Venetian Secretary, wrote of the bear gardens in his diary on July 10th, 1618 : " Then there is a certain theatre, a place belonging to the King, where he keeps a quantity of bears and other wild beasts, such as lynxes and tigers. In another part of it are a number of bulls. In separate kennels they have got over a hundred trained mastiffs. Every week they bait both bull and bear with dogs belonging to private individuals, such as butchers and others curious in these matters, as those of the kennel are only used on rare occasions in the presence of his Majesty or other grandees. We went one day by invitation to see this sight, and the result of our observations after various assaults was that both the bull and the bear over-power the courage of the dog, who, although he occasionally makes some good hits, yet in the end is frequently killed on the spot, either from being tossed by the one, or hugged, torn, and bitten by the other. This week a wager of hundreds of crowns was laid between one of the counties and these Londoners, their dogs being pitted in this very theatre. It was said that both sides displayed

2G

remarkable powers, but the Londoners won the day, under favour, it is believed, of those rufflers who attend the theatre, and who showed partiality either by setting on or taking off the dogs, which are detached from the bear by inserting between the teeth of that one of the two combatants who happens to be the griper, certain iron spattles with a wooden handle, whilst they take them off the bull, keeping at a greater distance, with certain flat iron hooks, which they apply to the thighs or even to the neck of the dog, whose tail is simultaneously dexterously seized by another of these rufflers. The bull can hardly get at anybody, as he wears a collar round his neck with only fifteen feet of rope, which is fastened to a stake deeply planted in the middle of the theatre. Other rufflers are at hand with long poles to put under the dog so as to break his fall after he has been tossed by the bull; the tips of these are covered with thick leather to prevent them from disembowelling the dogs. The most spirited stroke is considered to be that of the dog who seizes the bull's lip, clinging to it and pinning the animal for some time. The second best hit is to seize the eyebrows; the third, but far inferior, consists in seizing the bull's ear."

John Chamberlain, in a letter to Carleton on July 12th, 1623, wrote : " The Spanish Ambassador is much delighted in bear-baiting. He was the last week in Paris Garden, where they showed him all the pleasure they could, both with bull, bear, and horse, besides jackanapes, and then turned a white bear into the Thames, where the dogs baited him swimming, which was the best sport of all. The King of Spain hath sent hither five camels and an elephant, which, going through the town this day sevennight, past midnight, could not yet pass unseen."

Cock-fighting was eagerly pursued by the nobility and gentry, and the King went twice a week to see the sport in the cock-pit at Whitehall, when the Court was in residence there. Busino wrote in his diary on July 10th, 1618 : "I meant to stop here, in order to conclude my discourse, but it occurs to me that I have yet to tell of the enjoyable conflicts fought by crested cocks. In this kingdom they keep up a certain pugnacious breed of cocks with a jealousy equal to that observed at Padua over the beautiful birds of Spolverara. They have a place like an anatomical theatre, and in the middle of the circle, whose level is sunk and covered with matting, they place the two fighting cocks, who set to immediately. After a long and courageous battle one of them is killed, the other remaining with small life in him. They very frequently peck out each other's eyes, and at every first attack exchange very deep thrusts in the ribs with their spurs, and should one of them in action break a spur, if he has shewn courage in other respects, they immediately make another for him of silver. The spectators bet heavily, encouraging by support and exclamation the success of one or the other of the combatants."

Fishing with cormorants was a royal sport. On August 31st, 1618, an order issued to the Commissioners of the Treasury and the Under-Treasurer and Chamberlains of the Exchequer ran : " Whereas our servant Robert Wood, keeper of our cormorants, ospreys, and otters, hath, for the better bringing up and keeping of our said cormorants, ospreys, and otters, for our disport, compounded with our right trusty and well-beloved the Lord Danvers for a

lease for years of a parcel of ground within the
vine-garden, at Westminster, wherein the said
Wood hath undertaken to make nine fish ponds,
the same to be paled and stored with sundry sorts
of fish, with a sluice to bring water out of the Thames
to the said ponds, and also to build a house of brick
to keep the said cormorants, ospreys, and otters in, and
to perform other things requisite for such a work, the
charges of the whole amounting to the sum of £286."

Busino wrote, on July 10th of this year : " One
also sees various other hunts, namely, a duck put
into the water with a dog after her, but for the
most part she escapes, her pursuer becoming tired
and exhausted. Then there is another most
extravagant hunt, or rather fishery, effected by a
large bird called a cormorant, the site of whose
exploits belongs to the King. His Majesty
constantly has a pair of them hooded at this Court.
This very day he was to fish with them in the Thames
from a boat. They have a very wide craw, and
being well trained, dive in the ponds, or streams,
and after remaining some while under water, come
to the surface with the prey in their mouth, or even
in their craw, as they are unable to swallow because
their throat is bound with a lacet."

Hunting the stag was the favourite sport of
James I. ; and on May 7th, 1604, the Council
ordered Sir Thomas Fleming, the Solicitor-General,
to draw up a proclamation forbidding all ranks
of the people to hunt with hounds within four miles
of the Cities of London and Westminster, the only
exceptions being the King, Queen, and Prince Henry.
On September 9th, 1609—a few days after the King
had killed a stag at Windsor with his own hand—a
proclamation was issued from Hampton Court

against hunters, stealers, and killers of deer within any of the royal forests, chases, and parks.

Busino wrote, on July 10th, 1618 : " Concerning stag and deer hunting, I ought to be very accurate in drawing up a vigorous and sprightly narrative, for it is a worthy theme, fitted for great men, and more especially because the King here, now stricken in years, delights in it above all the sportsmen in the world. In various parts of this is and they carefully preserve more than half a million of animals, possibly without including t use of the forest, and therefore it is no wonder that they are here acquainted with the quintessence of these sports. The first and speediest way is to await the stag on his course armed with an arquebus or arbalest, from a bower formed in a shady tree like a small chamber, to which one ascends by a stair. The second is to set the dogs after him, having first given the animal a slight flesh wound in the least dangerous part of the body with a shot from a crossbow, so as to draw blood, so that the prey may be taken more speedily and with greater ease. The third and very noble manner is when his Majesty chooses to hunt without taking any advantage, to which effect he gives orders over night for one of the largest and fattest and strongest stags to be selected. On the following morning the hounds rouse him from his lair, pursuing him from natural instinct and never losing the scent, even should he hide himself in a thousand woods, or among as many other deer. The King, accompanied by a number of cavaliers riding the quickest horses, follows the game over the country, and often for the space of eight whole days, until it is quite exhausted and dead, and to effect this without killing the horses, relays are posted in various places. Being thus freshly mounted, the sportsmen are enabled to continue the hunt with greater spirit. On his Majesty coming up with the dead game, he dismounts, cuts its throat and opens it, sating the dogs with its blood, as the reward of their exertions. With his own imbued hands, moreover, he is wont to regale some of his nobility by touching their faces. This blood it is unlawful to remove or wash off, until it fall of its own accord, and the favoured individual thus be-daubed is considered to be dubbed a keen sportsman and chief of the hunt, and to have a certificate of his sovereign's cordial good-will. The same style is observed in hunting the deer, though from what I understand this sport is less fatiguing."

It was said of James that he returned from hunting, "clad all in grass green, with a green feather, shambling limbs, thick features, a spare beard, and a tongue too big for his mouth. He looks about him at the bye-standers half frightened ; yet he has ridden boldly, and been ' in at the death.' " Sir Roger Coke wrote, in 1619, that he was "excessively addicted to hunting and drinking, not ordinary French and Spanish wines, but strong Greek wines ; and though he would ' divide ' his hunting from drinking those wines (that is to say, have set times for them apart), yet he would ' compound ' his hunting with drinking those wines ; and to that purpose he was attended with a special officer, who was, as much as could be, always at hand to fill the King's cup in his hunting when he called for it. I have heard my father say that, being hunting with the King, after the King had drank of the wine, he also drank of it, and though he was young and of a healthful constitution, it so

disordered his head that it spoiled his pleasure, and
disordered him for three days after. Whether it
was from drinking these wines, or from some other
cause, the King became so lazy and unwieldy, that
he was thrust on horseback, and as he was set, so
he would ride, without otherwise poising himself
on his saddle ; nay, when his hat was set on his
head, he would not take the pains to alter it, but
it sat as it was upon him."

The game establishment of King James became
widely distributed and reached out as far afield as
Thetford in Norfolk. There were royal preserves of
pheasants at Windsor and Richmond, and in June,
1604, John Hall was appointed gamekeeper at
Windsor Castle, and George and Michael Kirkham
were appointed in the same capacity at Richmond.
A Hare Warren was maintained at Hampton Court,
and the keeper, Gilbert Wood, received 2s. per
diem. Royal game was preserved about Lambeth,
Wandsworth, and Clapham, and the keeper,
Alexander Glover, was paid 12d. per diem, and
26s. 8d. per annum for his livery. At Oatlands,
the gamekeeper, Robert Moore, received 12d. per
diem. The following appointments were made in
the reign—in 1606, Sampson Calvert as keeper of
game between Wandsworth Bridge and Merton ;
in 1608, William Duck and his son as keepers about
the honour of Hampton Court, from Staines Bridge
to Brentford Bridge ; and Thomas Tower as keeper
in Southwark, Lambeth, Clapham, Battersea, and
other places in Surrey ; in 1612, Ellis Holcombe as
keeper from Southwark to Lambeth Marsh ; in
1614, Charles Burton, on surrender of Michael
Kirkham, as keeper of the King's game of hare,
pheasants, etc., near Richmond, and Milon Gnaris-

borough as keeper at Richmond ; in 1616, Alexander and Vincent Glover as keepers in Lambeth Marsh, and Peregrin Guillun as keeper near Wandsworth ; in 1617, Richard Kerry, on surrender of George Ryman, as keeper of the Hare Warren and game of all sorts at Hampton Court ; and in 1623, Robert Stacey as keeper of the game at Chelsea, Kensington, Islington, and elsewhere in the neighbourhood of Westminster.

In February, 1608, a warrant of the Privy Council ordered John Powell to take away all guns and engines for destroying the King's game and fish from Wandsworth Bridge to Merton Abbey. In October, 1609, the King ordered Yonge Grove in Oatlands Park to be cleared and enclosed for breeding his pheasants.

Horatio Busino, describing Richmond Palace in July, 1618, wrote : " In this same place his Majesty's is now rearing with extraordinary care and attention the race of pheasants. They are placed in a small orchard beneath the palace windows with a few cherry and plum-trees, the grass being allowed to grow as pasture for the birds. This little fruitery is divided into six or eight compartments with wooden partitions, each containing a cock and five hens. They all have the tip of one of their wings clipped to prevent them from flying away, the site not being roofed in. Among them some are pied red, and all the rest white, very handsome to look at. For their food they give them a certain quantity of small peas and plenty of water. They make them go into their huts every night to roost. The hens lay their eggs in the grass, and they are carefully collected and placed in due time under clucking hens, who hatch them. Last month we saw eighty chicks already hatched under several brood hens, being reared in coops with two partitions, the hen being in the one, and the food of the young pheasants in the other, to which they have access at pleasure. The food consists of ants' eggs ; clean water is placed for them in shallow pans."

On the following September 17th, Busino wrote these further remarks : " I send you some observations which I have made about their way of breeding pheasants here. The first I saw was at Richmond, a place of the King, where there is a court, or rather a yard, enclosed by walls of some height. No one could enter except by the gate, which was always shut, so that the animals might not be disturbed by the traffic or curiosity of people. The place is divided by compartments about five feet high, into eight sections or squares, each with its own door. They might be about 18 feet long by 12 broad. All have turf, and they think this necessary as the birds can take exercise and feed there as well as lay their eggs. Trees protect them from the sun, and each place has its little wooden house, similar to and no larger than those used for watch-dogs. Each house has straw on the floor and a hatch at the side besides the door, and the birds retire thither at night, probably to protect them from being found by beasts of prey. There are five females and one male for each place, the white being separated from the speckled, and the common ones from the rest. They clip one wing only of each bird, so that they cannot fly. Their food varies. Some have wild peas, a very common vegetable here, found in great quantities. They give them in season handfuls of these, grain, etc. They are fond of mustard

seed and earth worms. The last are easily found in
damp places by simply turning the earth with a
fork. But the best thing is to give them what is
most abundant and costs least, as they will readily
eat lettuce, chopped cabbage, and all manner of
greens. I have seen them cover the young birds
with netting to protect them from birds of prey
and prevent them from escaping, as their wings
are not clipped."

Busino also wrote in his diary on July 10th :
" They also hunt rabbits with certain French beagles,
and we actually saw this the day before yesterday
in the park of the most fortunate Marquis of Buckingham. When they want to take a good many and
quickly for domestic purposes, or on any other
account, they employ a trained ferret thus : they
blind the animal partially with a red hot iron, and
put a bell round his neck. After surrounding the
warren with double nets, they let him loose in it,
whereupon he instantly drives out a quantity of
them, who rush terrified into the toils, in such
numbers, as to fill sacks, and these are much better
eating than the tame ones."

The upper ranks played tennis in covered
courts ; and King James recommended the game
to his son as becoming a prince. There were
courts at Blackfriars and Southwark, and royal
courts at Westminster. Early in 1604, Jehu Webb
was appointed Master of the King's Tennis Plays
at Westminster.

Prison Bar or Base was an old game practised by
the young and active, and football was played by
the city youths and apprentices in the fields.

Bowls had largely succeeded archery as a popular
pastime, and Stow wrote just before this time :

" Our bowes are turned into bowls." Many gardens by the river and elsewhere in the city and suburbs were converted into bowling alleys ; and so warmly was the game pursued that Stow said : "Common bowling alleyes are privy mothes that eat up the credit of many idle citizens." Howel wrote : " When the idle was tired of bowls, he had nothing to do but to step down to Queenhithe or the Temple," and have an afternoon's angling.

Fireworks had an enormous attraction for the populace, and the men who displayed them, fantastically dressed, were called " Green Men." A writer of the time said there were " abiding in the City of London men very skilful in the art of pyrotechnie or fireworkes." Card playing was in much favour, and from Allhallow Eve to the day following Christmas Day one of the principal sports was playing at cards for " counters, nails, and points."

Horatio Busino wrote on July 10th, 1618 : " It is also the custom in this kingdom to make the footmen run races of fifteen or twenty miles, and this very year a famous contest took place between the men of two of the leading nobles. It had something truly grand and magnificent about it, for they wagered an annual rental of 800 crowns. The master of the winner was pleased to present him with a life rent of 80 crowns. His Majesty takes pleasure in being present at such sports, especially when any of the Court favourites are concerned, and he chooses the winning footman to enter his service, as was the case lately. They likewise bet who can make the parish bells be heard at the greatest distance. In almost every belfry they ring seven or eight large bells in tune, just like a piece of music."

John Chamberlain wrote on July 31st, 1619, to Sir Dudley Carleton : " On St. James's Eve, upon a return, or wager, one went from Southwark to Calais and back again the same day, having almost an hour and a half to spare of his limited time, which was from broad daylight to sunset."

All ranks joined in Maying and May-games, and May-poles were erected on May Day morning. The two principal ones in sight of the river at London were near St. Clement Dane's Church in the Strand, and on St. Margaret's Hill, Southwark. A lord and lady of the May, adorned with scarves, ribbons, and other gay finery, presided over the games, and after the daytime dances and devices, the evening ushered in stage plays and bonfires in the streets. In 1611, Beaumont and Fletcher in " The Knight of the Burning Pestle," made the May-Lord thus discourse :

" London, to thee I do present
　　The merry month of May ;
Let each true subject be content
　　To hear me what I say :
For from the top of Conduit-Head,
　　As plainly may appear,
I will both tell my name to you,
　　And wherefore I came here.
My name is Ralph, by due descent
　　Though not ignoble I

" Yet far inferior to the flock
　　Of gracious grocery ;
And by the common counsel of
　　My fellows in the Strand,
With gilded staff and crossed scarf,
　　The May-Lord here I stand.
Rejoice, O English hearts, rejoice !
　　Rejoice, O lovers dear !
Rejoice, O City, town, and country !
　　Rejoice eke every shere !
　　.　.　.　.　.　.　.　.

Now little fish on tender stone
   Begin to cast their bellies,
And sluggish snails, that erst were mew'd
   Do creep out of their shellies ;
The rumbling rivers now do warm,
   For little boys to paddle ;
The sturdy steed now goes to grass,
   And up they hang his saddle.
The heavy hart, the bellowing buck,
   The rascal and the pricket,
Are now among the yeoman's pease,
   And leave the fearful thicket.

And be like them, O you, I say,
   Of this same noble Town,
And lift aloft your velvet heads,
   And slipping off your gown,
With bells on legs, and napkins clean
   Unto your shoulders tied,
With scarfs and garters as you please,
   And ' Hey for our town ! ' cried,
March out and show your willing minds,
   By twenty and by twenty,
To Hogsdon, or to Newington,
   Where ale and cakes are plenty !
And let it ne'er be said for shame,
   That we, the youths of London,
Lay thrumming of our caps at home,
And left our custom undone.
Up then, I say, both young and old,
   Both man and maid a-Maying,
With drums and guns that bounce aloud,
   And merry tabor playing !
Which to prolong, God save our King,
   And send his country peace,
And root out treason from the land !
   And so my friends I cease."

The following verses on the May Pole in the Strand,
in 1619, appeared in Pasquil's " Palinodia and
Progress to the Tavern " :

" Fairly we marched on, till our approach
   Within the spacious passage of the Strand,
Objected to our sight a summer broach
   Yclept a May Pole, which in all our land,

No city, town, nor street can parallel,
Nor can the lofty spire of Clerkenwell,
Although he have the advantage of a rock,
Perch up more high his turning weather-cock.

Stay, quoth my muse, and here behold a sign
  Of harmless mirth and honest neighbourhood,
Where all the parish did in one combine
    To mount the rod of peace, and none withstood ;
      Where no capricious constables disturb them,
      Nor justice of the peace did seem to curb them,
      Nor peevish puritan, in railing sort
      Nor over-wise churchwarden, spoil'd the sport.

Happy the age, and harmless were the days
  (For then true love and amity were found)
When every village did a May Pole raise,
    And Whitson-Ales and May-games did abound.
      And all the lusty yonkers, in a rout,
      With merry lasses danc'd the rod about,
      Then friendship to their banquets bid the guests,
      And poor men far'd the better for their feasts.

          .   .   .   .   .   .

Then lords of castles, manors, towns and towers
  Rejoiced when they beheld the farmers flourish,
And would come down into the summer-bowers
  To see the country gallants dance the morrice.

          .   .   .   .   .   .

But since the summer poles were overthrown,
  And all good sports and merriments decay'd
How times and men are chang'd, so well is known,
  It were but labour lost if more were said.

          .   .   .   .   .   .

But I do hope once more the day will come,
  That you shall mount and perch your cocks as high
As e'er you did, and that the pipe and drum
  Shall bid defiance to your enemy :
      And that all fiddlers, which in corners lurk,
      And have been almost starved for want of work,
      Shall draw their crowds, and, at your exaltation,
      Play many a fit of merry recreation."

Fairs were a great delight to the people, and the
coarse but good-natured fun was fast and furious.
All towns had their fairs at different periods of the

year.   The largest in London was St. Bartholomew's.
There was one at Westminster on St. James's Day,
July 25th ; and on September 7th, 8th, and 9th,
Southwark Fair was held.   This was opened by the
Lord Mayor and Sheriffs, all dressed in their scarlet
robes, without cloaks.   They rode to St. Magnus'
Church, after dinner at two o'clock in the afternoon,
attended by the Sword-bearer, in his embroidered
cap, and carrying the " pearl sword."   Being joined
at the church by the Aldermen, they all rode in
procession over the bridge, and passing through
the Fair continued on to St. George's Church,
Newington Bridge, or the stones marking the City
liberties at St. Thomas-a-Watering.   After returning
to the Bridge House, and partaking of a banquet,
the Aldermen took leave of the Lord Mayor, and all
went home across the bridge.

The bridge masters then gave a supper to the
City officers.

Probably after bull and bear baiting the most
popular of pleasures was the witnessing of stage
plays ; and the tragedies and comedies of Shakespeare and Ben Jonson, and a little later those
of Beaumont and Fletcher, drew applauding
crowds.

In the beginning of 1603, so accustomed and
hardened were the people to the constant peril of
the Plague, that when it was rapidly increasing
the number of its victims, especially in Southwark,
they were undeterred from flocking across the river
and over the bridge to the Bankside and applauding,
with a light heart, at the Swan Theatre in Paris
Garden, a performance named " England's Joy."
This was an apotheosis of Queen Elizabeth—now
dying at Richmond—with a cast of players, including

Old Vennor, called by Taylor, " the Water-poet,"
" that plain-dealing man."

At the same theatre, some months later, a contest
took place for a prize, and during its progress a man
named Turner was thrust in the eye and killed.

In the course of a few quiet days spent by King
James at Greenwich Palace, in May, soon after his
arrival, he granted a licence to Laurence Fletcher,
William Shakespeare, Richard Burbage, and six
others, to play comedies and dramatic pieces at the
Globe Theatre on Bankside.

On the last day of January, 1604, Edward
Kirkham, Alexander Hawkins, Thomas Kendall,
and Robert Payne were licensed to train a young
Society, to be named " Children of the Revels of
the Queen," and to exercise them in playing " within
the Blackfriars in London or elsewhere." This
band of players was dissolved in March, 1608, for
using lewd words in their performances.

The close intimacy of the dramatists, Francis
Beaumont and John Fletcher, dated from about
the year 1607. John Aubrey wrote of them :
" There was a wonderful consimility of fancy
between him (Beaumont) and Mr. Jo. Fletcher,
which caused that dearness of friendship between
them. . . . They lived together on the Bankside,
not far from the playhouse (Globe), both bachelors,
lay together, had one wench (servant maid) in the
house between them, which they did so admire,
the same clothes and cloak, etc."

About 1610 Francis Beaumont wrote in his letter
to Ben Jonson :

> " What things have we seen
> Done at the Mermaid ! heard words that have been
> So nimble, and so full of subtile flame,
> As if that every one from whence they came

Had meant to put his whole wit in a jest,
And had resolved to live a fool the rest
Of his dull life ; then when there hath been thrown
Wit able enough to justify the town
For three days past ; wit that might warrant be
For the whole city to talk foolishly
Till that were cancell'd ; and when that was gone,
We left on air behind us, which alone
Was able to make the two next companies
Right witty ; though but downright fools, more wise."

About August, 1611, Middleton's play, "A Chaste
Maid of Cheapside," was performed at the Swan
Theatre, Bankside. Moll, "the roaring drab," was
told how a knight, when seeing the last new play
at the Swan, lost his purse with seven angels
in it.

On St. Peter's Day, June 29th, 1613, the Globe
Theatre, Bankside, was destroyed by fire, including
the silken flag displayed during playing time, and
the ale-house adjoining. According to Winwood,
the mimic discharges in Shakespeare's play of
"Henry VIII." fired the rushes on the roof, and the
audience was so engrossed with the actors that the
mischief was not noticed till too late.

Fortunately few or no personal accidents occurred,
a circumstance alluded to in a ballad of the time,
of which the following is a portion :

"Now sit thee downe, Melpomene,
    Wrapt in a sea-coal robe ;
And tell the doleful tragedie
    That late was play'd at Globe :
For noe man that can singe and saye,
Was scar'd on St. Peter's daye.
Oh, sorrow, pittiful sorrow ; and yet all this
Is true.

> Out ran the knights, out ran the lords,
>   And there was great ado ;
> Some lost their hats, some lost their swords—
>   Then out ran Burbage too ;
> The reprobates, though drunk on Monday,
> Prayed for the fool and Henry Condy.
> Oh, sorrow, etc."

The next day the Rev. Thomas Lorkin, writing from London to Sir Thomas Puckering, said : " No longer since than yesterday, while Burbage's company were acting at the Globe the play of ' Henry VIII.,' and there shooting off certain chambers in way of triumph, the fire catched and fastened upon the thatch of the house, and there burned so furiously as it consumed the whole house, all in less than two hours, the people having enough to do to save themselves."

Sir Henry Wotton told the story of the fire in a letter to Sir Edmund Bacon : " Let matters of state sleep, I will entertain you at the present with what happened this week at the Bankside. The King's players had a new play, called ' All is True,' representing some principal pieces of the reign of Henry the Eighth, which was set forth with many extraordinary circumstances of pomp and majesty, even to the matting of the stage, the knights of the order with their Georges and Garters, the guards with their embroidered coats and the like. Now King Henry making a masque at the Cardinal Wolsey's house, and certain cannons being shot off at his entry, some of the paper or other stuff where- with one of them was stopped did light on the thatch, where being thought at first but an idle smoke, and their eyes more attentive to the show, it kindled inwardly and ran round like a train, consuming in less than an hour the whole house to the very ground ; nothing did perish but wood and straw and a few forsaken cloaks, and one man had his breeches set on fire."

In another letter he wrote : " But it was a great marvel and grace of God that the people had so little harm, having but two narrow doors to get out."

Ben Jonson witnessed the blaze, and in poetic fury launched his " Execration against Vulcan "— " that cruell stratagem against the Globe, the glory of the Banke."

John Taylor, the Water-poet, also " in action saw the Globe to burn."

A contract was entered into about now with Gilbert Katheren to pull down the old Bear Garden house, on the northern square courtilage of the lane called the " Bear Garden." He began rebuilding a bear-garden to be named the " Hope." " The Hope is to be in compass, form, wideness, like the play-house called the Swan in the lib'tie of Paris Garden."

In the spring of 1614 the rebuilding of the Globe Theatre, Bankside, was completed. John Taylor, the Water-poet, in his epigram, called it a stately playhouse :

> " As gold is better that's in fire tried,
> So is the Bankside Globe, that late was burn'd ;
> For when before it had a thatched hide,
> Now to a stately theatre is turn'd."

On the last day of October Ben Jonson's play, " Bartholomew Fair," was first acted at the " Hope " Theatre, on the Bankside, by the company called " Lady Elizabeth's servants." In his introduction the author spoke of the " special decorum " observed in the piece being performed there—"the place being as dirty as Smithfield, and as stinking every whit." In another passage he alluded to the "gathering of the broken apples for the bears within."

John Taylor, the Water-poet, and William Fennor, "the King's rhyming poet," created amusement this autumn by having a serious quarrel, the cause of which was thus described by the former : " Be it known unto all men, that I, John Taylor, waterman, did agree with William Fennor (who arrogantly and falsely entitles himself the King's Majesty's Rhyming Poet) to answer me at a trial of wit, on the 7th of October last, 1614, at the Hope stage on the Bankside . . . and when the day came that the play should have been performed, the house being filled with a great audience, who had spent their money extraordinarily, then this companion for an ass ran away and left me for a fool, amongst thousands of critical censurers."

Taylor had caused a thousand bills to be printed, announcing the contest and other expenses were incurred to the extent of twenty pounds ; and when the crowd in the theatre, who had paid a greater price for admission, realised that they were to be disappointed of their entertainment, the unlucky Water-poet was pelted and abused. In revenge he wrote : " Taylor's Revenge : or, the rhymer William Fenner, firk'd, ferrited and finely fetcht over the coales, etc."

On March 6th, 1616, Francis Beaumont, the dramatist, died, after a brief married life.

In 1617, Alleyn the actor commenced building a new Blackfriars Theatre.

In the course of September, 1618, Alleyn made the

following entry in his diary in connection with the building at the Blackfriars Theatre : " More disbursed for the building of the Blackfriars for this year and in anno 1617, when it first began with the £200 disbursed by my father ; buying in of leases, charges in law and the building itself is £1105 0s. 2d."

Early in 1619, the Lord Mayor—Sir Sebastian Harvey—and the Common Council of London issued an order for the discontinuance of the Playhouse at Blackfriars, " on petition of the inhabitants representing the inconvenience and blocking up of the thoroughfares occasioned by the great resort of people."

This did not at the time effect the abolition of the Theatre, for, on March 27th, a Licence was granted at Westminster to John Hemings, Richard Burbage, Henry Condall, John Lowen, Nicholas Tooley, John Underwood, Nathan Field, Robert Benfield, Robert Gough, William Ecclestone, Richard Robinson, John Shancks and their associates to act comedies, tragedies, histories, etc., " for the solace and pleasure of the King and his subjects," at the Globe Theatre, Bankside, and at their private playhouse in Blackfriars and elsewhere.

LORD MAYORS' DAYS.

1603. The Lord Mayor's Day at this time fell on the 29th of October, when a Water procession, composed of the city barge carrying the new chief Magistrate, the Aldermen, and other citizens and officers, escorted by the barges of the City Companies and others bearing emblematic devices and figures, all gay with flags and banners, and to the sound of lively music, went from Three Cranes Stairs to Westminster for the swearing in of the Lord Mayor. The return procession to the City was by land, and the pageantry of the Show was a huge delight to the crowd of all ranks, which made high festival of the occasion.

When King James came to the throne, Sir Robert Lee, a Merchant Taylor, was Lord Mayor of London; and he was succeeded in the autumn by Sir Thomas Bennet, a Mercer. On this occasion, the Plague being then at the height of its devastating fury, the pageantry of the river and land processions had no place in the quiet function. Men's minds were too full of grief and terror to admit of shows, and the quaint spectacle that the people rejoiced in, when free of calamity, would have been but a cruel mockery of their sorrows and sufferings.

1604. In 1604, Sir Thomas Lowe, a Haberdasher, was sworn in, and again the ceremony was attended with no special pageantry.

1605. Sir Leonard Hallyday, or Holliday, a Merchant Taylor, was sworn in on a Tuesday in 1605. The pageant, devised and written by Anthony Munday, citizen and Draper of London, represented the Triumphs of re-united Britannia, arising from the Union with Scotland, and was performed at the sole expense of the Merchant Taylors Company.

1606. No special features marked the Show in 1606, when Sir John Watts, a Clothworker, was sworn in at Westminster ; or the next year, **1607,** at the inauguration of Sir Henry Rowe, a Mercer.

1608. In 1608, Sir Humphrey Weld, a Grocer, became Chief Magistrate ; and he was succeeded the following year (**1609**) by Sir Thomas Cambell or Campbell, an Ironmonger, when the City Show, which had been neglected for several years, was revived by the King's order.

1610. In 1610 the new Lord Mayor was Sir William Craven, a Merchant Taylor, who as a poor Yorkshire boy had entered London in a carrier's cart to seek the fortune he attained, and was the father of the brave soldier who fought under Gustavus Adolphus of Sweden, and in after years was supposed to have privately married the widowed Queen of Bohemia, daughter of King James.

1711. Lord Mayor's Day in 1611 was on a Tuesday, and the pageant for the inauguration of Sir James Pemberton, a Goldsmith, performed at the expense of the Goldsmiths' Company, was devised and written by Anthony Munday, and named "Chryso-thriambos : the Triumphes of Golde." In the river show "a mare man and a mare maid" were introduced, "in a galley foist, with silk flags and silk pennons."

Six barrels of gunpowder were provided for a salute, in expectation of the attendance of the Queen.

1612. Sir John Swinnerton, a Merchant Taylor, was the new Lord Mayor in 1612, and his pageant, named "Troia Nova Triumphans; or, London Triumphing," was written by the poet Decker. The river show, consisting of four or five distinct pageants and others devices, was considered rather remarkable, but it was scattered, and almost suffered shipwreck from a great wind that was blowing. The barges of the City Companies were, with considerable difficulty and danger, either turned back or run aground, and the Lord Mayor himself was brought almost alone, only after a hard struggle, to Westminster. The Elector Palatine and his suite were entertained at the Guildhall banquet, when the Archbishop of Canterbury, the Bishop of London, and a crowd of noblemen and courtiers were present. The young prince was on the point of marrying Princess Elizabeth, the King's daughter, and the gallant bridegroom-elect established his popularity in the City by saluting the Lady Mayoress and her train. Two great gilt loving cups and a large basin and ewer, weighing 234 ounces, were presented to the Elector by the Chief Magistrate and his brethren.

1613. In 1613 the Lord Mayor was Sir Thomas Middleton, a Grocer, and brother of Sir Hugh Middleton, whose New River Head at Islington, was completed during his year of office. His pageant, called "The Triumph of Truth," was devised by himself, and he explained it as " all the shows, pageants, chariots, morning noon and night Triumphs, directed, written and redeem'd into

Form, from the ignorance of former Times, and their common Writer" (meaning Anthony Munday). This was one of the first attempts at scenic representation in the water spectacle, and was thus described: "The water pageant was truly picturesque; it did not consist merely of the gilded barges, but the river was decked in the richest glory to receive him, upon whose crystal bosom stands five islands, artfully garnished with all manner of Indian fruit trees, drugs, spiceries, and the like; the middle island with a faire castle especially beautiful." These islands rested on boats, and referred to the forts of the lately-established East India Company, and the whole intended as an emblem of the Grocers' Company. There was also a strange ship, with neither sailor nor pilot, bearing upon a white silk streamer the words "Veritate Gubernir" (I am steered by Truth), set in letters of gold. On board this vessel were a King of the Moors, his Queen, and two attendants of their own colour : the rest of their followers peopling the castle standing in the midst of the middle island. There were also six chariots, bearing Neptune and other characters, who addressed the Lord Mayor in his voyage to Westminster.

1614. In 1614, Sir Thomas Hayes, a Draper, was the new Lord Mayor. The pageant, written and devised by Anthony Munday, and performed at the expense of the Drapers' Company, was named "The Triumphs of Old Drapery, or the Rich Clothing of England."

1615. The 29th of October falling on a Sunday in 1615, the next day was chosen for the swearing in of Sir John Jolles, a Draper. The pageant, named "Metropolis Coronata ; the Triumphs of Ancient

Drapery, or Rich Clothing of England," was a reproduction of the Show of the previous year, "performed in heartie affection to him and at the bountifull charges of his worthie brethren the truely honourable Society of Drapers ; the first that received such dignitie in this Citie."

Anthony Munday, the author of the pageant, wrote : "According to ancient and most honourable custom the Lord Mayor being to pass by water to Westminster, in company of his worthy Brethren, and attended by all other Companies in their several barges made fit for triumph, after such manner as formerly hath been observed ; the first device that welcometh him to the water is an invention proper to that nature, and thought apt to conduct him in his passage. He being both a Draper and Stapler, and these two professions (in former times) appertaining to the Brethren of London's Drapery, trading only in wools and woollen-cloth, the then chief riches of the kingdom ; both these mysteries meeting together so conveniently in one man, I did account it as a sin in me to sunder them, and therefore made use of that crest or cognizance of the Golden Fleece, given by ancient heraldries to them both, and remaining still in firm force with the Draper, as their escutcheon of arms maketh manifest. In a goodly Argosy, shaped so near as art could yield it to that of such ancient and honourable fame as conveyed Jason and his valiant Argonauts of Greece to fetch away the Golden Fleece from Colchos, we make use of that memorable history as fit both for the time and occasion. Therein aloft sitteth Medea, whose love to Jason was his best means of obtaining the Golden Fleece ; and therefore, as still witnessing the fiery zeal of her

affection towards him, she sitteth playing with his
love-locks, and wantoning with him in all pleasing
dalliance, to compass the more settled assurance of
his constancy. His noble companions, as Hercules,
Telamon, Orpheus, Castor, Pollux, Calais and Zethes,
the sons of Boreas, are seated about him in their
several degrees, attired in fair gilt armours, bearing
triumphal lances, wreathed about with laurel,
shields, honoured with the impress of the Golden
Fleece, and their heads circled with laurels, according
to the manner of all famous conquerors. This
Argosy is rowed by divers comely eunuchs, which
continually attended on Medea, and she favouring
them but to pass under the Fleece of Gold, had all
their garments immediately sprinkled over with
gold, even as if it had showered down in drops
upon them ; and so they row on in Jason's triumph.
Having thus borrowed the help of this well-known
story, to honour the day of our London Jason, we
do poetically infer, that Neptune having declared
himself kind in their coming hither, and Thamesis
shewn herself as gracious in passing over her watery
bosom, to make his triumph more majestical, they
lend the assistance of their sea-chariot, wherein
they use to sport themselves on their watery regiment
(government), it being shaped like to a whale, or
the huge Leviathan of the sea. Therein is placed
the shadow of Sir Henry Fitz-Alwine, to grace
this day's honour both by land and water ;
and by him are seated eight royal virtues, bearing
the ensigns of arms of eight honourable Drapers
and Staplers, with beautiful shields that declare
each man's name to accompany them. . . .
No sooner is my Lord and his brethren seated in
their barge, and such silence obtained as the

season can best permit, but Fitz-Alwine saluteth
him in this manner."

Then followed a long rhymning speech delivered
on the water at the Three Cranes Stairs.

1616. In 1616, October 29th, fell on the Monday,
when Alderman John Leman, a Fishmonger, was
sworn in at Westminster. The pageant, again
devised and written by Anthony Munday, was
called "Chrysanaleia, or the Golden Fishing; or
Honour of Fishmongers," and was magnificently
performed "in hearty love to him, and at the charges
of his worthy brethren the ancient and right worshipful Company of Fishmongers." The water spectacle
contained "A Fishing Buss, in the true old shape,
forme, and proportion, yet dispensed in all with
some beautie for the daies honor, passing for the
one wherein St. Peter sate mending his nets."

There were islands on boats, on which appeared
mermen and mermaids, lemon trees, dolphins,
pelicans, etc. In the land procession were several
men in armour, one of whom bore the head of
Wat Tyler on a spear; there were also the effigies
of Walworth lying on his tomb, and an angel representing the genius of London calling on the dead
champion to arise and address the Lord Mayor in
a congratulatory speech.

1617. Alderman George Bolles or Bowles, a
Grocer, was the chosen of the City in 1617. The
pageant, entitled "The Triumphs of Honor and
Industry," was written and devised by Sir Thomas
Middleton, and contained islands, castles, Indian
chariots, ships, and other devices; costing the
Grocers' Company more than eight hundred
pounds.

Horatio Busino, Chaplain to the Venetian Ambassador, gave in his diary the following description of the show :

" His Excellency (the Venetian Ambassador) received a private invitation to view the first part of the pageant, which consists of ships, galleys, brigantines, foists and barges coming up the Thames, starting from the Lord Mayor's own house, and proceeding towards the palace or royal court, where he takes the oath of allegiance. On the present occasion the magistrate arranged his installation with the greatest pomp, but always with allusion to his trade of a grocer. At a very early hour his Excellency went to the mansion of a nobleman commanding a fine view of a bridge over the Thames. This runs through the City like our Grand Canal, but as wide as the Giudecca Canal. Scarcely had we arrived when a dense fleet of vessels hove in sight, accompanied by swarms of small boats to see the show, like the gondolas about the Bucintoro. The ships were beautifully decorated with balustrades and various paintings. They carried immense banners and countless pennons. Salutes were fired, and a number of persons bravely attired played on trumpets, fifes, and other instruments. The oarsmen rowed rapidly with the flood tide, while the discharges of the salutes were incessant We also saw highly ornamented stages with various devices, which subsequently served for the land pageant, for triumphal cars, when passing through the principal streets. When the gay squadron had reached a certain point it received a salute from the sakers, which made a great echo. The compliment was repeated even more loudly, when my Lord Mayor landed at the water stairs near the Court of Parliament, on his way to take the oath before the appointed judges.

" Bewildered by what we had seen, we proceeded to the Row, which is the finest part of the City, to the windows assigned to us in the house of a respectable goldsmith. Whilst the pageant was being marshalled we gazed about. The houses have many stories, and all the fronts are glazed so that the windows fill the entire space. On this occasion they were all crowded with the sweetest faces, looking like so many pretty pictures, with varied head-tire and rich dresses of every possible colour and texture, including cloth of gold and silver. This charming view was spoilt by two objects, namely two ugly Spanish women (as I may conscientiously call them, apart from our national prejudice), ill-dressed, lean, and livid, and with deep-set eyeballs, perfect hobgoblins, though we could not resist looking at them occasionally for the sake of comparing them with the English ladies nearest to them, whose beauty thus became more manifest.

" On looking into the street we saw a surging mass of people, moving in search of some resting place which a fresh mass of sightseers grouped higgled-piggledy rendered impossible. It was a fine medley ; there were old men in their dotage ; insolent youths and boys, especially the apprentices alluded to ; painted wenches and women of the lower classes carrying their children, all anxious to see the show. We noticed but few coaches and still fewer horsemen ; only a few gentlewomen coming in their carriages for a view at some house in the Row belonging to their friends or relations, for the insolence of the mob is extreme. They cling behind the coaches, and should the coachman use his whip, they jump down, and pelt him with mud. In this way we saw them bedaub the smart livery of one coachman, who was obliged to put up with it. In these great uproars no sword is ever unsheathed, everything ends in kicks, fisty cuffs and muddy faces. From the windows an incessant shower of squibs and crackers were thrown into the mass beneath, for which the boys scrambled when they were cold.

" On surveying the windows along the street as far as the eye could reach, we perceived sundry gallants in attendance on fine ladies. In our simplicity we imagined that for each lady there would have been a brother or a husband, but we were assured that the gallants were the servants of these ladies, which in plain language means their lovers, being much favoured by them and enjoying great liberty and familiarity. Foreigners are ill regarded not to say detested in London, so sensible people dress in the English fashion, or in that of France, which is adopted by nearly the whole Court, and thus mishaps are avoided, or passed over in silence. The Spaniards alone maintain the prerogative of wearing their own costume, so they are easily recognised and most mortally hated. Some of our party saw a wicked woman in a rage with an individual supposed to belong to the Spanish embassy. She urged the crowd to mob him, setting the example by belabouring him herself with a cabbage stalk, and calling him a Spanish rogue, and although in very brave array his garments were foully smeared, with a sort of soft and very stinking mud, which abounds here at all seasons, so that the place better deserves to be called ' Lorda ' (filth) than ' Londra ' (London). Had not the don saved himself in a shop they would assuredly have torn his eyes out, so hateful are the airs assumed by the Spaniards, whom the people of England consider harpies, which makes me think that they are less well known eslewhere.

" The companies of gownsmen now began to appear, for the mere purpose of lining the streets. They carried their maces, and there were officers to protect them from the crowd. Their gowns resemble those of a Doctor of Laws or the Doge, the sleeves being very wide in the shoulder and trimmed with various materials, such as plush, velvet, martens' fur, foynes, and a very beautiful kind of astrachan, while some wear sables. These gownsmen belonged exclusively to the Grocers' Company, to which the present Lord Mayor belongs, and they number more than a thousand. Over the left shoulder they wore a sort of satchel, one half of red cloth and the other black, fastened to a narrow stole. There were other gownsmen in long cloth gowns with satchels of red damask. These were younger men than the others, and their duty is to wait at table during the banquet. Others again wore another kind of appendage, also red, on the shoulder, and a fourth set had small stoles about the throat.

" To clear the way, the City Marshal, on horseback, with a gold collar round his neck, and two footmen in livery, kept parading up and down ; he was so smooth and sleek that we unhesitatingly pronounced him to be of the swinish race of jolly Bacchus. The way was also kept by a number of lusty youths and men armed with long fencing swords, which they manipulated very dexterously, but no sooner had a passage been forced in one place than the crowd closed in at another. There were also men masked as wild giants who by means of fireballs and wheels hurled sparks in the faces of the mob and over their persons, but all proved unavailing to make a free and ample thoroughfare.

" The first stages which made their appearance were harnessed to griffins ridden by lads in silk liveries. Others followed drawn by lions and camels and other large animals, laden with bales from which the lads took sundry confections, sugar, nutmegs, dates, and ginger, throwing them among the populace. The animals which drew these cars were all yoked with silken cords. The first pageant represented a lovely forest with fruit on the top of its trees, and peopled with children in Indian costume, with the black trees falling from the back of the head, their faces stained, imitating nudity, with the little apron fringed with red feathers and others of various hues. Then came a pastoral couple with fifes, one dressed entirely in red feathers, while the other represented a tiger, being wrapped in the animal's skin. This couple played the part of man and wife, performing on their instruments in the Indian fashion, the children danced all the while with much grace and great variety of gesture, moving the whole body, head, hands and feet, keeping excellent time and performing figures, first round one tree and then another, changing their positions, so as really to surprise everybody.

" Other large and handsome stages followed, one of which, I was told, represented the religion of the Indians ; the Sun shining aloft in the midst of other figures. On another stage was a fine castle ; while a third bore a beautiful ship, supposed to be just returned from the Indies with its crew and cargo. Other stages bore symbols of commerce, or the nations which trade with India. Among the figures represented was a Spaniard, wonderfully true to life, who imitated the gestures of that nation perfectly. He wore small black moustachios and a hat and cape in the Spanish fashion, with a ruff round his neck and others about his wrists, nine inches deep. He kept kissing his hands, right and left, but especially to the Spanish Ambassador, who was a short distance from us, in such wise as to elicit roars of laughter from the multitude.

" After this triumphant fleet the Archbishop of Canterbury appeared on horseback, which is as much as to say the Pope of England. On his left rode the Chief Baron, and they were preceded by forty gentlemen on foot, wearing gold chains. There were mace-bearers and footmen, and other officers in tabards of black velvet, most richly embroidered on the back in silk and gold with the rose of England. Then followed in pairs the earls, marquises, and other lords and treasurers of the Kingdom. Next came a display of sundry banners, one in particular of monstrous size belonging to the Grocers' Company, was carried by four of five men, who supported its staff by other small staves fixed in the main one, while others bore the train of the long streamer so that it really made a fine show. All these banners belonged to the Lord Mayor's own guild, each of the other companies having separate colours. They were followed by fifty old men, all in livery of long gowns down to the ground, of blue cloth with red sleeves and caps, carrying javelins. At night these men carry the Lord Mayor's torches. Immediately in rear of the javelin men came a tall man wearing a large hat of squirrel's fur, the size of a basket, and holding a handsome gilt truncheon. He preceded two small children also gaily dressed, each carrying a nosegay on the top of a wand.

" Finally the Lord Mayor elect made his appearance on a barbed horse, wearing a red robe and a gold collar round his neck, over which was a large order like the Fleece, given of yore by the King to the magistrate for having detected a conspiracy and killed the ringleader (Wat Tyler). This badge is of gold with a large and precious jewel in its centre. Fifteen or twenty aldermen came next, also on horseback, all in a costume of red cloth resembling my Lord Mayor's, and those with gold collars round their necks had previously filled the office. The last line of horsemen consisted of the two sheriffs, also dressed in red, though the shape of their gowns was somewhat different. They also wore gold chains, and these two individuals are those appointed to administer justice in London during the present year, as officials of this Lord Mayor.

" The whole of this fine company were to partake of the treat, and the line was closed by an endless train of vagrant hangers on, who all lay claim to the very sumptuous banquet, with open doors , for a whole year."

1618. In 1618, while the show of Sir Sebastian Harvey, an Ironmonger, was in progress, the unfortunate Sir Walter Raleigh was being executed in Old Palace Yard, Westminster. It was asserted that the time was specially chosen for drawing away the people from the sacrifice of a popular hero, and " from beholding," Aubrey wrote, " the tragedy of the gallantest worthy that England ever bred."

1619. The pageant of Alderman William Cockayn, a Skinner, in 1619, was written and devised by Sir Thomas Middleton, and entitled " The Triumphs of Love and Antiquity."

1620. Again October 29th fell on a Sunday in 1620, and the next day Alderman Francis Jones, a Haberdasher, was inaugurated. The pageant, devised and written by John Squire, was called " The Tryumphs of Peace," and was performed " at the particular cost and charge of the right Worshipful Society of the Haberdashers."

" The First Show or Presentment on the water was a chariot aptly contrived of two sea-monsters argent, and drawn by two sea-horses, set also off with pure silver ; on this chariot was one borne representing Oceanus his head wreathed with ' segges,' one hand grasping a sceptre of green reeds to shew his potent sway within his watery dominion, and the other curbing the forward fierceness of his horses ; his azure locks and beard o'er-grown, hung like the careless emblem of a reverend age, dishevelled o'er his naked limbs, which were shadowed off with a mantle of sea-green taffety, limned with waves and fishes. This first Presentment was on a stately well-built ship, bearing full sail, figuring the traffic or trade of the worthy to be esteemed noble Company of the Haberdashers. Behind the ship sat Æolus, the God of Winds, filling their sails with prosperous gusts ; and at each corner of the ship sat, upon small islands, the Four Parts of the World, Asia, Africa, America, and Europe, each of them inviting their trade unto their coasts. Asia was attired in an antique habit of peach-coloured satin, and buskins of the same, a coronet on her head, and a censor in her hand, reeking with Panchayian spices ; Africa, a blackamoor in a naked shape, adorned with beads, and in her hand a branch of a nutmeg tree ; America, a tawny Moor, upon her head a crown of features and bases of the same, at her back a quiver of shafts, and in her hand a Parthian bow ; Europe in a robe of crimson taffety, on her head an imperial crown conferred on her by the other three as Empress of the Earth, and holding in her hand a cluster of grapes to signify her fullswoln plenty."

These met the Lord Mayor when he embarked at the Three Cranes Wharf, and Oceanus and Æolus made him rhyming speeches.

" The Second and last Presentment on the water was Parnassus Mount, whereon the Nine Muses sat ; Clyo, the first, suited in a gown of purple taffety, and studiously employed in turning over books, she being the Historical Muse ; Melpomene was attired in a black taffety robe, her head decked with cypress, and playing on a therobo ; Thalia, the Comic Muse, in a light changeable taffety robe, and playing on a viol ; Euterpe, the Muse that first invented wind instruments, was richly apparelled, and played on a flute-recorder ; Terpsichore on the lute ; and the Geometrical Muse Erato with a scale and compass in her hand ; the Heroical Muse Calliope was shaped in a tawny silk robe, and her temples girt with bays ; the heavenly Muse Urania, that invented astrology, was decked in a robe of azure taffety, ' semined ' with stars, on her head she wore a coronet of stars, and her right hand supported a sphere ; Polymneia, the inventress of rhetoric, assumed her place nearest to Apollo, who sat on the top of the Mount in a robe of cloth of gold, under a laurel-tree, playing on a harp, alluding to that of Virgil : ' In medio residens complectitur omnia Phœbus.' And on the back of the Mount stood Mercury listening to their harmonious strains."

This latter part of the Show, discoursing a variety of music, went with the Lord Mayor to Westminster.

1621. Alderman Edward Barkham, a draper, was the new Lord Mayor in 1621, and his pageant, devised and written by Sir Thomas Middleton and performed with much splendour " at the sole cost and charges of the honourable and ancient Fraternity of Drapers," was named " The Sun in Aries."

1622. In 1622, Alderman Peter Proby became Chief Magistrate.

1623. Sir Martin Lumley, a Draper, was the next Lord Mayor, and his pageant was entitled " The Triumphs of Integrity."

1624. The last Lord Mayor of the reign was Alderman John Gore, or Goare, a Merchant Taylor, and his pageant, written by John Webster Taylor, and performed " at the charge and expense of the right worthy and worshipfull Fraternity of eminent Merchant Taylors," was called "The Monument of Honour." The East India Company allowed their "chambers" at Blackwall to be shot off at the time the oath was being taken at Westminster.

WORKS CONSULTED AND USED IN COMPILING "ON AND ALONG THE THAMES, JAMES I. 1603-1625."

AUTHOR		WORKS
Aikin, Lucy	..	Memoirs of the Court of James I. 1822.
Allen, Thomas	..	History and Antiquities of London, Westminster and Southward. 1827.
		The History and Antiquities of the Parish of Lambeth.
Ancaster, Earl of	..	MSS. of, at Grimsthorpe.
Anderson, Adam	..	An Historical and Chronological Deduction of the Origin of Commerce. 1787-9.
Andrews, William	..	Punishments in the Olden Times.
Arber, Edward	..	The Story of this Pilgrim Fathers 1603-23.
Asher, George Michael	..	Henry Hudson the Navigator. 1860.
Ashton, John	..	Humour, Wit and Satire of the 17th century. 1883.
Aubrey, John	..	Miscellanies upon Various Subjects. 1784.
		Lives and Letters of Eminent Men. 1813.
Aungier, George James	..	The History and Antiquities of Syon Monastery, etc. 1840.
Ballard, Adolphus	..	Chronicles of the Royal Borough of Woodstock. 1896.
Ballard, George	..	Memoirs of Learned Ladies. 1752.
Barrow, John	..	Voyages to the Arctic Regions.
Bayley, J.	..	The Tower of London. 1830.
Beaufort, Duke of, etc.	..	MSS. of
Beaumont, Francis	..	Letter to Ben Jonson.
Beaumont and Fletcher	..	The Knight of the Burning Pestle.
Belloc, Hilaire	..	The Historic Thames. 1907.
Besant, Sir Walter	..	London—in the Time of the Stuarts.
Birch, Thomas	..	The Life of Prince Henry.
		The Annals of King James.
		The Court and Times of James the First.
Birch, Walter de Gray	..	The Historical Charters and Constitutional Documents of the City of London.
Birdwood, Sir G.	..	Register of Letters of the Governor and Company of Merchants of London trading into the East Indies. 1600-19. 1893.

AUTHOR	WORKS
Boulton, William Biggs	The Amusements of Old London. 1901.
Brayley, Edward and Herbert	Lambeth Palace. 1806.
Brayley Edward Wedlake.	History of the Ancient Palace and late Houses of Parliament at Westminster. 1836.
	History of Surrey.
Brock, Arthur Clutton	Eton.
Brydges, Sir Samuel	Memoirs of the Peers of England during the Reign of James I.
Buccleuch and Queensberry, Duke of	MSS. of, at Montagu House, Whitehall.
Capper, Charles	The Port and Trade of London. 1862.
Cayley, Arthur	The Life of Sir Walter Raleigh. 1805.
Challenor, Bromley	Selections from the Records of the Borough of Abingdon, 1555—1897.
Challoner, Richard, Bishop of Debra	Catholic Book of Martyrs.
Chambers, Robert	The Life of King James the First.
Chancellor, E. Beresford	The History and Antiquities of Richmond. 1894.
Climenson, Emily J.	The History of Shiplake, Oxon. 1894.
	Guide to Henley-on-Thames. 1896.
Cobbett, Richard Stuteley	Memorials of Twickenham. 1872.
Collins, Arthur	Letters and Memorials of State.
	An History of the Ancient and Illustrious Family of the Percys, Barons Percy and Earls of Northumberland.
Collier, John Payne	The Egerton Papers. 1840.
	The Diary of P. Henslowe. 1591—1609.
Cunningham, Peter	Inigo Jones—A Life of the Architect, etc.
Daniel, William Barker	Rural Sports. 1801-2.
Decker, Thomas	The Wonderful Yeare, 1603. Wherein is shewed the picture of London lying Sicke of the Plague.
Deloney, Thomas	Strange Histories, consisting of Ballads and other Poems, principally by
Devereux, Walter Bouchier	Lives and Letters of the Devereux, Earls of Essex. 1853.
Devon, Frederick	Issues of the Exchequer, James I. 1836.
D'Ewes, Sir Simonds,	The Autobiography of
Ditchfield, P. H., and Page, William	The Victoria History of Berkshire.
Dixon, William Hepworth	Her Majesty's Tower.
	Royal Windsor. 1879.
	Personal History of Lord Bacon. 1861.
Donne, John	Letters to Several Persons of Honour. 1651.

AUTHOR	WORKS
Doubleday, H. Arthur, and Page, William	The Victoria History of Essex.
Drayton, Michael ..	Poly-olbion.
Ducarel, Andrew Coltee	Historical Particulars of Lambeth Parish and Lambeth Palace. 1791.
Dugdale, Gilbert ..	The Time Triumphant. Tract, 1604.
Edwards, Edward ..	The Life of Sir W. Raleigh. 1868.
Entick, John ..	History and Survey of London, etc. 1766. A New Naval History, or Compleat View of the British Marine. 1757.
Evans, John ..	Richmond and its Vicinity. 1824. An Excursion to Windsor. 1827.
Faulkner, Thomas ..	The History and Antiquities of Brentford, Ealing and Chiswick. 1845.
Fenton, John ..	King James, his Welcome to London. A Tract in Verse. 1603.
Fergusson, Thomas Colyer	The Marriage Registers of St. Dunstan's, Stepney, 1563—1719. 1898.
Finett, Sir John ..	Finetti Philoxenis: Observations touching Foreign Ambassadors. 1656.
F. R. ..	A Short History of the East India Company. 1793.
Francis, John ..	Chronicles and Character of the Stock Exchange. 1855.
Gardiner, S. R. ..	The First Two Stuarts and the Puritan Revolution: 1603—1660. 1874. Britain under James I. 1904.
Garnett, Richard ..	Richmond on Thames. 1896.
Goodman, Godfrey ..	The Court of King James the First. 1839.
Gosse, Edmund ..	The Life and Letters of John Donne, Dean of St. Paul's. 1899.
Granger, James ..	Biographical History of England.
Grant, Sir Robert ..	A Sketch of the History of the East India Company, etc., to 1773. 1813.
Guilding, J. M. ..	Reading Records—The Diary of the Corporation.
Hall, Hubert ..	A History of the Custom-Revenue in England. 1885.
Harris, J. ..	An Historical Account of the Intercourse between the Inhabitants of Great Britain and the people of the East Indies. 1744.
Harrison, Walter ..	A New and Universal History, etc., of London and Westminster. 1775.

AUTHOR	WORKS
Hasted, Edward ..	History of Kent. 1778.
	History of Kent—The Hundred of Black-heath. 1886.
Heckethorn, Charles William	London Memories.
Herbert, William ..	The History of the Twelve Great Livery Companies of London.
Hickey, T. ..	East Indian Chronologist.
Howe, Edmund ..	Continuation of Stow's Survey of London.
Howell, James ..	Londinopolis. 1657.
	Familiar Letters on Important Subjects. 1753.
Humpherus, Henry ..	History of the Origin and Progress of the Company of Watermen and Lightermen of the River Thames. 1887.
Hunt, Leigh ..	The Town.
Hutchinson, Francis ..	An Historical Essay concerning Witchcraft.
Ironside, Edward ..	History and Antiquities of Twickenham. 1701.
Isaacson, Henry ..	Saturni Ephemerides—Chronological Tables. 1633.
	Life and Death of Lancelot Andrewes. 1829.
Jesse, John Heneage ..	Memoirs of the Court of England during the Reign of the Stuarts. 1855.
Jonson, Ben ..	Poems, etc., The Forest.
Knight, Charles ..	Once upon a Time.
Lambert, B. ..	History and Survey of London and its Environs. 1806.
Laud, William, Arch-bishop.	The Diary of
Law, Ernest ..	History of Hampton Court Palace. 1885-91.
L'Estrange, A. G. K. ..	The Village of Palaces ; or, Chronicle of Chelsea. 1880.
	The Palace and the Hospital; or, Chronicles of Greenwich. 1886.
Lilly, William ..	History of his Life and Times. 1715.
Littledale, Willoughby, A.	The Registers of St. Bene't and St. Peter, Paul's Wharf, London.
Lodge, Edmund ..	Illustration of British History. 1781
Lysons, Daniel ..	Environs of London.
Macpherson, David ..	The History of European Commerce with India. 1812.
Maitland, William ..	History of London

AUTHOR	WORKS
Malcolm, James Peller ..	Londinium Redivivum. 1803.
	Anecdotes of the Manners and Customs of London. 1811.
Malden, H. E. ..	The Victorian History of Surrey.
Man, John ..	The History and Antiquities of Reading. 1816
Manning, Owen ..	History and Antiquities of Surrey.
Markham, Sir Clement Robert	The Voyages of William Baffin. 1612-22.
Montagu of Beaulieu, Lord	MSS. of
Nichols, John	The Progresses, etc., of James I.
	The Progresses, etc., of Queen Elizabeth.
Nichols, John Bowyer ..	The Cries of London. 1824.
	Account of the Royal Hospital and Collegiate Church of St. Katherine near the Tower of London. 1824.
Nichols, John Gough ..	London Pageants. 1831.
Noorthouck, John ..	A New History of London, including Westminster and Southwark. 1773.
Norden, John ..	An intended Guyde for English Travailers, etc. 1625.
Oldys, William ..	Life of Sir Walter Raleigh. 1736.
Osborne, F ..	Traditionall Memoyres on the Raigne of King James. 1658.
Overall, W. H. and H. C.	Analytical Index to the Series of Records known as the Remembrancia. 1579—1664.
Page, William ..	The Victoria History of Buckingham.
	The Victoria History of Oxfordshire.
	The Victoria History of Kent.
	The Victoria History of Gloucester.
Page, William, and Round, Horace.	The Victoria History of Essex.
Paget, Sir James ..	Records of Harvey. 1846.
Pasquil ..	Palinodia and Progress in the Tavern.
Paule, Sir George ..	The Life of John Whitgift, Archbishop of Canterbury. 1612.
Pauli, Reinhold ..	Pictures of Old England.
Pennant, Thomas ..	Some Account of London. 1793.
Percy, Sholto and Reuben	London.
Phillimore, W. P. W. ..	The London and Middlesex Notebook. 1892.
Phillimore, William Phillimore Watts, and Ragg, F. W.	Buckinghamshire Parish Registers.
Phillimore, W. P. W. and Whitear, Walter Henry	Historical Collections relating to Chiswick. 1897.
Portland, Duke of ..	MSS. of, at Welbeck

AUTHOR		WORKS
Prynne, William	..	The Coronation of King James, etc.
Purchas, Samuel	..	Purchas, His Pilgrimes.
Rendle, W.	..	The Playhouses of Bankside in the Time of Shakespeare.
		The Globe Playhouse.
Roberts, Henry	..	Tract on the Visit of the King of Denmark. 1606.
Roots, George	..	The Charters of the Town of Kingston-upon-Thames, translated into English by. 1797.
Rushworth, John	..	Historical Collections.
Rymer, Thomas	..	Fœdera.
Salmon, Thomas	..	Chronological Historian.
Scott, Sir Walter	..	The Fortunes of Nigel.
		Secret History of the Court of James I. 1811.
Seymour, Robert	..	Survey of the Cities of London and Westminster. 1734.
Sharpe, Reginald Robinson		A Short Account of the Worshipful Company of Shipwrights. 1876.
		London and the Kingdom. A History derived mainly from the Archives at Guildhall, 1894.
Sheppard, James Edgar	..	The Old Royal Palace of Whitehall, 1902.
Simpson, Edwin	..	The History of Kew. 1849.
Smith, John Thomas	..	The Antiquities of Westminster.
		Ancient Topography of London.
		The Cries of London.
Smith, L. P.	..	The Life and Letters of Sir Henry Wotton. 1907.
Somers, John	..	A Collection of Scarce and Valuable Tracts. 1748.
		A Second Collection of Scarce and Valuable Tracts. 1750.
		A Third Collection of Scarce and Valuable Tracts. 1751.
		A Fourth Collection of Scarce and Valuable Tracts. 1751-52.
Spedding, James	..	The Letters and Life of Francis Bacon. 1861-72.
Squire, John Traviss	..	The Registers of the Parish of Wandsworth, 1603—1787. 1889.
Stanley, Arthur Penrhyn		Historical Memorials of Westminster Abbey.
Stebbing, William	..	Sir Walter Raleigh—A Biography. 1891.
St. John, James Augustus		Life of Sir Walter Raleigh. 1869.
Stow, John	..	Survey of London.
Strutt, Joseph	..	Sports and Pastimes of the People of England.
Strype, John	..	The Life and Acts of John Whitgift. 1718.

AUTHOR	WORKS
Tanswell, John	.. The History and Antiquities of Lambeth. 1858.
Taylor, John—the Water Poet	Thief. The World runs on Wheels. Tract, 1623.
Thompson, Richard	.. Chronicles of London Bridge.
Thornbury and Walford.	.. Haunted London.
Thornton, William	.. History, Description and Survey of London, Westminster, Southwark, etc. 1784.
Tiler, Arthur	.. The History and Antiquities of St. Saviour's, Southwark. 1765.
Timbs, John	.. The Romance of London.
Toone, W.	.. The Chronological Historian.
Turner, William	.. A Compleat History of the most Remarkable Providences both of Judgment and Mercy, etc.
Tyler, Patrick Fraser	.. Life of Sir Walter Raleigh. 1833.
Visscher, Nikolaas	.. Londinum florentissima Britanniæ urbs, etc., 1616. View of London on the Thames
Wade, John	.. British Chronology.
Walcott, Mackenzie, E. C.	Memorials of Westminster.
Walker, J. W.	.. A Calendar of the Ancient Charters and Documents of the Corporation of Maidenhead. 1908.
Weldon, Sir Anthony	.. The Court and Character of King James. 1811.
Whitten, Wilfred	.. London in Song.
Wilkinson, R.	.. Londina Illustrata. 1819. Illustrations.
Williams, Robert Folkestone	The Court and Times of James the First. 1848.
Wilson, Arthur	.. The Life and Reign of King James the First. 1653.
Winwood, Sir Ralph	.. Memorials of Affairs of State.
Wotton, Sir Henry	.. Reliquiæ Wottonianæ. 1651.
Wright, Thomas	.. The History and Topography of Essex. 1836.

Tract.—The Royal Entertainment of the Right Honourable the Earl of Nottingham, sent Ambassador from his Majestie to the King of Spaine. 1605.

The Interpreter, 1622, Rhymes.

The True Description of the Royall Masque presented at Hampton Court upon Sunday night, being the Eight of January, 1604, and personated by the Queenes most Excellent Majestie, attended by eleven Ladies of Honour. 1604.

Manner of the Coronation of Charles I., with James I. added.

Tract.—The True Narrative of the Entertainment of his Royal Majesty from the time of his departure from Edinburgh till his receiving at London. 1603.

The Secret History of the four last Monarchs of Great Britain. 1691.

Historical Memoires of the Reigns of Queen Elizabeth and King James. 1658.

Letters of Queen Elizabeth and James VI. 1849.

The Annals of King James and King Charles the First. 1681.

Tract.—A Briefe Declaration of the Reasons that moved King James of blessed Memory and the state to erect a Colledge of Divines, and other learned Men at Chelsey. 1645.

Miscellaneous State Papers from 1501 to 1726. Edited by P. Y., 1778.

Harleian Miscellany.

The Dawn of British Trade to the East Indies : as recorded in the Court Minutes of the East India Company, 1599—1603.

The Register of Letters, etc., of the Governors and Company of Merchants of London trading into the East Indies, 1600—1619. (The first Letter Book of the East India Company.)

The East Indian Chronologist. (Historical Events respecting the East India Company.)

Antiquarian Repertory.

Acts of the Privy Council of England, 1601—1604.

Acts of the Privy Council of England. Colonial Series : 1613—1680.

Calendar of State Papers—Domestic Series : 1580—1625 ; 1603—1610 ; 1611—1618 ; 1619—1623 ; 1623—1625.

Calendar of State Papers—Colonial Series : 1513—1616 ; 1574—1660 ; 1617—1621 ; 1622—1624.

Calendar of State Papers—Irish Series : 1615—1625.

Calendar of State Papers—Venetian Series : 1603—1607 ; 1607—1610 ; 1610—1613 ; 1613—1615 ; 1615—1617 ; 1617—1619.

Calendar of the Clarendon State Papers : 1523—1649.

Calendar of the Carew Manuscripts : 1603—1624.

An English Garner—Social England—17th cent. Tracts.

MSS. of Southwell Cathedral.

Annals of England—Oxford.

A Chronology of the most remarkable events that have occurred in the Parishes of Gravesend, Milton and Denton. 1790.

Oxoniana.

Gentleman's Magazine. 1780.

Dictionary of National Biography.

A New View of London. 1708.

History of the Public Schools, etc.—Eton.

Eton—Things Old and New.

INDEX OF PLACES, PERSONS, ETC.

2L